COLORADO'S
BEST FISHING WATERS™

213 Detailed Maps of 73 of the Best Rivers, Lakes, and Streams

BEST FISHING WATERS™

Wilderness
Adventures
Press, Inc.™

Belgrade, Montana

Wilderness Adventures Press is dedicated to making these angling maps as accurate as possible. Please contact us at books@wildadvpress.com to let us know about any information in this book that you feel needs to be corrected. We appreciate your help.

Special thanks to Chuck Rizuto at Rizuto's San Juan River Lodge, for detailed map information on the special trout water of the San Juan River (map 7 of 7, page 139).

Rizuto's San Juan River Lodge
PO Box 6309
Navajo Dam, NM 87419
505-632-3893 or 505-632-1411

Published by Wilderness Adventures Press, Inc.™
45 Buckskin Road
Belgrade, MT 59714
866-400-2012
Website: www.wildadvpress.com
Email: books@wildadvpress.com

Second Edition 2008

Printed in the Singapore

ISBN 978-1-932098-57-0 (1-932098-57-7)

TABLE OF CONTENTS

RIVERS

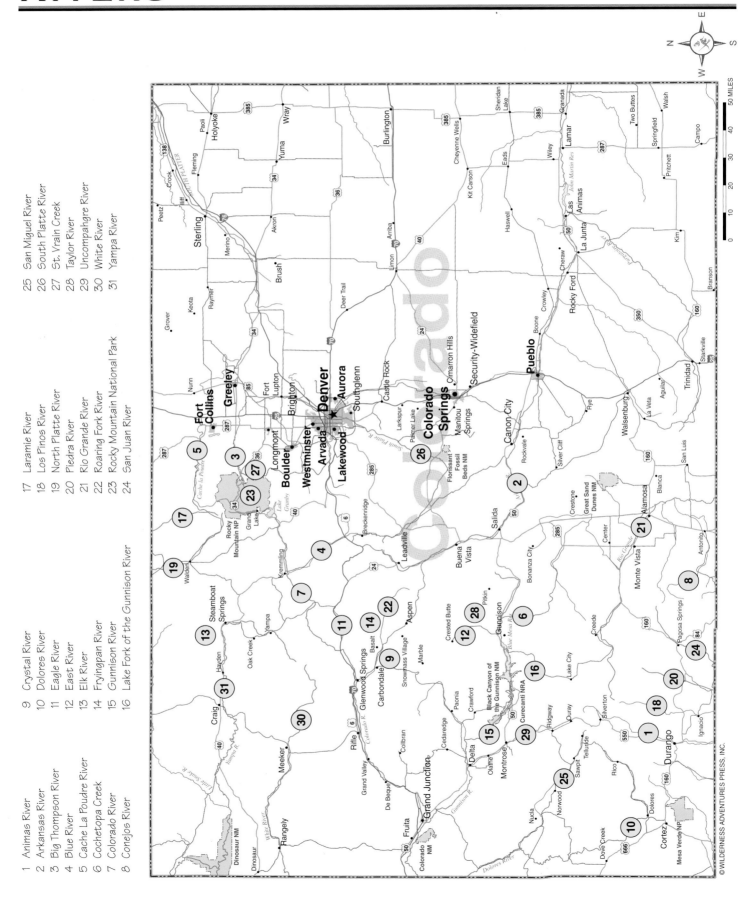

1 Animas River
2 Arkansas River
3 Big Thompson River
4 Blue River
5 Cache La Poudre River
6 Cochetopa Creek
7 Colorado River
8 Conejos River
9 Crystal River
10 Dolores River
11 Eagle River
12 East River
13 Elk River
14 Fryingpan River
15 Gunnison River
16 Lake Fork of the Gunnison River
17 Laramie River
18 Los Pinos River
19 North Platte River
20 Piedra River
21 Rio Grande River
22 Roaring Fork River
23 Rocky Mountain National Park
24 San Juan River
25 San Miguel River
26 South Platte River
27 St. Vrain Creek
28 Taylor River
29 Uncompahgre River
30 White River
31 Yampa River

© WILDERNESS ADVENTURES PRESS, INC.

LAKES

1 Aurora Reservoir
2 Bonny Reservoir
3 Blue Mesa Reservoir
4 Chambers Lake
5 Chatfield Reservoir
6 Cherry Creek Reservoir
7 Delaney Butte Lakes
8 Elevenmile Reservoir

9 Grand Lake and
   Shadow Mountain Lake
10 Grand Mesa Lakes, East
11 Grand Mesa Lakes, West
12 Green Mountain Reservoir
13 Hohnholz Lakes
14 Horseshoe Reservoir and
    Martin Lake
15 Horsetooth Reservoir

16 Jackson Reservoir
17 John Martin Reservoir
18 Lake Granby
19 Lake John
20 Lon Hagler Reservoir
21 McPhee Reservoir
22 Neenoshe, Neegronda,
    and Queens Reservoirs
23 North Sterling Reservoir

24 Pearl Lake
25 Pueblo Reservoir
26 Quincy Reservoir
27 Red Feather Lakes
28 Sanchez Reservoir
29 Spinney Mountain Reservoir
30 Stagecoach Reservoir
31 Steamboat Lake

32 Taylor Park Reservoir
33 Trappers Lake
34 Turquoise Lake
35 Vallecito Reservoir
36 Vega Reservoir
37 Williams Fork Reservoir
38 Wolford Mountain Reservoir

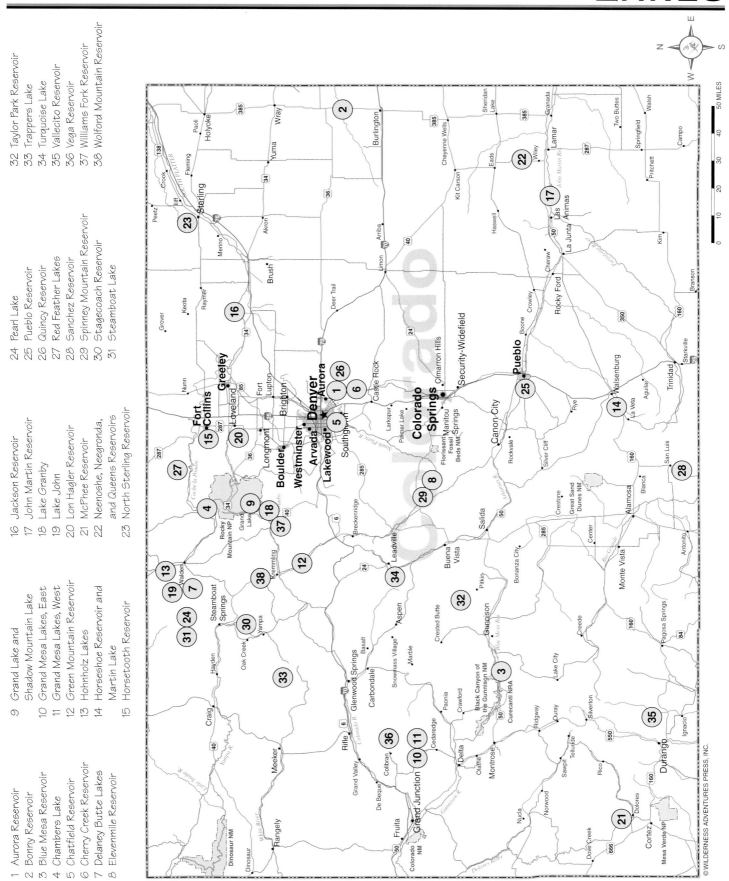

INTRODUCTION

The state of Colorado has long been famous for its fishing. From tiny high-country lakes and creeks to world-renowned rivers like the South Platte and Colorado Rivers to massive reservoirs like Blue Mesa or Pueblo, anglers of all types will find water here that suits them. Rainbow, brown, cutthroat, lake, and brook trout are available, as are kokanee salmon, arctic grayling, and hybrid trout like splake. Many warmwater species are present too, such as northern pike, largemouth and smallmouth bass, walleye, wipers, tiger muskie, and crappie, among others.

Much has been written about the state's amazing fisheries over the years, but good maps that anglers can actually use to pinpoint key areas are a rarity. This book changes all of that. The maps herein are based on U.S. Geological Survey maps, and a wealth of useful angling information is included on each one, along with an overview of the fishing.

The land along Colorado's most popular waters is usually a mix of private and public land and heavy fishing pressure in the most popular public areas can detract from the overall angling experience. So it pays to know every out-of-the-way access that casual anglers might overlook. The Department of Wildlife has worked hard to provide anglers with good access to their favorite waters through state wildlife areas and easements, and BLM and Forest Service lands also border many fisheries. The angler who can quickly identify all of these areas will find a whole new world of fishing opportunities.

The waters are listed in alphabetical order for easy reference without the need to consult an index for specific page numbers. Please note: Lake depths are shown on some of the reservoirs but these are approximations only, as siltation and drought can affect depths and water levels over time.

For the best information on up-to-the-minute water conditions for all of the rivers and lakes covered here, contact outdoor stores and fly shops near the water you're planning to fish. And it's always a good idea to acquire a copy of the latest fishing regulations. These are free for the asking by contacting:

Colorado Department of Wildlife
6060 Broadway
Denver, CO 80216
303-297-1192
www.wildlife.state.co.us

LEGEND

——	Interstate		BLM - Public Land	⛏	Picnic Area
══	Primary Highway		State - Public Land	✈	Airport
——	Road or Street		Indian Reservation		Rapids
········	Trails		National Forest	▬	Dam
70	Interstate Route	⚓	Fishing Access	▪▪▪▪	Continental Divide
131	State Route	◢	Boat Launch	┼┼┼	Railroad
192	U.S. Route	▲	Campsite	GPS	GPS Coordinates

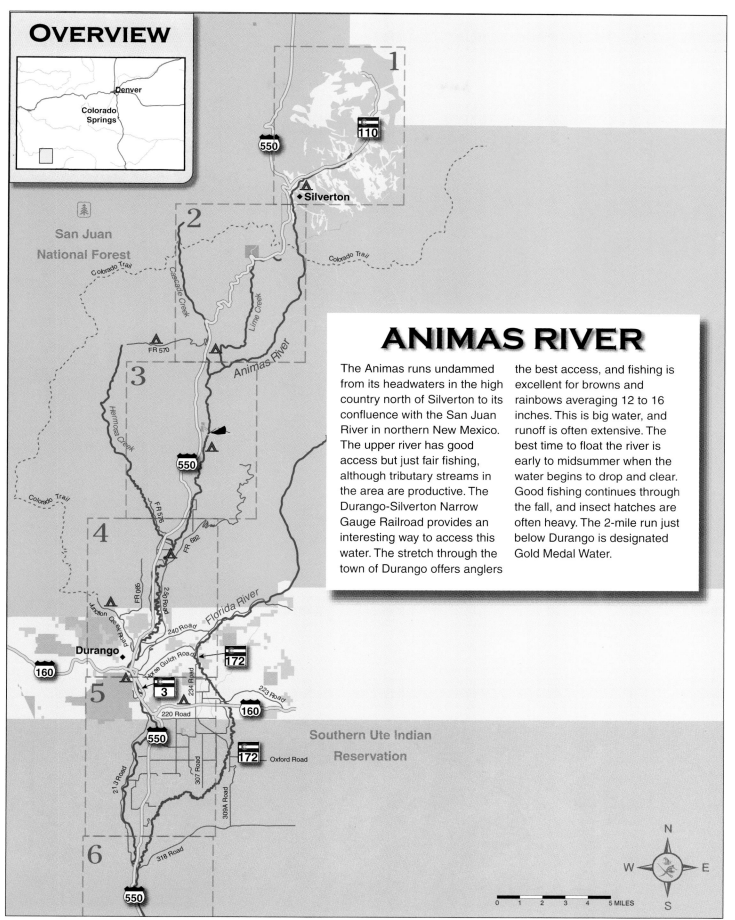

ANIMAS RIVER

The Animas runs undammed from its headwaters in the high country north of Silverton to its confluence with the San Juan River in northern New Mexico. The upper river has good access but just fair fishing, although tributary streams in the area are productive. The Durango-Silverton Narrow Gauge Railroad provides an interesting way to access this water. The stretch through the town of Durango offers anglers the best access, and fishing is excellent for browns and rainbows averaging 12 to 16 inches. This is big water, and runoff is often extensive. The best time to float the river is early to midsummer when the water begins to drop and clear. Good fishing continues through the fall, and insect hatches are often heavy. The 2-mile run just below Durango is designated Gold Medal Water.

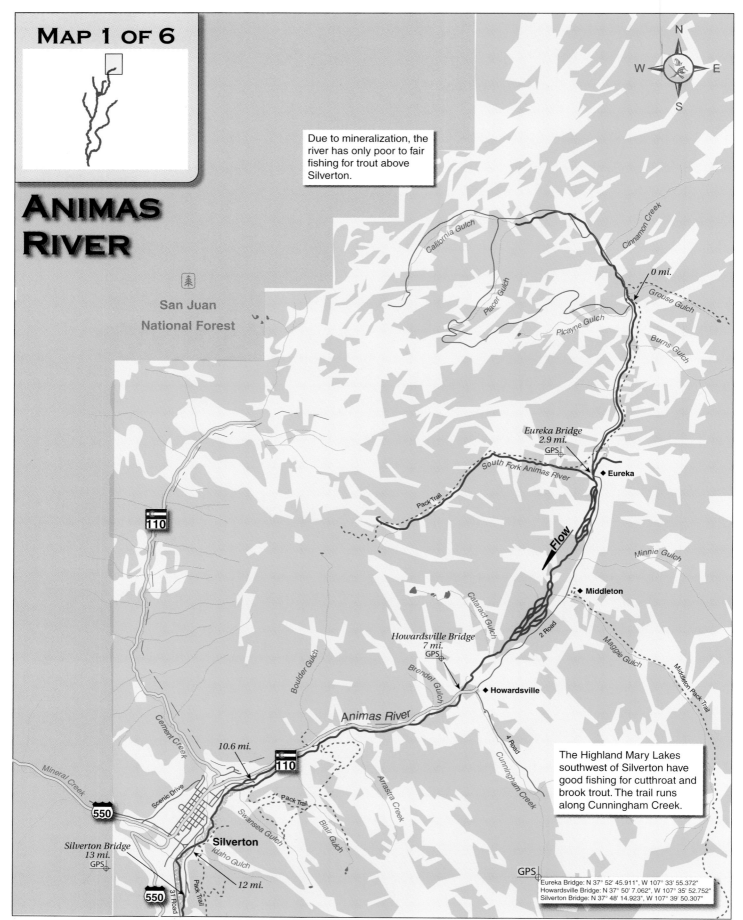

MAP 1 OF 6

ANIMAS RIVER

Due to mineralization, the river has only poor to fair fishing for trout above Silverton.

San Juan National Forest

California Gulch

Cinnamon Creek

Placer Gulch

Picayne Gulch

Grouse Gulch

0 mi.

Burns Gulch

Eureka Bridge
2.9 mi.
GPS

South Fork Animas River

Pack Trail

◆ Eureka

Flow

Minnie Gulch

Cataract Gulch

◆ Middleton

2 Road

Howardsville Bridge
7 mi.
GPS

Magpie Gulch

Brendel Gulch

◆ Howardsville

Middleton Pack Trail

Boulder Gulch

Animas River

4 Road

Cunningham Creek

10.6 mi.

The Highland Mary Lakes southwest of Silverton have good fishing for cutthroat and brook trout. The trail runs along Cunningham Creek.

Cement Creek

Scenic Drive

Mineral Creek

Swansea Gulch

Pack Trail

Arrastra Creek

Blair Gulch

Silverton

Idaho Gulch

Silverton Bridge
13 mi.
GPS

12 mi.

3" Road

Pack Trail

GPS

Eureka Bridge: N 37° 52' 45.911", W 107° 33' 55.372"
Howardsville Bridge: N 37° 50' 7.062", W 107° 35' 52.752"
Silverton Bridge: N 37° 48' 14.923", W 107° 39' 50.307"

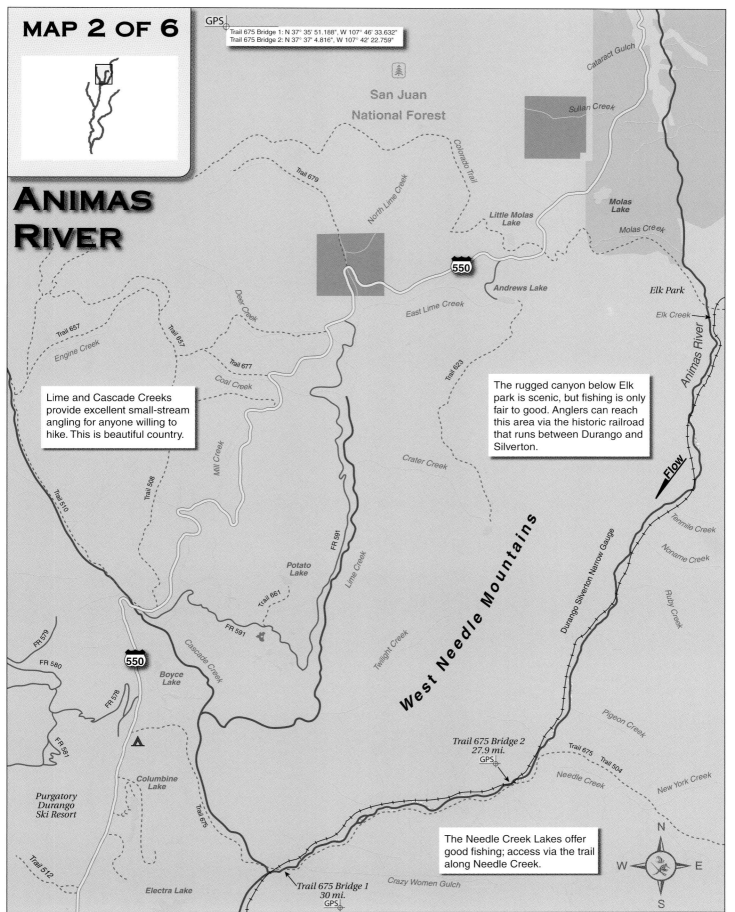

MAP 2 OF 6

ANIMAS RIVER

GPS
Trail 675 Bridge 1: N 37° 35' 51.188", W 107° 46' 33.632"
Trail 675 Bridge 2: N 37° 37' 4.816", W 107° 42' 22.759"

San Juan
National Forest

Lime and Cascade Creeks provide excellent small-stream angling for anyone willing to hike. This is beautiful country.

The rugged canyon below Elk park is scenic, but fishing is only fair to good. Anglers can reach this area via the historic railroad that runs between Durango and Silverton.

The Needle Creek Lakes offer good fishing; access via the trail along Needle Creek.

West Needle Mountains

Trail 675 Bridge 2
27.9 mi.
GPS

Trail 675 Bridge 1
30 mi.
GPS

Purgatory Durango Ski Resort

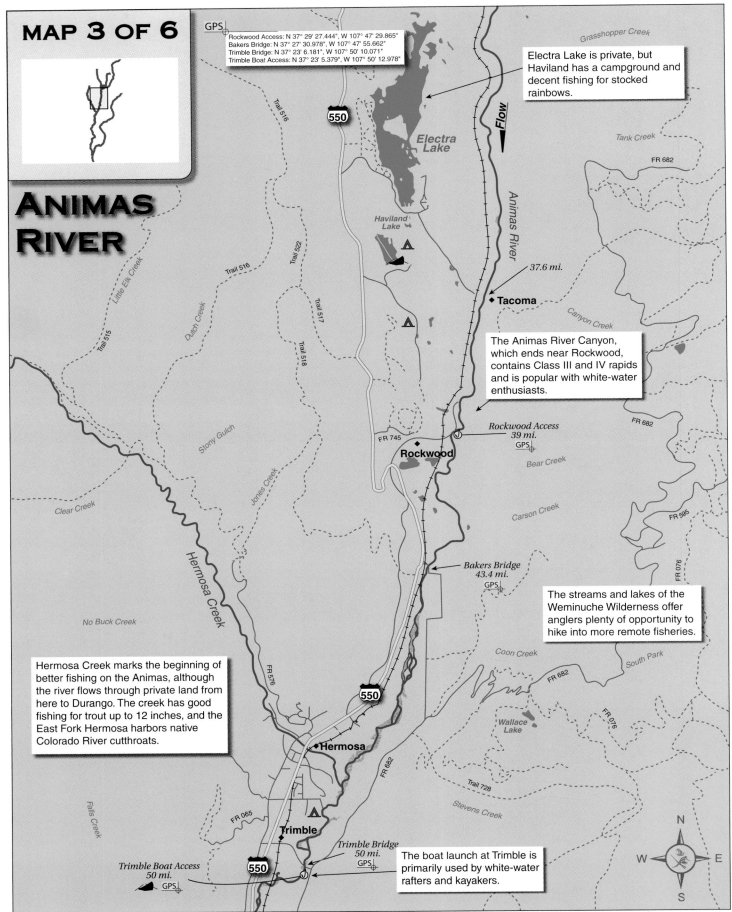

MAP 3 OF 6

ANIMAS RIVER

Rockwood Access: N 37° 29' 27.444", W 107° 47' 29.865"
Bakers Bridge: N 37° 27' 30.978", W 107° 47' 55.662"
Trimble Bridge: N 37° 23' 6.181", W 107° 50' 10.071"
Trimble Boat Access: N 37° 23' 5.379", W 107° 50' 12.978"

Electra Lake is private, but Haviland has a campground and decent fishing for stocked rainbows.

The Animas River Canyon, which ends near Rockwood, contains Class III and IV rapids and is popular with white-water enthusiasts.

The streams and lakes of the Weminuche Wilderness offer anglers plenty of opportunity to hike into more remote fisheries.

Hermosa Creek marks the beginning of better fishing on the Animas, although the river flows through private land from here to Durango. The creek has good fishing for trout up to 12 inches, and the East Fork Hermosa harbors native Colorado River cutthroats.

The boat launch at Trimble is primarily used by white-water rafters and kayakers.

Electra Lake

Haviland Lake

37.6 mi.

◆ Tacoma

Rockwood Access
39 mi.
GPS

FR 745

◆ **Rockwood**

Bakers Bridge
43.4 mi.
GPS

Bear Creek

Carson Creek

Coon Creek

Wallace Lake

South Park

Trail 728

Stevens Creek

◆ **Hermosa**

FR 065

◆ **Trimble**

Trimble Bridge
50 mi.
GPS

Trimble Boat Access
50 mi.
GPS

Grasshopper Creek

Tank Creek

FR 682

Canyon Creek

FR 682

FR 595

FR 076

FR 076

FR 682

Little Elk Creek

Trail 516

Trail 522

Trail 516

Trail 517

Trail 518

Trail 515

Dutch Creek

Stony Gulch

Jones Creek

Clear Creek

Hermosa Creek

No Buck Creek

FR 576

Falls Creek

550

550

550

550

Flow

Animas River

N
W   E
S

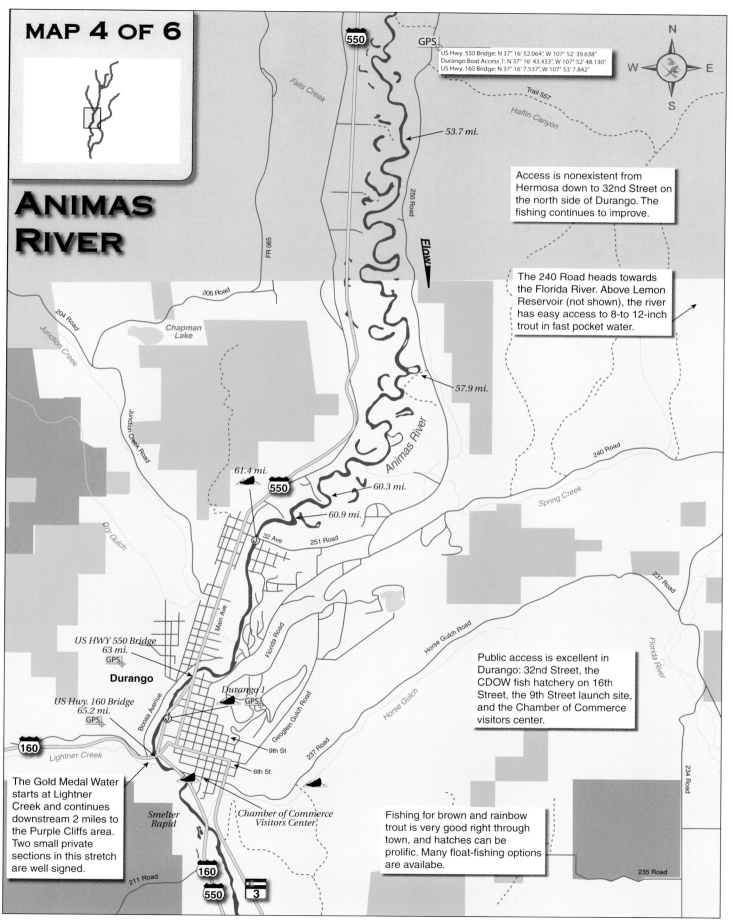

MAP 4 OF 6

ANIMAS RIVER

US Hwy. 550 Bridge: N 37° 16' 52.064", W 107° 52' 39.638"
Durango Boat Access 1: N 37° 16' 43.433", W 107° 52' 48.130"
US Hwy. 160 Bridge: N 37° 16' 7.537", W 107° 53' 7.842"

GPS

550

Trail 557

Haflin Canyon

Falls Creek

53.7 mi.

250 Road

Flow

Access is nonexistent from Hermosa down to 32nd Street on the north side of Durango. The fishing continues to improve.

The 240 Road heads towards the Florida River. Above Lemon Reservoir (not shown), the river has easy access to 8-to 12-inch trout in fast pocket water.

205 Road

204 Road

Junction Creek

Chapman Lake

FR 065

57.9 mi.

Junction Creek Road

Animas River

240 Road

Spring Creek

61.4 mi.

550

60.3 mi.

60.9 mi.

Dry Gulch

32 Ave

251 Road

237 Road

Florida River

Main Ave

US HWY 550 Bridge 63 mi.
GPS

Horse Gulch Road

Public access is excellent in Durango: 32nd Street, the CDOW fish hatchery on 16th Street, the 9th Street launch site, and the Chamber of Commerce visitors center.

Durango

US Hwy. 160 Bridge 65.2 mi.
GPS

Durango 1
GPS

Boosa Avenue

Geoglein Gulch Road

Horse Gulch

160

Lightner Creek

9th St

237 Road

234 Road

The Gold Medal Water starts at Lightner Creek and continues downstream 2 miles to the Purple Cliffs area. Two small private sections in this stretch are well signed.

6th St

Smelter Rapid

Chamber of Commerce Visitors Center

Fishing for brown and rainbow trout is very good right through town, and hatches can be prolific. Many float-fishing options are availabe.

211 Road

160

550

3

235 Road

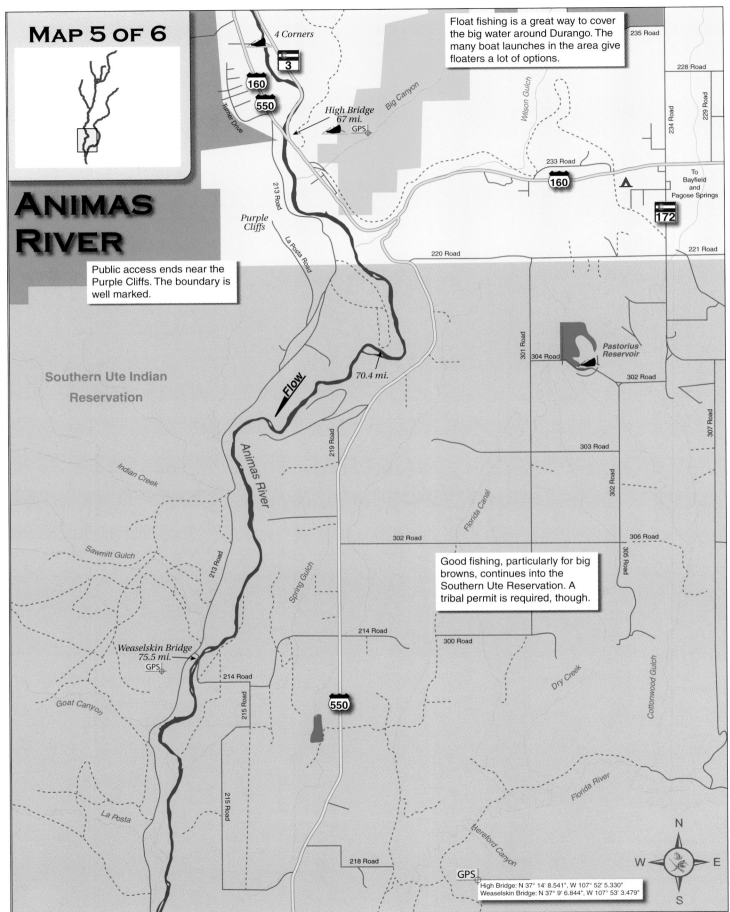

MAP 5 OF 6

ANIMAS RIVER

4 Corners

3

160

550

Turner Drive

High Bridge
67 mi.
GPS

Big Canyon

213 Road

Purple Cliffs

La Posta Road

Float fishing is a great way to cover the big water around Durango. The many boat launches in the area give floaters a lot of options.

235 Road

228 Road

229 Road

234 Road

Wilson Gulch

233 Road

160

To Bayfield and Pagose Springs

172

Public access ends near the Purple Cliffs. The boundary is well marked.

220 Road

221 Road

Southern Ute Indian Reservation

Flow

70.4 mi.

301 Road

304 Road

Pastorius Reservoir

302 Road

Animas River

219 Road

303 Road

302 Road

307 Road

Indian Creek

Florida Canal

Sawmitt Gulch

213 Road

302 Road

306 Road

305 Road

Spring Gulch

Good fishing, particularly for big browns, continues into the Southern Ute Reservation. A tribal permit is required, though.

214 Road

300 Road

Dry Creek

Cottonwood Gulch

Weaselskin Bridge
75.5 mi.
GPS

214 Road

215 Road

Goat Canyon

550

215 Road

Florida River

La Posta

218 Road

GPS

Hereford Canyon

N

W   E

S

High Bridge: N 37° 14' 8.541", W 107° 52' 5.330"
Weaselskin Bridge: N 37° 9' 6.844", W 107° 53' 3.479"

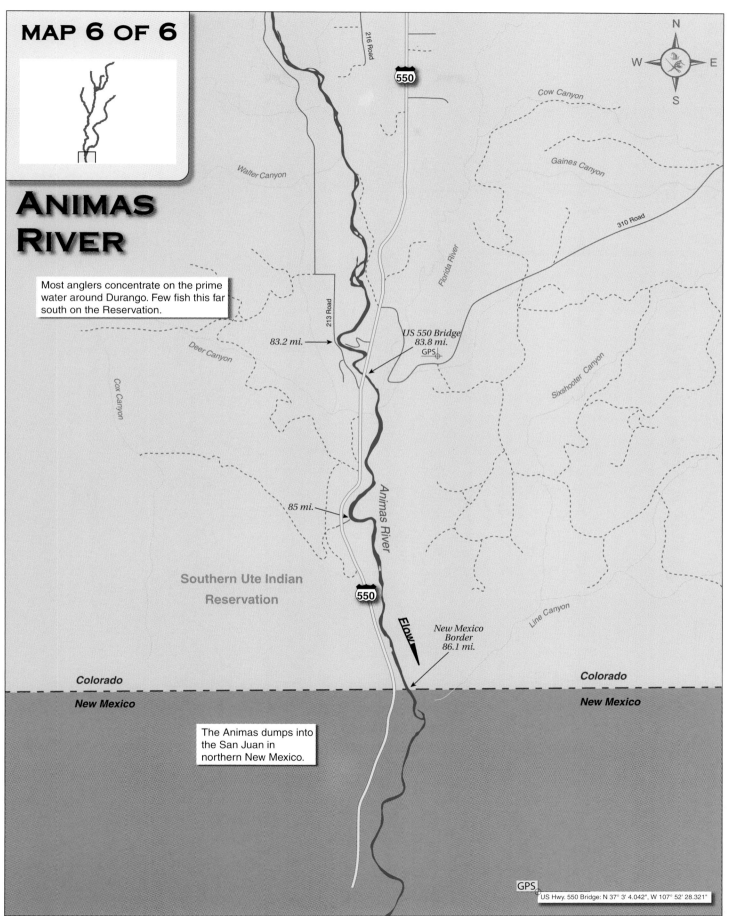

MAP 6 OF 6

ANIMAS RIVER

Most anglers concentrate on the prime water around Durango. Few fish this far south on the Reservation.

216 Road

550

Cow Canyon

Gaines Canyon

310 Road

Walter Canyon

Florida River

213 Road

Deer Canyon

Sixshooter Canyon

83.2 mi.

US 550 Bridge
83.8 mi.
GPS

Cox Canyon

Animas River

85 mi.

Southern Ute Indian
Reservation

550

Line Canyon

FLOW

New Mexico
Border
86.1 mi.

Colorado

Colorado

New Mexico

New Mexico

The Animas dumps into the San Juan in northern New Mexico.

GPS

US Hwy. 550 Bridge: N 37° 3' 4.042", W 107° 52' 28.321"

OVERVIEW

ARKANSAS RIVER

The mighty Arkansas begins in the Sawatch Mountains above Leadville and runs 300-odd miles to the Kansas border. For anglers, the headwaters down to Canon City and the Pueblo Reservoir tailwater are of most interest. Access is intermittent but plentiful and the fishing for browns and a few rainbows and cutthroats averaging 12 to 14 inches is excellent. As this is one of the country's most popular whitewater rafting rivers, boat launches are seemingly everywhere. Summer recreation use is high, but with well over 100 miles of prime trout water, there's usually room to have some water to yourself.

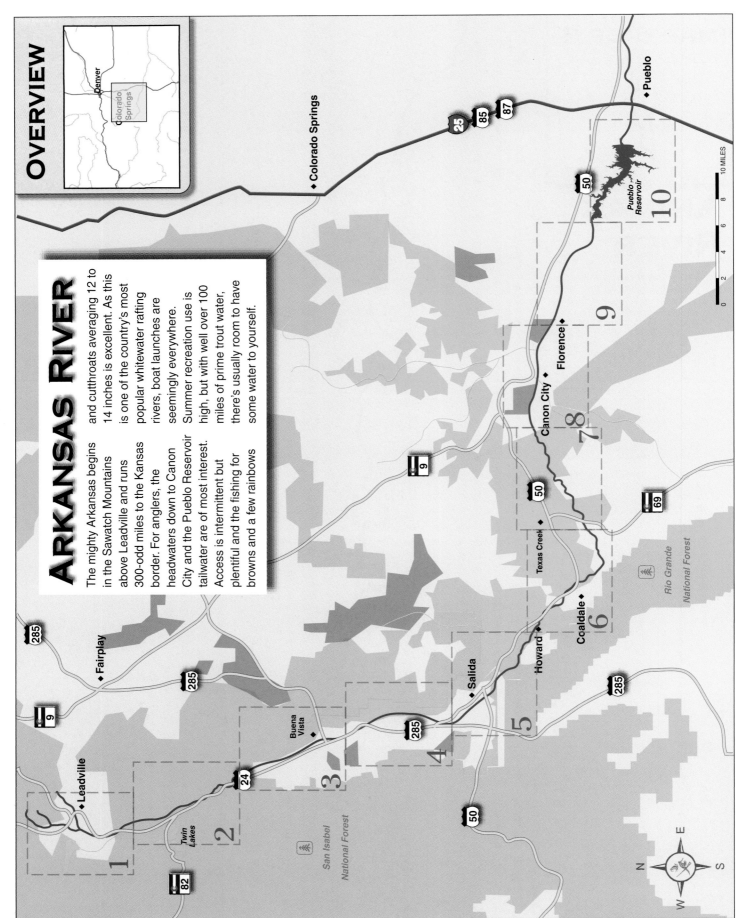

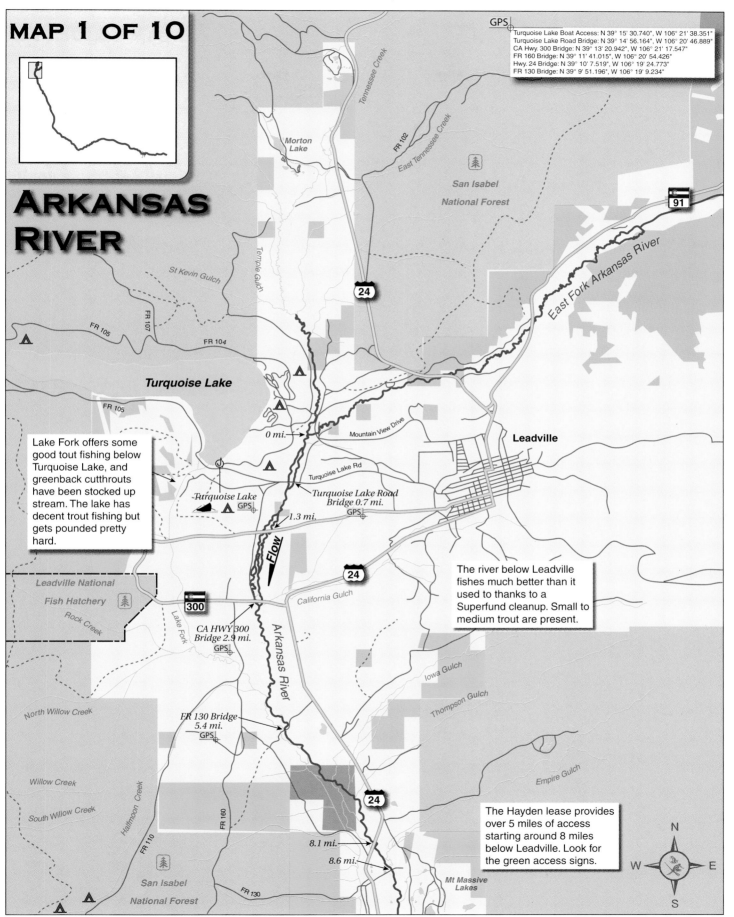

MAP 1 OF 10

ARKANSAS RIVER

GPS

Turquoise Lake Boat Access: N 39° 15' 30.740", W 106° 21' 38.351"
Turquoise Lake Road Bridge: N 39° 14' 56.164", W 106° 20' 46.889"
CA Hwy. 300 Bridge: N 39° 13' 20.942", W 106° 21' 17.547"
FR 160 Bridge: N 39° 11' 41.015", W 106° 20' 54.426"
Hwy. 24 Bridge: N 39° 10' 7.519", W 106° 19' 24.773"
FR 130 Bridge: N 39° 9' 51.196", W 106° 19' 9.234"

Morton Lake

Tennessee Creek

East Tennessee Creek

FR 102

San Isabel National Forest

East Fork Arkansas River

91

St Kevin Gulch

Temple Gulch

24

FR 107

FR 105

FR 104

Turquoise Lake

Leadville

Lake Fork offers some good tout fishing below Turquoise Lake, and greenback cutthrouts have been stocked up stream. The lake has decent trout fishing but gets pounded pretty hard.

FR 105

0 mi.

Mountain View Drive

Turquoise Lake
GPS

Turquoise Lake Rd

Turquoise Lake Road Bridge 0.7 mi.
GPS

1.3 mi.

Flow

The river below Leadville fishes much better than it used to thanks to a Superfund cleanup. Small to medium trout are present.

24

Leadville National Fish Hatchery

Rock Creek

300

California Gulch

CA HWY 300 Bridge 2.9 mi.
GPS

Lake Fork

Arkansas River

Iowa Gulch

Thompson Gulch

North Willow Creek

FR 130 Bridge 5.4 mi.
GPS

Willow Creek

Empire Gulch

South Willow Creek

Halfmoon Creek

24

FR 160

8.1 mi.

The Hayden lease provides over 5 miles of access starting around 8 miles below Leadville. Look for the green access signs.

FR 110

8.6 mi.

N

San Isabel National Forest

FR 130

Mt Massive Lakes

W   E

S

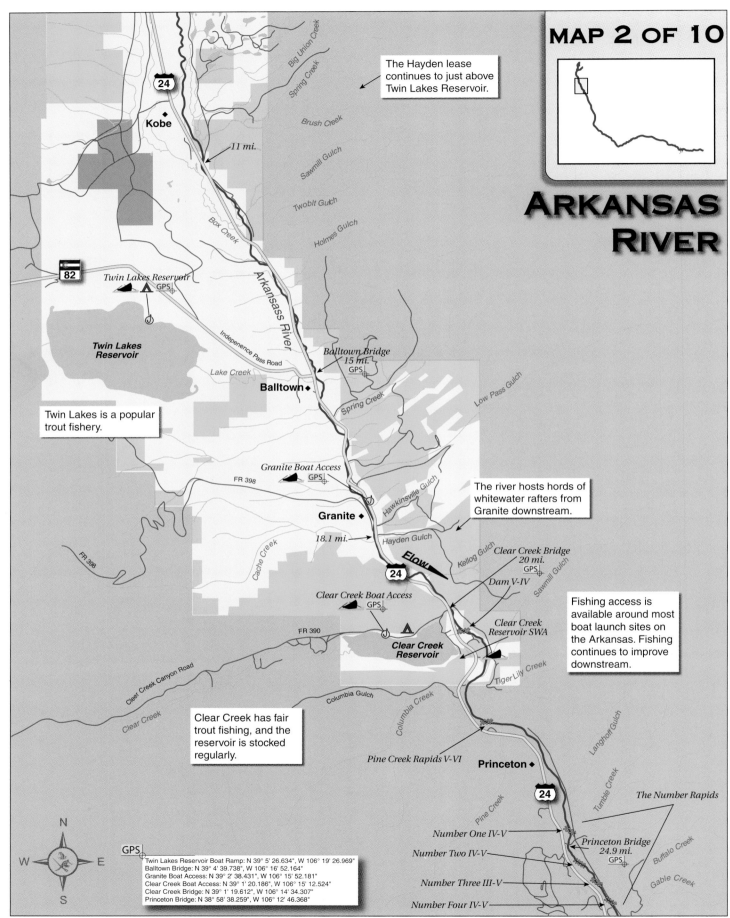

MAP 2 OF 10

ARKANSAS RIVER

The Hayden lease continues to just above Twin Lakes Reservoir.

Kobe

11 mi.

Big Union Creek

Spring Creek

Brush Creek

Sawmill Gulch

Twoblt Gulch

Holmes Gulch

Box Creek

Arkansass River

Twin Lakes Reservoir
GPS

Independence Pass Road

Twin Lakes Reservoir

Twin Lakes is a popular trout fishery.

Lake Creek

Balltown Bridge
15 mi.
GPS

Balltown

Spring Creek

Low Pass Gulch

Granite Boat Access
GPS

FR 398

Hawkinsville Gulch

The river hosts hords of whitewater rafters from Granite downstream.

Granite

18.1 mi.

Hayden Gulch

FR 398

Cache Creek

Flow

Kellog Gulch

Clear Creek Bridge
20 mi.
GPS

Dam V-IV

Sawmill Gulch

Clear Creek Boat Access
GPS

Clear Creek Reservoir SWA

Fishing access is available around most boat launch sites on the Arkansas. Fishing continues to improve downstream.

FR 390

Clear Creek Reservoir

Clear Creek Canyon Road

Tiger Lily Creek

Clear Creek

Columbia Gulch

Columbia Creek

Clear Creek has fair trout fishing, and the reservoir is stocked regularly.

Pine Creek Rapids V-VI

Princeton

Langhoff Gulch

The Number Rapids

Pine Creek

Tumble Creek

Number One IV-V

Princeton Bridge
24.9 mi.
GPS

Number Two IV-V

Buffalo Creek

Number Three III-V

Gable Creek

Number Four IV-V

N
W E
S

GPS

Twin Lakes Reservoir Boat Ramp: N 39° 5' 26.634", W 106° 19' 26.969"
Balltown Bridge: N 39° 4' 39.738", W 106° 16' 52.164"
Granite Boat Access: N 39° 2' 38.431", W 106° 15' 52.181"
Clear Creek Boat Access: N 39° 1' 20.186", W 106° 15' 12.524"
Clear Creek Bridge: N 39° 1' 19.612", W 106° 14' 34.307"
Princeton Bridge: N 38° 58' 38.259", W 106° 12' 46.368"

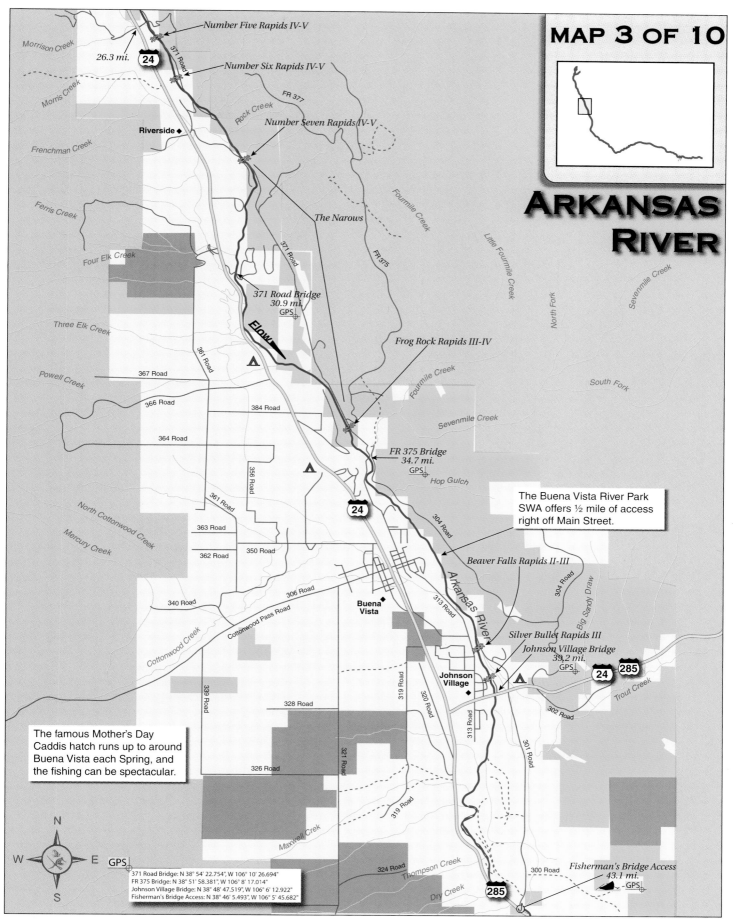

Number Five Rapids IV-V

26.3 mi.

Number Six Rapids IV-V

Riverside ◆

Number Seven Rapids IV-V

The Narows

371 Road Bridge
30.9 mi.
GPS

MAP 3 OF 10

ARKANSAS RIVER

Frog Rock Rapids III-IV

FR 375 Bridge
34.7 mi.
GPS

The Buena Vista River Park
SWA offers ½ mile of access
right off Main Street.

Beaver Falls Rapids II-III

Buena Vista ◆

Silver Bullet Rapids III

Johnson Village Bridge
39.2 mi.
GPS

Johnson Village ◆

The famous Mother's Day
Caddis hatch runs up to around
Buena Vista each Spring, and
the fishing can be spectacular.

N
W   E
S

GPS

371 Road Bridge: N 38° 54' 22.754", W 106° 10' 26.694"
FR 375 Bridge: N 38° 51' 58.381", W 106° 8' 17.014"
Johnson Village Bridge: N 38° 48' 47.519", W 106° 6' 12.922"
Fisherman's Bridge Access: N 38° 46' 5.493", W 106° 5' 45.682"

Fisherman's Bridge Access
43.1 mi.
GPS

© 2008 Wilderness Adventures Press, Inc.

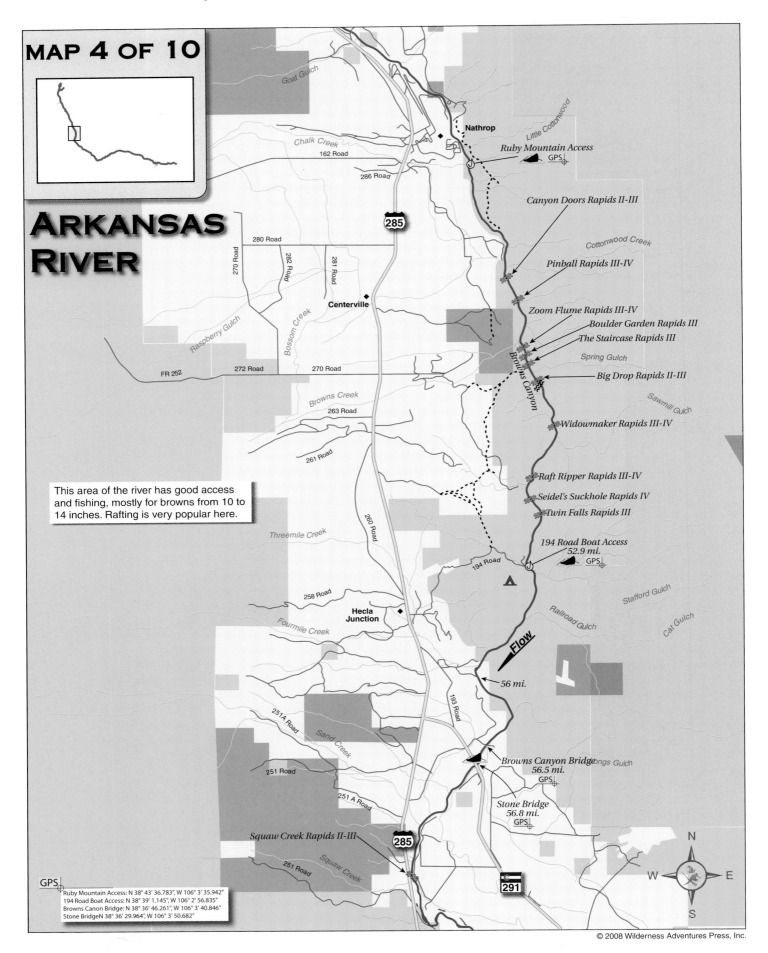

MAP 4 OF 10

ARKANSAS RIVER

Goat Gulch

Chalk Creek

162 Road

286 Road

Nathrop

Little Cottonwood

Ruby Mountain Access GPS

Canyon Doors Rapids II-III

US 285

Cottonwood Creek

280 Road

270 Road

282 Road

281 Road

Pinball Rapids III-IV

Centerville

Zoom Flume Rapids III-IV

Boulder Garden Rapids III

The Staircase Rapids III

Spring Gulch

Raspberry Gulch

Bossom Creek

FR 252

272 Road

270 Road

Big Drop Rapids II-III

Browns Canyon

Sawmill Gulch

Browns Creek

263 Road

Widowmaker Rapids III-IV

261 Road

Raft Ripper Rapids III-IV

This area of the river has good access and fishing, mostly for browns from 10 to 14 inches. Rafting is very popular here.

Seidel's Suckhole Rapids IV

Twin Falls Rapids III

260 Road

Threemile Creek

194 Road Boat Access
52.9 mi.
GPS

194 Road

Stafford Gulch

258 Road

Hecla Junction

Railroad Gulch

Cat Gulch

Fourmile Creek

Flow

56 mi.

193 Road

251 A Road

Sand Creek

Longs Gulch

Browns Canyon Bridge
56.5 mi.
GPS

251 Road

Stone Bridge
56.8 mi.
GPS

251 A Road

US 285

Squaw Creek Rapids II-III

251 Road

Squaw Creek

CO 291

GPS

Ruby Mountain Access: N 38° 43' 36.783", W 106° 3' 35.942"
194 Road Boat Access: N 38° 39' 1.145", W 106° 2' 56.835"
Browns Canon Bridge: N 38° 36' 46.261", W 106° 3' 40.846"
Stone Bridge N 38° 36' 29.964", W 106° 3' 50.682"

N
W E
S

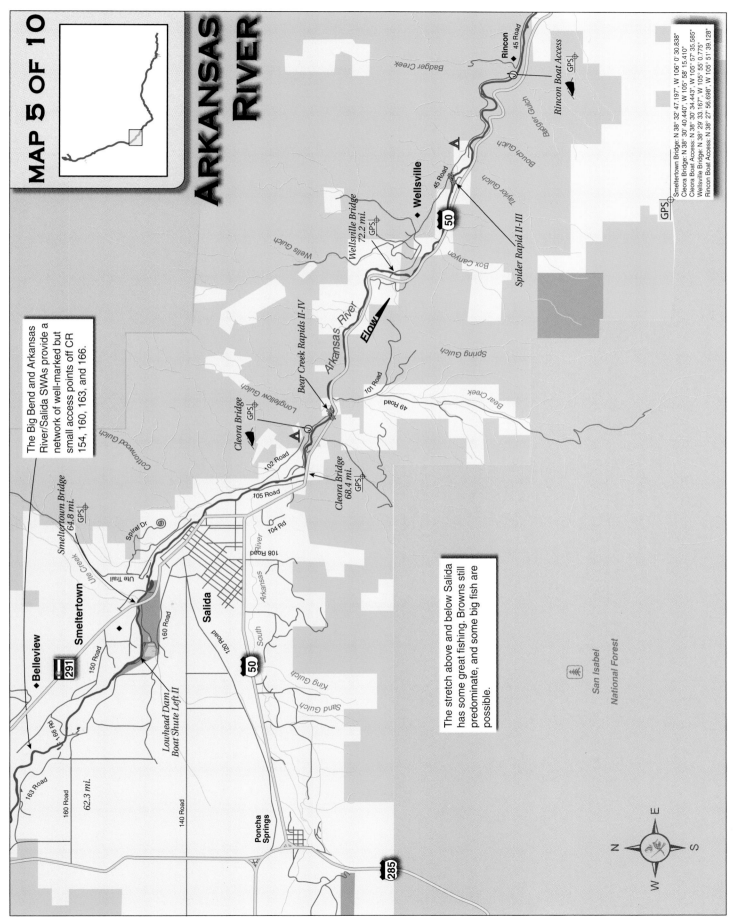

MAP 5 OF 10

ARKANSAS RIVER

The Big Bend and Arkansas River/Salida SWAs provide a network of well-marked but small access points off CR 154, 160, 163, and 166.

The stretch above and below Salida has some great fishing. Browns still predominate, and some big fish are possible.

Smeltertown Bridge: N 38° 32' 47.197", W 106° 0' 30.838"
Cleora Bridge: N 38° 30' 40.440", W 105° 58' 15.410"
Cleora Boat Access: N 38° 30' 34.443", W 105° 57' 35.585"
Wellsville Bridge: N 38° 29' 33.167", W 105° 55' 0.775"
Rincon Boat Access: N 38° 27' 56.698', W 105° 51' 39.128"

Rincon

Rincon Boat Access

Badger Creek

Badger Gulch

Bouch Gulch

45 Road

Spider Rapid II-III

Taylor Gulch

Box Canyon

Wellsville

50

Wellsville Bridge
72.2 mi.

Wells Gulch

Spring Gulch

Bear Creek Rapids II-IV

Arkansas River

Flow

101 Road

49 Road

Bear Creek

San Isabel National Forest

Cleora Bridge

Longfellow Gulch

Cottonwood Gulch

102 Road

105 Road

104 Rd

Cleora Bridge
68.4 mi.

108 Road

Arkansas River

South Arkansas River

Smeltertown Bridge
64.8 mi.

Ute Creek

Spiral Dr

Ute Trail

Smeltertown

Belleview

291

150 Road

160 Road

166 Rd

Lowhead Dam
Boat Shute Left II

Salida

50

120 Road

King Gulch

Sand Gulch

163 Road

160 Road

62.3 mi.

140 Road

Poncha Springs

285

N E S W

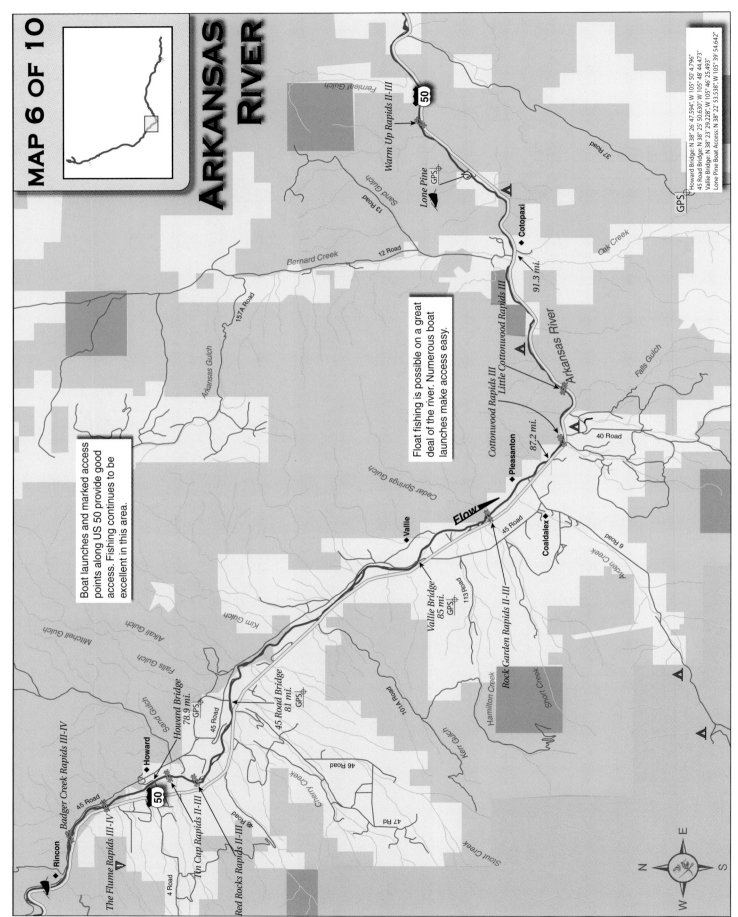

MAP 6 OF 10

ARKANSAS RIVER

Boat launches and marked access points along US 50 provide good access. Fishing continues to be excellent in this area.

Float fishing is possible on a great deal of the river. Numerous boat launches make access easy.

Warm Up Rapids II-III

Fernleaf Gulch

Lone Pine
GPS

Sand Gulch

13 Road

37 Road

Bernard Creek

12 Road

Cotopaxi

91.3 mi.

Oak Creek

157A Road

Arkansas Gulch

Little Cottonwood Rapids III

Cottonwood Rapids III

Arkansas River

Falls Gulch

40 Road

87.2 mi.

Cedar Springs Gulch

Pleasanton

Vallie

Flow

45 Road

Coaldalex

6 Road

Arden Creek

Mitchell Gulch

Alkali Gulch

Falls Gulch

Kim Gulch

Vallie Bridge
85 mi.
GPS

113 Road

Rock Garden Rapids II-III

Hamilton Creek

Short Creek

Sand Gulch

Howard Bridge
78.9 mi.
GPS

45 Road

45 Road Bridge
81 mi.
GPS

10A Road

Kerr Gulch

Badger Creek Rapids III-IV

Howard

50

46 Road

Cherry Creek

47 Rd

48 Road

Rincon

The Flume Rapids III-IV

Tin Cup Rapids II-III

Red Rocks Rapids II-III

45 Road

4 Road

Stout Creek

N E S W

Howard Bridge: N 38° 26' 47.594" W 105° 50' 4.796"
45 Road Bridge: N 38° 25' 50.630" W 105° 48' 44.473"
Vallie Bridge: N 38° 23' 29.228" W 105° 46' 25.493"
Lone Pine Boat Access: N 38° 22' 53.538" W 105° 39' 54.642"

GPS

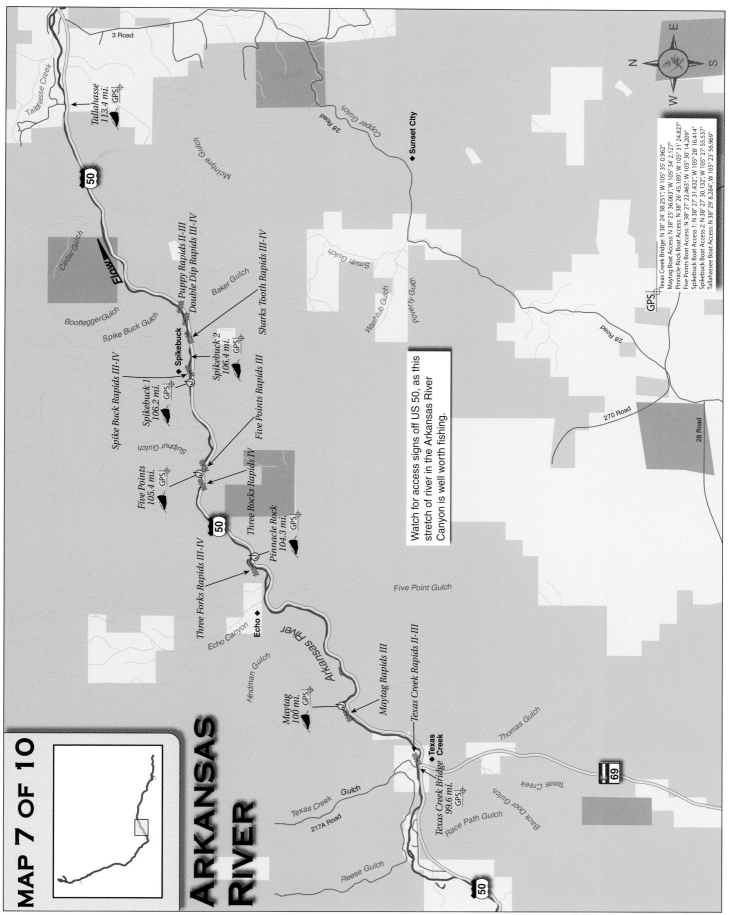

MAP 7 OF 10

ARKANSAS RIVER

3 Road

Tallahasse Creek

Tallahasse
113.4 mi.
GPS

50

Cedar Gulch

FLOW

Bootlegger Gulch

McIntyre Gulch

Spike Buck Gulch

Puppy Rapids II-III
Double Dip Rapids III-IV

Baker Gulch

Sharks Tooth Rapids III-IV

Spikebuck

Spike Buck Rapids III-IV

Spikebuck 1
106.2 mi.
GPS

Spikebuck 2
106.4 mi.
GPS

Five Points Rapids III

Sulphur Gulch

Five Points
105.4 mi.
GPS

Three Rocks Rapids IV

50

Three Forks Rapids III-IV

Pinnacle Rock
104.3 mi.
GPS

Echo Canyon

Echo

Hindman Gulch

Arkansas River

Maytag
100 mi.
GPS

Maytag Rapids III

Texas Creek Rapids II-III

Texas Creek

Texas Creek Bridge
99.6 mi.
GPS

Texas Creek Gulch

217A Road

Reese Gulch

Race Path Gulch

Back Door Gulch

Thomas Gulch

Texas Creek

69

50

Five Point Gulch

Sunset City

Copper Gulch

28 Road

Smith Gulch

Washtub Gulch

Poverty Gulch

28 Road

270 Road

28 Road

Watch for access signs off US 50, as this stretch of river in the Arkansas River Canyon is well worth fishing.

GPS

Texas Creek Bridge: N 38° 24′ 38.251″; W 105° 35′ 0.962″
Maytag Boat Access: N 38° 25′ 36.063′; W 105° 34′ 2.127″
Pinnacle Rock Boat Access: N 38° 26′ 45.189′; W 105° 31′ 24.827″
Five Points Boat Access: N 38° 27′ 22.463′; W 105° 30′ 14.209″
Spikebuck Boat Access 1: N 38° 27′ 31.432′; W 105° 28′ 16.414″
Spikebuck Boat Access 2: N 38° 27′ 30.132′; W 105° 27′ 55.537″
Tallahassee Boat Access: N 38° 29′ 8.284″ W 105° 23′ 56.969′

N E S W

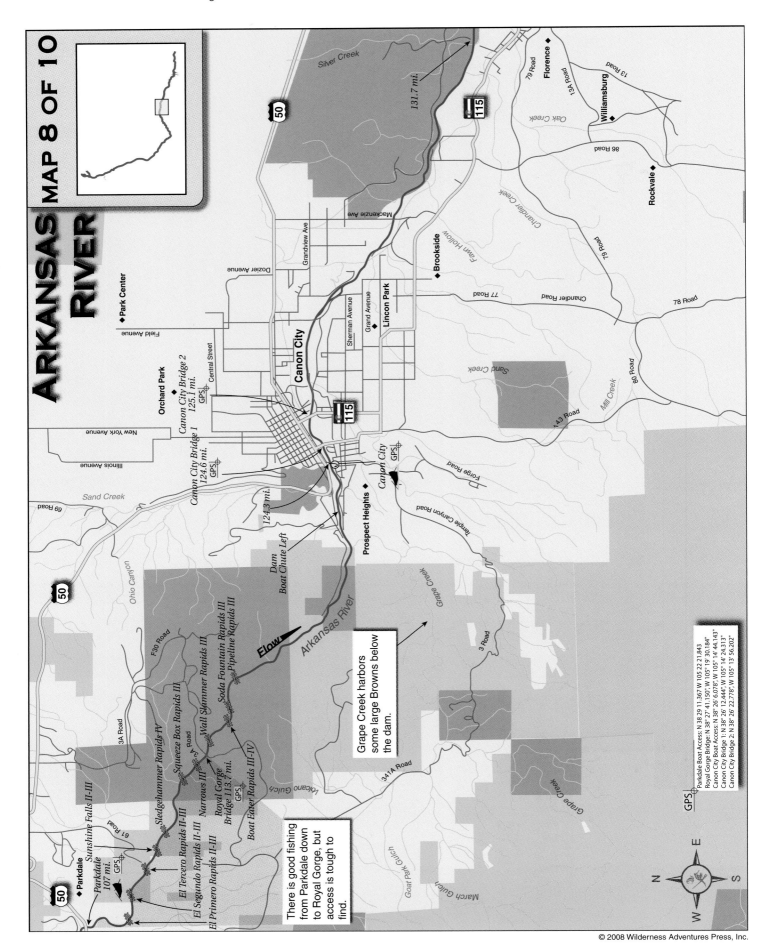

ARKANSAS MAP 8 OF 10 RIVER

There is good fishing from Parkdale down to Royal Gorge, but access is tough to find.

Grape Creek harbors some large Browns below the dam.

Parkdale Boat Access: N 38 29 11.367' W 105 22 21.843
Royal Gorge Bridge: N 38° 27 41.150'; W 105° 19 30.184"
Canon City Boat Access: N 38° 26 6.078'; W 105° 14 44.143"
Canon City Bridge 1: N 38° 26' 12.444'; W 105° 14' 24.313"
Canon City Bridge 2: N 38° 26' 22.778'; W 105° 13' 56.202"

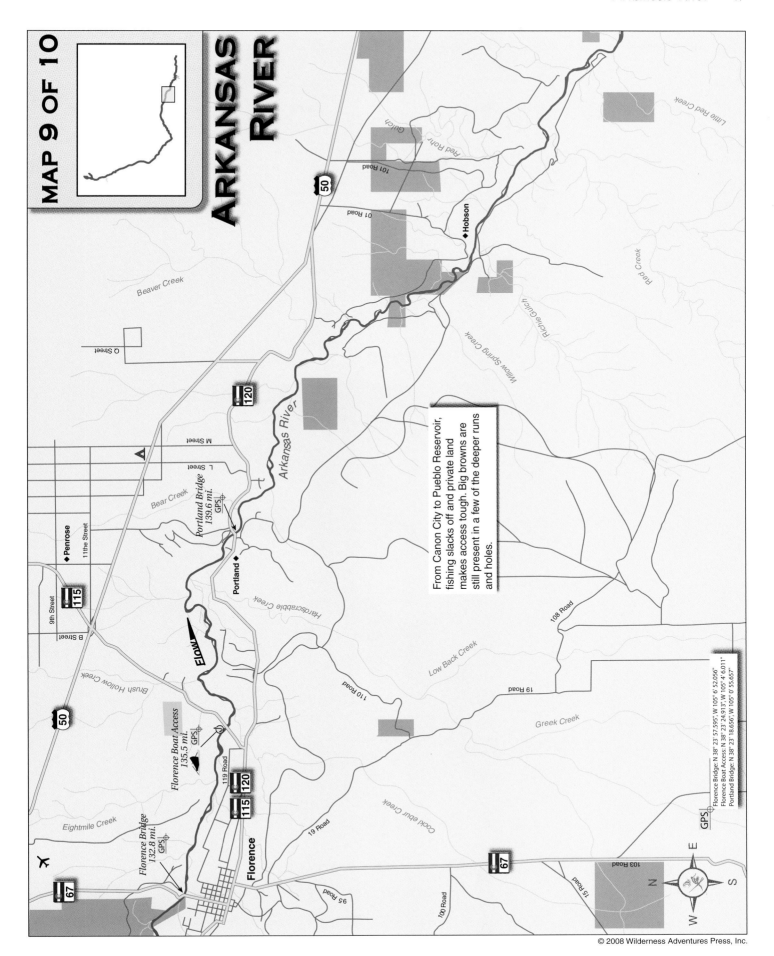

MAP 9 OF 10

ARKANSAS RIVER

From Canon City to Pueblo Reservoir, fishing slacks off and private land makes access tough. Big browns are still present in a few of the deeper runs and holes.

Florence Bridge: N 38° 23' 57.595"; W 105° 6' 52.056"
Florence Boat Access: N 38° 23' 24.913"; W 105° 4' 6.011"
Portland Bridge: N 38° 23' 18.656"; W 105° 0' 55.657"

Portland Bridge 139.6 mi.

Florence Boat Access 135.5 mi.

Florence Bridge 132.8 mi.

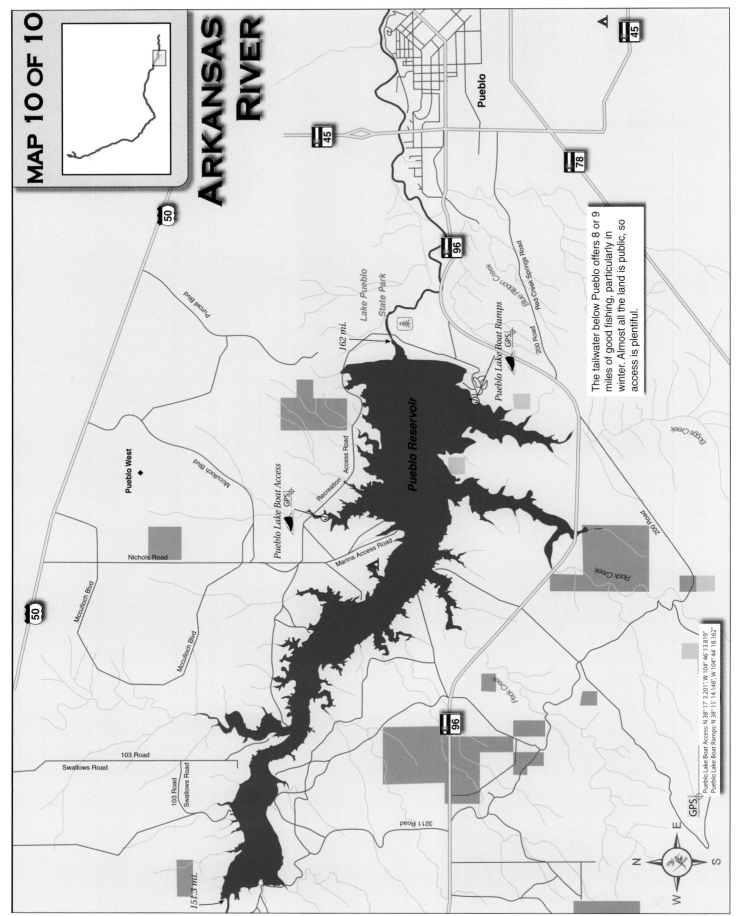

MAP 10 OF 10

ARKANSAS RIVER

Pueblo

Pueblo West

Pueblo Reservoir

Lake Pueblo State Park

Pueblo Lake Boat Access
GPS

Pueblo Lake Boat Ramps
GPS

The tailwater below Pueblo offers 8 or 9 miles of good fishing, particularly in winter. Almost all the land is public, so access is plentiful.

Purcell Blvd
Mcculloch Blvd
Mcculloch Blvd
Nichols Road
Marina Access Road
Recreation Access Road
162 mi.
151.3 mi.
103 Road
Swallows Road
3211 Road
200 Road
Rock Creek
Boggs Creek
Red Creek Springs Road
Blue Ribbon Creek

GPS Pueblo Lake Boat Access: N 38° 17' 3.201", W 104° 46' 13.819"
Pueblo Lake Boat Ramps: N 38° 15' 14.148", W 104° 44' 18.162"

© 2008 Wilderness Adventures Press, Inc.

BIG THOMPSON RIVER

The Big Thompson begins just east of the Continental Divide in Rocky Mountain National Park. It starts small but grows in size on its run to the South Platte River near Greeley. Above Estes Lake, Moraine Park gives anglers a chance at smaller brook, brown, and cutthroat trout. The stretch of river between Lake Estes and Waltonia has special regulations in place, and a lot of anglers concentrate on this section. While the river below

Olympus Dam is technically a tailwater, it fishes more like a freestone river due to the schedule of water releases. Good fishing for brown and rainbow trout continues downstream through Big Thompson Canyon.

The many lakes in and around Rocky Mountain National Park offer anglers plenty of opportunities to fish for greenback cutthroats away from the summer crowds.

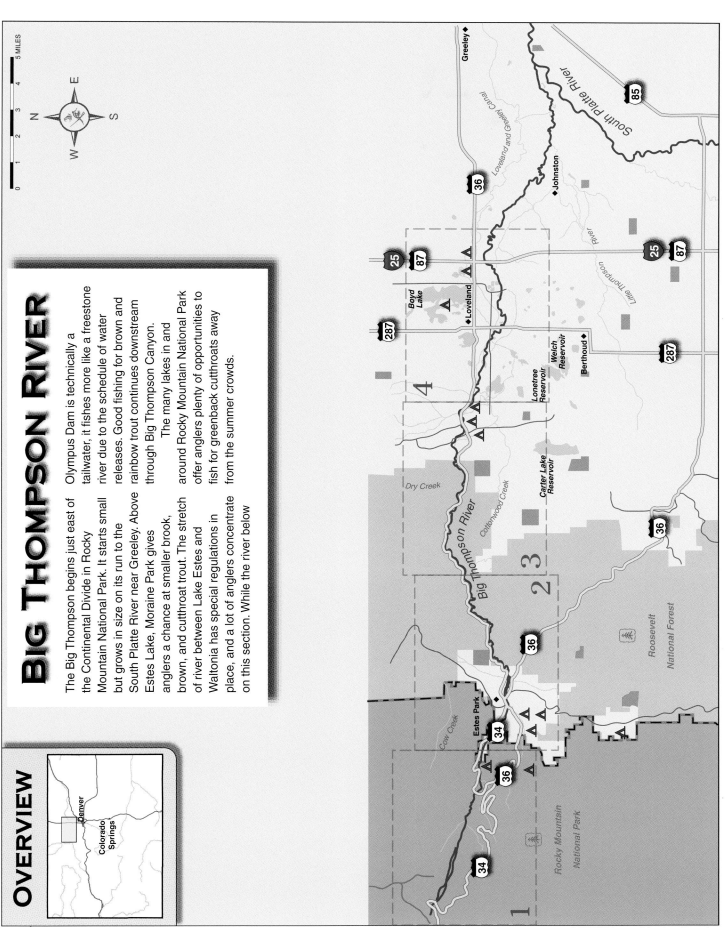

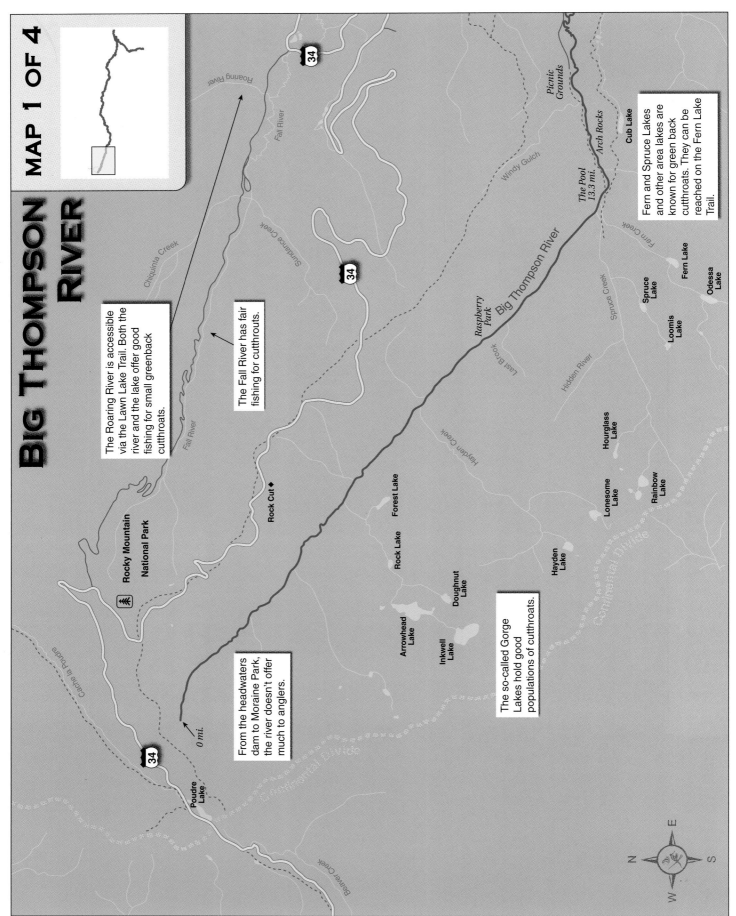

BIG THOMPSON RIVER

MAP 1 OF 4

The Roaring River is accessible via the Lawn Lake Trail. Both the river and the lake offer good fishing for small greenback cutthroats.

The Fall River has fair fishing for cutthroats.

From the headwaters dam to Moraine Park, the river doesn't offer much to anglers.

The so-called Gorge Lakes hold good populations of cutthroats.

Fern and Spruce Lakes and other area lakes are known for green back cutthroats. They can be reached on the Fern Lake Trail.

Rocky Mountain National Park

Rock Cut ◆

The Pool 13.3 mi.

0 mi.

Picnic Grounds

Arch Rocks

Cub Lake

Spruce Lake

Fern Lake

Loomis Lake

Odessa Lake

Hourglass Lake

Lonesome Lake

Rainbow Lake

Hayden Lake

Arrowhead Lake

Doughnut Lake

Inkwell Lake

Rock Lake

Forest Lake

Raspberry Park

Big Thompson River

Last Brook

Hidden River

Hayden Creek

Spruce Creek

Fern Creek

Windy Gulch

Chiquinta Creek

Sundance Creek

Fall River

Roaring River

Fall River

Cache la Poudre

Poudre Lake

Beaver Creek

Continental Divide

34

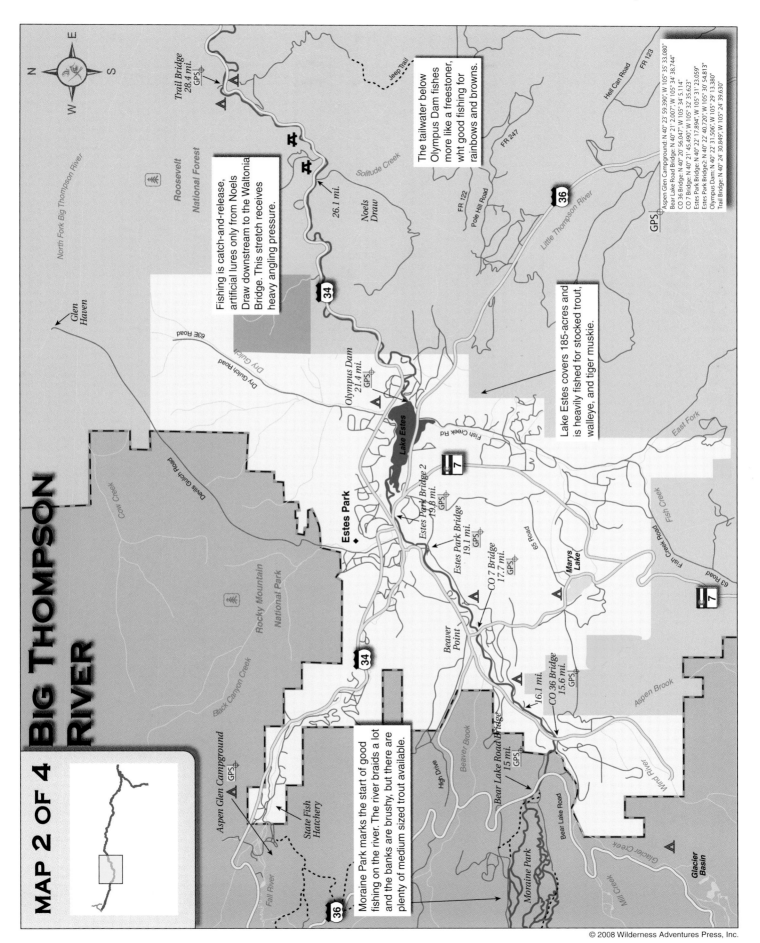

MAP 2 OF 4

BIG THOMPSON RIVER

Moraine Park marks the start of good fishing on the river. The river braids a lot and the banks are brushy, but there are plenty of medium sized trout available.

Fishing is catch-and-release, artificial lures only from Noels Draw downstream to the Waltonia Bridge. This stretch receives heavy angling pressure.

The tailwater below Olympus Dam fishes more like a freestoner, wht good fishing for rainbows and browns.

Lake Estes covers 185-acres and is heavily fished for stocked trout, walleye, and tiger muskie.

Trail Bridge 28.4 mi. GPS

26.1 mi.

Olympus Dam 21.4 mi. GPS

Lake Estes

Estes Park

Estes Park Bridge 2 19.8 mi. GPS

Estes Park Bridge 19.1 mi. GPS

CO 7 Bridge 17.7 mi. GPS

16.1 mi.

CO 36 Bridge 15.6 mi. GPS

Bear Lake Road Bridge 15 mi. GPS

Aspen Glen Campground GPS

State Fish Hatchery

Moraine Park

Glacier Basin

Beaver Point

Marys Lake

Glen Haven

Roosevelt National Forest

Rocky Mountain National Park

North Fork Big Thompson River

Solitude Creek

Noels Draw

Little Thompson River

Fall River

Cow Creek

Black Canyon Creek

Devils Gulch Road

Dry Gulch Road

63E Road

Fish Creek Rd

65 Road

63 Road

Fish Creek Road

Fish Creek

East Fork

Aspen Brook

Beaver Brook

High Drive

Wind River

Bear Lake Road

Glacier Creek

Mill Creek

Hell Can Road

Pole Hill Road

FR 122

FR 247

FR 123

Jeep Trail

Aspen Glen Campground: N 40° 23' 59.390'; W 105° 35' 33.080'
Bear Lake Road Bridge: N 40° 21' 2.007'; W 105° 34 38.744'
CO 36 Bridge: N 40° 20' 56.047'; W 105° 34 5.114'
CO 7 Bridge: N 40° 21' 45.490'; W 105° 32 35.623'
Estes Park Bridge: N 40° 22' 17.894'; W 105° 31' 23.059'
Estes Park Bridge2: N 40° 22' 40.720'; W 105° 30 54.813'
Olympus Dam: N 40° 22' 31.506'; W 105° 29 13.380'
Trail Bridge: N 40° 24' 30.849'; W 105° 24' 39.630'

GPS

N E S W

© 2008 Wilderness Adventures Press, Inc.

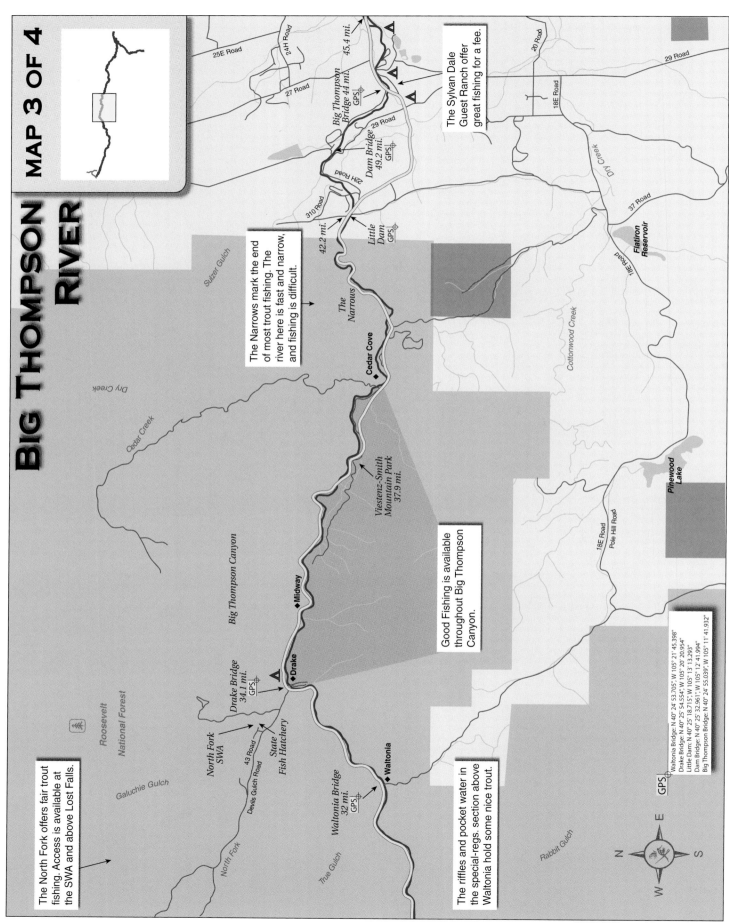

MAP 3 OF 4

BIG THOMPSON RIVER

The North Fork offers fair trout fishing. Access is available at the SWA and above Lost Falls.

The Sylvan Dale Guest Ranch offer great fishing for a fee.

The Narrows mark the end of most trout fishing. The river here is fast and narrow, and fishing is difficult.

Good Fishing is available throughout Big Thompson Canyon.

The riffles and pocket water in the special-regs. section above Waltonia hold some nice trout.

Roosevelt National Forest

Galuchie Gulch

Dry Creek

Cedar Creek

Sulzer Gulch

North Fork

Devils Gulch Road

43 Road

North Fork SWA

State Fish Hatchery

Drake Bridge 34.1 mi. GPS

Waltonia Bridge 32 mi. GPS

True Gulch

Rabbit Gulch

◆ Waltonia

◆ Drake

◆ Midway

Big Thompson Canyon

Viestenz-Smith Mountain Park 37.9 mi.

◆ Cedar Cove

The Narrows

42.2 mi.

Little Dam GPS

Dam Bridge 49.2 mi. GPS

Big Thompson Bridge 44 mi. GPS

45.4 mi.

310 Road

32H Road

29 Road

27 Road

24H Road

25E Road

29 Road

20 Road

18E Road

Dry Creek

37 Road

18E Road

Flatiron Reservoir

Cottonwood Creek

18E Road

Pole Hill Road

Pinewood Lake

GPS

Waltonia Bridge: N 40° 24' 53.705'; W 105° 21' 45.398"
Drake Bridge: N 40° 25' 54.554'; W 105° 20' 20.954"
Little Dam: N 40° 25' 18.715'; W 105° 13' 13.293"
Dam Bridge: N 40° 25' 32.961'; W 105° 12' 41.994"
Big Thompson Bridge: N 40° 24' 55.039'; W 105° 11' 41.932"

N E W S

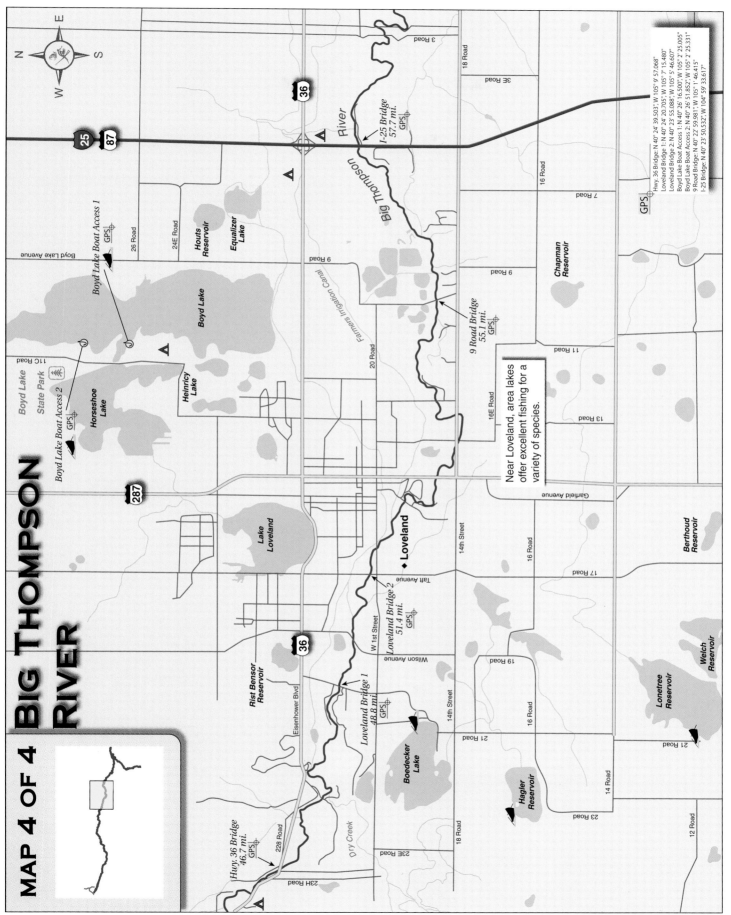

MAP 4 OF 4

BIG THOMPSON RIVER

Near Loveland, area lakes offer excellent fishing for a variety of species.

Hwy. 36 Bridge: N 40° 24' 39.503"; W 105° 9' 57.068"
Loveland Bridge 1: N 40° 24' 20.705"; W 105° 7' 15.480"
Loveland Bridge 2: N 40° 23' 55.088"; W 105° 5' 46.607"
Boyd Lake Boat Access 1: N 40° 26' 16.500"; W 105° 2' 25.005"
Boyd Lake Boat Access 2: N 40° 26' 51.852"; W 105° 2' 25.331"
9 Road Bridge: N 40° 22' 59.981"; W 105° 1' 46.415"
I-25 Bridge: N 40° 23' 50.532"; W 104° 59' 33.617"

I-25 Bridge 57.7 mi.
GPS

9 Road Bridge 55.1 mi.
GPS

Loveland Bridge 2 51.4 mi.
GPS

Loveland Bridge 1 48.8 mi.
GPS

Hwy. 36 Bridge 46.7 mi.
GPS

Boyd Lake Boat Access 1
GPS

Boyd Lake Boat Access 2
GPS

Boyd Lake State Park

Boyd Lake

Horseshoe Lake

Heinricy Lake

Houts Reservoir

Equalizer Lake

Chapman Reservoir

Lake Loveland

♦ Loveland

Rist Bensor Reservoir

Boedecker Lake

Hagler Reservoir

Lonetree Reservoir

Welch Reservoir

Berthoud Reservoir

Big Thompson River

Farmers Irrigation Canal

Dry Creek

Boyd Lake Avenue
11C Road
26 Road
24E Road
Road 6
20 Road
9 Road
11 Road
16E Road
13 Road
16 Road
7 Road
18 Road
3E Road
3 Road
Garfield Avenue
17 Road
19 Road
14 Road
21 Road
23 Road
12 Road
Eisenhower Blvd
228 Road
23H Road
23E Road
18 Road
14th Street
W 1st Street
Wilson Avenue
Taft Avenue
14th Street

25 87

36

36

287

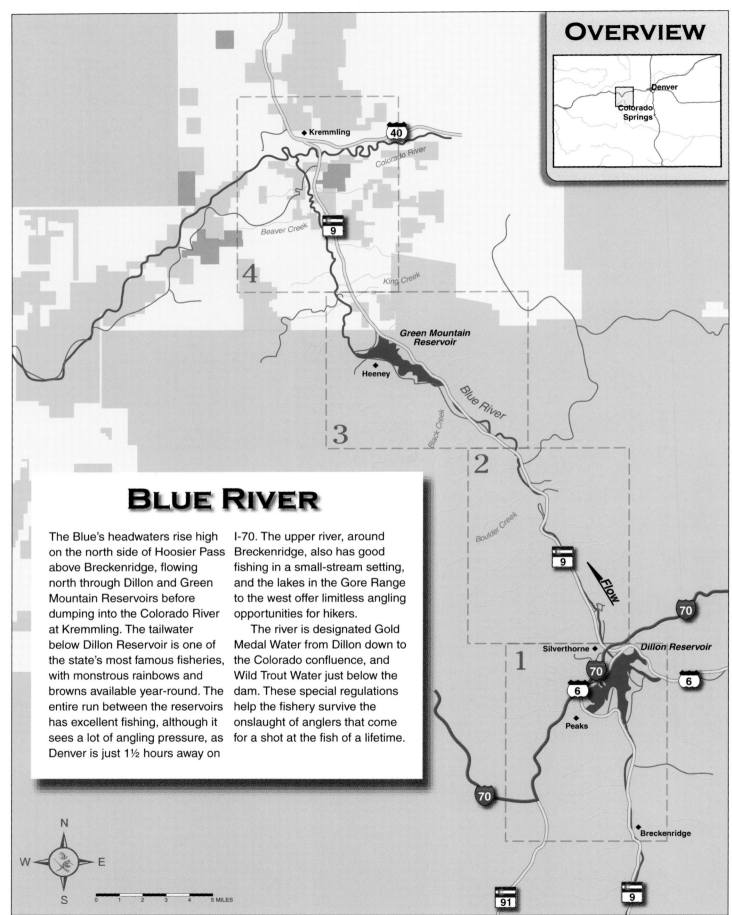

OVERVIEW

Denver

Colorado
Springs

Kremmling

Colorado River

40

Beaver Creek

9

4

King Creek

Green Mountain
Reservoir

Heeney

Blue River

Black Creek

3

2

Boulder Creek

9

Flow

70

Silverthorne

Dillon Reservoir

1

70

6

6

Peaks

70

Breckenridge

BLUE RIVER

The Blue's headwaters rise high on the north side of Hoosier Pass above Breckenridge, flowing north through Dillon and Green Mountain Reservoirs before dumping into the Colorado River at Kremmling. The tailwater below Dillon Reservoir is one of the state's most famous fisheries, with monstrous rainbows and browns available year-round. The entire run between the reservoirs has excellent fishing, although it sees a lot of angling pressure, as Denver is just 1½ hours away on

I-70. The upper river, around Breckenridge, also has good fishing in a small-stream setting, and the lakes in the Gore Range to the west offer limitless angling opportunities for hikers.

The river is designated Gold Medal Water from Dillon down to the Colorado confluence, and Wild Trout Water just below the dam. These special regulations help the fishery survive the onslaught of anglers that come for a shot at the fish of a lifetime.

N
W   E
S

0   1   2   3   4   5 MILES

91

9

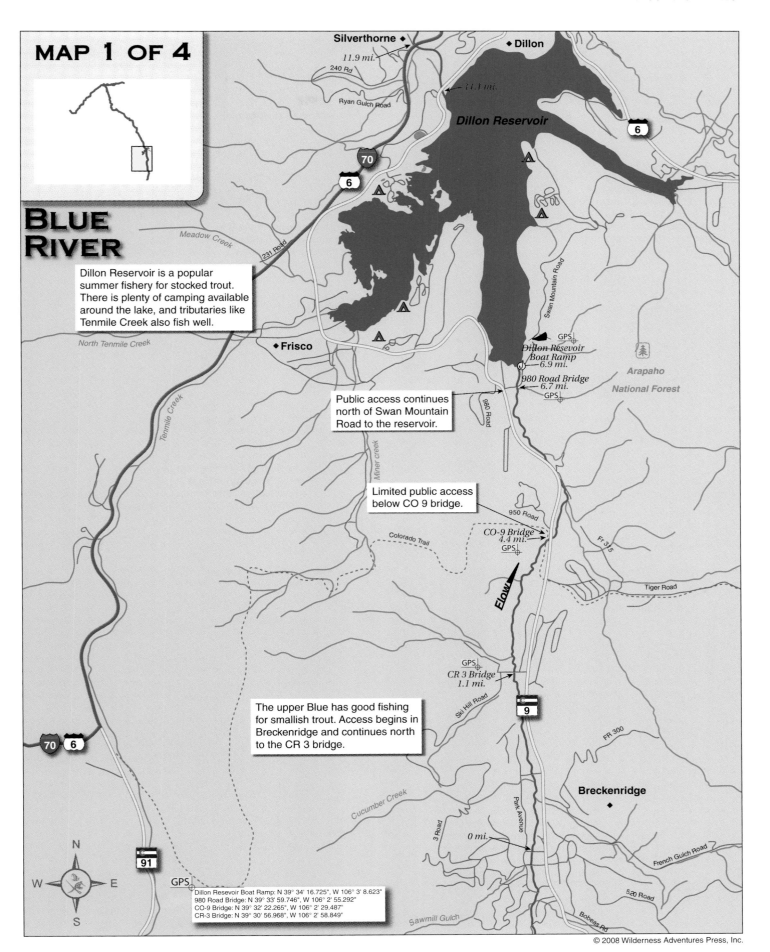

MAP 1 OF 4

BLUE RIVER

Dillon Reservoir is a popular summer fishery for stocked trout. There is plenty of camping available around the lake, and tributaries like Tenmile Creek also fish well.

Public access continues north of Swan Mountain Road to the reservoir.

Limited public access below CO 9 bridge.

The upper Blue has good fishing for smallish trout. Access begins in Breckenridge and continues north to the CR 3 bridge.

Silverthorne ◆
11.9 mi.
240 Rd
Ryan Gulch Road

◆ Dillon

11.1 mi.

Dillon Reservoir

6

70
6

Meadow Creek

231 Road

North Tenmile Creek

◆ Frisco

Tenmile Creek

Miner creek

Swan Mountain Road

Arapaho National Forest

GPS
Dillon Resevoir Boat Ramp
6.9 mi.
980 Road Bridge
6.7 mi.
GPS

980 Road

950 Road

Colorado Trail

CO-9 Bridge
4.4 mi.
GPS

Ft 315

Tiger Road

Flow

GPS
CR 3 Bridge
1.1 mi.

Ski Hill Road

9

FR 300

Breckenridge ◆

Park Avenue

3 Road

0 mi.

Cucumber Creek

70 6

N
W E
S

91

GPS

French Gulch Road

520 Road

Bobcas Rd

Sawmill Gulch

Dillon Resevoir Boat Ramp: N 39° 34' 16.725", W 106° 3' 8.623"
980 Road Bridge: N 39° 33' 59.746", W 106° 2' 55.292"
CO-9 Bridge: N 39° 32' 22.265", W 106° 2' 29.487"
CR-3 Bridge: N 39° 30' 56.968", W 106° 2' 58.849"

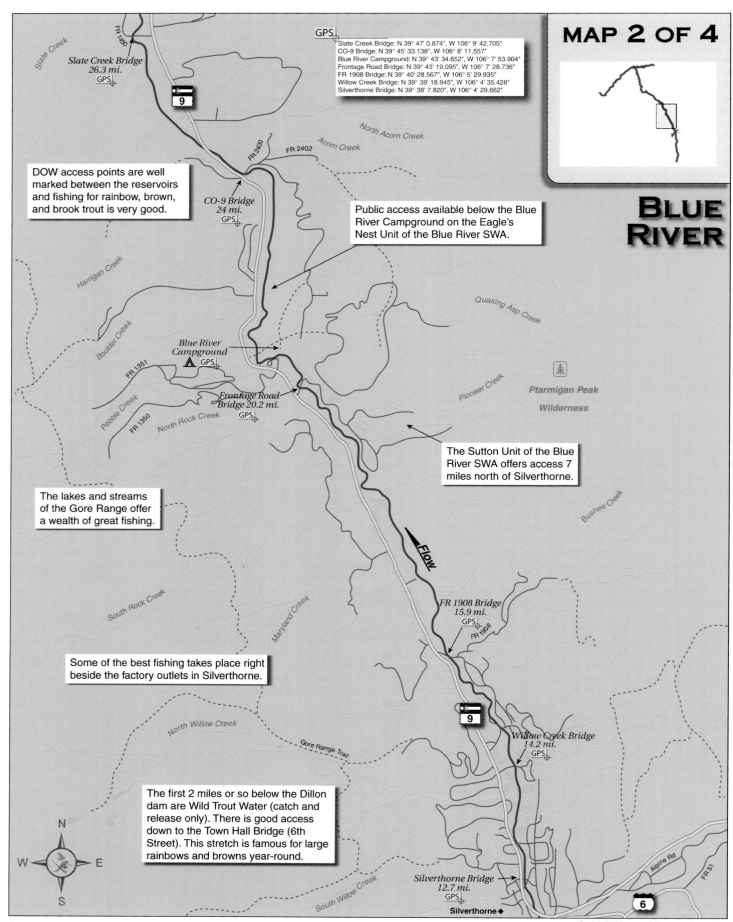

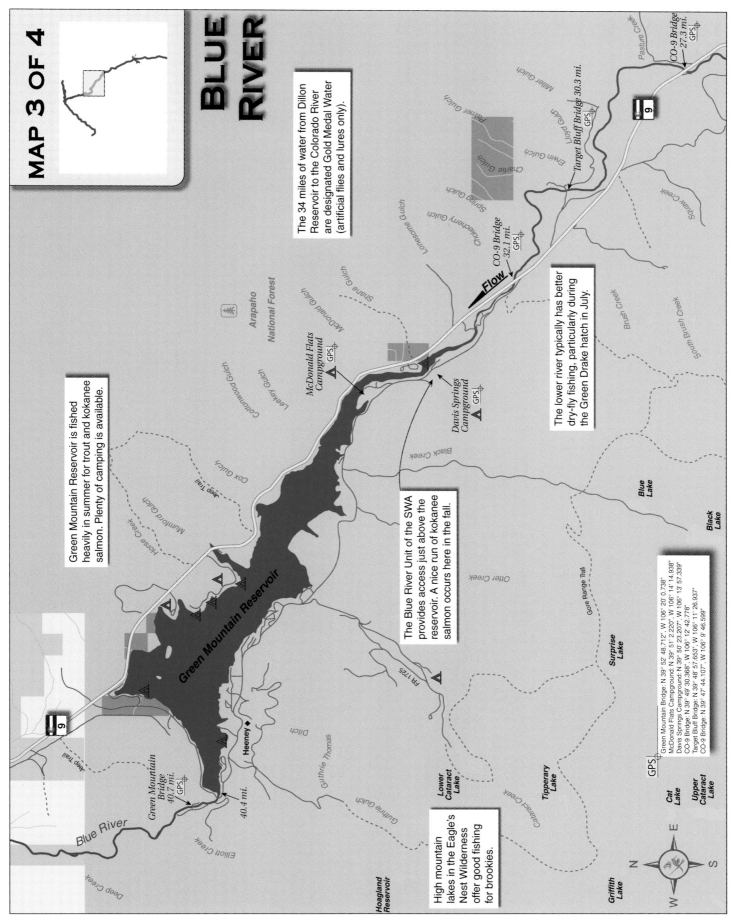

MAP 3 OF 4

BLUE RIVER

The 34 miles of water from Dillon Reservoir to the Colorado River are designated Gold Medal Water (artificial flies and lures only).

Green Mountain Reservoir is fished heavily in summer for trout and kokanee salmon. Plenty of camping is available.

The Blue River Unit of the SWA provides access just above the reservoir. A nice run of kokanee salmon occurs here in the fall.

The lower river typically has better dry-fly fishing, particularly during the Green Drake hatch in July.

High mountain lakes in the Eagle's Nest Wilderness offer good fishing for brookies.

Green Mountain Reservoir

Arapaho National Forest

Flow

GPS: Green Mountain Bridge: N 39° 52' 48.712", W 106° 20' 0.738"
McDonald Flats Campground: N 39° 51' 2.220", W 106° 14' 14.938"
Davis Springs Campground: N 39° 50' 23.207", W 106° 13' 57.339"
CO-9 Bridge: N 39° 49' 30.368", W 106° 12' 42.778"
Target Bluff Bridge: N 39° 48' 57.653", W 106° 11' 26.937"
CO-9 Bridge: N 39° 47' 44.107", W 106° 9' 46.599"

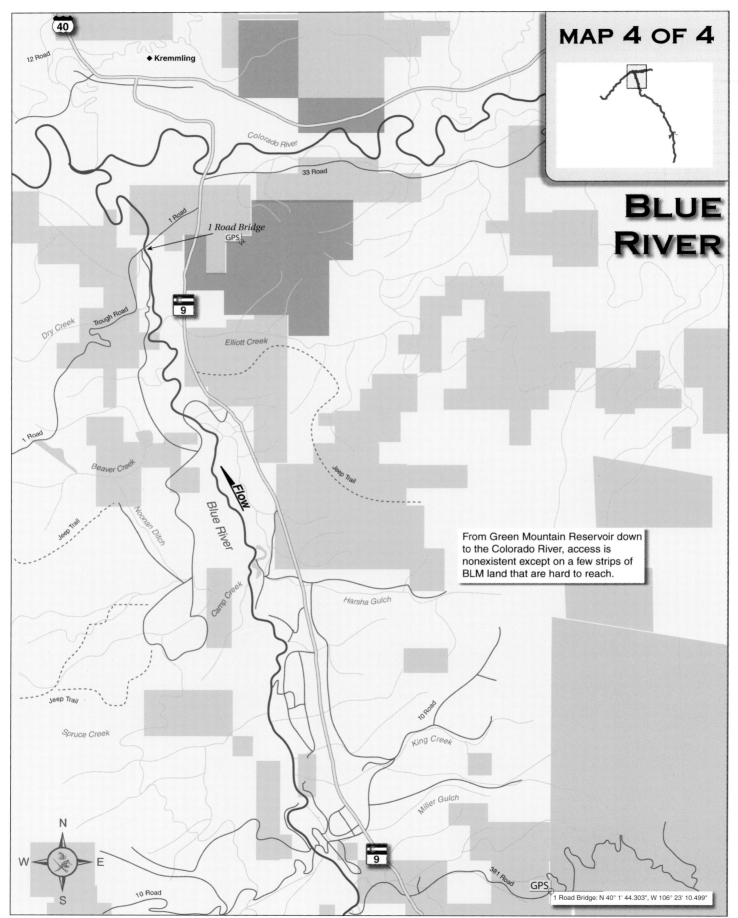

MAP **4** OF **4**

BLUE RIVER

US 40

12 Road

◆ Kremmling

Colorado River

33 Road

1 Road

1 Road Bridge
GPS

9

Dry Creek

Trough Road

Elliott Creek

Jeep Trail

1 Road

Beaver Creek

Flow

Blue River

Jeep Trail

Noonan Ditch

From Green Mountain Reservoir down to the Colorado River, access is nonexistent except on a few strips of BLM land that are hard to reach.

Camp Creek

Harsha Gulch

Jeep Trail

Spruce Creek

10 Road

King Creek

Miller Gulch

N
W E
S

9

381 Road

GPS

10 Road

1 Road Bridge: N 40° 1' 44.303", W 106° 23' 10.499"

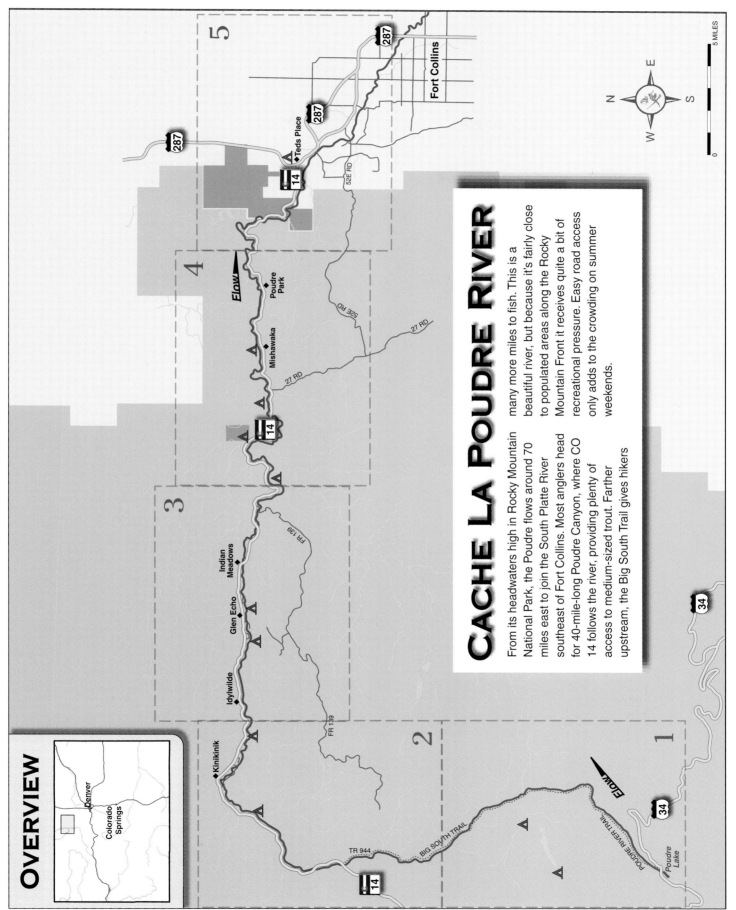

CACHE LA POUDRE RIVER

From its headwaters high in Rocky Mountain National Park, the Poudre flows around 70 miles east to join the South Platte River southeast of Fort Collins. Most anglers head for 40-mile-long Poudre Canyon, where CO 14 follows the river, providing plenty of access to medium-sized trout. Farther upstream, the Big South Trail gives hikers many more miles to fish. This is a beautiful river, but because it's fairly close to populated areas along the Rocky Mountain Front it receives quite a bit of recreational pressure. Easy road access only adds to the crowding on summer weekends.

OVERVIEW

Denver

Colorado Springs

Fort Collins

Teds Place

Poudre Park

Mishawaka

Indian Meadows

Glen Echo

Idylwilde

Kinikinik

Poudre Lake

287

287

287

14

14

14

34

34

52E RD

27 RD

27 RD

S2E RD

FR 139

FR 139

TR 944

BIG SOUTH TRAIL

POUDRE RIVER TRAIL

Flow

Flow

1

2

3

4

5

N

E

S

W

0   5 MILES

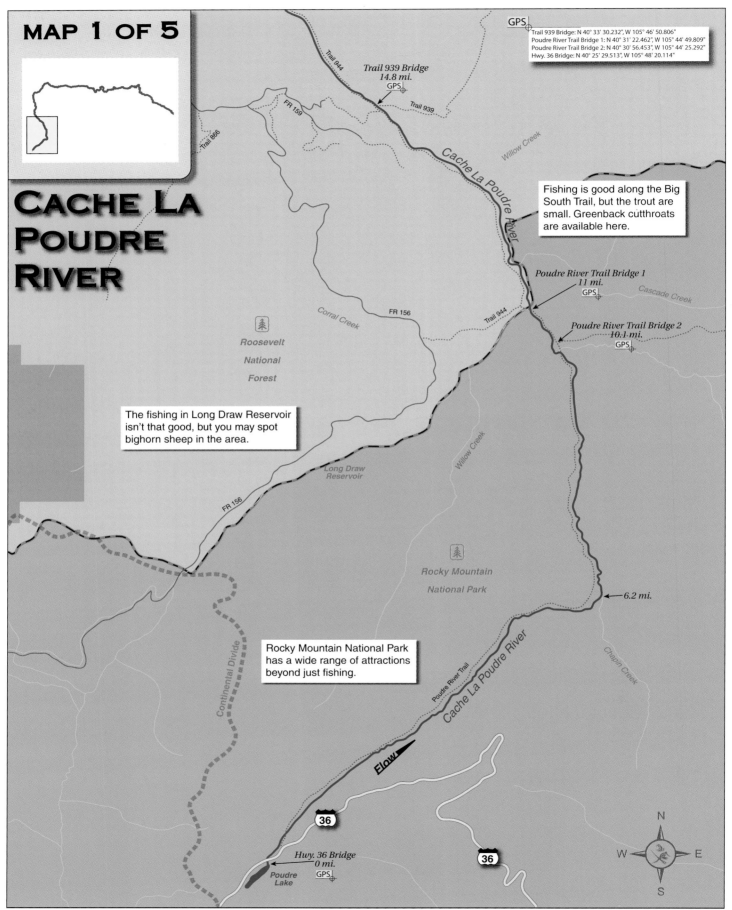

MAP 1 OF 5

CACHE LA POUDRE RIVER

GPS

Trail 939 Bridge: N 40° 33' 30.232", W 105° 46' 50.806"
Poudre River Trail Bridge 1: N 40° 31' 22.462", W 105° 44' 49.809"
Poudre River Trail Bridge 2: N 40° 30' 56.453", W 105° 44' 25.292"
Hwy. 36 Bridge: N 40° 25' 29.513", W 105° 48' 20.114"

Trail 944

Trail 939 Bridge
14.8 mi.
GPS

FR 159

Trail 939

Trail 866

Willow Creek

Cache La Poudre River

Fishing is good along the Big South Trail, but the trout are small. Greenback cutthroats are available here.

Poudre River Trail Bridge 1
11 mi.
GPS

Cascade Creek

Corral Creek

FR 156

Trail 944

Poudre River Trail Bridge 2
10.1 mi.
GPS

Roosevelt

National

Forest

The fishing in Long Draw Reservoir isn't that good, but you may spot bighorn sheep in the area.

Willow Creek

Long Draw
Reservoir

FR 156

Rocky Mountain

National Park

6.2 mi.

Continental Divide

Rocky Mountain National Park has a wide range of attractions beyond just fishing.

Poudre River Trail

Chapin Creek

Cache La Poudre River

Flow

36

N

W   E

S

36

Hwy. 36 Bridge
0 mi.
GPS

Poudre
Lake

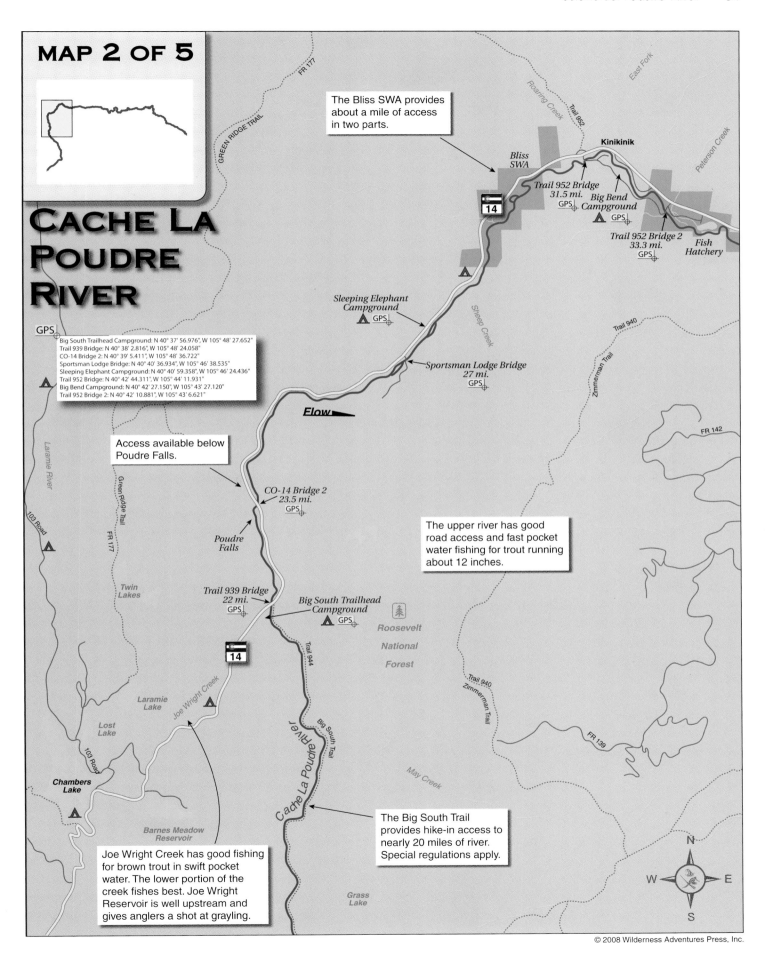

MAP 2 OF 5

CACHE LA POUDRE RIVER

The Bliss SWA provides about a mile of access in two parts.

Bliss SWA

Kinikinik

Trail 952 Bridge 31.5 mi.
GPS

Big Bend Campground
GPS

Trail 952 Bridge 2 33.3 mi.
GPS

Fish Hatchery

GPS
Big South Trailhead Campground: N 40° 37' 56.976", W 105° 48' 27.652"
Trail 939 Bridge: N 40° 38' 2.816", W 105° 48' 24.058"
CO-14 Bridge 2: N 40° 39' 5.411", W 105° 48' 36.722"
Sportsman Lodge Bridge: N 40° 40' 36.934", W 105° 46' 38.535"
Sleeping Elephant Campground: N 40° 40' 59.358", W 105° 46' 24.436"
Trail 952 Bridge: N 40° 42' 44.311", W 105° 44' 11.931"
Big Bend Campground: N 40° 42' 27.150", W 105° 43' 27.120"
Trail 952 Bridge 2: N 40° 42' 10.881", W 105° 43' 6.621"

Sleeping Elephant Campground
GPS

Sportsman Lodge Bridge 27 mi.
GPS

Flow

Access available below Poudre Falls.

CO-14 Bridge 2 23.5 mi.
GPS

The upper river has good road access and fast pocket water fishing for trout running about 12 inches.

Poudre Falls

Trail 939 Bridge 22 mi.
GPS

Big South Trailhead Campground
GPS

Roosevelt National Forest

Twin Lakes

Laramie Lake

Lost Lake

Chambers Lake

Barnes Meadow Reservoir

The Big South Trail provides hike-in access to nearly 20 miles of river. Special regulations apply.

Joe Wright Creek has good fishing for brown trout in swift pocket water. The lower portion of the creek fishes best. Joe Wright Reservoir is well upstream and gives anglers a shot at grayling.

Grass Lake

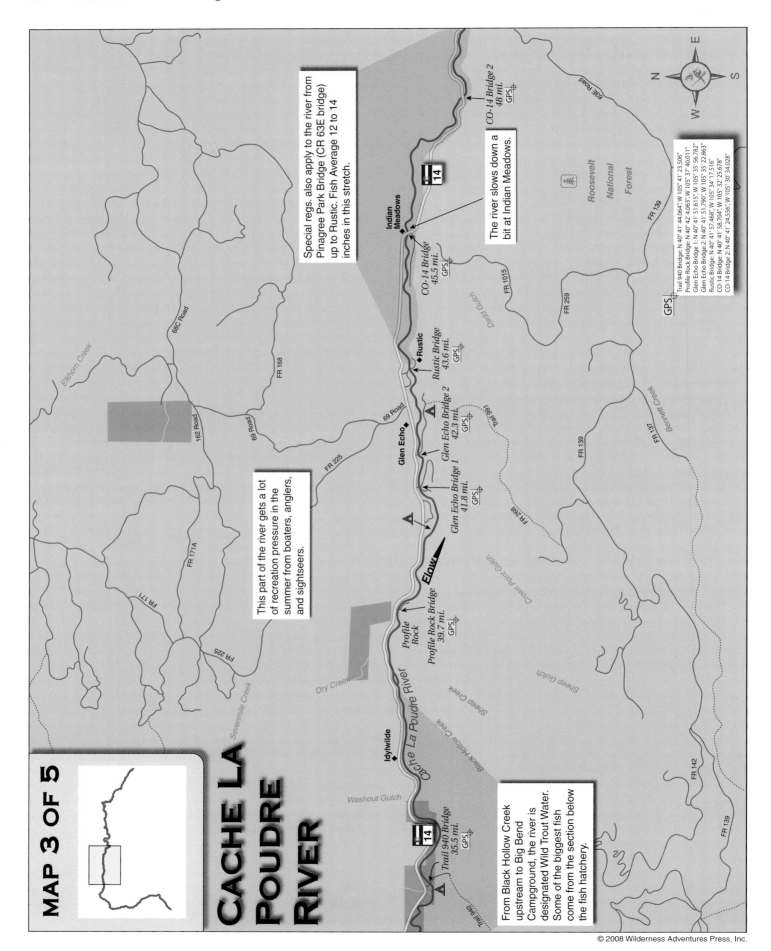

MAP 3 OF 5

CACHE LA POUDRE RIVER

Special regs. also apply to the river from Pinagree Park Bridge (CR 63E bridge) up to Rustic. Fish Average 12 to 14 inches in this stretch.

The river slows down a bit at Indian Meadows.

This part of the river gets a lot of recreation pressure in the summer from boaters, anglers, and sightseers.

From Black Hollow Creek upstream to Big Bend Campground, the river is designated Wild Trout Water. Some of the biggest fish come from the section below the fish hatchery.

CO-14 Bridge 2 48 mi. GPS

Indian Meadows

CO-14 Bridge 45.5 mi. GPS

Rustic
Rustic Bridge 43.6 mi. GPS

Glen Echo
Glen Echo Bridge 2 42.3 mi. GPS

Glen Echo Bridge 1 41.8 mi. GPS

Flow

Profile Rock
Profile Rock Bridge 39.7 mi. GPS

Idylwilde

Trail 940 Bridge 35.5 mi. GPS

GPS

Trail 940 Bridge: N 40° 41' 44.064'; W 105° 41' 23.506"
Profile Rock Bridge: N 40° 42' 4.063'; W 105° 37' 40.011"
Glen Echo Bridge 1: N 40° 41' 51.615'; W 105° 35' 56.782'
Glen Echo Bridge 2: N 40° 41' 51.790'; W 105° 35' 22.863'
Rustic Bridge: N 40° 41' 57.468'; W 105° 34' 17.516"
CO-14 Bridge: N 40° 41' 58.704'; W 105° 32' 25.678"
CO-14 Bridge 2: N 40° 41' 24.556'; W 105° 30' 34.028"

Roosevelt National Forest

Elkhorn Creek
Sevenmile Creek
Dry Creek
Black Hollow Creek
Washout Gulch
Sheep Gulch
Crown Point Gulch
Dead Gulch
Bennett Creek

68C Road
69C Road
162 Road
69 Road
FR 168
FR 225
FR 171A
FR 171
FR 225
FR 259
FR 1015
FR 139
FR 139
FR 137
FR 142
FR 139
63E Road
Trail 991
FR 268
Trail 940

Cache La Poudre River

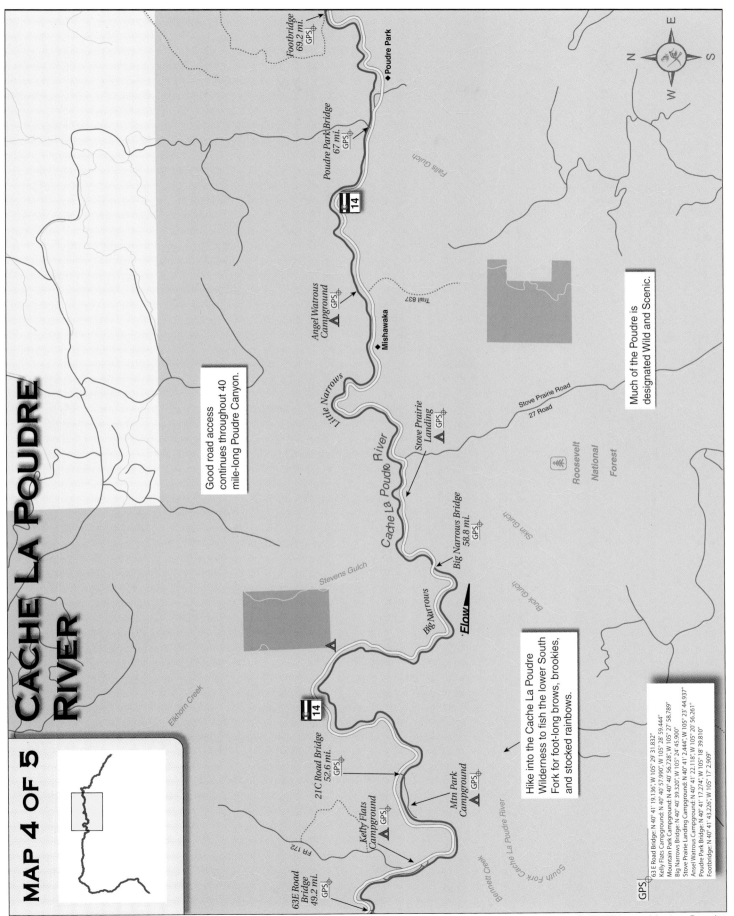

MAP 4 OF 5

CACHE LA POUDRE RIVER

Footbridge
69.2 mi.
GPS

● Poudre Park

Poudre Park Bridge
67 mi.
GPS

14

Falls Gulch

Angel Watrous
Campground
GPS

◆ Mishawaka

Trail 837

Little Narrows

Much of the Poudre is
designated Wild and Scenic.

Good road access
continues throughout 40
mile-long Poudre Canyon.

Cache La Poudre River

Stove Prairie
Landing
GPS

Stove Prairie Road

27 Road

Roosevelt
National
Forest

Big Narrows Bridge
58.8 mi.
GPS

Skin Gulch

Big Narrows

◀ Flow

Stevens Gulch

Buck Gulch

Hike into the Cache La Poudre
Wilderness to fish the lower South
Fork for foot-long brows, brookies,
and stocked rainbows.

14

Elkhorn Creek

21C Road Bridge
52.6 mi.
GPS

Kelly Flats
Campground
GPS

FR 172

Mtn Park
Campground
GPS

South Fork Cache La Poudre River

63E Road
Bridge
49.2 mi.
GPS

Bennett Creek

GPS
63 E Road Bridge: N 40° 41' 19.136', W 105° 29' 31.832"
Kelly Flats Campground: N 40° 40' 57.990', W 105° 28' 59.444"
Mountain Park Campground: N 40° 40' 56.728', W 105° 27' 58.789'
Big Narrows Bridge: N 40° 40' 39.320', W 105° 24' 45.900"
Stove Prairie Landing Campground: N 40° 41' 2.444', W 105° 23' 44.937"
Ansel Watrous Campground: N 40° 41' 22.118', W 105° 20' 56.261"
Poudre Park Bridge: N 40° 41' 17.274', W 105° 18' 39.810'
Footbridge: N 40° 41' 43.226', W 105° 17' 2.909'

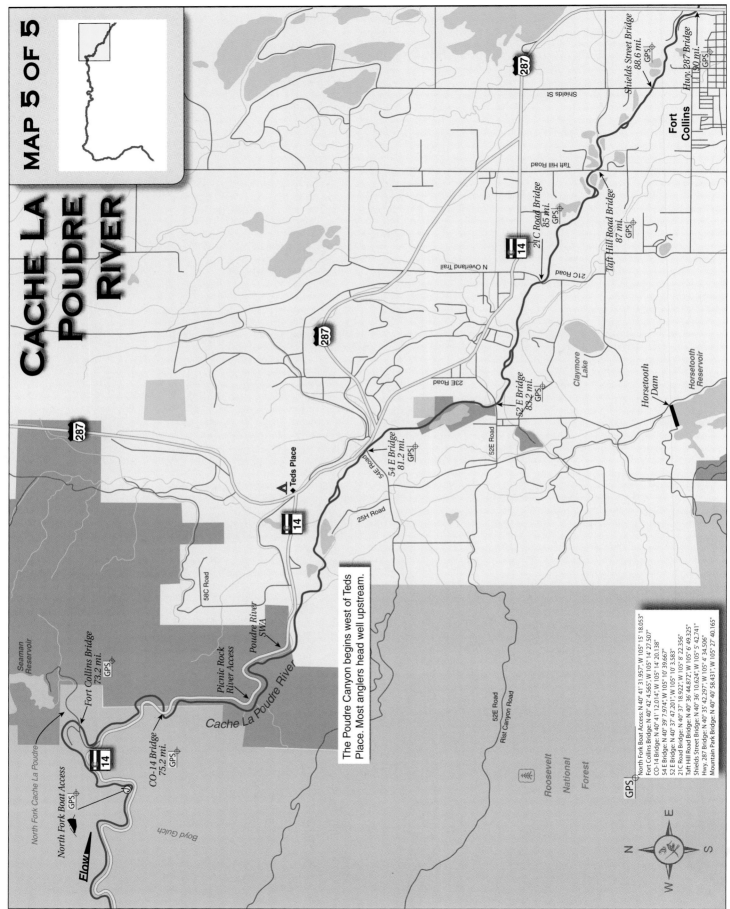

MAP 5 OF 5

CACHE LA POUDRE RIVER

Fort Collins

Shields Street Bridge 88.6 mi. GPS

Hwy. 287 Bridge 90 mi. GPS

Shields St

Taft Hill Road

21C Road Bridge 85 mi. GPS

14

N Overland Trail

Taft Hill Road Bridge 87 mi. GPS

21C Road

52 E Bridge 83.2 mi. GPS

23E Road

Claymore Lake

Horsetooth Dam

Horsetooth Reservoir

52E Road

54 E Bridge 81.2 mi. GPS

S4E Road

Teds Place

14

25H Road

58C Road

The Poudre Canyon begins west of Teds Place. Most anglers head well upstream.

Picnic Rock River Access

Poudre River SWA

Cache La Poudre River

Seaman Reservoir

Fort Collins Bridge 73.2 mi. GPS

North Fork Cache La Poudre

CO-14 Bridge 75.2 mi. GPS

14

North Fork Boat Access GPS

North Fork Boat Access

Boyd Gulch

Flow

52E Road

Rist Canyon Road

Roosevelt National Forest

GPS
North Fork Boat Access: N 40° 41' 31.957", W 105° 15' 18.053"
Fort Collins Bridge: N 40° 42' 4.565", W 105° 14' 27.507"
CO-14 Bridge: N 40° 41' 12.014", W 105° 14' 20.138"
54 E Bridge: N 40° 39' 7.974", W 105° 10' 39.667"
52 E Bridge: N 40° 37' 47.201", W 105° 10' 3.583"
21C Road Bridge: N 40° 37' 18.922", W 105° 8' 22.356"
Taft Hill Road Bridge: N 40° 36' 44.872", W 105° 6' 49.325"
Shields Street Bridge: N 40° 36' 10.624", W 105° 5' 42.741"
Hwy. 287 Bridge: N 40° 35' 42.297", W 105° 4' 34.506"
Mountain Park Bridge: N 40° 40' 58.431", W 105° 27' 40.165"

N W E S

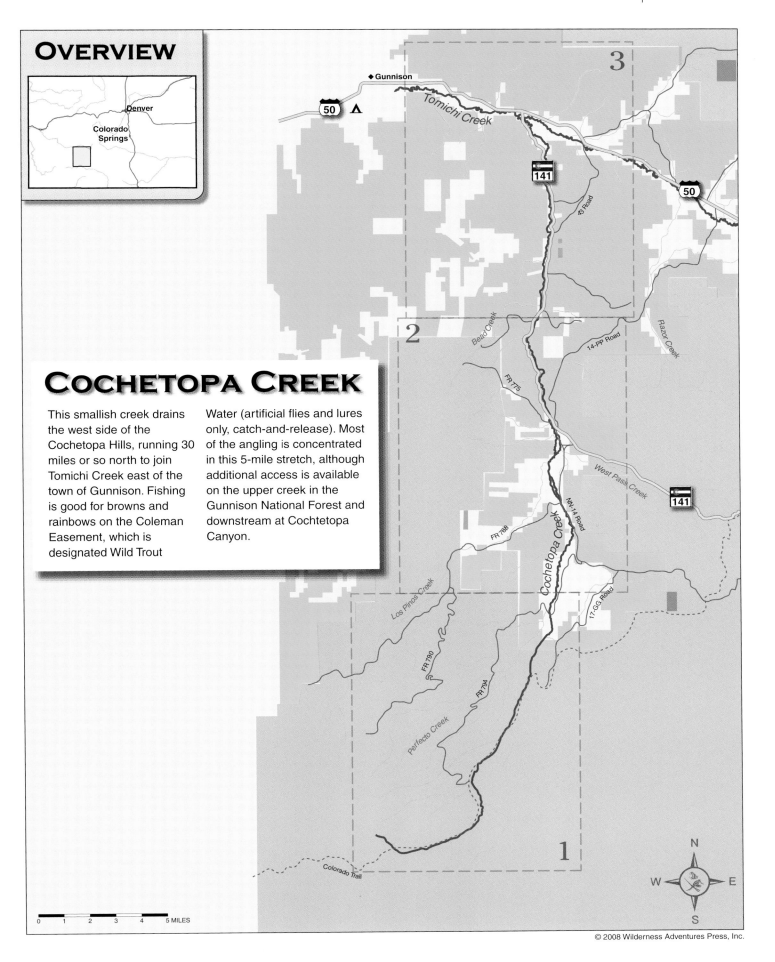

OVERVIEW

Denver

Colorado Springs

COCHETOPA CREEK

This smallish creek drains the west side of the Cochetopa Hills, running 30 miles or so north to join Tomichi Creek east of the town of Gunnison. Fishing is good for browns and rainbows on the Coleman Easement, which is designated Wild Trout

Water (artificial flies and lures only, catch-and-release). Most of the angling is concentrated in this 5-mile stretch, although additional access is available on the upper creek in the Gunnison National Forest and downstream at Cochtetopa Canyon.

◆ Gunnison

Tomichi Creek

43 Road

Bead Creek

14-PP Road

Razor Creek

FR 775

West Pass Creek

NN-14 Road

FR 788

Los Pinos Creek

17-GG Road

FR 790

FR 794

Cochetopa Creek

Perfecto Creek

Colorado Trail

0 1 2 3 4 5 MILES

N
W E
S

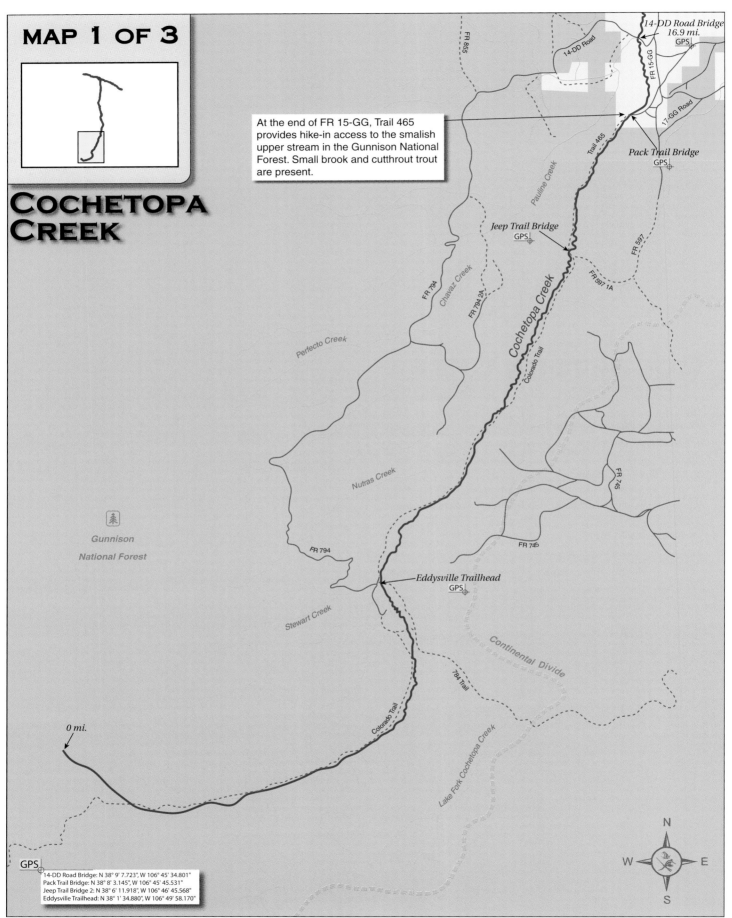

MAP 1 OF 3

COCHETOPA CREEK

At the end of FR 15-GG, Trail 465 provides hike-in access to the smalish upper stream in the Gunnison National Forest. Small brook and cutthrout trout are present.

14-DD Road Bridge
16.9 mi.
GPS

Pack Trail Bridge
GPS

Jeep Trail Bridge
GPS

FR 855

14-DD Road

FR 15-GG

17-GG Road

Trail 465

Pauline Creek

FR 597

FR 597 1A

Cochetopa Creek

Colorado Trail

Chavaz Creek

FR 794

FR 794 2A

Perfecto Creek

Nutras Creek

FR 745

FR 745

Gunnison National Forest

Stewart Creek

Eddysville Trailhead
GPS

Continental Divide

784 Trail

Colorado Trail

0 mi.

Lake Fork Cochetopa Creek

GPS
14-DD Road Bridge: N 38° 9' 7.723", W 106° 45' 34.801"
Pack Trail Bridge: N 38° 8' 3.145", W 106° 45' 45.531"
Jeep Trail Bridge 2: N 38° 6' 11.918", W 106° 46' 45.568"
Eddysville Trailhead: N 38° 1' 34.880", W 106° 49' 58.170"

© 2008 Wilderness Adventures Press, Inc.

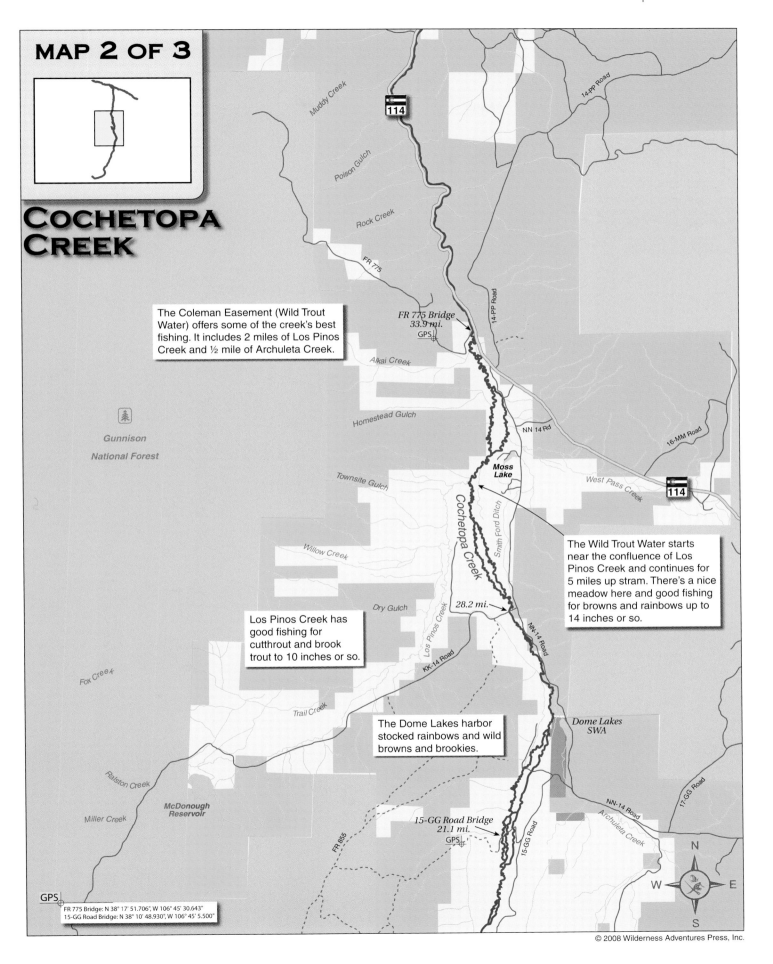

MAP 2 OF 3

COCHETOPA CREEK

The Coleman Easement (Wild Trout Water) offers some of the creek's best fishing. It includes 2 miles of Los Pinos Creek and ½ mile of Archuleta Creek.

Gunnison

National Forest

Muddy Creek

Poison Gulch

Rock Creek

FR 775

Alkai Creek

Homestead Gulch

Townsite Gulch

Willow Creek

Dry Gulch

Los Pinos Creek has good fishing for cutthrout and brook trout to 10 inches or so.

Trail Creek

Fox Creek

Ralston Creek

Miller Creek

McDonough Reservoir

FR 855

14-PP Road

114

FR 775 Bridge 33.9 mi. GPS

14-PP Road

NN 14 Rd

Moss Lake

Cochetopa Creek

Smith Ford Ditch

West Pass Creek

16-MM Road

114

The Wild Trout Water starts near the confluence of Los Pinos Creek and continues for 5 miles up stram. There's a nice meadow here and good fishing for browns and rainbows up to 14 inches or so.

28.2 mi.

Los Pinos Creek

KK-14 Road

NN-14 Road

Dome Lakes SWA

The Dome Lakes harbor stocked rainbows and wild browns and brookies.

15-GG Road Bridge 21.1 mi. GPS

15-GG Road

NN-14 Road

Archuleta Creek

17-GG Road

N
W   E
S

GPS

FR 775 Bridge: N 38° 17' 51.706", W 106° 45' 30.643"
15-GG Road Bridge: N 38° 10' 48.930", W 106° 45' 5.500"

© 2008 Wilderness Adventures Press, Inc.

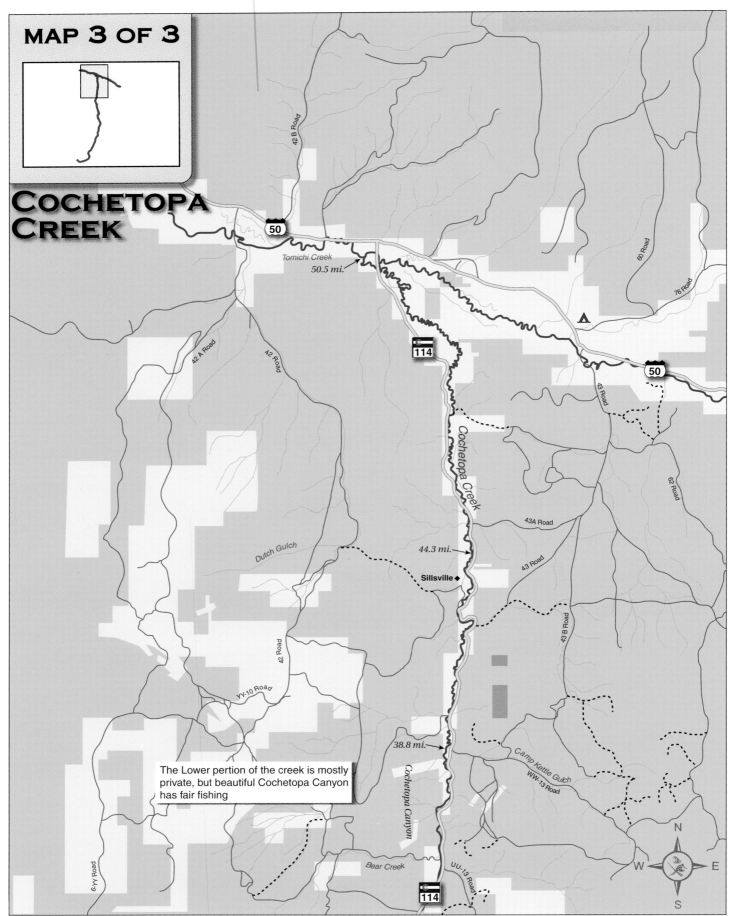

MAP 3 OF 3

COCHETOPA CREEK

Tomichi Creek

50.5 mi.

Cochetopa Creek

44.3 mi.

Sillsville ◆

38.8 mi.

Cochetopa Canyon

The Lower pertion of the creek is mostly private, but beautiful Cochetopa Canyon has fair fishing

Dutch Gulch

Bear Creek

Camp Kettle Gulch

42 B Road

42 A Road

42 Road

42 Road

YY-10 Road

6-YY Road

60 Road

76 Road

43 Road

62 Road

43A Road

43 Road

43 B Road

WW-13 Road

UU-13 Road

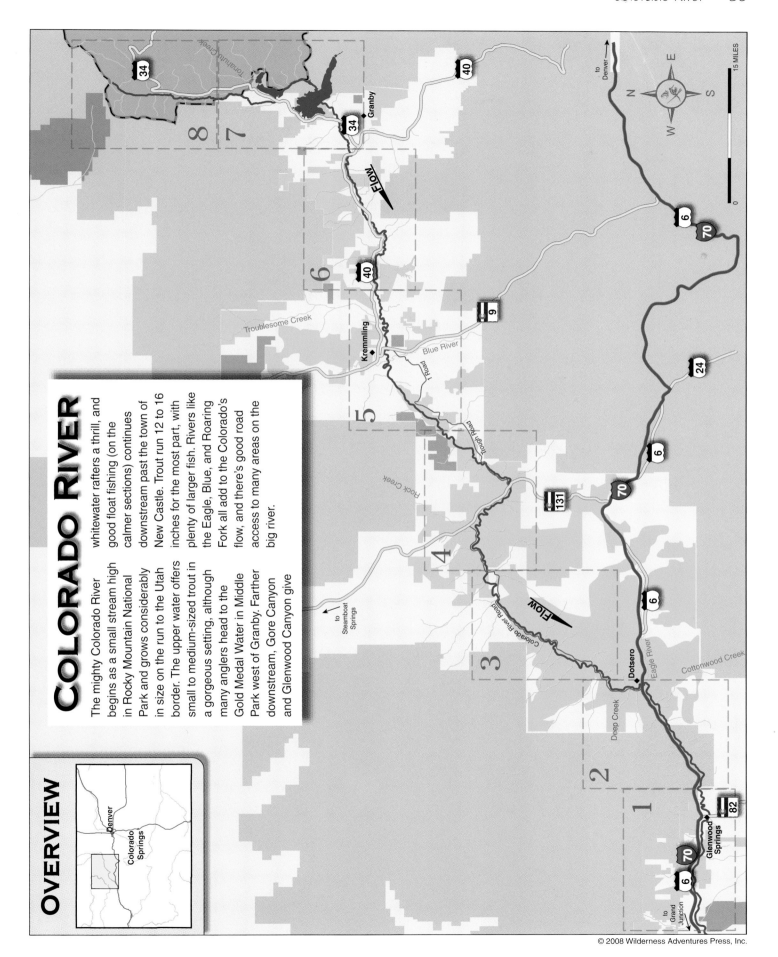

Colorado River

Overview

The mighty Colorado River begins as a small stream high in Rocky Mountain National Park and grows considerably in size on the run to the Utah border. The upper water offers small to medium-sized trout in a gorgeous setting, although many anglers head to the Gold Medal Water in Middle Park west of Granby. Farther downstream, Gore Canyon and Glenwood Canyon give whitewater rafters a thrill, and good float fishing (on the calmer sections) continues downstream past the town of New Castle. Trout run 12 to 16 inches for the most part, with plenty of larger fish. Rivers like the Eagle, Blue, and Roaring Fork all add to the Colorado's flow, and there's good road access to many areas on the big river.

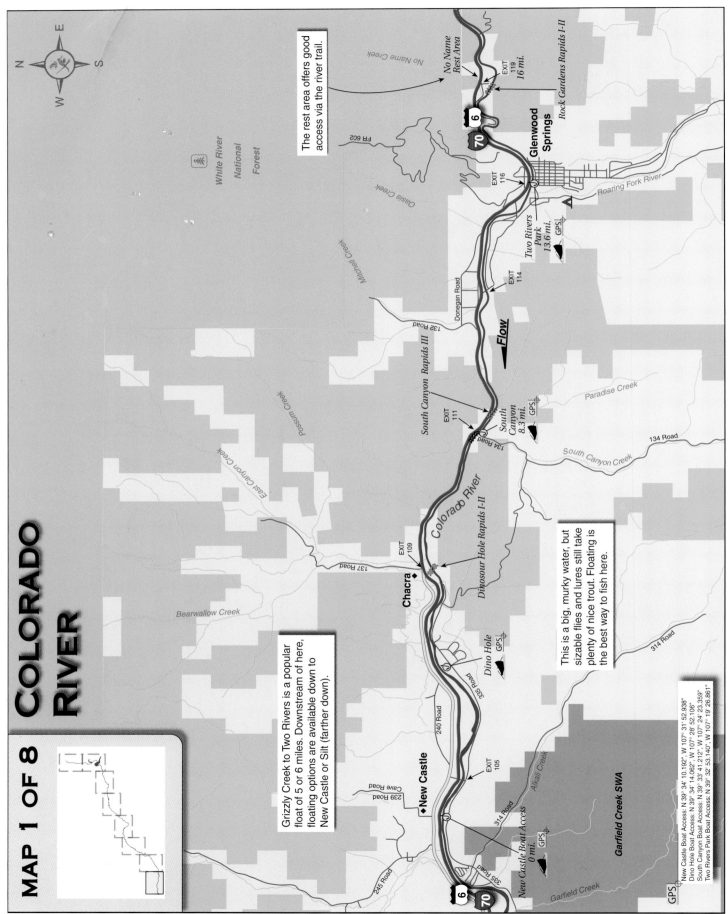

MAP 1 OF 8

COLORADO RIVER

The rest area offers good access via the river trail.

No Name Rest Area

EXIT 119 16 mi.

Rock Gardens Rapids I-II

6
70

Glenwood Springs

No Name Creek

FR 602

Oasis Creek

Roaring Fork River

EXIT 116

Two Rivers Park 13.6 mi.

GPS

EXIT 114

Donegan Road

132 Road

Flow

White River National Forest

Mitchell Creek

South Canyon Rapids III

EXIT 111

South Canyon 8.3 mi.

134 Road

GPS

Paradise Creek

South Canyon Creek

134 Road

Possum Creek

East Canyon Creek

Colorado River

Dinosour Hole Rapids I-II

EXIT 109

137 Road

Chacra

This is a big, murky water, but sizable flies and lures still take plenty of nice trout. Floating is the best way to fish here.

Bearwallow Creek

335 Road

Dino Hole

GPS

240 Road

EXIT 105

Grizzly Creek to Two Rivers is a popular float of 5 or 6 miles. Downstream of here, floating options are available down to New Castle or Silt (farther down).

New Castle

239 Road
Cave Road

314 Road

Alkali Creek

314 Road

New Castle Boat Access 0 mi.

GPS

Garfield Creek SWA

245 Road

335 Road

6
70

Garfield Creek

GPS

New Castle Boat Access: N 39° 34' 10.192", W 107° 31' 52.938"
Dino Hole Boat Access: N 39° 34' 14.062", W 107° 28' 52.106"
South Canyon Boat Access: N 39° 33' 41.212", W 107° 24' 23.359"
Two Rivers Park Boat Access: N 39° 32' 53.140", W 107° 19' 26.861"

© 2008 Wilderness Adventures Press, Inc.

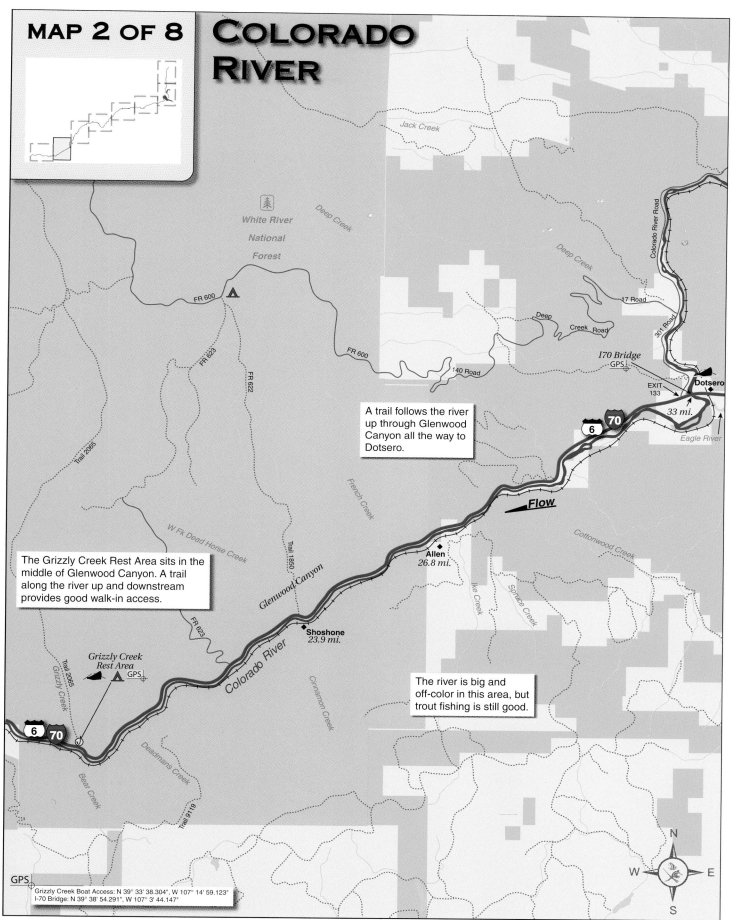

MAP 2 OF 8 COLORADO RIVER

Jack Creek

White River

National

Forest

Deep Creek

FR 600

Deep Creek

Deep

Creek Road

17 Road

Colorado River Road

301 Road

FR 600

140 Road

I70 Bridge
GPS

Dotsero

EXIT
133

33 mi.

6 70

Eagle River

A trail follows the river up through Glenwood Canyon all the way to Dotsero.

FR 623

FR 622

Flow

Trail 2065

French Creek

Cottonwood Creek

Allen
26.8 mi.

The Grizzly Creek Rest Area sits in the middle of Glenwood Canyon. A trail along the river up and downstream provides good walk-in access.

W Fk Dead Horse Creek

Trail 1850

Glenwood Canyon

Ike Creek

Spruce Creek

FR 623

Shoshone
23.9 mi.

Colorado River

Cinnamon Creek

Grizzly Creek
Rest Area GPS

Trail 2065

Grizzly Creek

6 70

The river is big and off-color in this area, but trout fishing is still good.

Deadmans Creek

Bear Creek

Trail 9119

N
W   E
S

GPS

Grizzly Creek Boat Access: N 39° 33' 38.304", W 107° 14' 59.123"
I-70 Bridge: N 39° 38' 54.291", W 107° 3' 44.147"

© 2008 Wilderness Adventures Press, Inc.

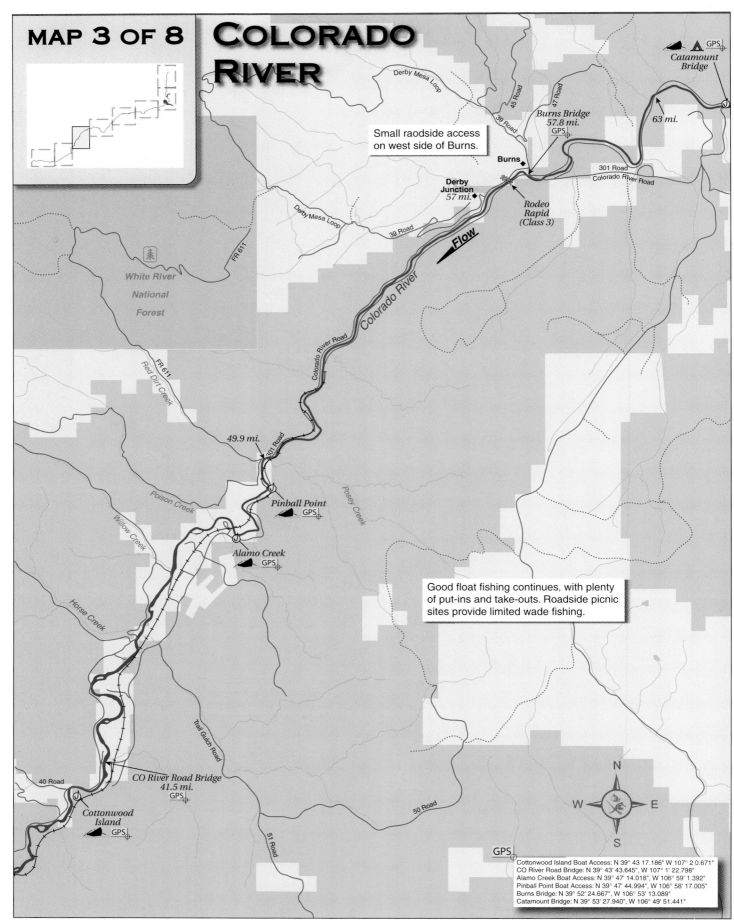

MAP 3 OF 8

COLORADO RIVER

Derby Mesa Loop

Catamount Bridge

GPS

63 mi.

Burns Bridge
57.8 mi.
GPS

Small raodside access
on west side of Burns.

Burns

301 Road

Colorado River Road

Derby
Junction
57 mi.

Rodeo
Rapid
(Class 3)

Flow

39 Road

Colorado River

Derby Mesa Loop

FR 611

White River
National
Forest

Colorado River Road

Red Dirt Creek

FR 611

Posey Creek

49.9 mi.

301 Road

Poison Creek

Pinball Point
GPS

Alamo Creek
GPS

Willow Creek

Good float fishing continues, with plenty
of put-ins and take-outs. Roadside picnic
sites provide limited wade fishing.

Horse Creek

Trail Gulch Road

N
W   E
S

40 Road

CO River Road Bridge
41.5 mi.
GPS

Cottonwood
Island
GPS

50 Road

51 Road

GPS

Cottonwood Island Boat Access: N 39° 43 17.186" W 107° 2 0.671"
CO River Road Bridge: N 39° 43' 43.645", W 107° 1' 22.798"
Alamo Creek Boat Access: N 39° 47' 14.018", W 106° 59' 1.392"
Pinball Point Boat Access: N 39° 47' 44.994", W 106° 58' 17.005"
Burns Bridge: N 39° 52' 24.667", W 106° 53' 13.089"
Catamount Bridge: N 39° 53' 27.940", W 106° 49' 51.441"

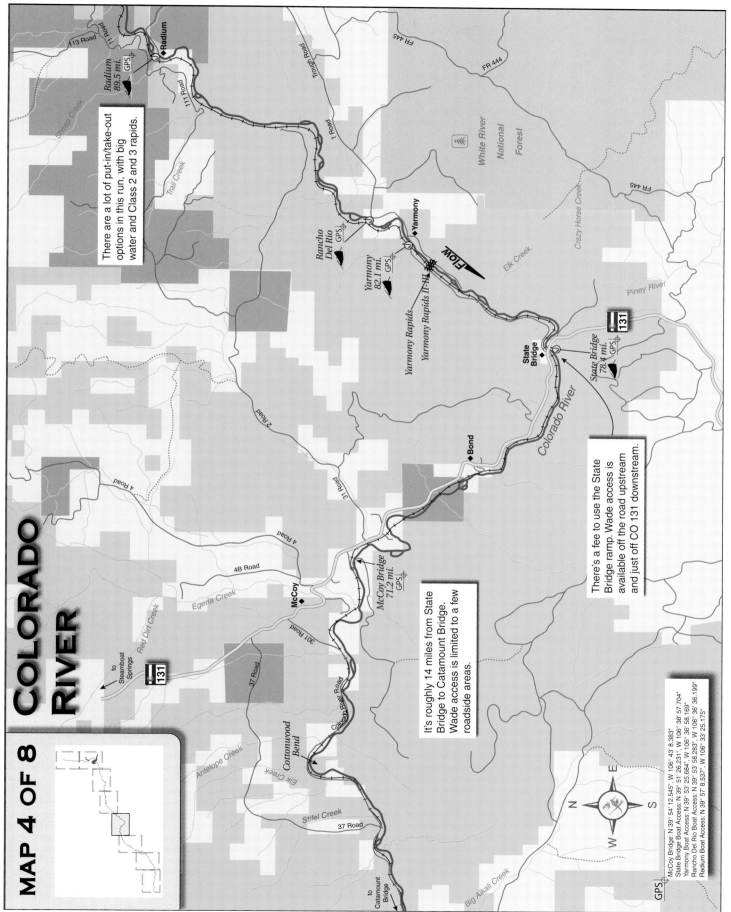

MAP 4 OF 8

COLORADO RIVER

There are a lot of put-in/take-out options in this run, with big water and Class 2 and 3 rapids.

Radium
89.5 mi.

Rancho Del Rio

Yarmony
82.1 mi.

Yarmony Rapids
Yarmony Rapids II–III

Flow

State Bridge
78.4 mi.

There's a fee to use the State Bridge boat ramp. Wade access is available off the road upstream and just off CO 131 downstream.

It's roughly 14 miles from State Bridge to Catamount Bridge. Wade access is limited to a few roadside areas.

McCoy Bridge
71.2 mi.

to Steamboat Springs

Cottonwood Bend

to Catamount Bridge

White River National Forest

Colorado River

McCoy Bridge: N 39° 54' 12.545", W 106° 43' 8.383"
State Bridge Boat Access: N 39° 51' 26.231", W 106° 38' 57.704"
Yarmony Boat Access: N 39° 53' 25.684", W 106° 36' 58.169"
Rancho Del Rio Boat Access: N 39° 53' 58.283", W 106° 36' 36.199"
Radium Boat Access: N 39° 57' 8.537", W 106° 33' 25.175"

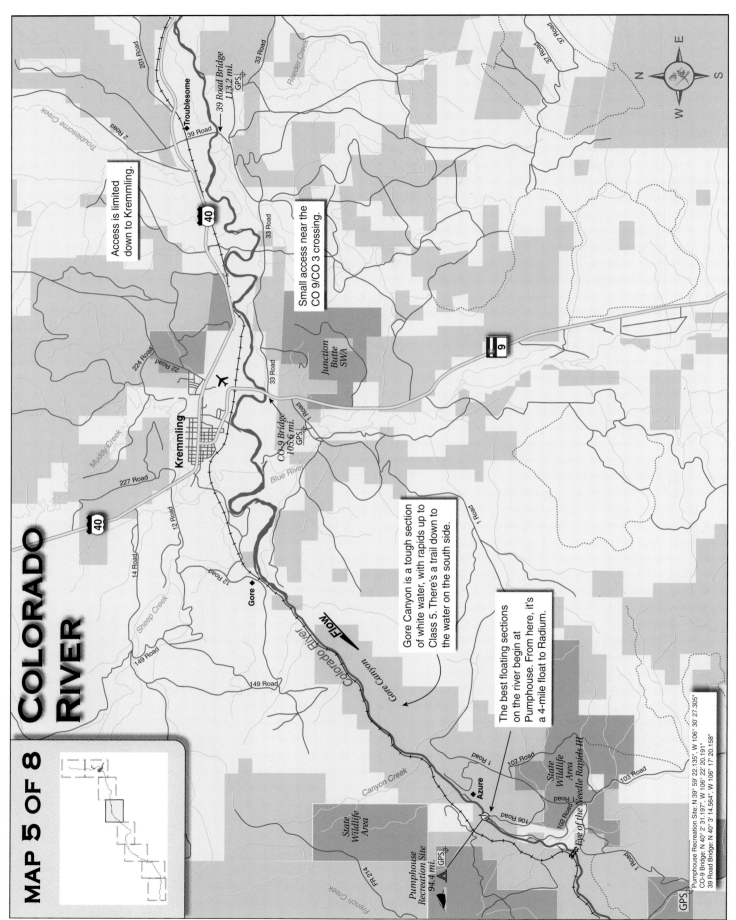

MAP 5 OF 8

COLORADO RIVER

Access is limited down to Kremmling.

Small access near the CO 9/CO 3 crossing.

Gore Canyon is a tough section of white water, with rapids up to Class 5. There's a trail down to the water on the south side.

The best floating sections on the river begin at Pumphouse. From here, it's a 4-mile float to Radium.

39 Road Bridge 113.2 mi. GPS

CO-9 Bridge 105.6 mi. GPS

Pumphouse Recreation Site 94.4 mi. GPS

Troublesome

Kremmling

Gore

Azure

Junction Butte SWA

State Wildlife Area

State Wildlife Area

Eye of the Needle Rapids

FLOW

Colorado River

Gore Canyon

Blue River

Reeder Creek

Troublesome Creek

Muddy Creek

Sheep Creek

Canyon Creek

French Creek

Pumphouse Recreation Site: N 39° 59' 22.135", W 106° 30' 27.305"
CO-9 Bridge: N 40° 2' 31.197", W 106° 22' 20.191"
39 Road Bridge: N 40° 3' 14.564" W 106° 17' 20.158"

GPS

© 2008 Wilderness Adventures Press, Inc.

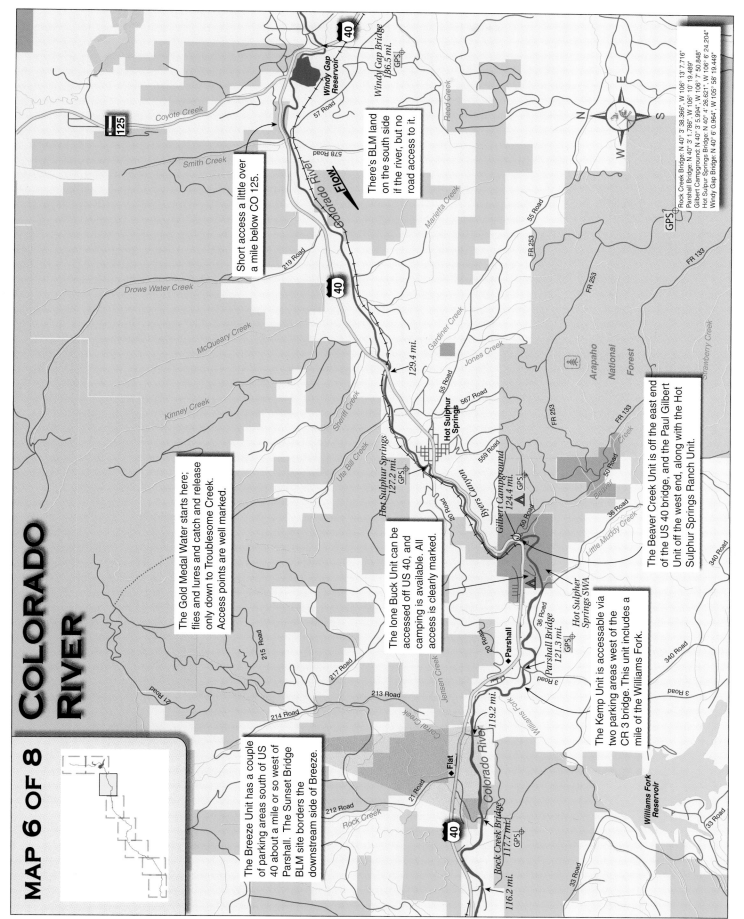

MAP 6 OF 8

COLORADO RIVER

The Gold Medal Water starts here; flies and lures and catch and release only down to Troublesome Creek. Access points are well marked.

The Breeze Unit has a couple of parking areas south of US 40 about a mile or so west of Parshall. The Sunset Bridge BLM site borders the downstream side of Breeze.

Short access a little over a mile below CO 125.

There's BLM land on the south side if the river, but no road access to it.

The lone Buck Unit can be accessed off US 40, and camping is available. All access is clearly marked.

The Kemp Unit is accessible via two parking areas west of the CR 3 bridge. This unit includes a mile of the Williams Fork.

The Beaver Creek Unit is off the east end of the US 40 bridge, and the Paul Gilbert Unit off the west end, along with the Hot Sulphur Springs Ranch Unit.

Windy Gap Reservoir

Windy Gap Bridge 136.5 mi. GPS

FLOW

Colorado River

129.4 mi.

Hot Sulphur Springs

Hot Sulphur Springs 127.2 mi. GPS

Byers Canyon

Gilbert Campground 124.4 mi. GPS

Hot Sulpher Springs SWA

Parshall

Parshall Bridge 121.3 mi. GPS

Flat

119.2 mi.

Colorado River

Rock Creek Bridge 117.7 mi. GPS

116.2 mi.

Williams Fork

Williams Fork Reservoir

Coyote Creek

Smith Creek

Drows Water Creek

McQueary Creek

Kinney Creek

Sheriff Creek

Ute Bill Creek

Reed Creek

Marietta Creek

Gardiner Creek

Jones Creek

Beaver Creek

Little Muddy Creek

Strawberry Creek

Jensen Creek

Corral Creek

Rock Creek

Arapaho National Forest

57 Road

578 Road

219 Road

215 Road

214 Road

212 Road

21 Road

217 Road

213 Road

27 Road

20 Road

20 Road

55 Road

567 Road

559 Road

55 Road

50 Road

36 Road

36 Road

36 Road

3 Road

340 Road

340 Road

33 Road

33 Road

3 Road

FR 253

FR 253

FR 253

FR 133

FR 133

GPS

© 2008 Wilderness Adventures Press, Inc.

Rock Creek Bridge: N 40° 3' 38.366", W 106° 13' 7.716"
Parshall Bridge: N 40° 3' 1.786", W 106° 10' 19.489"
Gilbert Campground: N 40° 3' 5.994", W 106° 7' 50.848"
Hot Sulpur Springs Bridge: N 40° 4' 26.621", W 106° 6' 24.204"
Windy Gap Bridge: N 40° 6' 0.964", W 105° 58' 19.449"

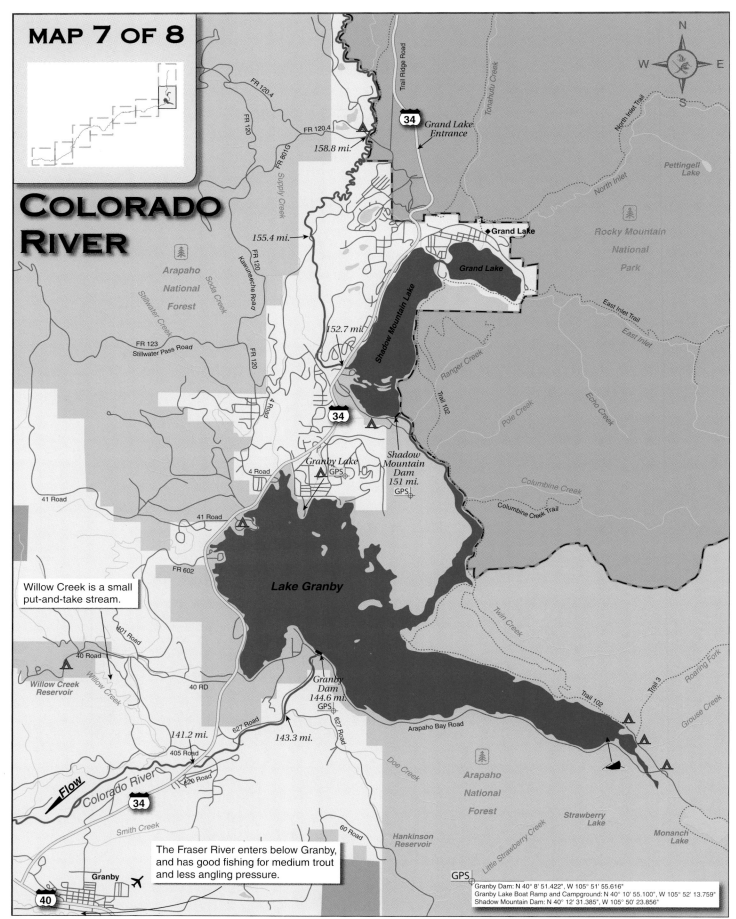

MAP 7 OF 8

COLORADO RIVER

Arapaho National Forest

Willow Creek is a small put-and-take stream.

The Fraser River enters below Granby, and has good fishing for medium trout and less angling pressure.

Grand Lake Entrance

158.8 mi.

155.4 mi.

152.7 mi.

Grand Lake

Shadow Mountain Lake

Rocky Mountain National Park

Pettingell Lake

Shadow Mountain Dam 151 mi. GPS

Granby Lake GPS

Lake Granby

Granby Dam 144.6 mi. GPS

143.3 mi.

141.2 mi.

Colorado River

Flow

Willow Creek Reservoir

Arapaho National Forest

Strawberry Lake

Monarch Lake

Granby

GPS

Granby Dam: N 40° 8' 51.422", W 105° 51' 55.616"
Granby Lake Boat Ramp and Campground: N 40° 10' 55.100", W 105° 52' 13.759"
Shadow Mountain Dam: N 40° 12' 31.385", W 105° 50' 23.856"

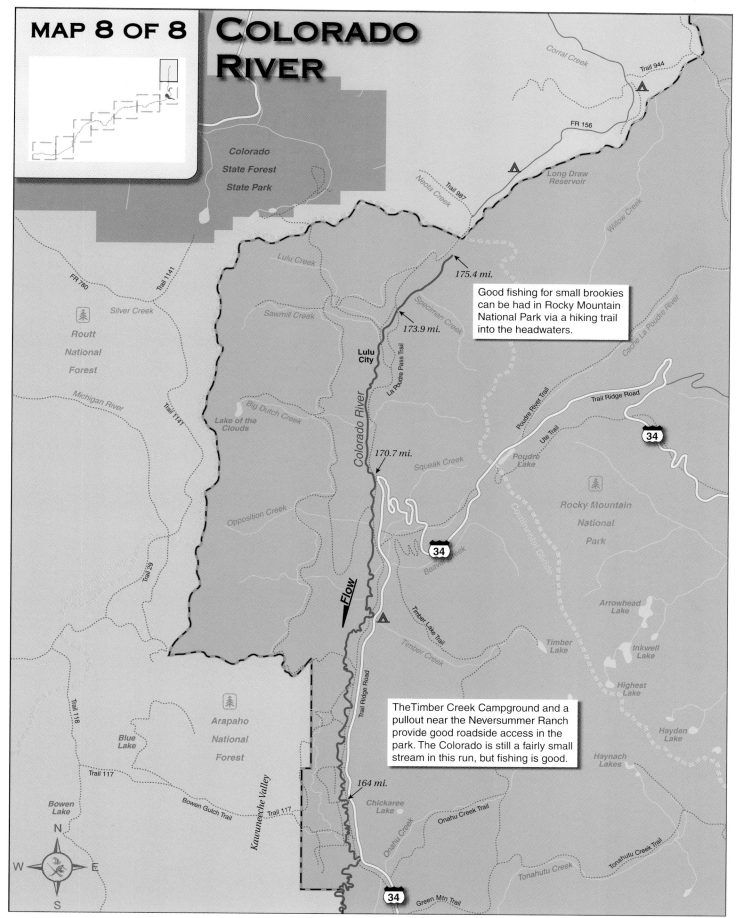

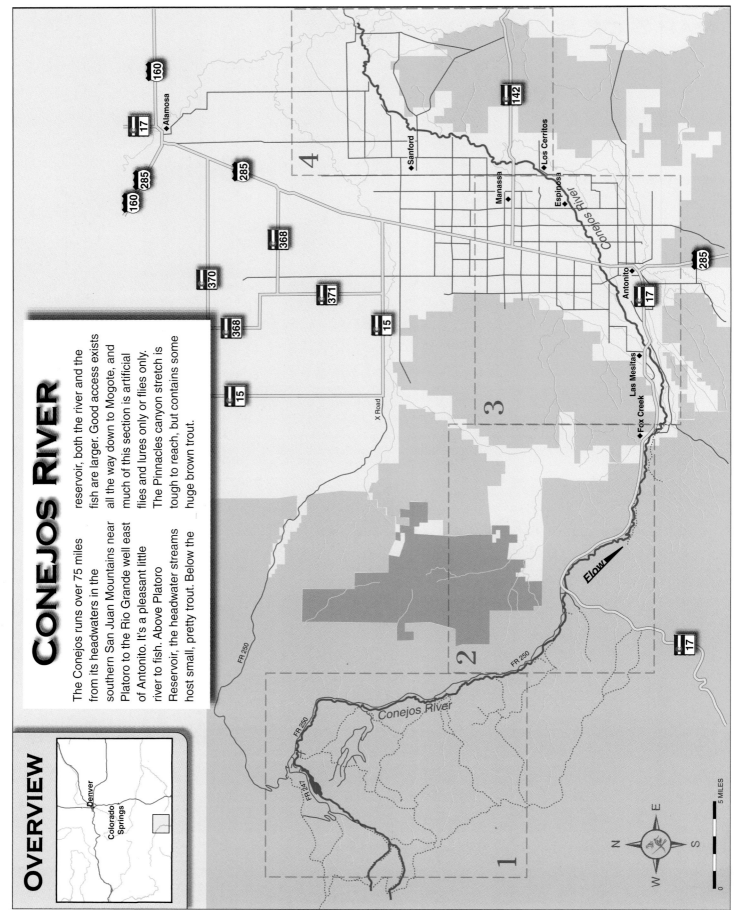

CONEJOS RIVER

The Conejos runs over 75 miles from its headwaters in the southern San Juan Mountains near Platoro to the Rio Grande well east of Antonito. It's a pleasant little river to fish. Above Platoro Reservoir, the headwater streams host small, pretty trout. Below the reservoir, both the river and the fish are larger. Good access exists all the way down to Mogote, and much of this section is artificial flies and lures only or flies only. The Pinnacles canyon stretch is tough to reach, but contains some huge brown trout.

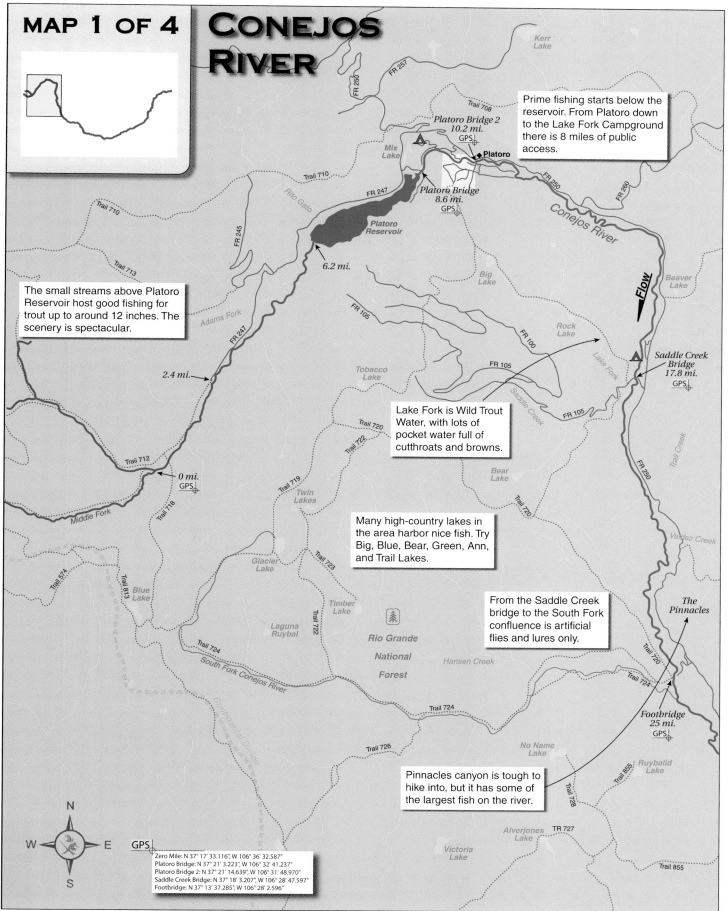

MAP 1 OF 4 CONEJOS RIVER

Prime fishing starts below the reservoir. From Platoro down to the Lake Fork Campground there is 8 miles of public access.

Platoro Bridge 2
10.2 mi.
GPS

Platoro Bridge
8.6 mi.
GPS

Platoro Reservoir

6.2 mi.

The small streams above Platoro Reservoir host good fishing for trout up to around 12 inches. The scenery is spectacular.

2.4 mi.

0 mi.
GPS

Saddle Creek Bridge
17.8 mi.
GPS

Lake Fork is Wild Trout Water, with lots of pocket water full of cutthroats and browns.

Many high-country lakes in the area harbor nice fish. Try Big, Blue, Bear, Green, Ann, and Trail Lakes.

From the Saddle Creek bridge to the South Fork confluence is artificial flies and lures only.

The Pinnacles

Footbridge
25 mi.
GPS

Pinnacles canyon is tough to hike into, but it has some of the largest fish on the river.

Rio Grande National Forest

N W E S
GPS

Zero Mile: N 37° 17' 33.116", W 106° 36' 32.587"
Platoro Bridge: N 37° 21' 3.223", W 106° 32' 41.237"
Platoro Bridge 2: N 37° 21' 14.639", W 106° 31' 48.970"
Saddle Creek Bridge: N 37° 18' 3.207", W 106° 28' 47.597"
Footbridge: N 37° 13' 37.285", W 106° 28' 2.596"

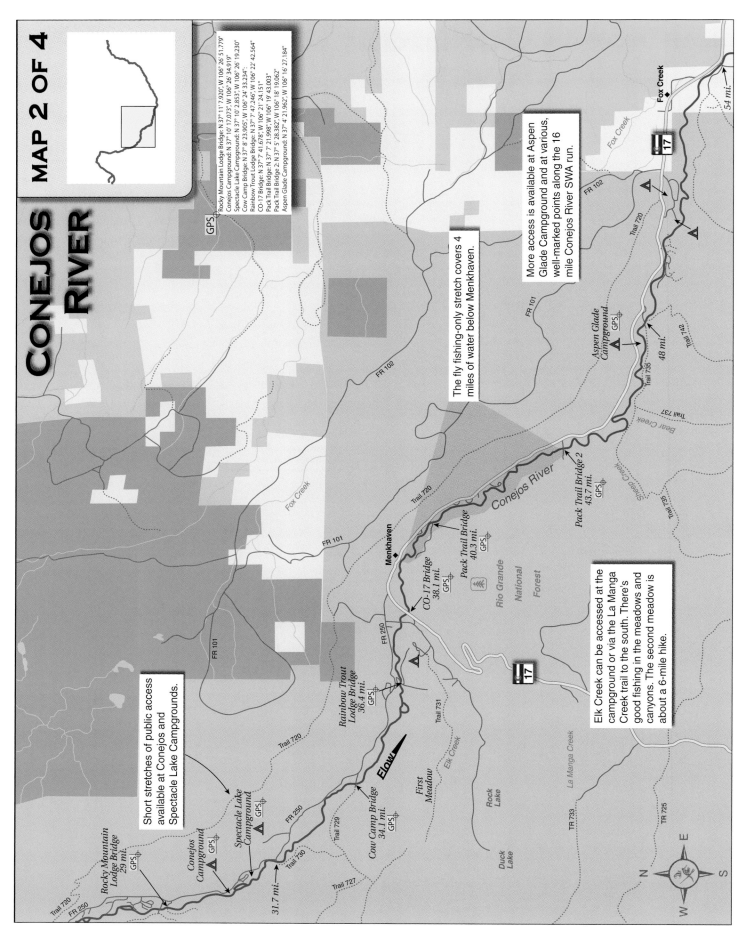

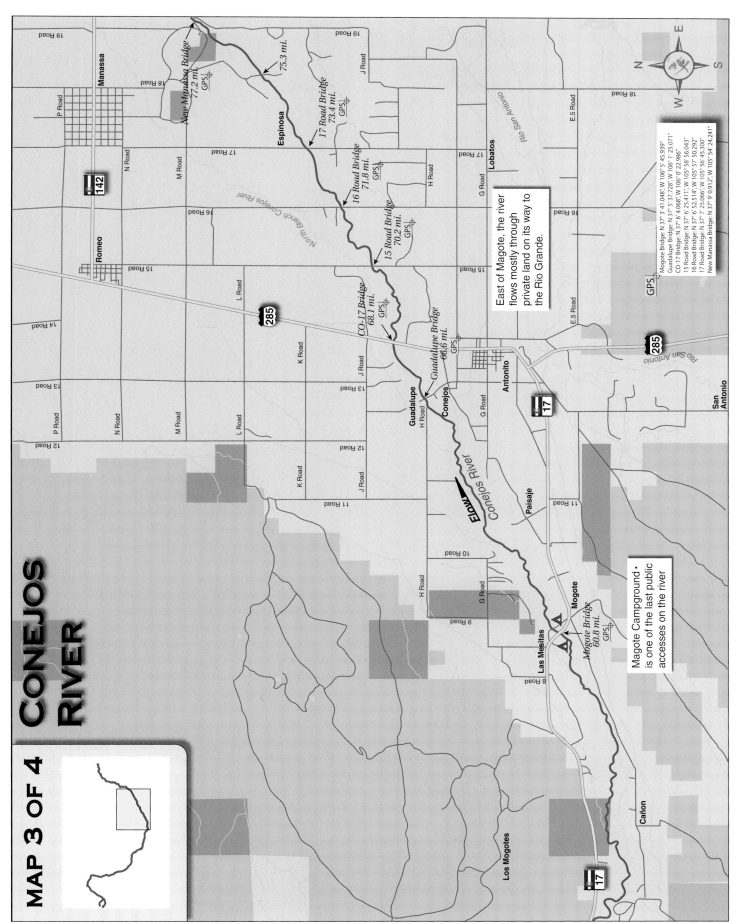

MAP 3 OF 4

CONEJOS RIVER

New Manassa Bridge
77.2 mi.
GPS

75.3 mi.

17 Road Bridge
73.4 mi.
GPS

16 Road Bridge
71.8 mi.
GPS

15 Road Bridge
70.2 mi.
GPS

CO-17 Bridge
68.1 mi.
GPS

Guadalupe Bridge
66.6 mi.
GPS

Mogote Bridge
60.8 mi.
GPS

East of Magote, the river flows mostly through private land on its way to the Rio Grande.

Magote Campground is one of the last public accesses on the river

Mogote Bridge: N 37° 3' 41.048'; W 106° 5' 45.939"
Guadalupe Bridge: N 37° 5' 37.728'; W 106° 1' 25.071"
CO-17 Bridge: N 37° 6' 4.068'; W 106° 0' 22.986"
15 Road Bridge: N 37° 6' 25.411'; W 105° 58' 56.043"
16 Road Bridge: N 37° 6' 52.514'; W 105° 57' 50.292"
17 Road Bridge: N 37° 7' 25.066'; W 105° 56' 45.300"
New Manassa Bridge: N 37° 9' 0.912'; W 105° 54' 24.241"

Manassa
Romeo
Espinosa
Lobatos
Antonito
Guadalupe
Conejos
Paisaje
Mogote
Las Mesitas
Los Mogotes
Cañon
San Antonio

North Branch Conejos River
Conejos River
FLOW
Rio San Antonio

142
285
17

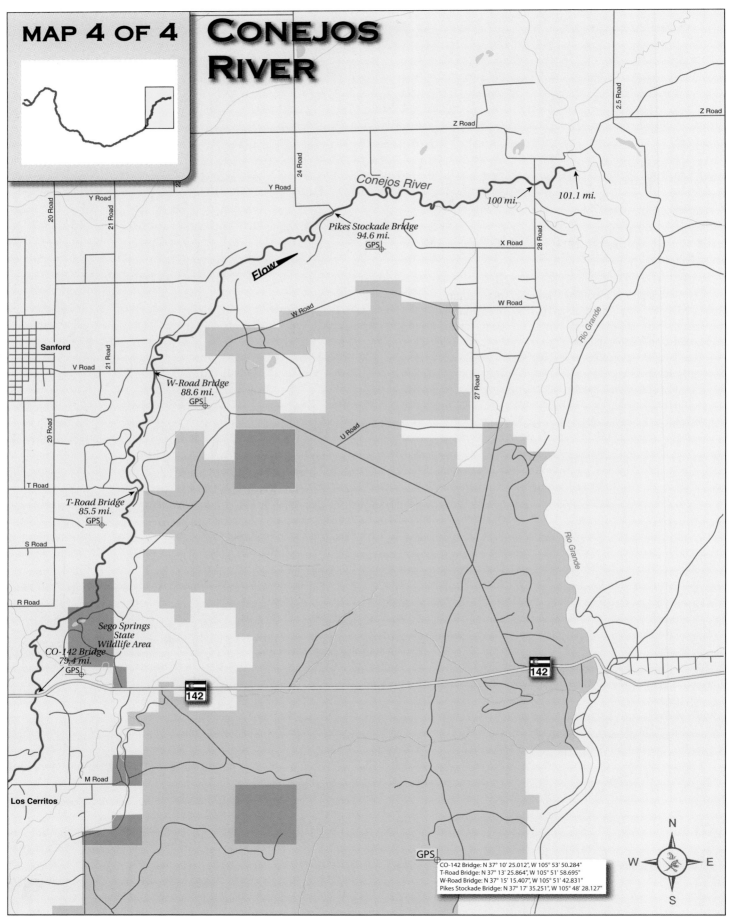

MAP 4 OF 4

CONEJOS RIVER

Conejos River

100 mi.

101.1 mi.

Pikes Stockade Bridge
94.6 mi.
GPS

Flow

W-Road Bridge
88.6 mi.
GPS

T-Road Bridge
85.5 mi.
GPS

Sanford

Sego Springs
State
Wildlife Area

CO-142 Bridge
79.4 mi.
GPS

Los Cerritos

Rio Grande

GPS

CO-142 Bridge: N 37° 10' 25.012", W 105° 53' 50.284"
T-Road Bridge: N 37° 13' 25.864", W 105° 51' 58.695"
W-Road Bridge: N 37° 15' 15.407", W 105° 51' 42.831"
Pikes Stockade Bridge: N 37° 17' 35.251", W 105° 48' 28.127"

N
W E
S

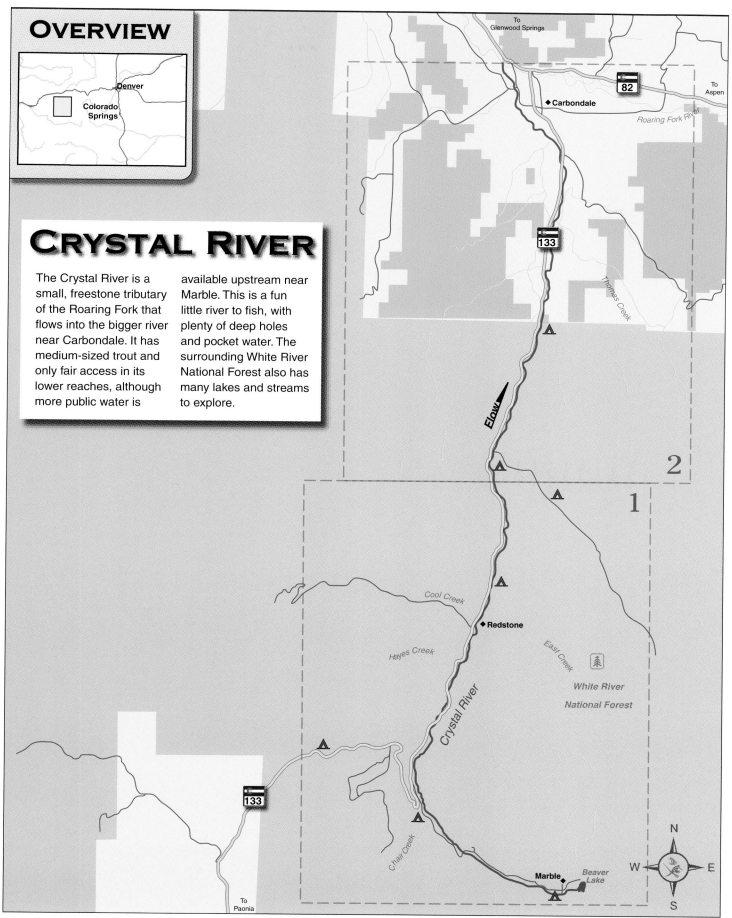

OVERVIEW

Denver
Colorado
Springs

CRYSTAL RIVER

The Crystal River is a small, freestone tributary of the Roaring Fork that flows into the bigger river near Carbondale. It has medium-sized trout and only fair access in its lower reaches, although more public water is available upstream near Marble. This is a fun little river to fish, with plenty of deep holes and pocket water. The surrounding White River National Forest also has many lakes and streams to explore.

To
Glenwood Springs

82

To
Aspen

Carbondale

Roaring Fork River

133

Thomas Creek

Flow

2

1

Cool Creek

Redstone

East Creek

Hayes Creek

White River

National Forest

Crystal River

133

Chair Creek

Marble

Beaver
Lake

To
Paonia

N
W   E
S

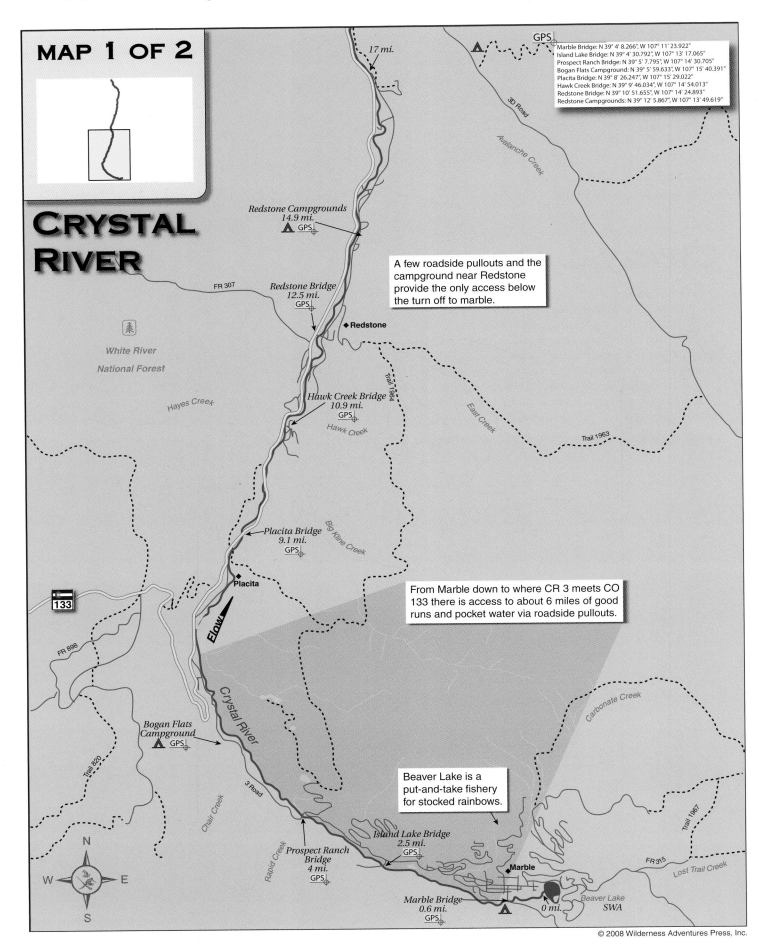

MAP 1 OF 2

CRYSTAL RIVER

Marble Bridge: N 39° 4' 8.266", W 107° 11' 23.922"
Island Lake Bridge: N 39° 4' 30.792", W 107° 13' 17.065"
Prospect Ranch Bridge: N 39° 5' 7.795", W 107° 14' 30.705"
Bogan Flats Campground: N 39° 5' 59.633", W 107° 15' 40.391"
Placita Bridge: N 39° 8' 26.247", W 107° 15' 29.022"
Hawk Creek Bridge: N 39° 9' 46.034", W 107° 14' 54.013"
Redstone Bridge: N 39° 10' 51.655", W 107° 14' 24.893"
Redstone Campgrounds: N 39° 12' 5.867", W 107° 13' 49.619"

17 mi.

GPS

3D Road

Avalanche Creek

East Creek

Trail 1963

Trail 1964

Redstone Campgrounds
14.9 mi.
GPS

A few roadside pullouts and the campground near Redstone provide the only access below the turn off to marble.

FR 307

Redstone Bridge
12.5 mi.
GPS

◆ Redstone

White River
National Forest

Hayes Creek

Hawk Creek Bridge
10.9 mi.
GPS

Hawk Creek

Placita Bridge
9.1 mi.
GPS

Big Kline Creek

◆ Placita

Flow

133

From Marble down to where CR 3 meets CO 133 there is access to about 6 miles of good runs and pocket water via roadside pullouts.

Carbonate Creek

FR 898

Bogan Flats
Campground
GPS

Crystal River

Trail 820

Chair Creek

3 Road

Rapid Creek

Beaver Lake is a put-and-take fishery for stocked rainbows.

Island Lake Bridge
2.5 mi.
GPS

Trail 1967

FR 315

Lost Trail Creek

Prospect Ranch
Bridge
4 mi.
GPS

◆ Marble

Marble Bridge
0.6 mi.
GPS

0 mi.

Beaver Lake
SWA

N
W   E
S

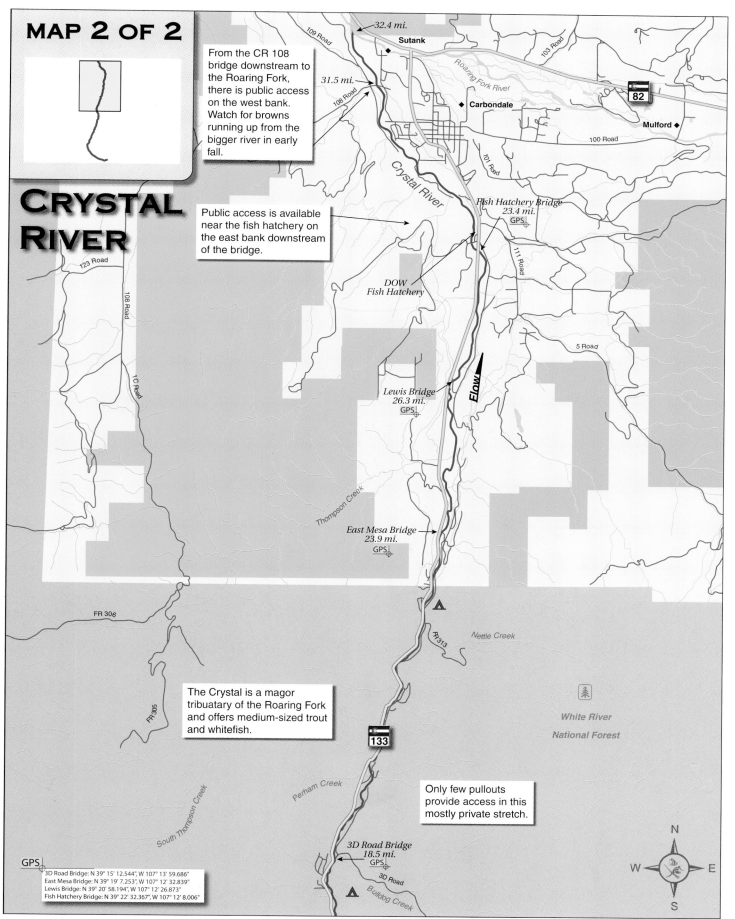

MAP 2 OF 2

CRYSTAL RIVER

From the CR 108 bridge downstream to the Roaring Fork, there is public access on the west bank. Watch for browns running up from the bigger river in early fall.

Public access is available near the fish hatchery on the east bank downstream of the bridge.

32.4 mi.

Sutank

31.5 mi.

Carbondale

Mulford

82

100 Road

Roaring Fork River

109 Road

103 Road

108 Road

101 Road

Crystal River

Fish Hatchery Bridge
23.4 mi.
GPS

111 Road

DOW
Fish Hatchery

5 Road

Lewis Bridge
26.3 mi.
GPS

Flow

123 Road

108 Road

1C Road

Thompson Creek

East Mesa Bridge
23.9 mi.
GPS

FR 306

FR 313

Nettle Creek

The Crystal is a magor tribuatary of the Roaring Fork and offers medium-sized trout and whitefish.

FR 305

White River
National Forest

133

Only few pullouts provide access in this mostly private stretch.

South Thompson Creek

Perham Creek

3D Road Bridge
18.5 mi.
GPS

3D Road

Bulldog Creek

N
W   E
S

GPS

3D Road Bridge: N 39° 15' 12.544", W 107° 13' 59.686"
East Mesa Bridge: N 39° 19' 7.253", W 107° 12' 32.839"
Lewis Bridge: N 39° 20' 58.194", W 107° 12' 26.873"
Fish Hatchery Bridge: N 39° 22' 32.367", W 107° 12' 8.006"

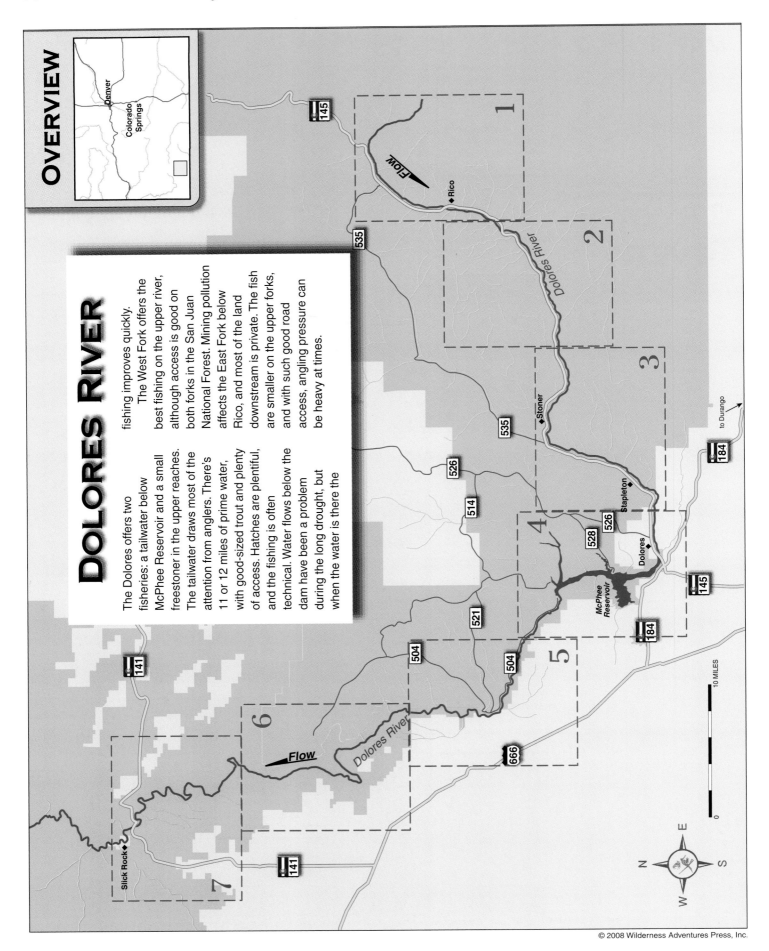

OVERVIEW

DOLORES RIVER

The Dolores offers two fisheries: a tailwater below McPhee Reservoir and a small freestoner in the upper reaches. The tailwater draws most of the attention from anglers. There's 11 or 12 miles of prime water, with good-sized trout and plenty of access. Hatches are plentiful, and the fishing is often technical. Water flows below the dam have been a problem during the long drought, but when the water is there the

fishing improves quickly.

The West Fork offers the best fishing on the upper river, although access is good on both forks in the San Juan National Forest. Mining pollution affects the East Fork below Rico, and most of the land downstream is private. The fish are smaller on the upper forks, and with such good road access, angling pressure can be heavy at times.

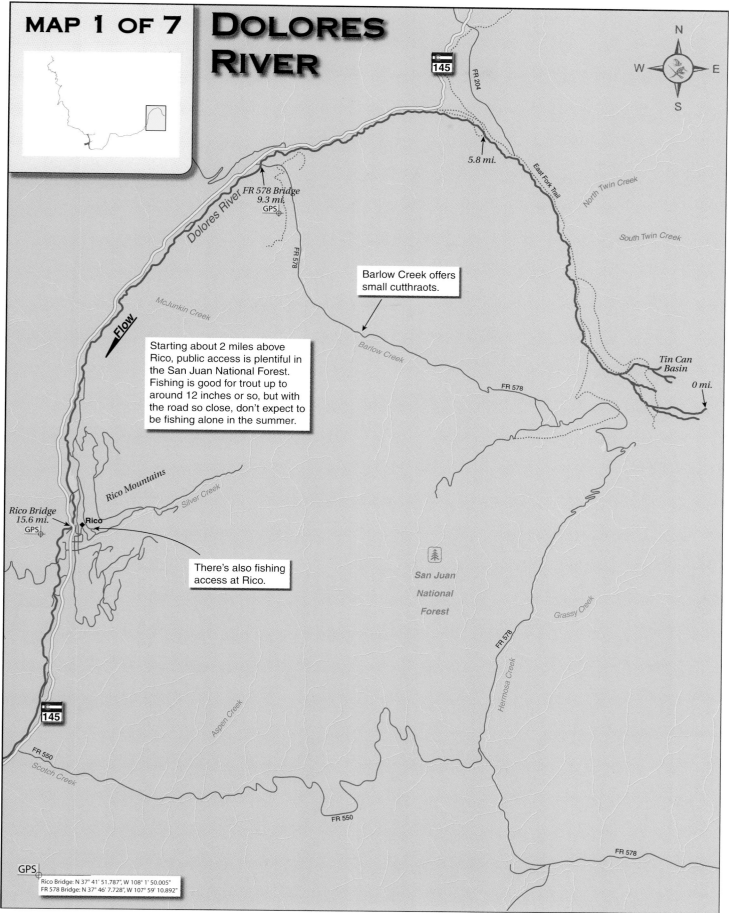

MAP 1 OF 7 **DOLORES RIVER**

145

FR 204

N
W E
S

5.8 mi.

North Twin Creek

South Twin Creek

Dolores River

FR 578 Bridge
9.3 mi.
GPS

FR 578

Flow

McJunkin Creek

East Fork Trail

Barlow Creek offers
small cutthraots.

Tin Can
Basin

0 mi.

Barlow Creek

FR 578

Starting about 2 miles above
Rico, public access is plentiful in
the San Juan National Forest.
Fishing is good for trout up to
around 12 inches or so, but with
the road so close, don't expect to
be fishing alone in the summer.

Rico Mountains

Silver Creek

Rico Bridge
15.6 mi.
GPS

Rico

San Juan

National

Forest

There's also fishing
access at Rico.

Grassy Creek

Hermosa Creek

Aspen Creek

145

FR 550

Scotch Creek

FR 550

FR 578

GPS
Rico Bridge: N 37° 41' 51.787", W 108° 1' 50.005"
FR 578 Bridge: N 37° 46' 7.728", W 107° 59' 10.892"

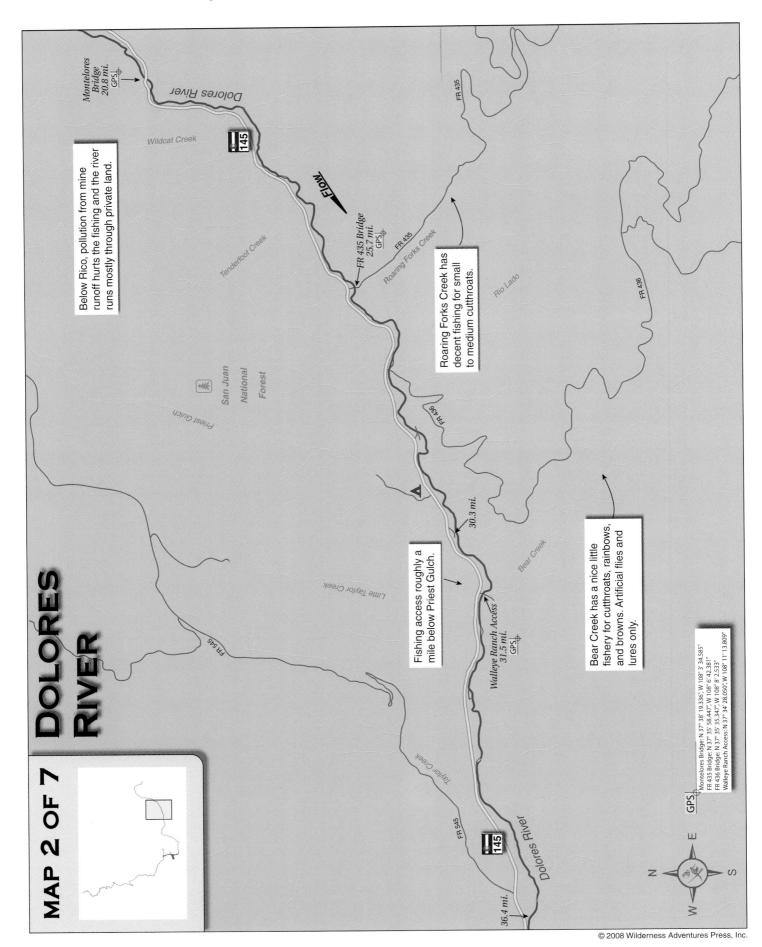

MAP 2 OF 7

DOLORES RIVER

Below Rico, pollution from mine runoff hurts the fishing and the river runs mostly through private land.

Roaring Forks Creek has decent fishing for small to medium cutthroats.

Fishing access roughly a mile below Priest Gulch.

Bear Creek has a nice little fishery for cutthroats, rainbows, and browns. Artificial flies and lures only.

Montelores Bridge
20.8 mi.
GPS

FR 435 Bridge
25.7 mi.
GPS

30.3 mi.

Walleye Ranch Access
31.5 mi.
GPS

36.4 mi.

Dolores River

Wildcat Creek

Tenderfoot Creek

Priest Gulch

San Juan National Forest

Little Taylor Creek

Taylor Creek

Roaring Forks Creek

Rio Lado

Bear Creek

FLOW

FR 435

FR 436

FR 436

FR 545

FR 545

GPS
Montelores Bridge: N 37° 38' 19.336', W 108° 3' 34.585'
FR 435 Bridge: N 37° 35' 58.447', W 108° 6' 42.381'
FR 436 Bridge: N 37° 35' 35.347', W 108° 8' 2.533'
Walleye Ranch Access: N 37° 34' 28.050', W 108° 11' 13.809'

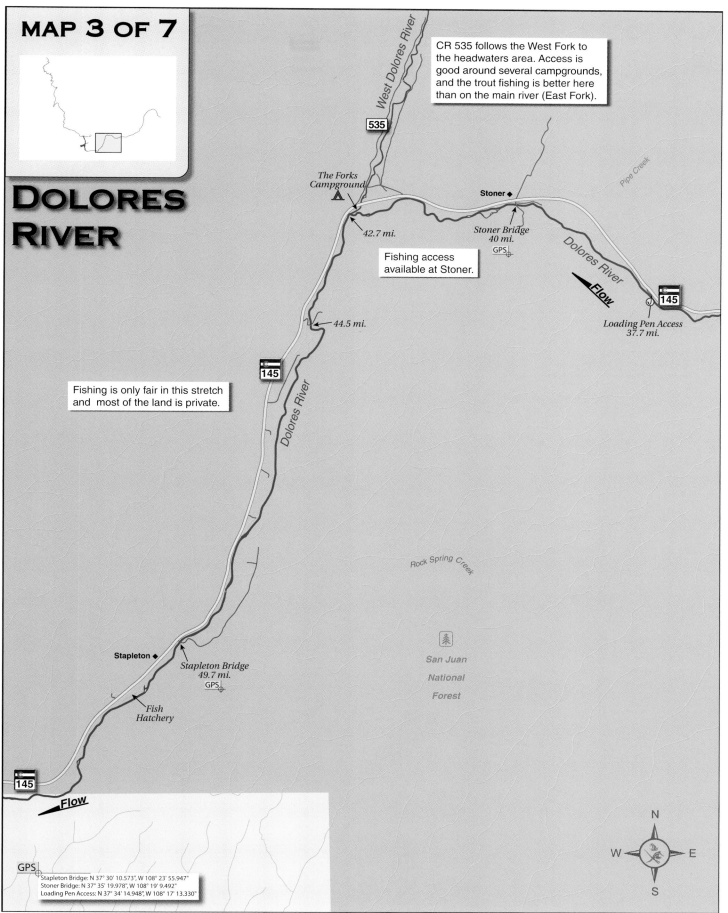

MAP 3 OF 7

DOLORES RIVER

West Dolores River

CR 535 follows the West Fork to the headwaters area. Access is good around several campgrounds, and the trout fishing is better here than on the main river (East Fork).

535

The Forks Campground

42.7 mi.

Fishing access available at Stoner.

Stoner ◆

Stoner Bridge 40 mi. GPS

Dolores River

Flow

145

Loading Pen Access 37.7 mi.

44.5 mi.

145

Fishing is only fair in this stretch and most of the land is private.

Dolores River

Pipe Creek

Rock Spring Creek

San Juan National Forest

Stapleton ◆

Stapleton Bridge 49.7 mi. GPS

Fish Hatchery

145

Flow

N
W   E
S

GPS

Stapleton Bridge: N 37° 30' 10.573", W 108° 23' 55.947"
Stoner Bridge: N 37° 35' 19.978", W 108° 19' 9.492"
Loading Pen Access: N 37° 34' 14.948", W 108° 17' 13.330"

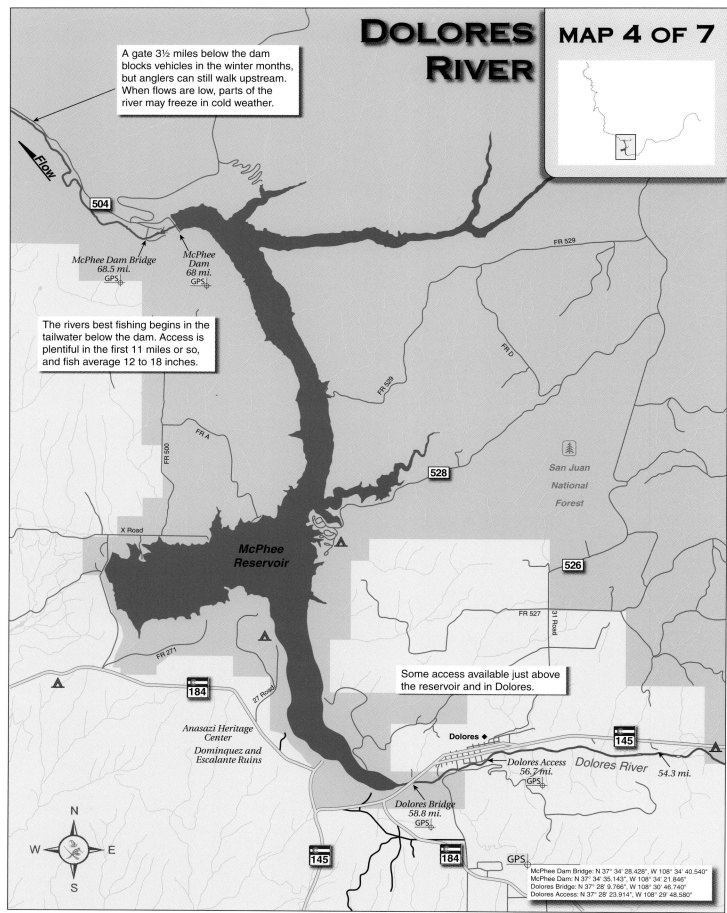

A gate 3½ miles below the dam blocks vehicles in the winter months, but anglers can still walk upstream. When flows are low, parts of the river may freeze in cold weather.

Flow

504

McPhee Dam Bridge 68.5 mi. GPS

McPhee Dam 68 mi. GPS

FR 529

FR D

The rivers best fishing begins in the tailwater below the dam. Access is plentiful in the first 11 miles or so, and fish average 12 to 18 inches.

FR 529

FR A

FR 500

528

San Juan National Forest

X Road

McPhee Reservoir

526

FR 527

31 Road

FR 271

184

27 Road

Some access available just above the reservoir and in Dolores.

Anasazi Heritage Center
Dominquez and Escalante Ruins

Dolores ◆

145

Dolores Access 56.7 mi. GPS

Dolores River

54.3 mi.

Dolores Bridge 58.8 mi. GPS

N W E S

145

184

GPS

McPhee Dam Bridge: N 37° 34' 28.428", W 108° 34' 40.540°
McPhee Dam: N 37° 34' 35.143", W 108° 34' 21.846°
Dolores Bridge: N 37° 28' 9.766", W 108° 30' 46.740°
Dolores Access: N 37° 28' 23.914", W 108° 29' 48.580°

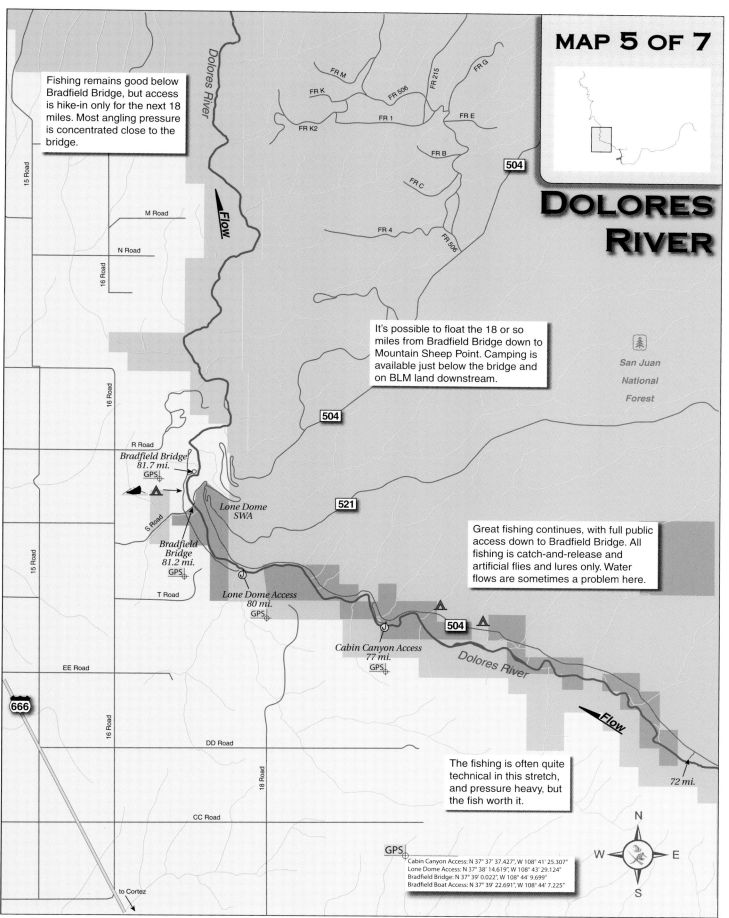

MAP 5 OF 7

DOLORES RIVER

Fishing remains good below Bradfield Bridge, but access is hike-in only for the next 18 miles. Most angling pressure is concentrated close to the bridge.

FR M
FR K
FR 506
FR 215
FR G
FR K2
FR 1
FR E
FR B
504
FR C
FR 4
FR 506

Dolores River

Flow

15 Road

M Road

N Road

16 Road

16 Road

R Road

It's possible to float the 18 or so miles from Bradfield Bridge down to Mountain Sheep Point. Camping is available just below the bridge and on BLM land downstream.

San Juan

National

Forest

504

Bradfield Bridge 81.7 mi.
GPS

Lone Dome SWA

521

S Road

Bradfield Bridge 81.2 mi.
GPS

15 Road

T Road

Lone Dome Access 80 mi.
GPS

504

Great fishing continues, with full public access down to Bradfield Bridge. All fishing is catch-and-release and artificial flies and lures only. Water flows are sometimes a problem here.

Cabin Canyon Access 77 mi.
GPS

Dolores River

666

EE Road

16 Road

DD Road

18 Road

Flow

The fishing is often quite technical in this stretch, and pressure heavy, but the fish worth it.

72 mi.

CC Road

N
W E
S

to Cortez

GPS
Cabin Canyon Access: N 37° 37' 37.427", W 108° 41' 25.307"
Lone Dome Access: N 37° 38' 14.619", W 108° 43' 29.124"
Bradfield Bridge: N 37° 39' 0.022", W 108° 44' 9.699"
Bradfield Boat Access: N 37° 39' 22.691", W 108° 44' 7.225"

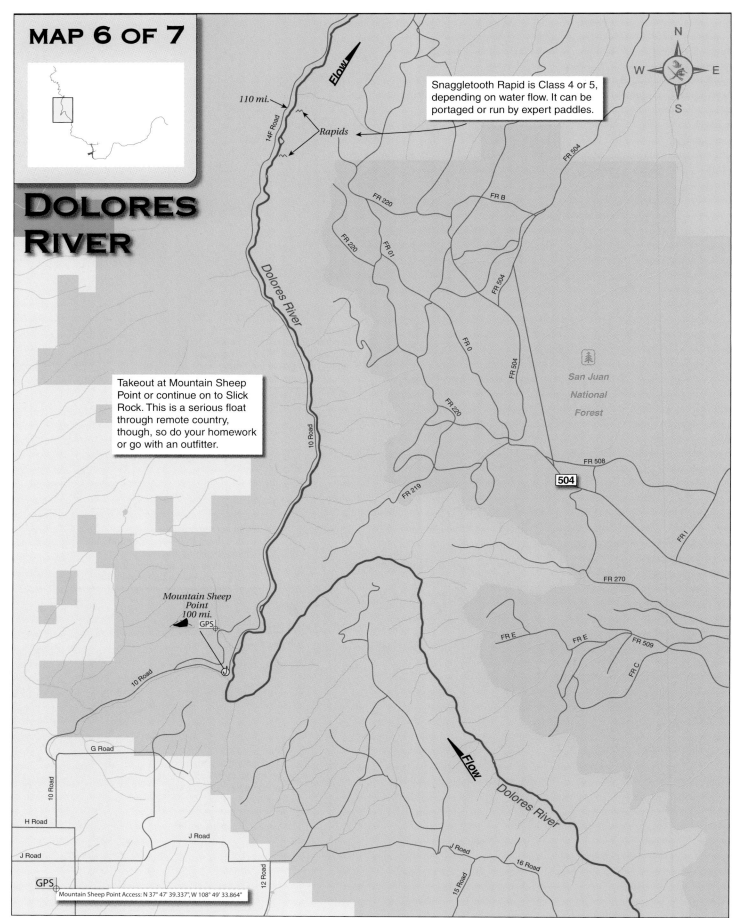

MAP 6 OF 7

DOLORES RIVER

Flow

110 mi.

14F Road

Rapids

Snaggletooth Rapid is Class 4 or 5, depending on water flow. It can be portaged or run by expert paddles.

FR 504

FR 220

FR 220

FR 01

FR B

FR 504

FR 0

FR 504

San Juan National Forest

Dolores River

Takeout at Mountain Sheep Point or continue on to Slick Rock. This is a serious float through remote country, though, so do your homework or go with an outfitter.

FR 508

504

FR 219

FR 220

FR 270

FR 1

10 Road

Mountain Sheep Point 100 mi.
GPS

FR E

FR E

FR 509

FR C

10 Road

G Road

Flow

Dolores River

10 Road

H Road

J Road

J Road

J Road

12 Road

15 Road

16 Road

GPS

Mountain Sheep Point Access: N 37° 47' 39.337", W 108° 49' 33.864"

© 2008 Wilderness Adventures Press, Inc.

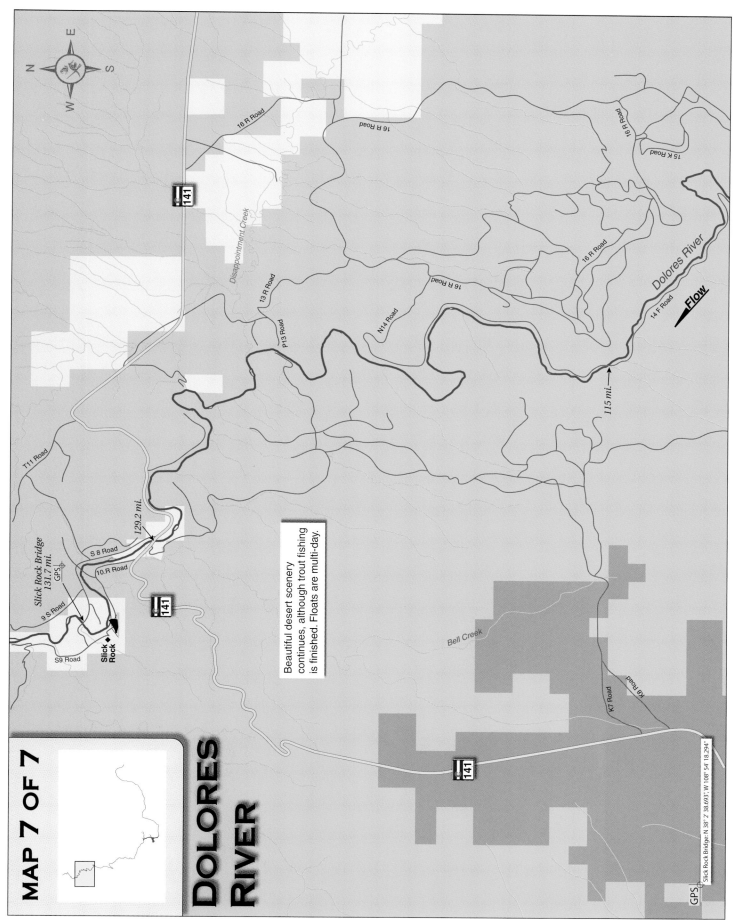

Beautiful desert scenery continues, although trout fishing is finished. Floats are multi-day.

Slick Rock Bridge 131.7 mi.

129.2 mi.

115 mi.

Flow

Dolores River

16 R Road

16 R Road

15 K Road

16 R Road

16 R Road

14 F Road

13 R Road

P13 Road

N14 Road

Disappointment Creek

T11 Road

S 8 Road

10 R Road

9 S Road

S9 Road

Slick Rock

Bell Creek

K7 Road

K8 Road

GPS

GPS

GPS

141

141

141

141

MAP 7 OF 7

DOLORES RIVER

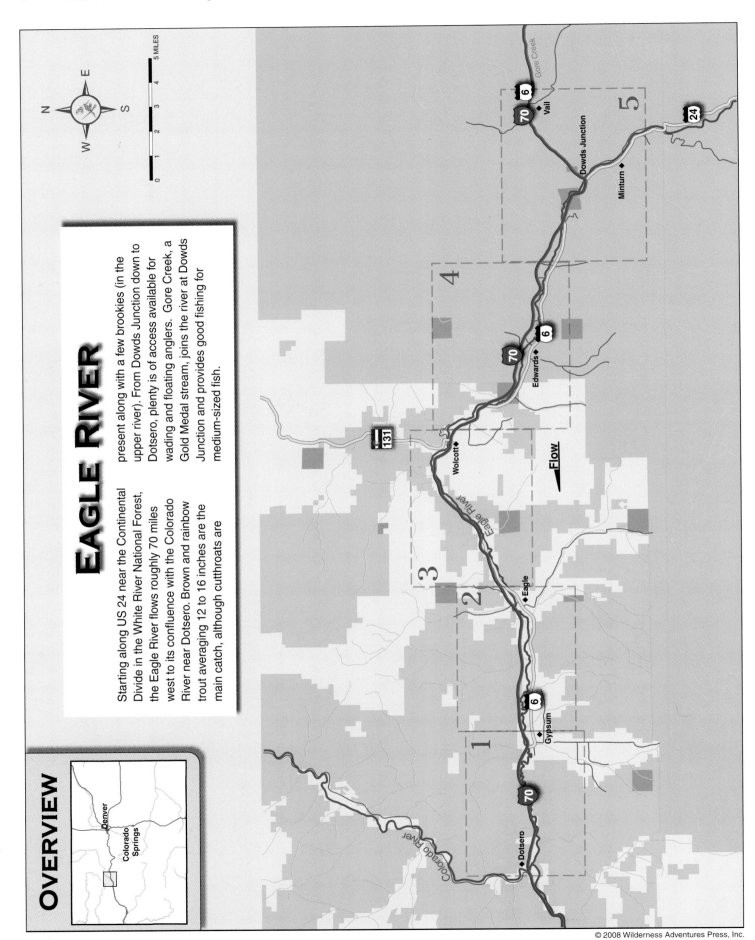

EAGLE RIVER

Starting along US 24 near the Continental Divide in the White River National Forest, the Eagle River flows roughly 70 miles west to its confluence with the Colorado River near Dotsero. Brown and rainbow trout averaging 12 to 16 inches are the main catch, although cutthroats are present along with a few brookies (in the upper river). From Dowds Junction down to Dotsero, plenty of access available for wading and floating anglers. Gore Creek, a Gold Medal stream, joins the river at Dowds Junction and provides good fishing for medium-sized fish.

OVERVIEW

Denver

Colorado Springs

Gore Creek

Vail

Dowds Junction

Minturn

Edwards

Wolcott

Eagle River

Flow

Eagle

Gypsum

Dotsero

Colorado River

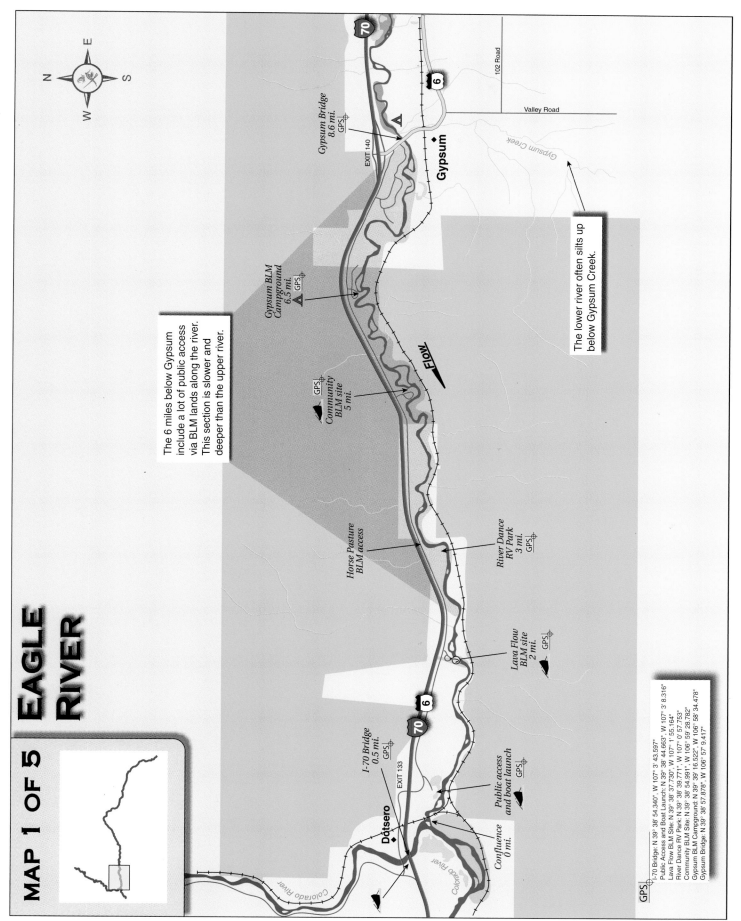

MAP 1 OF 5

EAGLE RIVER

The 6 miles below Gypsum include a lot of public access via BLM lands along the river. This section is slower and deeper than the upper river.

The lower river often silts up below Gypsum Creek.

Gypsum Bridge
8.6 mi.

Gypsum BLM Campground
6.5 mi.

Community BLM site
5 mi.

Horse Pasture BLM access

River Dance RV Park
3 mi.

Lava Flow BLM site
2 mi.

I-70 Bridge
0.5 mi.

Public access and boat launch

Confluence
0 mi.

Dotsero

Gypsum

Flow

Valley Road

102 Road

Gypsum Creek

Colorado River

EXIT 140

EXIT 133

GPS I-70 Bridge: N 39° 38' 54.340", W 107° 3' 43.597"
Public Access and Boat Launch: N 39° 38' 44.663", W 107° 3' 8.316"
Lava Flow BLM Site: N 39° 38' 37.730", W 107° 1' 55.164"
River Dance RV Park: N 39° 38' 39.771", W 107° 0' 57.753"
Community BLM Site: N 39° 38' 54.991", W 106° 59' 28.782"
Gypsum BLM Campground: N 39° 39' 16.522", W 106° 58' 34.478"
Gypsum Bridge: N 39° 38' 57.878", W 106° 57' 9.417"

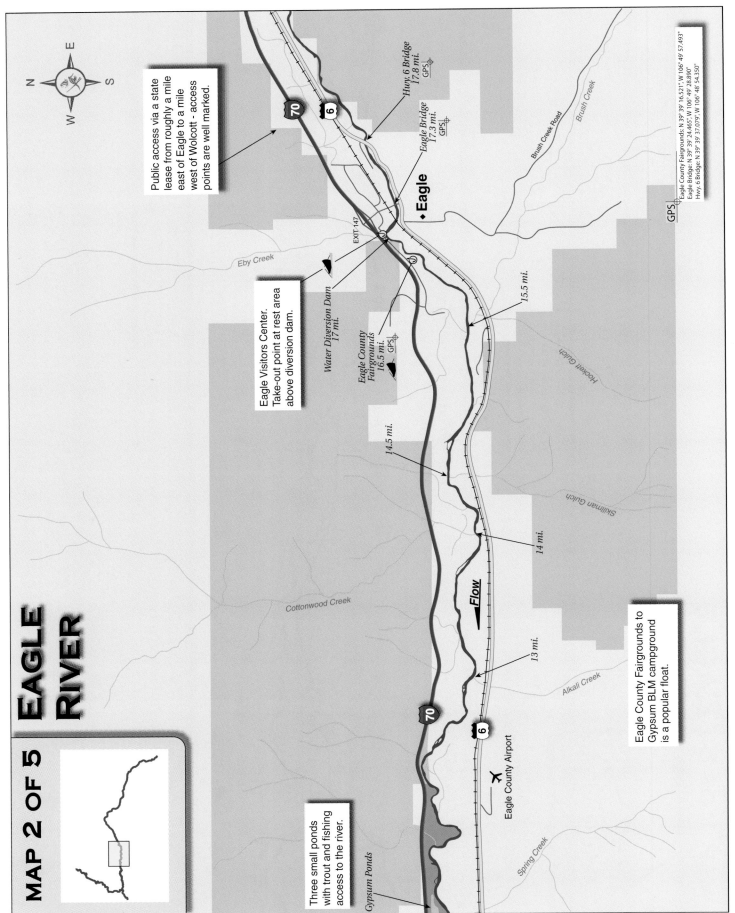

MAP 2 OF 5

EAGLE RIVER

Public access via a state lease from roughly a mile east of Eagle to a mile west of Wolcott - access points are well marked.

Eagle Visitors Center. Take-out point at rest area above diversion dam.

Three small ponds with trout and fishing access to the river.

Eagle County Fairgrounds to Gypsum BLM campground is a popular float.

Hwy. 6 Bridge 17.8 mi. GPS

Eagle Bridge 17.3 mi. GPS

Water Diversion Dam 17 mi.

Eagle County Fairgrounds 16.5 mi. GPS

15.5 mi.

14.5 mi.

14 mi.

13 mi.

◆ Eagle

EXIT 147

Eby Creek

Cottonwood Creek

Alkali Creek

Spring Creek

Gypsum Ponds

Eagle County Airport

Flow

Brush Creek Road

Brush Creek

Hockett Gulch

Skillman Gulch

GPS

Eagle County Fairgrounds: N 39° 39' 16.521", W 106° 49' 57.493"
Eagle Bridge: N 39° 39' 24.465", W 106° 49' 28.890"
Hwy. 6 Bridge: N 39° 39' 37.079", W 106° 48' 54.350"

© 2008 Wilderness Adventures Press, Inc.

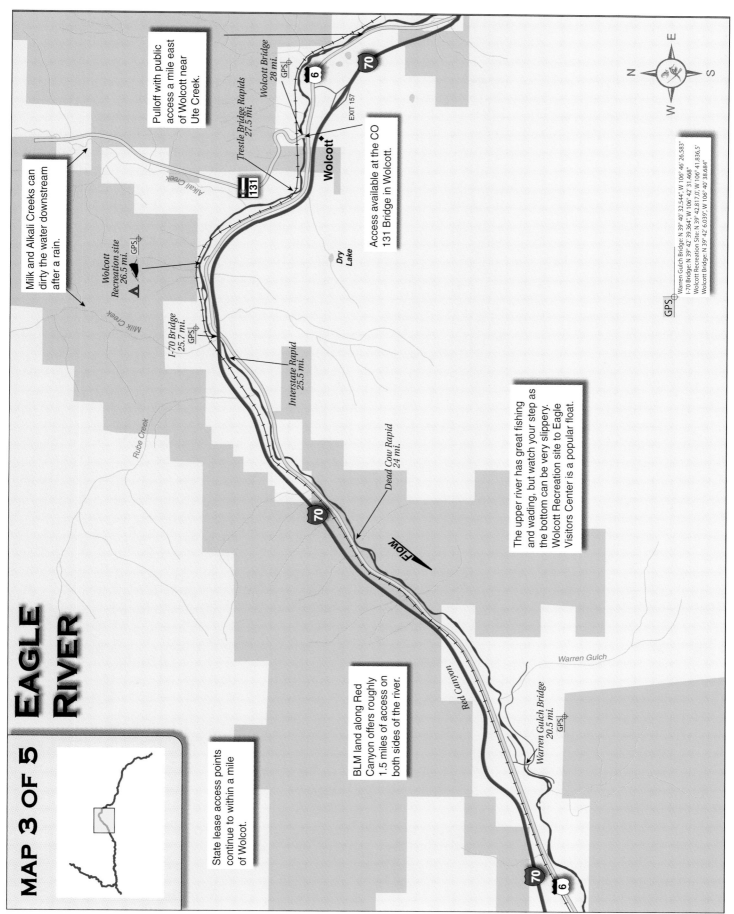

MAP 3 OF 5 EAGLE RIVER

State lease access points continue to within a mile of Wolcott.

BLM land along Red Canyon offers roughly 1.5 miles of access on both sides of the river.

The upper river has great fishing and wading, but watch your step as the bottom can be very slippery. Wolcott Recreation site to Eagle Visitors Center is a popular float.

Milk and Alkali Creeks can dirty the water downstream after a rain.

Pulloff with public access a mile east of Wolcott near Ute Creek.

Access available at the CO 131 Bridge in Wolcott.

Trestle Bridge Rapids 27.5 mi.

Wolcott Bridge 28 mi.

Wolcott Recreation site 26.5 mi.

I-70 Bridge 25.7 mi.

Interstate Rapid 25.5 mi.

Dead Cow Rapid 24 mi.

Warren Gulch Bridge 20.5 mi.

Wolcott

Dry Lake

EXIT 157

Alkali Creek

Milk Creek

Rube Creek

Red Canyon

Warren Gulch

Flow

GPS
Warren Gulch Bridge: N 39° 40' 32.544'; W 106° 46' 26.583"
I-70 Bridge: N 39° 42' 39.364'; W 106° 42' 31.468"
Wolcott Recreation Site: N 39° 42' 42.817.0'; W 106° 41' 836.5'
Wolcott Bridge: N 39° 42' 6.039'; W 106° 40' 38.684"

© 2008 Wilderness Adventures Press, Inc.

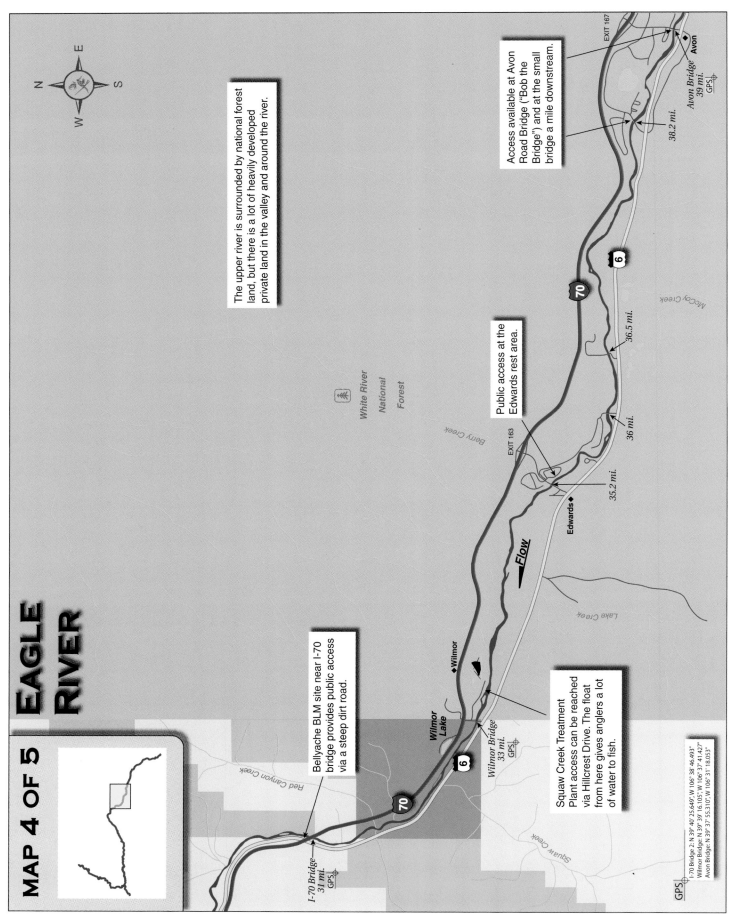

MAP 4 OF 5

EAGLE RIVER

The upper river is surrounded by national forest land, but there is a lot of heavily developed private land in the valley and around the river.

Access available at Avon Road Bridge ("Bob the Bridge") and at the small bridge a mile downstream.

Public access at the Edwards rest area.

Bellyache BLM site near I-70 bridge provides public access via a steep dirt road.

Squaw Creek Treatment Plant access can be reached via Hillcrest Drive. The float from here gives anglers a lot of water to fish.

White River National Forest

Avon

Avon Bridge 39 mi. GPS

38.2 mi.

36.5 mi.

36 mi.

35.2 mi.

Edwards

EXIT 167

EXIT 163

McCoy Creek

Berry Creek

Lake Creek

Flow

Wilmor

Wilmor Lake

Wilmor Bridge 33 mi. GPS

I-70 Bridge 31 mi. GPS

Red Canyon Creek

Squaw Creek

GPS
I-70 Bridge 2: N 39° 40' 25.649'; W 106° 38' 46.493"
Wilmor Bridge: N 39° 39' 16.105'; W 106° 37' 41.427"
Avon Bridge: N 39° 37' 55.310'; W 106° 31' 18.053"

© 2008 Wilderness Adventures Press, Inc.

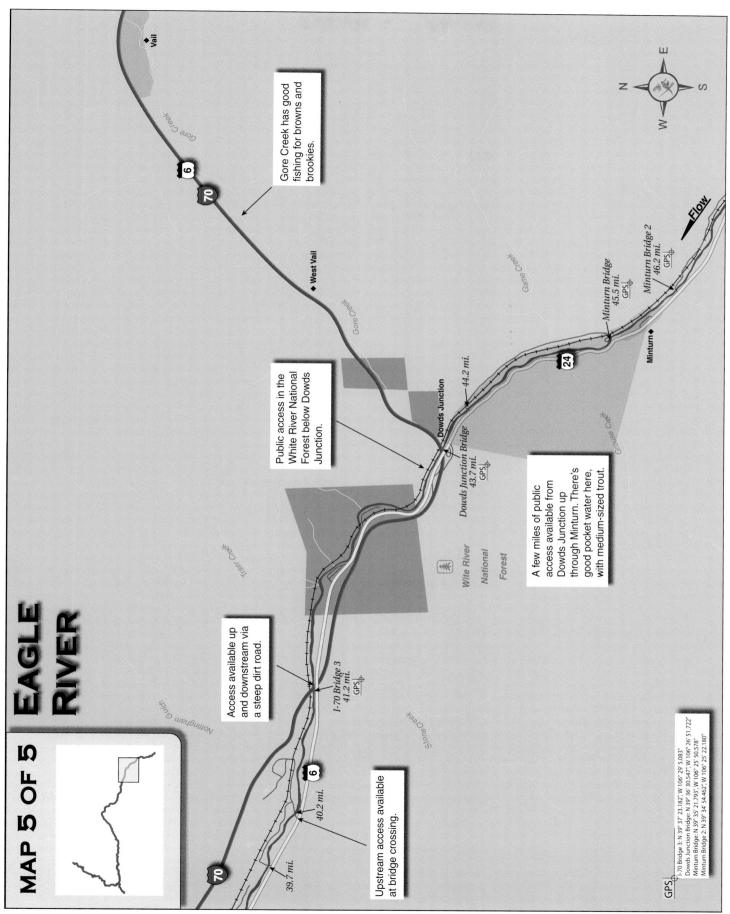

MAP 5 OF 5

EAGLE RIVER

Gore Creek has good fishing for browns and brookies.

Public access in the White River National Forest below Dowds Junction.

A few miles of public access available from Dowds Junction up through Minturn. There's good pocket water here, with medium-sized trout.

Access available up and downstream via a steep dirt road.

Upstream access available at bridge crossing.

Vail

West Vail

Dowds Junction

Minturn

Dowds Junction Bridge
43.7 mi.
GPS

Minturn Bridge
45.5 mi.
GPS

Minturn Bridge 2
46.2 mi.
GPS

44.2 mi.

I-70 Bridge 3
41.2 mi.
GPS

40.2 mi.

39.7 mi.

Wite River
National
Forest

Gore Creek

Game Creek

Grouse Creek

Trier Creek

Nottingham Gulch

Stone Creek

Flow

GPS
I-70 Bridge 3: N 39° 37' 23.182"; W 106° 29' 5.083"
Dowds Junction Bridge: N 39° 36' 30.547"; W 106° 26' 51.722"
Minturn Bridge: N 39° 35' 21.793"; W 106° 25' 50.578"
Minturn Bridge 2: N 39° 34' 54.462"; W 106° 25' 22.180"

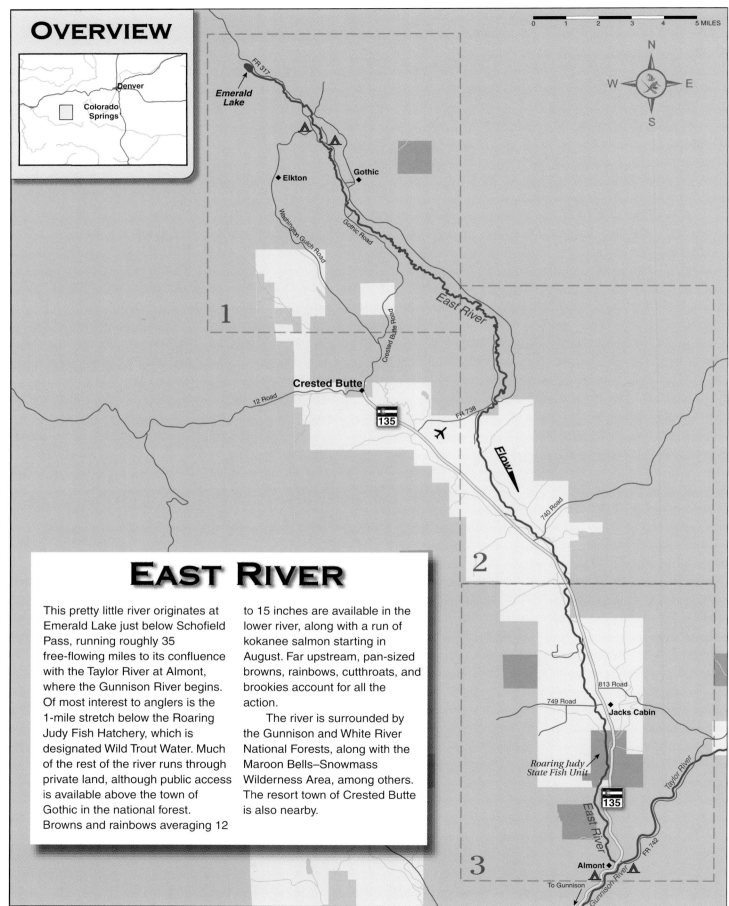

OVERVIEW

EAST RIVER

This pretty little river originates at Emerald Lake just below Schofield Pass, running roughly 35 free-flowing miles to its confluence with the Taylor River at Almont, where the Gunnison River begins. Of most interest to anglers is the 1-mile stretch below the Roaring Judy Fish Hatchery, which is designated Wild Trout Water. Much of the rest of the river runs through private land, although public access is available above the town of Gothic in the national forest. Browns and rainbows averaging 12 to 15 inches are available in the lower river, along with a run of kokanee salmon starting in August. Far upstream, pan-sized browns, rainbows, cutthroats, and brookies account for all the action.

The river is surrounded by the Gunnison and White River National Forests, along with the Maroon Bells–Snowmass Wilderness Area, among others. The resort town of Crested Butte is also nearby.

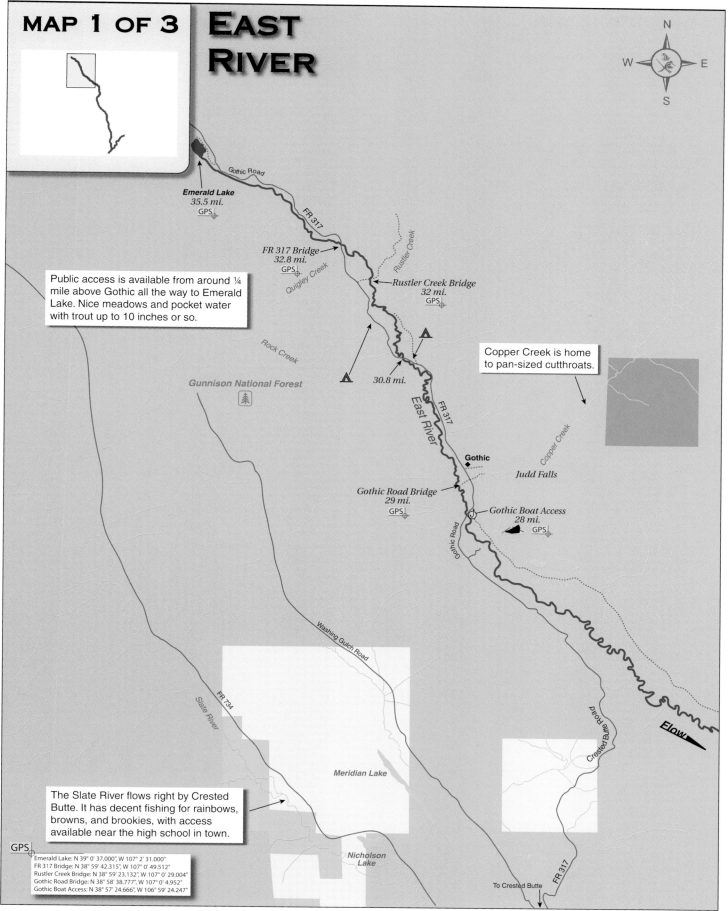

MAP 1 OF 3

EAST RIVER

N
W E
S

Gothic Road

Emerald Lake
35.5 mi.
GPS

FR 317

Rustler Creek

FR 317 Bridge
32.8 mi.
GPS

Public access is available from around ¼ mile above Gothic all the way to Emerald Lake. Nice meadows and pocket water with trout up to 10 inches or so.

Quigley Creek

Rustler Creek Bridge
32 mi.
GPS

Rock Creek

Copper Creek is home to pan-sized cutthroats.

30.8 mi.

Gunnison National Forest

East River

FR 317

Copper Creek

Gothic

Judd Falls

Gothic Road Bridge
29 mi.
GPS

Gothic Boat Access
28 mi.
GPS

Gothic Road

Washing Gulch Road

FR 734

Slate River

Crested Butte Road

Flow

Meridian Lake

The Slate River flows right by Crested Butte. It has decent fishing for rainbows, browns, and brookies, with access available near the high school in town.

GPS
Emerald Lake: N 39° 0' 37.000", W 107° 2' 31.000"
FR 317 Bridge: N 38° 59' 42.315", W 107° 0' 49.512"
Rustler Creek Bridge: N 38° 59' 23.132", W 107° 0' 29.004"
Gothic Road Bridge: N 38° 58' 38.777", W 107° 0' 4.952"
Gothic Boat Access: N 38° 57' 24.666", W 106° 59' 24.247"

Nicholson Lake

To Crested Butte

FR 317

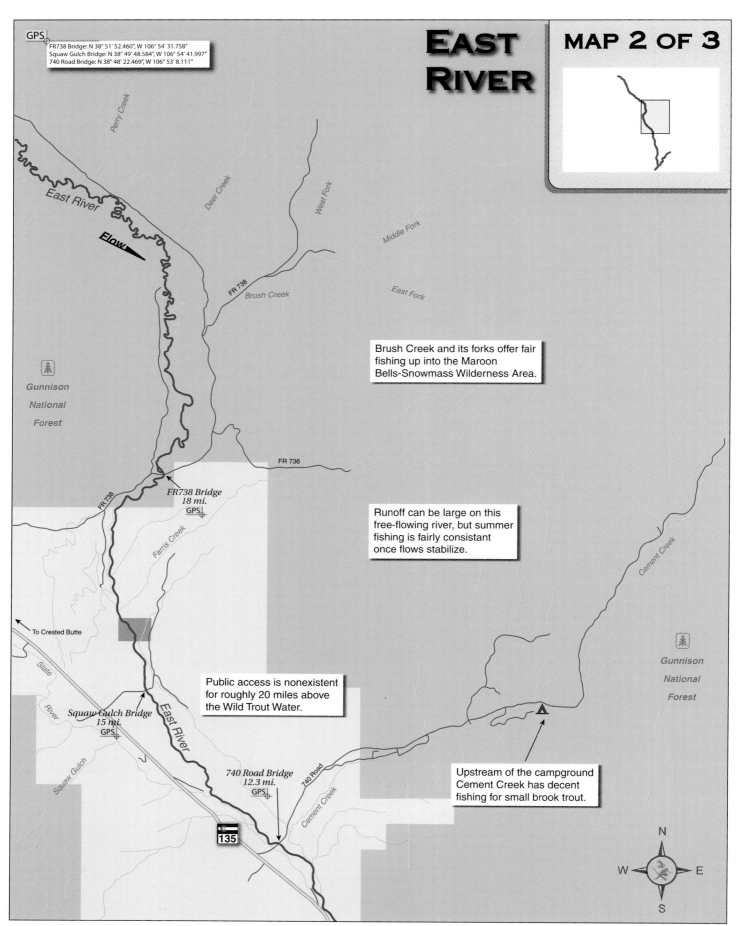

GPS
FR738 Bridge: N 38° 51' 52.460", W 106° 54' 31.758"
Squaw Gulch Bridge: N 38° 49' 48.584", W 106° 54' 41.997"
740 Road Bridge: N 38° 48' 22.469", W 106° 53' 8.111"

Perry Creek

East River

Flow

Deer Creek

West Fork

Middle Fork

East Fork

FR 738

Brush Creek

Brush Creek and its forks offer fair
fishing up into the Maroon
Bells-Snowmass Wilderness Area.

Gunnison
National
Forest

FR 736

FR738 Bridge
18 mi.
GPS

FR 738

Farris Creek

Runoff can be large on this
free-flowing river, but summer
fishing is fairly consistant
once flows stabilize.

Cement Creek

To Crested Butte

Slate

River

Public access is nonexistent
for roughly 20 miles above
the Wild Trout Water.

Gunnison
National
Forest

Squaw Gulch Bridge
15 mi.
GPS

East River

Squaw Gulch

740 Road Bridge
12.3 mi.
GPS

740 Road

Cement Creek

Upstream of the campground
Cement Creek has decent
fishing for small brook trout.

135

N
W   E
S

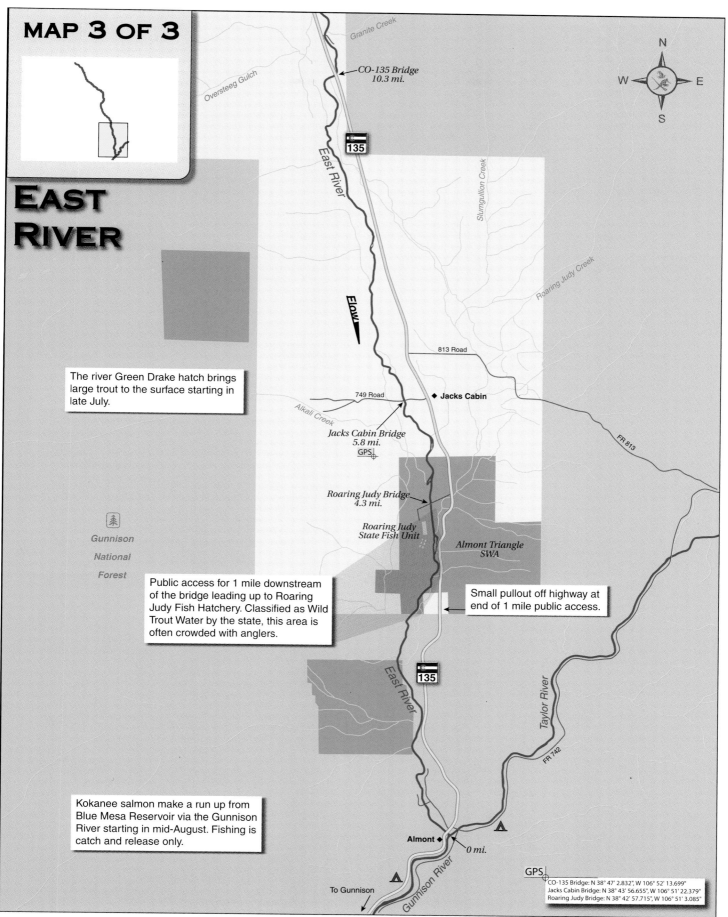

MAP 3 OF 3

EAST RIVER

Granite Creek

CO-135 Bridge
10.3 mi.

Oversteeg Gulch

135

East River

Flow

Slumgullion Creek

Roaring Judy Creek

813 Road

The river Green Drake hatch brings
large trout to the surface starting in
late July.

749 Road

◆ **Jacks Cabin**

Alkali Creek

Jacks Cabin Bridge
5.8 mi.
GPS

FR 813

Roaring Judy Bridge
4.3 mi.

Roaring Judy
State Fish Unit

Almont Triangle
SWA

🌲

Gunnison

National

Forest

Public access for 1 mile downstream
of the bridge leading up to Roaring
Judy Fish Hatchery. Classified as Wild
Trout Water by the state, this area is
often crowded with anglers.

Small pullout off highway at
end of 1 mile public access.

East River

135

Taylor River

FR 742

Kokanee salmon make a run up from
Blue Mesa Reservoir via the Gunnison
River starting in mid-August. Fishing is
catch and release only.

Almont ◆

⛺

0 mi.

GPS

CO-135 Bridge: N 38° 47' 2.832", W 106° 52' 13.699"
Jacks Cabin Bridge: N 38° 43' 56.655", W 106° 51' 22.379"
Roaring Judy Bridge: N 38° 42' 57.715", W 106° 51' 3.085"

⛺

To Gunnison

Gunnison River

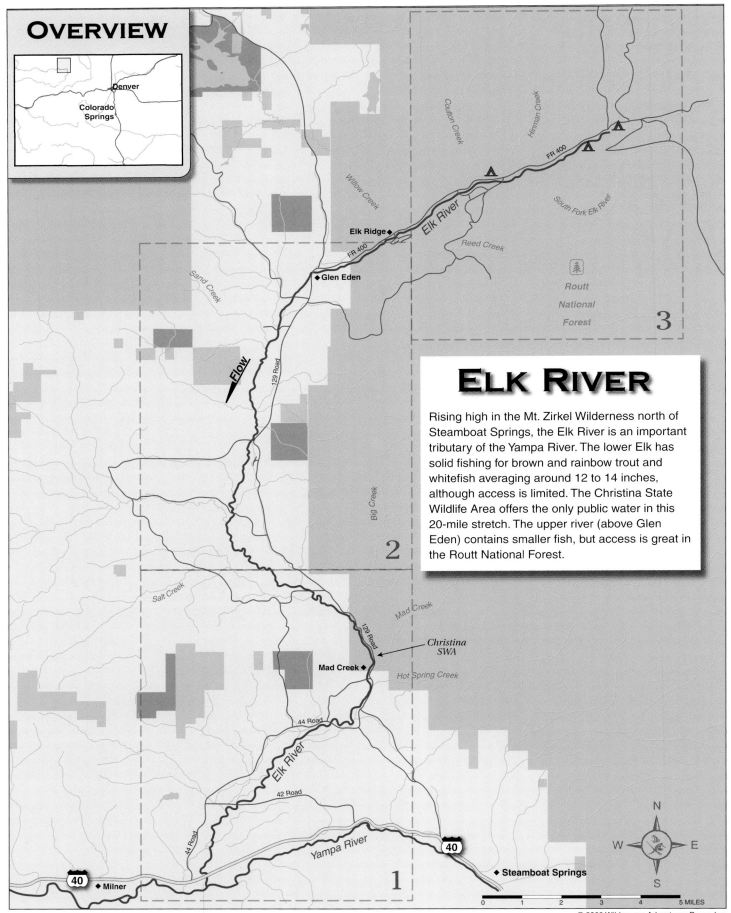

OVERVIEW

Denver

Colorado
Springs

ELK RIVER

Rising high in the Mt. Zirkel Wilderness north of
Steamboat Springs, the Elk River is an important
tributary of the Yampa River. The lower Elk has
solid fishing for brown and rainbow trout and
whitefish averaging around 12 to 14 inches,
although access is limited. The Christina State
Wildlife Area offers the only public water in this
20-mile stretch. The upper river (above Glen
Eden) contains smaller fish, but access is great in
the Routt National Forest.

Coulton Creek

Hinman Creek

Willow Creek

FR 400

South Fork Elk River

Elk River

Elk Ridge ◆

Reed Creek

Routt

FR 400

◆ Glen Eden

National

Sand Creek

Forest

3

129 Road

Flow

Big Creek

2

Salt Creek

Mad Creek

129 Road

Christina
SWA

Mad Creek ◆

Hot Spring Creek

44 Road

Elk River

42 Road

44 Road

N

Yampa River

40

W   E

S

1

◆ Steamboat Springs

40 ◆ Milner

0   1   2   3   4   5 MILES

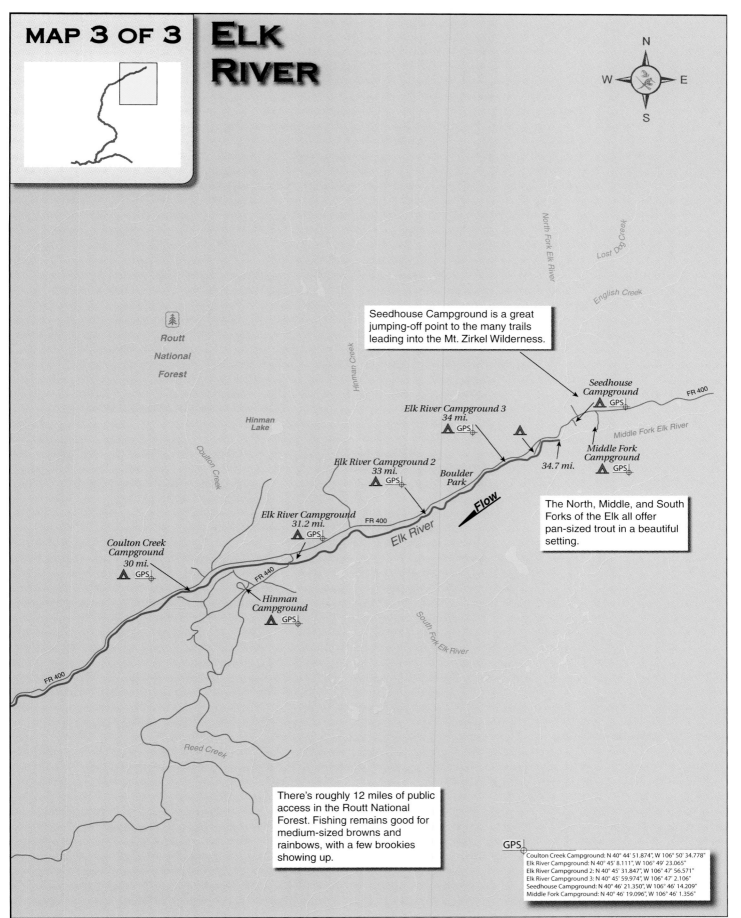

MAP 3 OF 3

ELK RIVER

Seedhouse Campground is a great jumping-off point to the many trails leading into the Mt. Zirkel Wilderness.

Routt National Forest

Hinman Lake

Seedhouse Campground
GPS
FR 400

Elk River Campground 3
34 mi.
GPS

Middle Fork Campground
GPS

Middle Fork Elk River

North Fork Elk River

Lost Dog Creek

English Creek

Hinman Creek

Coulton Creek

34.7 mi.

Elk River Campground 2
33 mi.
GPS

Boulder Park

Flow

Elk River

FR 400

The North, Middle, and South Forks of the Elk all offer pan-sized trout in a beautiful setting.

Elk River Campground
31.2 mi.
GPS

Coulton Creek Campground
30 mi.
GPS

FR 440

Hinman Campground
GPS

South Fork Elk River

FR 400

Reed Creek

There's roughly 12 miles of public access in the Routt National Forest. Fishing remains good for medium-sized browns and rainbows, with a few brookies showing up.

GPS
Coulton Creek Campground: N 40° 44' 51.874", W 106° 50' 34.778"
Elk River Campground: N 40° 45' 8.111", W 106° 49' 23.065"
Elk River Campground 2: N 40° 45' 31.847", W 106° 47' 56.571"
Elk River Campground 3: N 40° 45' 59.974", W 106° 47' 2.106"
Seedhouse Campground: N 40° 46' 21.350", W 106° 46' 14.209"
Middle Fork Campground: N 40° 46' 19.096", W 106° 46' 1.356"

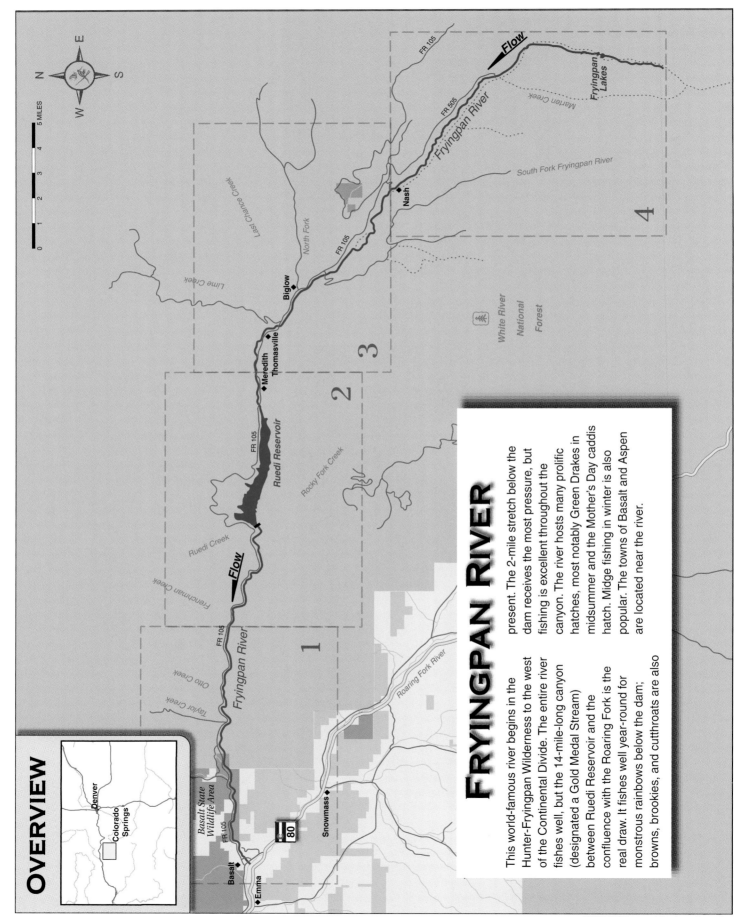

FRYINGPAN RIVER

This world-famous river begins in the Hunter-Fryingpan Wilderness to the west of the Continental Divide. The entire river fishes well, but the 14-mile-long canyon between Ruedi Reservoir and the confluence with the Roaring Fork is the real draw. It fishes well year-round for monstrous rainbows below the dam; browns, brookies, and cutthroats are also present. The 2-mile stretch below the dam receives the most pressure, but fishing is excellent throughout the canyon. The river hosts many prolific hatches, most notably Green Drakes in midsummer and the Mother's Day caddis hatch. Midge fishing in winter is also popular. The towns of Basalt and Aspen are located near the river.

OVERVIEW

FRYINGPAN RIVER

MAP 1 OF 4

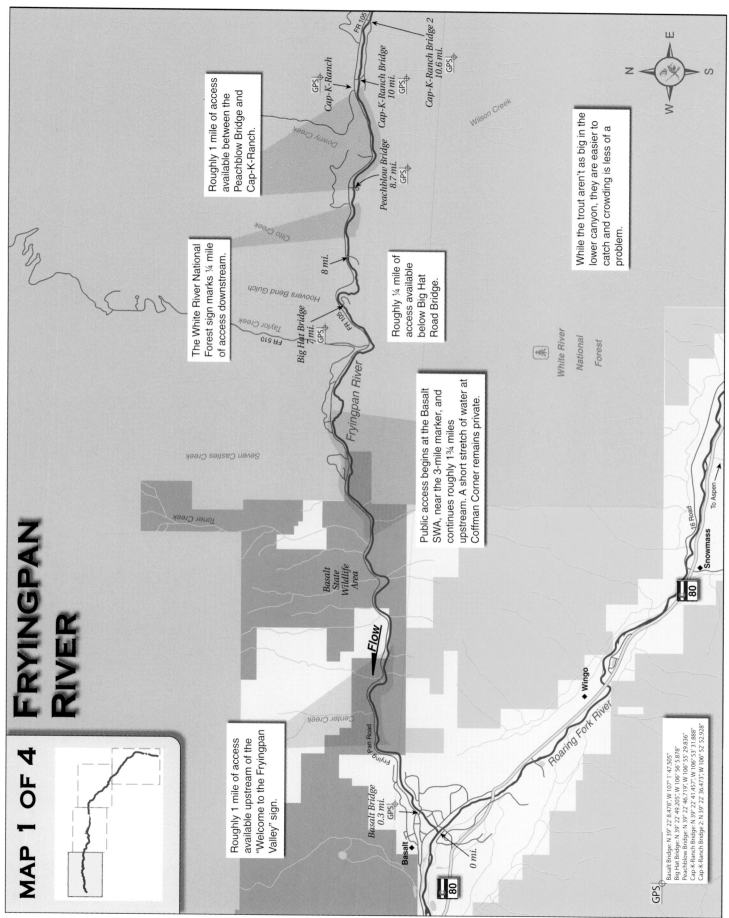

Roughly 1 mile of access available between the Peachblow Bridge and Cap-K-Ranch.

The White River National Forest sign marks ¼ mile of access downstream.

Roughly ¼ mile of access available below Big Hat Road Bridge.

While the trout aren't as big in the lower canyon, they are easier to catch and crowding is less of a problem.

Public access begins at the Basalt SWA, near the 3-mile marker, and continues roughly 1¾ miles upstream. A short stretch of water at Coffman Corner remains private.

Roughly 1 mile of access available upstream of the "Welcome to the Fryingpan Valley" sign.

FR 105

Cap-K-Ranch

Cap-K-Ranch Bridge 10 mi.
GPS

Cap-K-Ranch Bridge 2 10.6 mi.
GPS

Wilson Creek

Downy Creek

Peachblow Bridge 8.7 mi.
GPS

Otto Creek

8 mi.

Hoovers Bend Gulch

Taylor Creek

Big Hat Bridge 7 mi.
GPS

FR 510

FR 105

Fryingpan River

Seven Castles Creek

Toner Creek

Basalt State Wildlife Area

Flow

White River National Forest

Center Creek

Fryingpan Road

Basalt Bridge 0.3 mi.
GPS

Basalt

80

0 mi.

Wingo

Roaring Fork River

Snowmass

80

16 Road

To Aspen

N E S W

GPS
Basalt Bridge: N 39° 22' 8.478"; W 107° 1' 47.505"
Big Hat Bridge: N 39° 22' 49.205"; W 106° 56' 5.878"
Peachblow Bridge: N 39° 22' 46.719"; W 106° 55' 29.836"
Cap-K-Ranch Bridge: N 39° 22' 41.457"; W 106° 53' 31.888"
Cap-K-Ranch Bridge 2: N 39° 22' 36.473"; W 106° 52' 52.928"

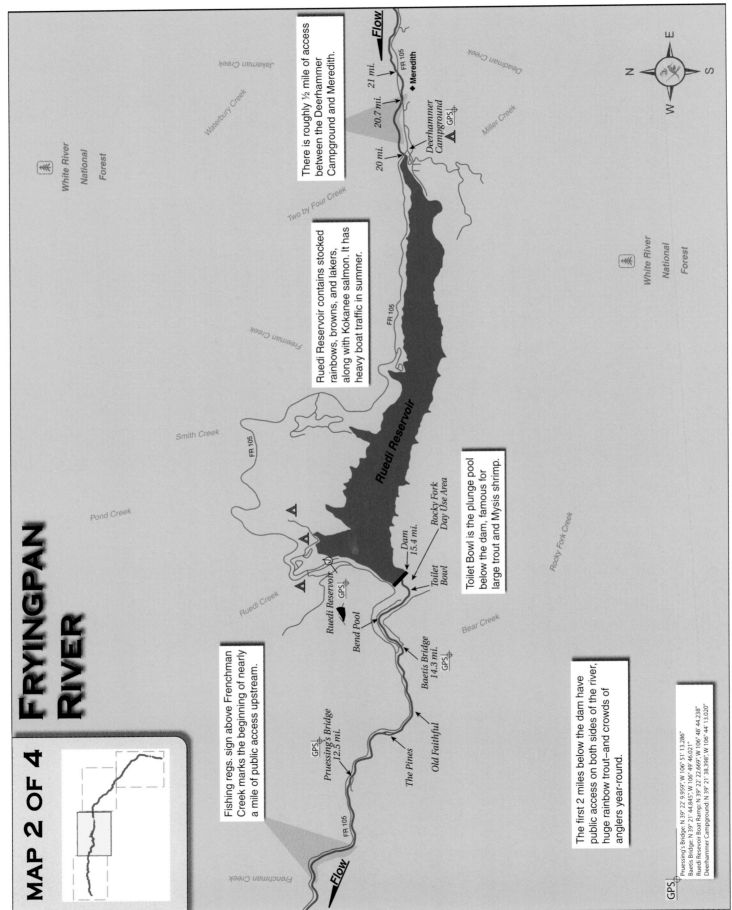

MAP 2 OF 4

FRYINGPAN RIVER

There is roughly ½ mile of access between the Deerhammer Campground and Meredith.

Ruedi Reservoir contains stocked rainbows, browns, and lakers, along with Kokanee salmon. It has heavy boat traffic in summer.

Toilet Bowl is the plunge pool below the dam, famous for large trout and Mysis shrimp.

Fishing regs. sign above Frenchman Creek marks the beginning of nearly a mile of public access upstream.

The first 2 miles below the dam have public access on both sides of the river, huge rainbow trout—and crowds of anglers year-round.

White River National Forest

White River National Forest

Jakeman Creek

Waterbury Creek

Deadman Creek

Two by Four Creek

Miller Creek

Freeman Creek

Smith Creek

Pond Creek

Ruedi Reservoir

Ruedi Creek

Rocky Fork Creek

Bear Creek

FR 105

FR 105

FR 105

FR 105

Flow

Flow

Flow

Meredith

Deerhammer Campground GPS

21 mi.
20.7 mi.
20 mi.

Dam
15.4 mi.

Rocky Fork Day Use Area

Toilet Bowl

Ruedi Reservoir GPS

Bend Pool

Baetis Bridge 14.3 mi. GPS

Old Faithful

The Pines

Pruessing's Bridge 12.5 mi. GPS

Frenchman Creek

N E S W

GPS
Pruessing's Bridge: N 39° 22' 9.959"; W 106° 51' 13.286"
Baetis Bridge: N 39° 21' 44.845"; W 106° 49' 46.021"
Ruedi Resevoir Boat Ramp: N 39° 22' 22.669"; W 106° 48' 44.238"
Deerhammer Campground: N 39° 21' 38.398"; W 106° 44' 13.020"

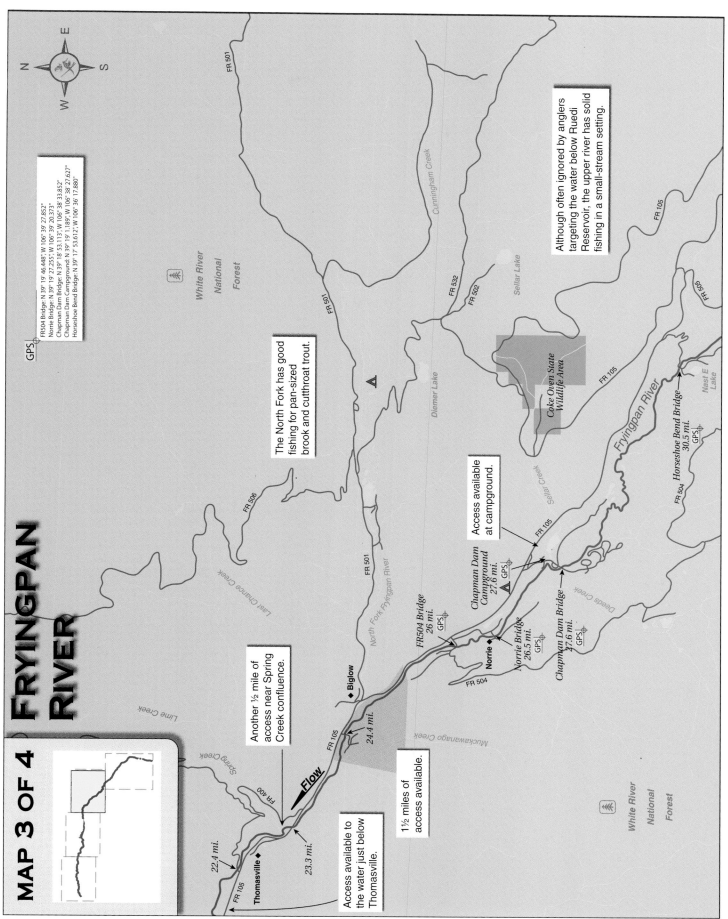

MAP 3 OF 4

FRYINGPAN RIVER

© 2008 Wilderness Adventures Press, Inc.

GPS

FR504 Bridge: N 39° 19' 46.448"; W 106° 39' 27.852"
Norrie Bridge: N 39° 19' 27.255"; W 106° 39' 20.373"
Chapman Dam Bridge: N 39° 18' 53.113"; W 106° 38' 33.852"
Chapman Dam Campground: N 39° 19' 1.189'; W 106° 38' 27.627"
Horseshoe Bend Bridge: N 39° 17' 53.612'; W 106 36' 17.880"

Although often ignored by anglers targeting the water below Ruedi Reservoir, the upper river has solid fishing in a small-stream setting.

The North Fork has good fishing for pan-sized brook and cutthroat trout.

Access available at campground.

Another ½ mile of access near Spring Creek confluence.

1½ miles of access available.

Access available to the water just below Thomasville.

White River National Forest

White River National Forest

Coke Oven State Wildlife Area

Sellar Lake

Diemer Lake

Nast E Lake

Fryingpan River

North Fork Fryingpan River

Cunningham Creek

Sellar Creek

Deeds Creek

Muckawanago Creek

Last Chance Creek

Lime Creek

Spring Creek

Flow

Thomasville ◆

◆ Biglow

Norrie ◆

FR 501
FR 501
FR 501
FR 506
FR 105
FR 105
FR 105
FR 400
FR 504
FR 504
FR 502
FR 532
FR 505

FR504 Bridge 26 mi. GPS
Norrie Bridge 26.5 mi. GPS
Chapman Dam Bridge 27.6 mi. GPS
Chapman Dam Campground 27.6 mi. GPS
Horseshoe Bend Bridge 30.5 mi. GPS

22.4 mi.
23.3 mi.
24.4 mi.

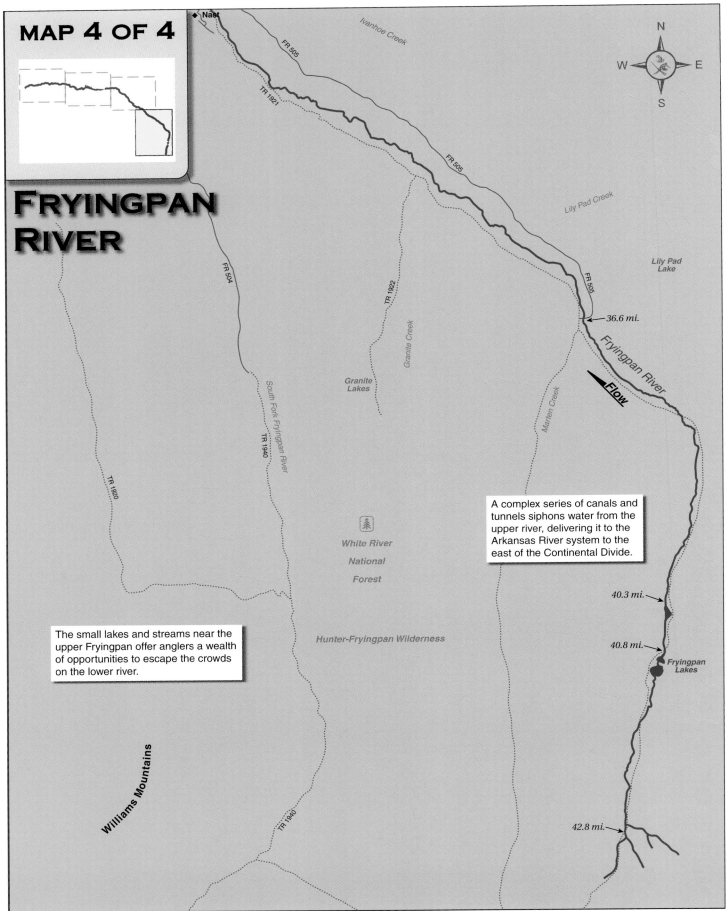

MAP 4 OF 4

FRYINGPAN RIVER

Nast

Ivanhoe Creek

FR 505

TR 1921

FR 504

TR 1922

Granite Creek

Granite Lakes

South Fork Fryingpan River

TR 1940

TR 1920

White River

National

Forest

Hunter-Fryingpan Wilderness

TR 1940

Williams Mountains

Lily Pad Creek

Lily Pad Lake

FR 505

36.6 mi.

Fryingpan River

Flow

Marten Creek

A complex series of canals and tunnels siphons water from the upper river, delivering it to the Arkansas River system to the east of the Continental Divide.

40.3 mi.

40.8 mi.

Fryingpan Lakes

The small lakes and streams near the upper Fryingpan offer anglers a wealth of opportunities to escape the crowds on the lower river.

42.8 mi.

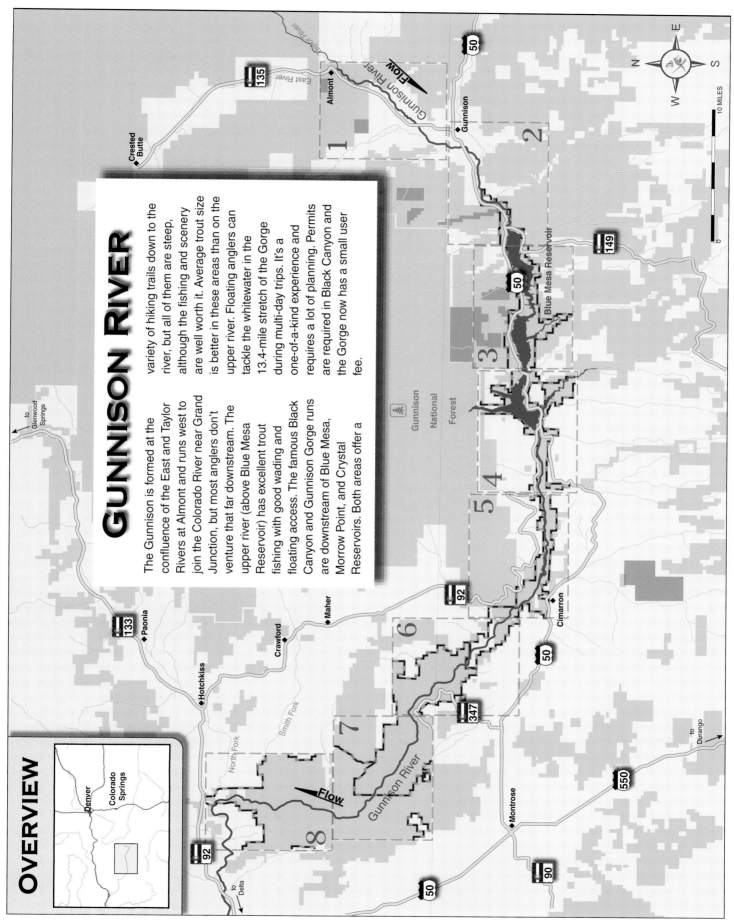

GUNNISON RIVER

The Gunnison is formed at the confluence of the East and Taylor Rivers at Almont and runs west to join the Colorado River near Grand Junction, but most anglers don't venture that far downstream. The upper river (above Blue Mesa Reservoir) has excellent trout fishing with good wading and floating access. The famous Black Canyon and Gunnison Gorge runs are downstream of Blue Mesa, Morrow Point, and Crystal Reservoirs. Both areas offer a variety of hiking trails down to the river, but all of them are steep, although the fishing and scenery are well worth it. Average trout size is better in these areas than on the upper river. Floating anglers can tackle the whitewater in the 13.4-mile stretch of the Gorge during multi-day trips. It's a one-of-a-kind experience and requires a lot of planning. Permits are required in Black Canyon and the Gorge now has a small user fee.

OVERVIEW

MAP 1 OF 8 GUNNISON RIVER

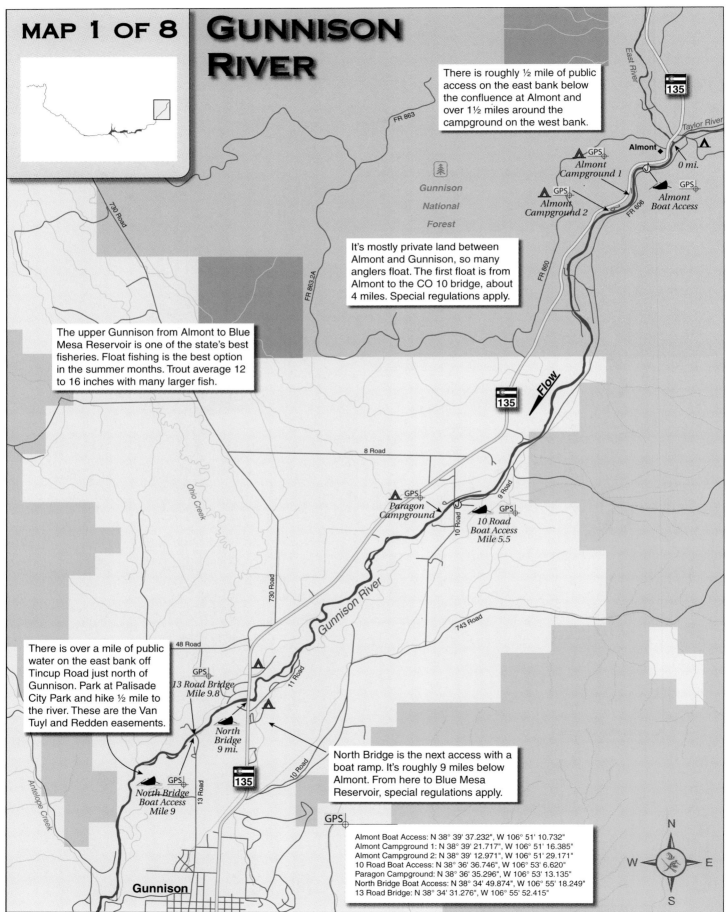

There is roughly ½ mile of public access on the east bank below the confluence at Almont and over 1½ miles around the campground on the west bank.

It's mostly private land between Almont and Gunnison, so many anglers float. The first float is from Almont to the CO 10 bridge, about 4 miles. Special regulations apply.

The upper Gunnison from Almont to Blue Mesa Reservoir is one of the state's best fisheries. Float fishing is the best option in the summer months. Trout average 12 to 16 inches with many larger fish.

There is over a mile of public water on the east bank off Tincup Road just north of Gunnison. Park at Palisade City Park and hike ½ mile to the river. These are the Van Tuyl and Redden easements.

North Bridge is the next access with a boat ramp. It's roughly 9 miles below Almont. From here to Blue Mesa Reservoir, special regulations apply.

Gunnison National Forest

FR 863

FR 863.2A

730 Road

East River

135

Taylor River

Almont

0 mi.

Almont Campground 1

GPS

Almont Campground 2

GPS

FR 606

Almont Boat Access

GPS

FR 860

Flow

135

8 Road

9 Road

Ohio Creek

Paragon Campground

GPS

10 Road

GPS

10 Road Boat Access Mile 5.5

730 Road

Gunnison River

743 Road

11 Road

48 Road

GPS

13 Road Bridge Mile 9.8

North Bridge 9 mi.

North Bridge Boat Access Mile 9

GPS

13 Road

135

10 Road

Antelope Creek

GPS

Gunnison

Almont Boat Access: N 38° 39' 37.232", W 106° 51' 10.732"
Almont Campground 1: N 38° 39' 21.717", W 106° 51' 16.385"
Almont Campground 2: N 38° 39' 12.971", W 106° 51' 29.171"
10 Road Boat Access: N 38° 36' 36.746", W 106° 53' 6.620"
Paragon Campground: N 38° 36' 35.296", W 106° 53' 13.135"
North Bridge Boat Access: N 38° 34' 49.874", W 106° 55' 18.249"
13 Road Bridge: N 38° 34' 31.276", W 106° 55' 52.415"

N
W E
S

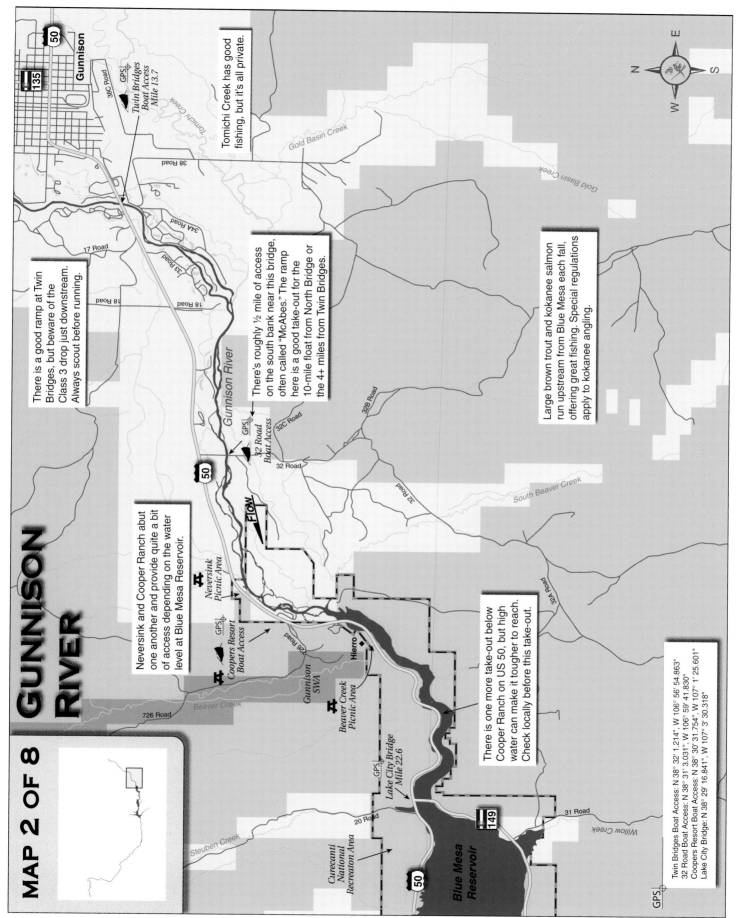

MAP 2 OF 8

GUNNISON RIVER

There is a good ramp at Twin Bridges, but beware of the Class 3 drop just downstream. Always scout before running.

Neversink and Cooper Ranch abut one another and provide quite a bit of access depending on the water level at Blue Mesa Reservoir.

Tomichi Creek has good fishing, but it's all private.

There's roughly ½ mile of access on the south bank near this bridge, often called "McAbes." The ramp here is a good take-out for the 10-mile float from North Bridge or the 4+ miles from Twin Bridges.

Large brown trout and kokanee salmon run upstream from Blue Mesa each fall, offering great fishing. Special regulations apply to kokanee angling.

There is one more take-out below Cooper Ranch on US 50, but high water can make it tougher to reach. Check locally before this take-out.

Twin Bridges Boat Access: N 38° 32' 1.214", W 106° 56' 54.863"
32 Road Boat Access: N 38° 31' 3.031", W 106° 59' 41.830"
Coopers Resort Boat Access: N 38° 30' 31.754", W 107° 1' 25.601"
Lake City Bridge: N 38° 29' 16.841", W 107° 3' 30.318"

Gunnison

Twin Bridges Boat Access Mile 13.7

38C Road
38 Road
34A Road
33 Road
17 Road
18 Road

Gunnison River

32C Road
32 Road
32B Road
32 Road

Gold Basin Creek

South Beaver Creek

FLOW

Neversink Picnic Area

Coopers Resort Boat Access

726 Road

Beaver Creek

Gunnison SWA

Beaver Creek Picnic Area

Hierro

Lake City Bridge Mile 22.6

20 Road

Curecanti National Recreation Area

Steuben Creek

Blue Mesa Reservoir

31 Road

Willow Creek

32A Road

Tomichi Creek

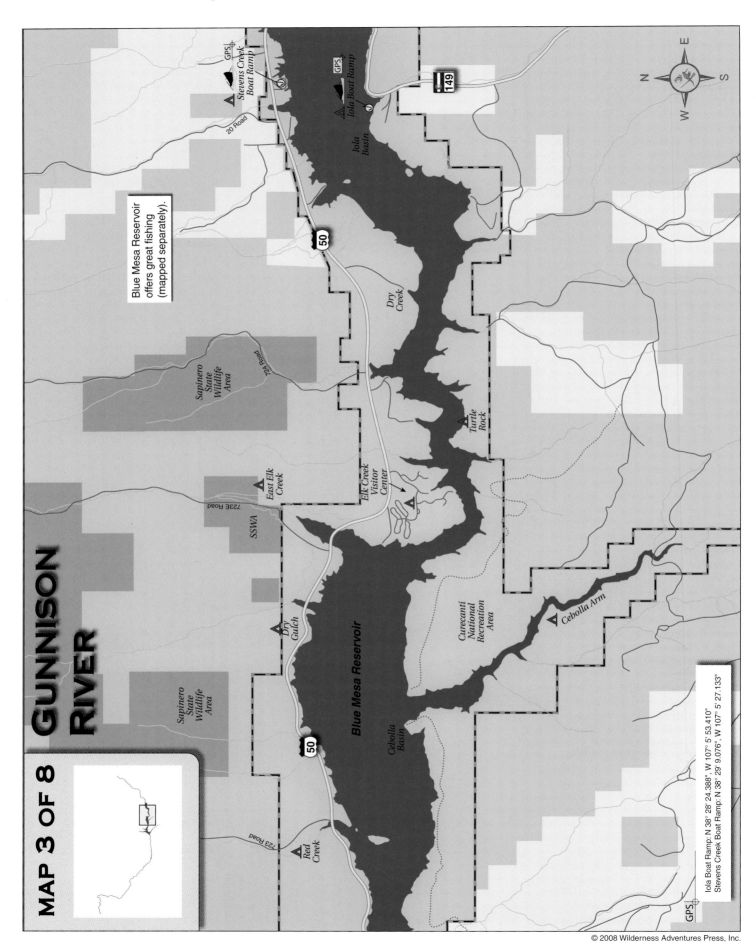

MAP 3 OF 8 **GUNNISON RIVER**

Sapinero State Wildlife Area

Blue Mesa Reservoir offers great fishing (mapped separately).

20 Road

Stevens Creek Boat Ramp

GPS

Iola Boat Ramp

GPS

149

Iola Basin

50

Dry Creek

124 Road

Sapinero State Wildlife Area

East Elk Creek

723E Road

SSWA

Turtle Rock

Elk Creek Visitor Center

Curecanti National Recreation Area

Cebolla Arm

Dry Gulch

Blue Mesa Reservoir

Cebolla Basin

50

723 Road

Red Creek

GPS

Iola Boat Ramp: N 38° 28' 24.388', W 107° 5' 53.410"
Stevens Creek Boat Ramp: N 38° 29 9.076', W 107° 5' 27.133"

© 2008 Wilderness Adventures Press, Inc.

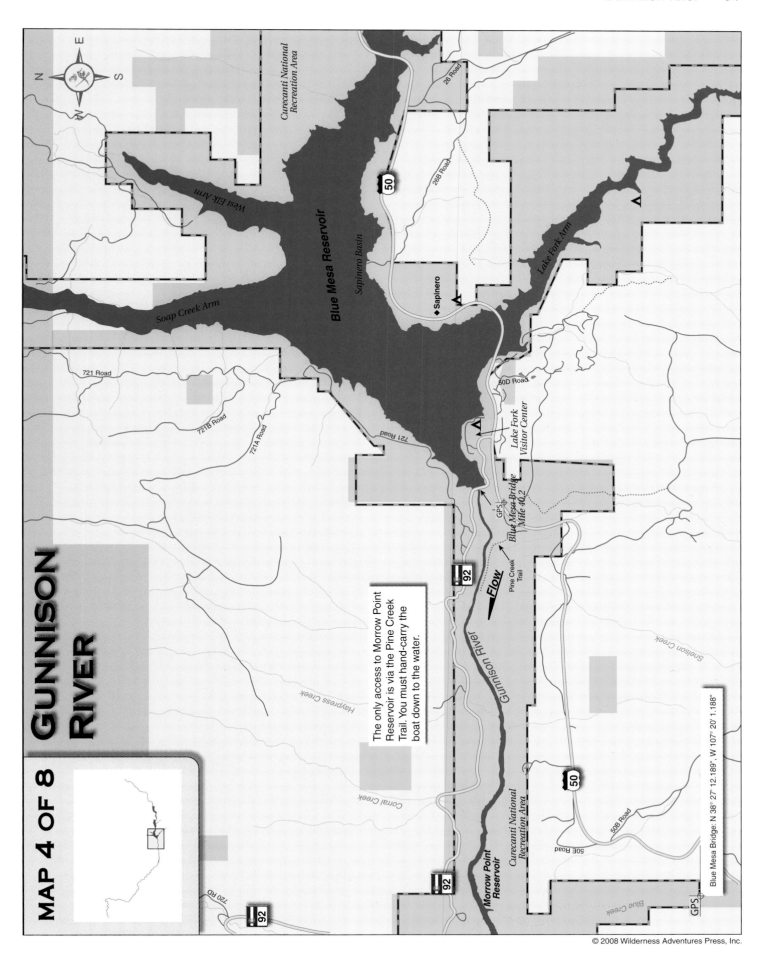

MAP 4 OF 8
GUNNISON RIVER

The only access to Morrow Point Reservoir is via the Pine Creek Trail. You must hand-carry the boat down to the water.

Blue Mesa Bridge: N 38° 27' 12.189", W 107° 20' 1.188"

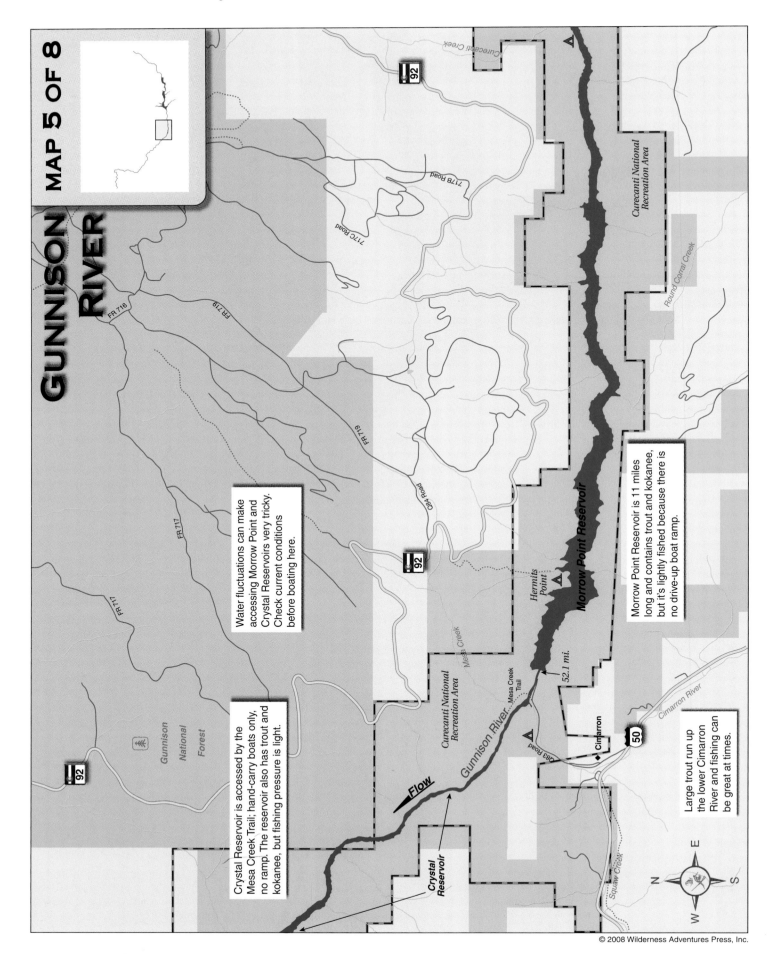

MAP 5 OF 8

GUNNISON RIVER

Curecanti Creek

92

717B Road

717C Road

Curecanti National Recreation Area

Round Corral Creek

FR 716

FR 719

FR 719

FR 717

FR 717

Gunnison National Forest

Water fluctuations can make accessing Morrow Point and Crystal Reservoirs very tricky. Check current conditions before boating here.

Q84 Road

92

Hermits Point

Morrow Point Reservoir

Morrow Point Reservoir is 11 miles long and contains trout and kokanee, but it's lightly fished because there is no drive-up boat ramp.

52.1 mi.

Mesa Creek

Curecanti National Recreation Area

Mesa Creek Trail

Cimarron River

Crystal Reservoir is accessed by the Mesa Creek Trail; hand-carry boats only, no ramp. The reservoir also has trout and kokanee, but fishing pressure is light.

92

Gunnison River

Flow

Q83 Road

Cimarron

50

Large trout run up the lower Cimarron River and fishing can be great at times.

Crystal Reservoir

Squaw Creek

N
W   E
S

© 2008 Wilderness Adventures Press, Inc.

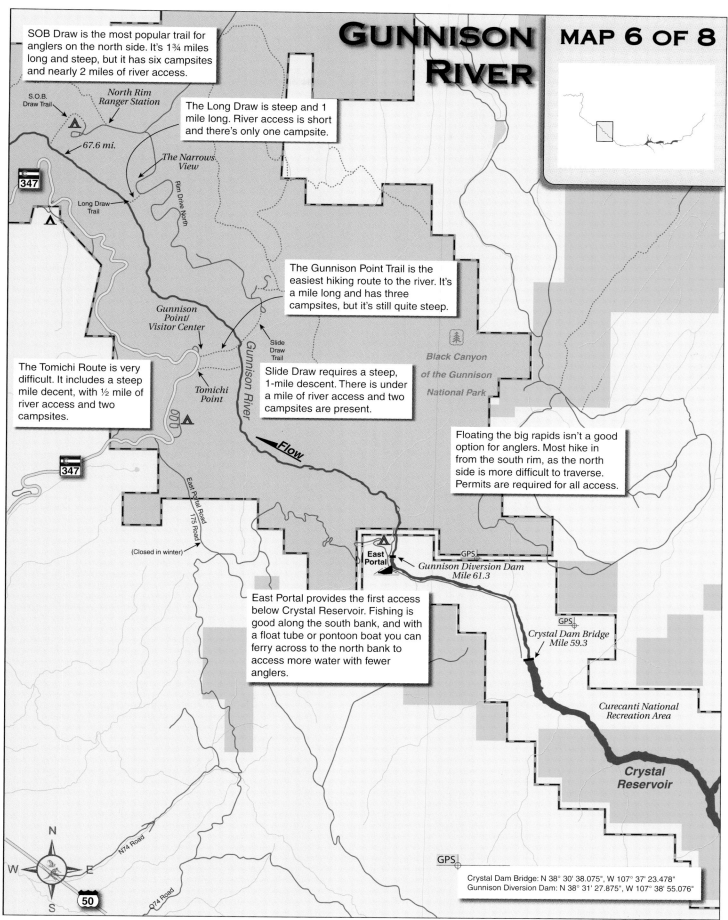

SOB Draw is the most popular trail for anglers on the north side. It's 1¾ miles long and steep, but it has six campsites and nearly 2 miles of river access.

GUNNISON RIVER

MAP 6 OF 8

North Rim Ranger Station

S.O.B. Draw Trail

The Long Draw is steep and 1 mile long. River access is short and there's only one campsite.

← 67.6 mi.

The Narrows View

347

Rim Drive North

Long Draw Trail

The Gunnison Point Trail is the easiest hiking route to the river. It's a mile long and has three campsites, but it's still quite steep.

Gunnison Point/ Visitor Center

Slide Draw Trail

Black Canyon of the Gunnison National Park

The Tomichi Route is very difficult. It includes a steep mile decent, with ½ mile of river access and two campsites.

Tomichi Point

Gunnison River

Slide Draw requires a steep, 1-mile descent. There is under a mile of river access and two campsites are present.

Floating the big rapids isn't a good option for anglers. Most hike in from the south rim, as the north side is more difficult to traverse. Permits are required for all access.

→ Flow

347

East Portal Road

175 Road

(Closed in winter) →

East Portal provides the first access below Crystal Reservoir. Fishing is good along the south bank, and with a float tube or pontoon boat you can ferry across to the north bank to access more water with fewer anglers.

East Portal

← *Gunnison Diversion Dam Mile 61.3*

GPS

GPS

Crystal Dam Bridge Mile 59.3

Curecanti National Recreation Area

Crystal Reservoir

N
W   E
S

N74 Road

50

Q74 Road

GPS

Crystal Dam Bridge: N 38° 30' 38.075", W 107° 37' 23.478"
Gunnison Diversion Dam: N 38° 31' 27.875", W 107° 38' 55.076"

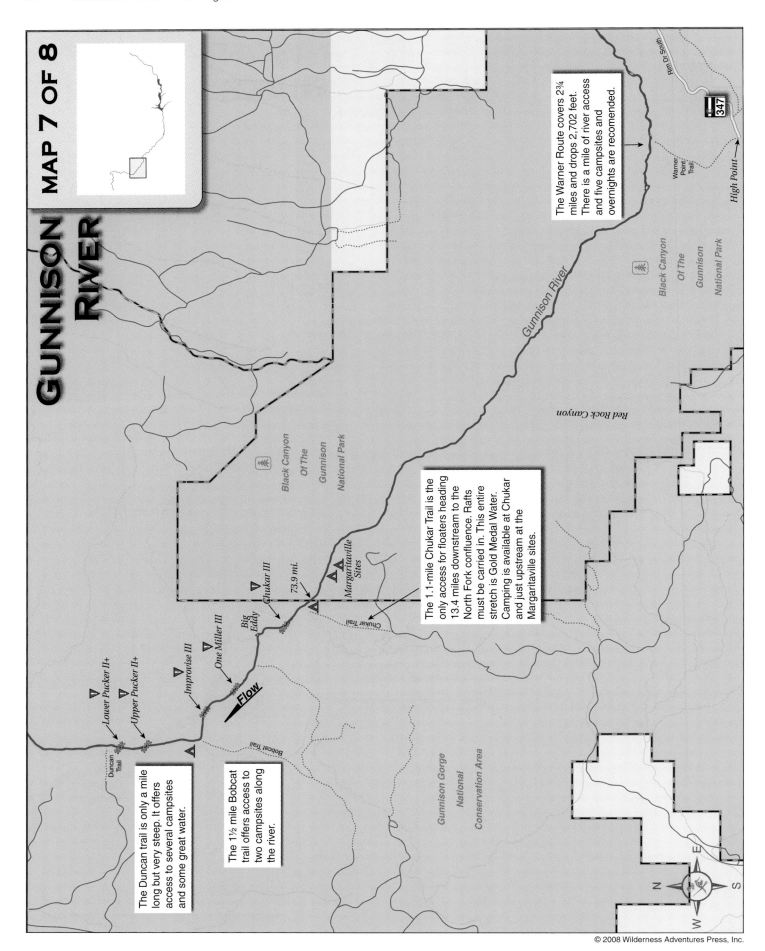

GUNNISON RIVER

MAP 7 OF 8

The Warner Route covers 2¾ miles and drops 2,702 feet. There is a mile of river access and five campsites and overnights are recomended.

Rim Dr South

347

Warner Point Trail

High Point

Gunnison River

Black Canyon Of The Gunnison National Park

Red Rock Canyon

Black Canyon Of The Gunnison National Park

The 1.1-mile Chukar Trail is the only access for floaters heading 13.4 miles downstream to the North Fork confluence. Rafts must be carried in. This entire stretch is Gold Medal Water. Camping is available at Chukar and just upstream at the Margaritaville sites.

Chukar III

73.9 mi.

Margaritaville Sites

Chukar Trail

Big Eddy

One Miller III

Improvise III

Upper Pucker II+

Lower Pucker II+

Duncan Trail

Flow

Bobcat Trail

Gunnison Gorge National Conservation Area

The Duncan trail is only a mile long but very steep. It offers access to several campsites and some great water.

The 1½ mile Bobcat trail offers access to two campsites along the river.

N E S W

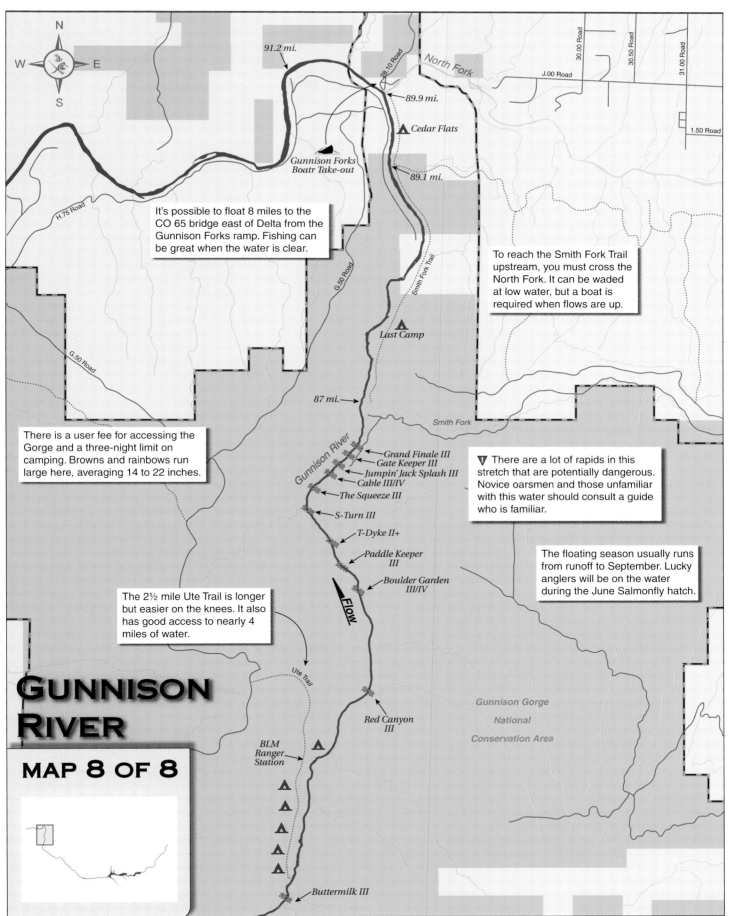

91.2 mi.

North Fork

28.10 Road

30.00 Road
30.50 Road
31.00 Road

J.00 Road

89.9 mi.

1.50 Road

Cedar Flats

Gunnison Forks
Boatr Take-out

89.1 mi.

H.75 Road

It's possible to float 8 miles to the CO 65 bridge east of Delta from the Gunnison Forks ramp. Fishing can be great when the water is clear.

To reach the Smith Fork Trail upstream, you must cross the North Fork. It can be waded at low water, but a boat is required when flows are up.

G.50 Road

Smith Fork Trail

Last Camp

G.50 Road

87 mi.

Smith Fork

There is a user fee for accessing the Gorge and a three-night limit on camping. Browns and rainbows run large here, averaging 14 to 22 inches.

Gunnison River

Grand Finale III
Gate Keeper III
Jumpin' Jack Splash III
Cable III/IV
The Squeeze III

There are a lot of rapids in this stretch that are potentially dangerous. Novice oarsmen and those unfamiliar with this water should consult a guide who is familiar.

S-Turn III

T-Dyke II+

Paddle Keeper III

The floating season usually runs from runoff to September. Lucky anglers will be on the water during the June Salmonfly hatch.

Boulder Garden III/IV

Flow

The 2½ mile Ute Trail is longer but easier on the knees. It also has good access to nearly 4 miles of water.

Ute Trail

Red Canyon III

Gunnison Gorge

National

Conservation Area

GUNNISON RIVER

MAP 8 OF 8

BLM Ranger Station

Buttermilk III

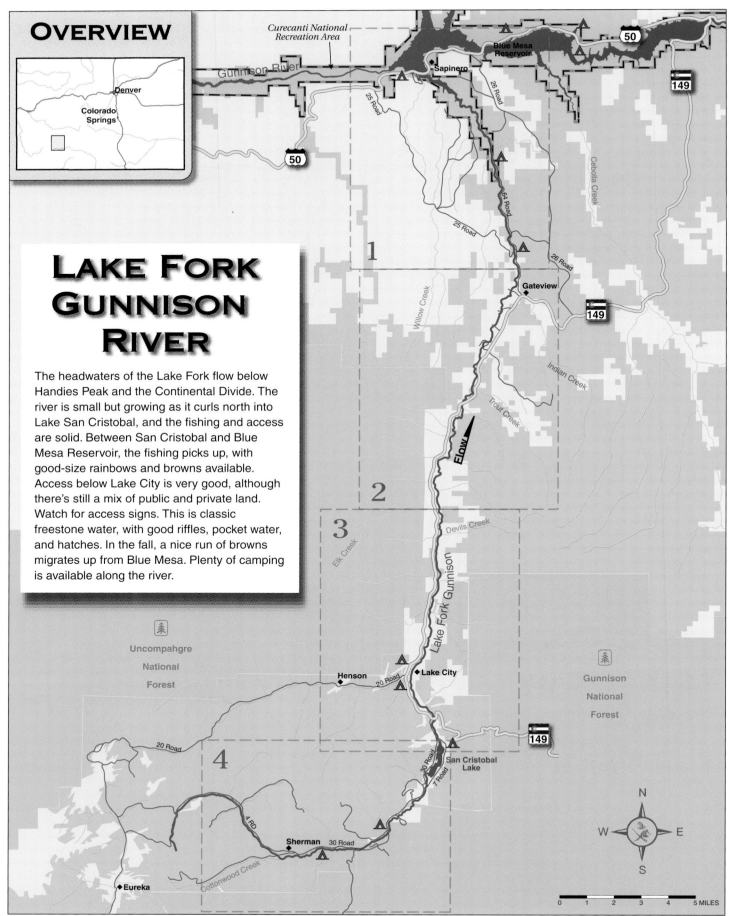

LAKE FORK GUNNISON RIVER

The headwaters of the Lake Fork flow below Handies Peak and the Continental Divide. The river is small but growing as it curls north into Lake San Cristobal, and the fishing and access are solid. Between San Cristobal and Blue Mesa Reservoir, the fishing picks up, with good-size rainbows and browns available. Access below Lake City is very good, although there's still a mix of public and private land. Watch for access signs. This is classic freestone water, with good riffles, pocket water, and hatches. In the fall, a nice run of browns migrates up from Blue Mesa. Plenty of camping is available along the river.

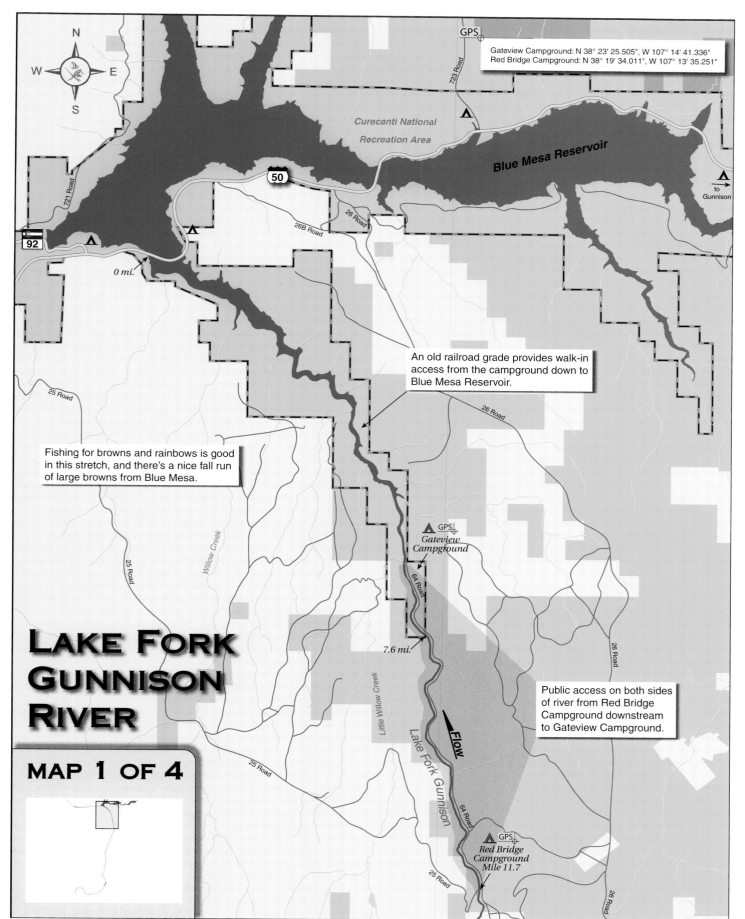

N
W · E
S

Curecanti National
Recreation Area

Blue Mesa Reservoir

723 Road

50

26B Road

26 Road

92

0 mi.

to
Gunnison

An old railroad grade provides walk-in
access from the campground down to
Blue Mesa Reservoir.

25 Road

26 Road

Fishing for browns and rainbows is good
in this stretch, and there's a nice fall run
of large browns from Blue Mesa.

Willow Creek

25 Road

GPS
Gateview
Campground

64 Road

**LAKE FORK
GUNNISON
RIVER**

Little Willow Creek

Lake Fork Gunnison

Flow

7.6 mi.

Public access on both sides
of river from Red Bridge
Campground downstream
to Gateview Campground.

MAP 1 OF 4

25 Road

26 Road

64 Road

GPS
Red Bridge
Campground
Mile 11.7

25 Road

26 Road

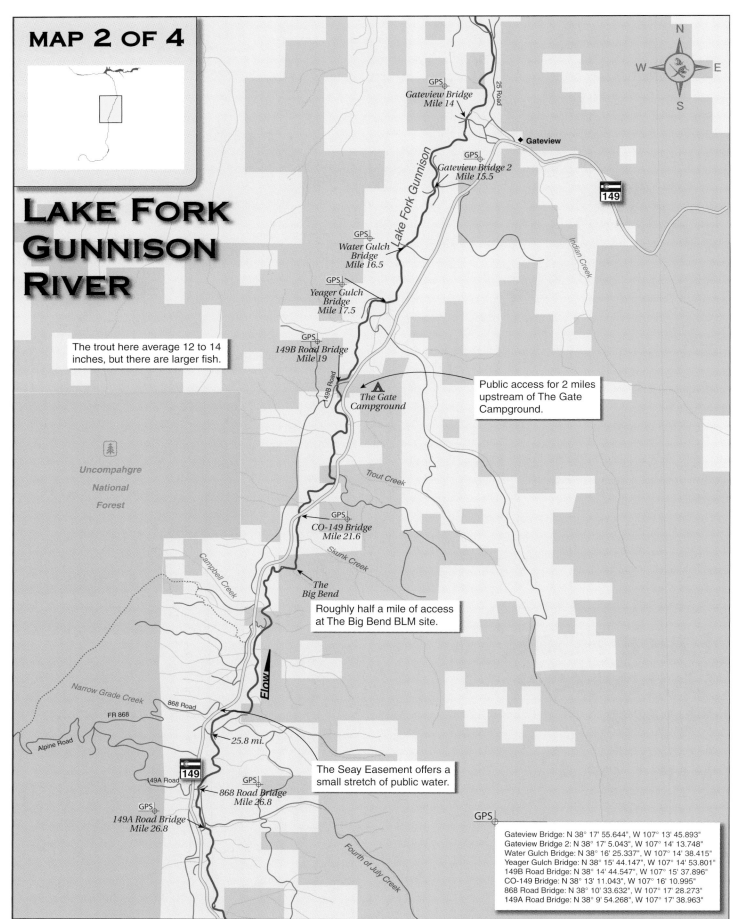

MAP 2 OF 4

LAKE FORK GUNNISON RIVER

The trout here average 12 to 14 inches, but there are larger fish.

Public access for 2 miles upstream of The Gate Campground.

Roughly half a mile of access at The Big Bend BLM site.

The Seay Easement offers a small stretch of public water.

Gateview Bridge
Mile 14

Gateview

Gateview Bridge 2
Mile 15.5

Water Gulch
Bridge
Mile 16.5

Yeager Gulch
Bridge
Mile 17.5

149B Road Bridge
Mile 19

The Gate
Campground

Uncompahgre National Forest

Trout Creek

CO-149 Bridge
Mile 21.6

Skunk Creek

The Big Bend

Campbell Creek

Narrow Grade Creek

868 Road

FR 868

Alpine Road

25.8 mi.

149A Road

868 Road Bridge
Mile 26.8

149A Road Bridge
Mile 26.8

Fourth of July Creek

Indian Creek

Lake Fork Gunnison

Flow

Gateview Bridge: N 38° 17' 55.644", W 107° 13' 45.893"
Gateview Bridge 2: N 38° 17' 5.043", W 107° 14' 13.748"
Water Gulch Bridge: N 38° 16' 25.337", W 107° 14' 38.415"
Yeager Gulch Bridge: N 38° 15' 44.147", W 107° 14' 53.801"
149B Road Bridge: N 38° 14' 44.547", W 107° 15' 37.896"
CO-149 Bridge: N 38° 13' 11.043", W 107° 16' 10.995"
868 Road Bridge: N 38° 10' 33.632", W 107° 17' 28.273"
149A Road Bridge: N 38° 9' 54.268", W 107° 17' 38.963"

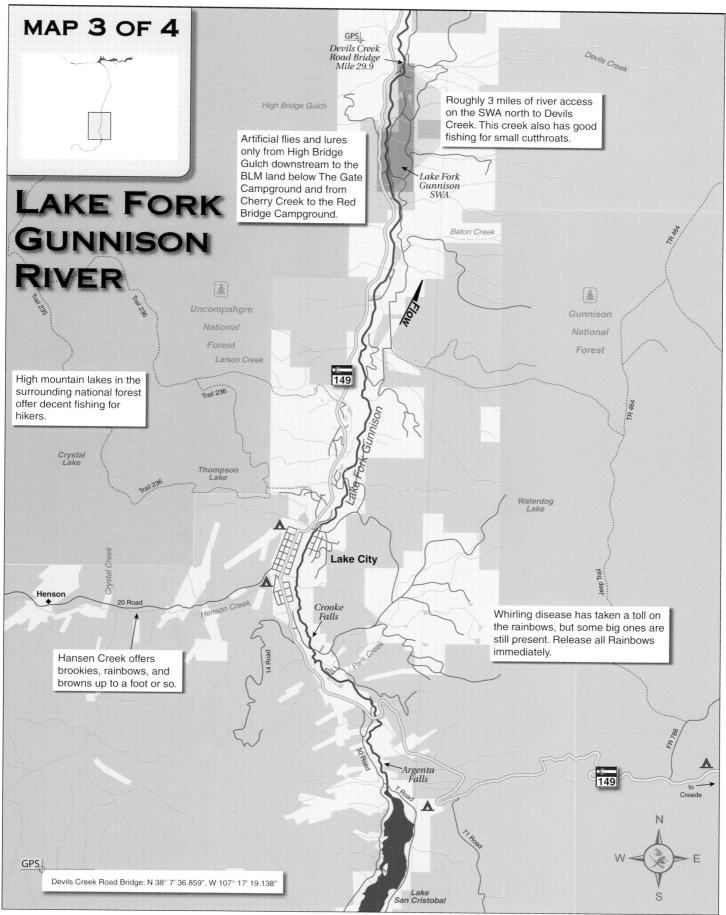

MAP 3 OF 4

LAKE FORK GUNNISON RIVER

Devils Creek Road Bridge Mile 29.9

GPS

Devils Creek

High Bridge Gulch

Roughly 3 miles of river access on the SWA north to Devils Creek. This creek also has good fishing for small cutthroats.

Artificial flies and lures only from High Bridge Gulch downstream to the BLM land below The Gate Campground and from Cherry Creek to the Red Bridge Campground.

Lake Fork Gunnison SWA

Baton Creek

TR 464

FLOW

Uncompahgre National Forest

Larson Creek

Gunnison National Forest

Trail 235

Trail 236

Trail 236

149

TR 464

High mountain lakes in the surrounding national forest offer decent fishing for hikers.

Crystal Lake

Thompson Lake

Trail 236

Lake Fork Gunnison

Waterdog Lake

Jeep Trail

Crystal Creek

Lake City

Henson

20 Road

Henson Creek

Crooke Falls

Whirling disease has taken a toll on the rainbows, but some big ones are still present. Release all Rainbows immediately.

Hansen Creek offers brookies, rainbows, and browns up to a foot or so.

14 Road

Park Creek

30 Road

Argenta Falls

T Road

71 Road

FR 788

149

to Creede

N
W   E
S

GPS

Devils Creek Road Bridge: N 38° 7' 36.859", W 107° 17' 19.138"

Lake San Cristobal

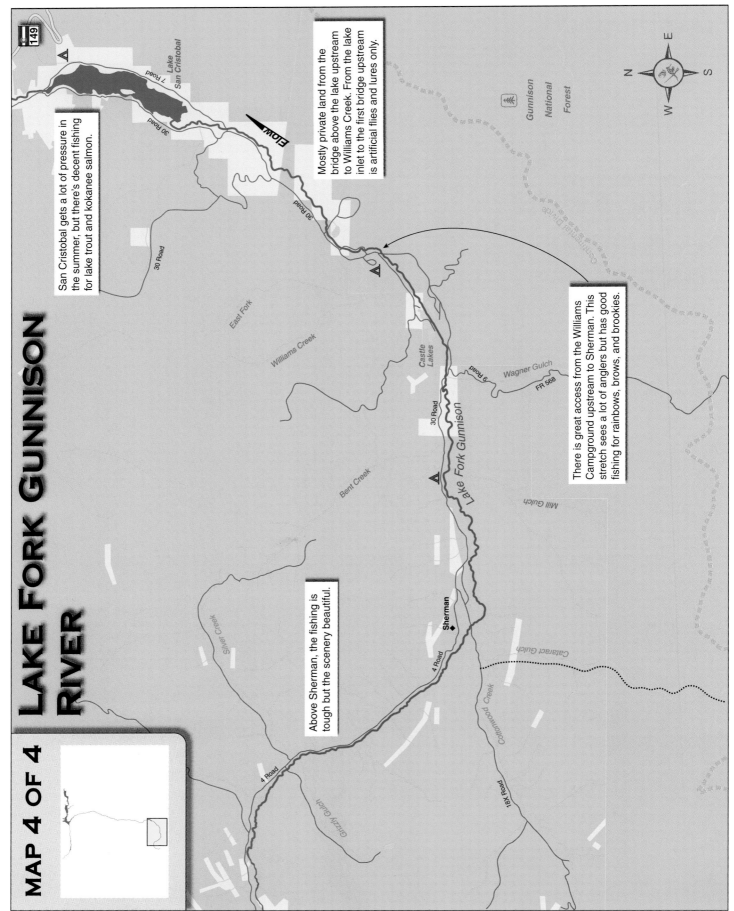

MAP 4 OF 4

LAKE FORK GUNNISON RIVER

San Cristobal gets a lot of pressure in the summer, but there's decent fishing for lake trout and kokanee salmon.

Mostly private land from the bridge above the lake upstream to Williams Creek. From the lake inlet to the first bridge upstream is artificial flies and lures only.

There is great access from the Williams Campground upstream to Sherman. This stretch sees a lot of anglers but has good fishing for rainbows, brows, and brookies.

Above Sherman, the fishing is tough but the scenery beautiful.

Lake San Cristobal

7 Road

30 Road

Flow

East Fork

Williams Creek

Castle Lakes

30 Road

9 Road

Wagner Gulch

FR 568

Bent Creek

Lake Fork Gunnison

Mill Gulch

Gunnison National Forest

Continental Divide

Silver Creek

Sherman

4 Road

Cataract Gulch

Cottonwood Creek

18X Road

Grizzly Gulch

4 Road

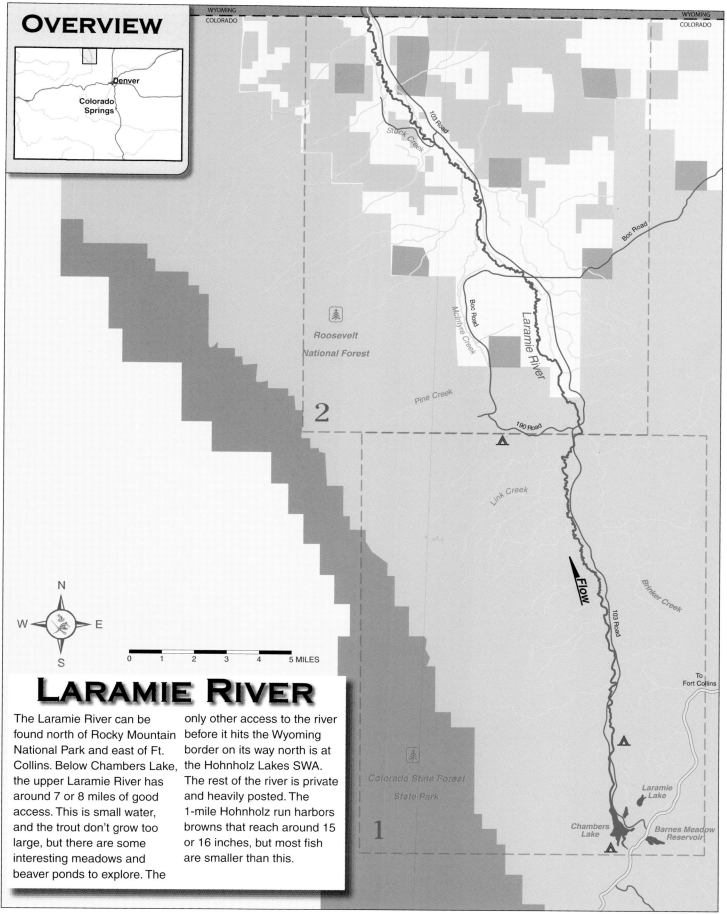

OVERVIEW

Denver

Colorado
Springs

WYOMING
COLORADO

WYOMING
COLORADO

Stuck Creek

103 Road

Boc Road

Boc Road

McIntyre Creek

Laramie River

Roosevelt
National Forest

Pine Creek

2

190 Road

Link Creek

Flow

Brinker Creek

103 Road

To
Fort Collins

Colorado State Forest
State Park

1

Laramie
Lake

Chambers
Lake

Barnes Meadow
Reservoir

N
W   E
S

0   1   2   3   4   5 MILES

LARAMIE RIVER

The Laramie River can be found north of Rocky Mountain National Park and east of Ft. Collins. Below Chambers Lake, the upper Laramie River has around 7 or 8 miles of good access. This is small water, and the trout don't grow too large, but there are some interesting meadows and beaver ponds to explore. The only other access to the river before it hits the Wyoming border on its way north is at the Hohnholz Lakes SWA. The rest of the river is private and heavily posted. The 1-mile Hohnholz run harbors browns that reach around 15 or 16 inches, but most fish are smaller than this.

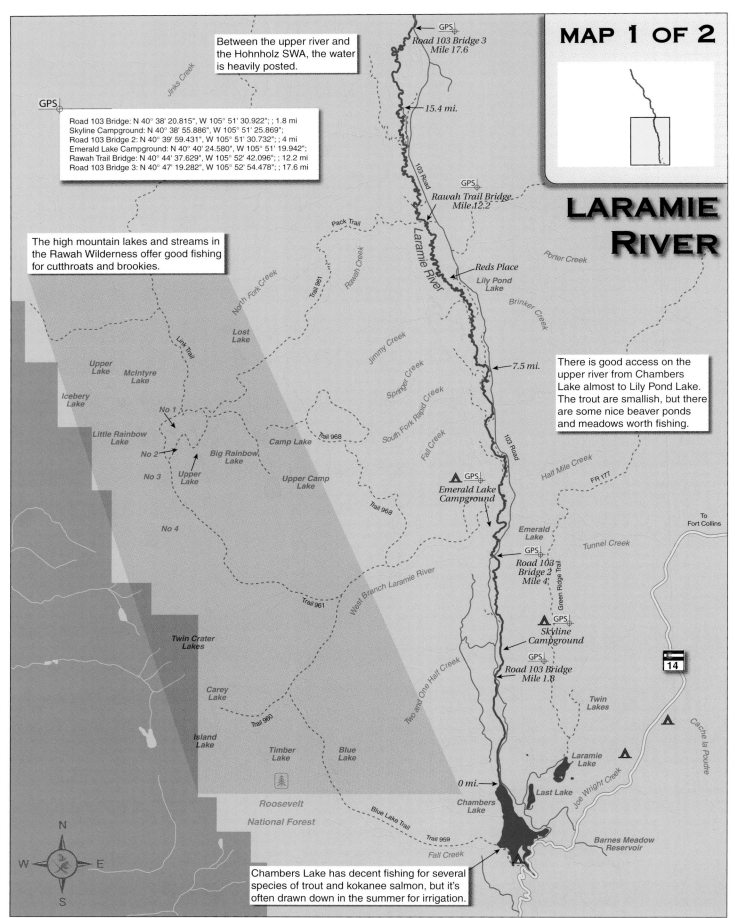

Between the upper river and the Hohnholz SWA, the water is heavily posted.

Road 103 Bridge 3
Mile 17.6

15.4 mi.

GPS

Road 103 Bridge: N 40° 38' 20.815", W 105° 51' 30.922"; ; 1.8 mi
Skyline Campground: N 40° 38' 55.886", W 105° 51' 25.869";
Road 103 Bridge 2: N 40° 39' 59.431", W 105° 51' 30.732"; ; 4 mi
Emerald Lake Campground: N 40° 40' 24.580", W 105° 51' 19.942";
Rawah Trail Bridge: N 40° 44' 37.629", W 105° 52' 42.096"; ; 12.2 mi
Road 103 Bridge 3: N 40° 47' 19.282", W 105° 52' 54.478"; ; 17.6 mi

Rawah Trail Bridge
Mile 12.2

Reds Place
Lily Pond Lake

Porter Creek

Brinker Creek

The high mountain lakes and streams in the Rawah Wilderness offer good fishing for cutthroats and brookies.

Jinks Creek

Pack Trail

North Fork Creek

Rawah Creek

Trail 961

Lost Lake

Jimmy Creek

Springer Creek

7.5 mi.

There is good access on the upper river from Chambers Lake almost to Lily Pond Lake. The trout are smallish, but there are some nice beaver ponds and meadows worth fishing.

Upper Lake

McIntyre Lake

Link Trail

Icebery Lake

No 1

South Fork Rapid Creek

Fall Creek

Little Rainbow Lake

No 2

Big Rainbow Lake

Camp Lake

Trail 968

No 3

Upper Lake

Upper Camp Lake

Half Mile Creek

FR 177

No 4

Trail 968

Emerald Lake Campground

To Fort Collins

Tunnel Creek

Emerald Lake

Road 103 Bridge 2
Mile 4

West Branch Laramie River

Trail 961

Green Ridge Trail

Skyline Campground

Twin Crater Lakes

Road 103 Bridge
Mile 1.8

14

Carey Lake

Trail 960

Twin Lakes

Island Lake

Timber Lake

Blue Lake

Two and One Half Creek

Laramie Lake

Cache la Poudre

Roosevelt

National Forest

0 mi.

Last Lake

Joe Wright Creek

Barnes Meadow Reservoir

N
W E
S

Blue Lake Trail

Chambers Lake

Trail 959

Fall Creek

Chambers Lake has decent fishing for several species of trout and kokanee salmon, but it's often drawn down in the summer for irrigation.

MAP 1 OF 2

LARAMIE RIVER

Laramie River

103 Road

© 2008 Wilderness Adventures Press, Inc.

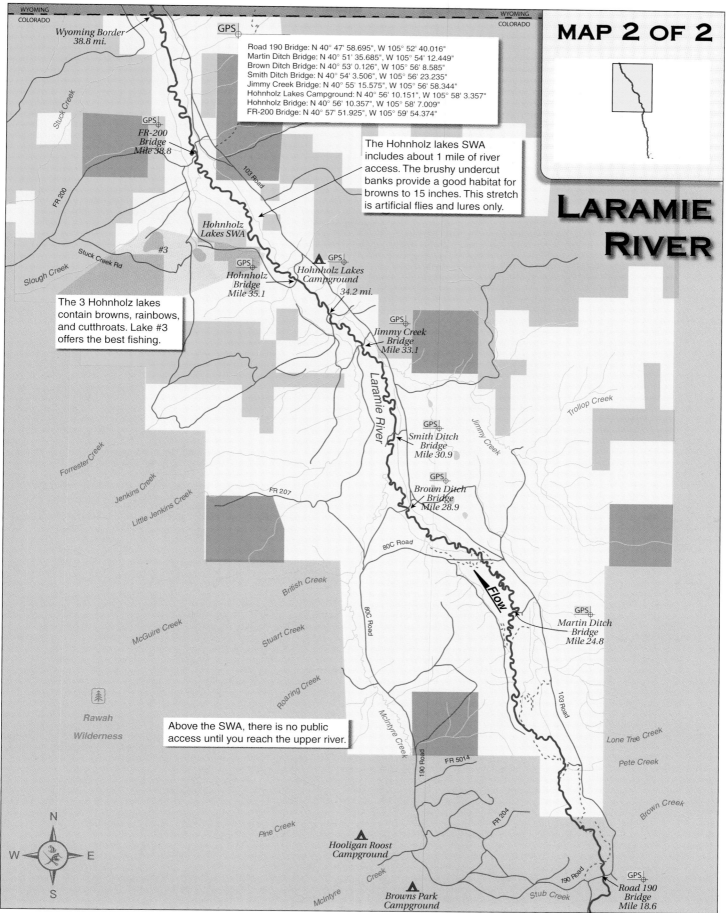

MAP 2 OF 2

LARAMIE RIVER

Road 190 Bridge: N 40° 47' 58.695", W 105° 52' 40.016"
Martin Ditch Bridge: N 40° 51' 35.685", W 105° 54' 12.449"
Brown Ditch Bridge: N 40° 53' 0.126", W 105° 56' 8.585"
Smith Ditch Bridge: N 40° 54' 3.506", W 105° 56' 23.235"
Jimmy Creek Bridge: N 40° 55' 15.575", W 105° 56' 58.344"
Hohnholz Lakes Campground: N 40° 56' 10.151", W 105° 58' 3.357"
Hohnholz Bridge: N 40° 56' 10.357", W 105° 58' 7.009"
FR-200 Bridge: N 40° 57' 51.925", W 105° 59' 54.374"

The Hohnholz lakes SWA includes about 1 mile of river access. The brushy undercut banks provide a good habitat for browns to 15 inches. This stretch is artificial flies and lures only.

The 3 Hohnholz lakes contain browns, rainbows, and cutthroats. Lake #3 offers the best fishing.

Above the SWA, there is no public access until you reach the upper river.

Wyoming Border 38.8 mi.
FR-200 Bridge Mile 38.8
Hohnholz Lakes SWA
Hohnholz Bridge Mile 35.1
Hohnholz Lakes Campground
34.2 mi.
Jimmy Creek Bridge Mile 33.1
Smith Ditch Bridge Mile 30.9
Brown Ditch Bridge Mile 28.9
Martin Ditch Bridge Mile 24.8
Road 190 Bridge Mile 18.6

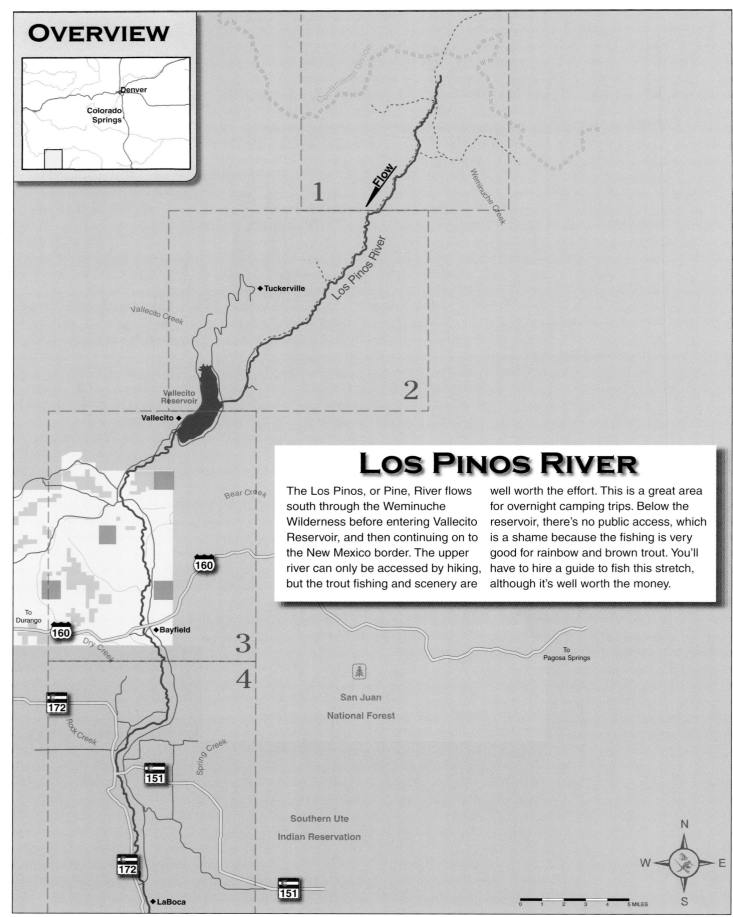

OVERVIEW

Denver

Colorado Springs

Flow

1

Weminuche Creek

Los Pinos River

Tuckerville

Vallecito Creek

2

Vallecito Reservoir

Vallecito

Bear Creek

LOS PINOS RIVER

The Los Pinos, or Pine, River flows south through the Weminuche Wilderness before entering Vallecito Reservoir, and then continuing on to the New Mexico border. The upper river can only be accessed by hiking, but the trout fishing and scenery are well worth the effort. This is a great area for overnight camping trips. Below the reservoir, there's no public access, which is a shame because the fishing is very good for rainbow and brown trout. You'll have to hire a guide to fish this stretch, although it's well worth the money.

160

To Pagosa Springs

To Durango

160

Bayfield

Dry Creek

3

4

San Juan

National Forest

172

Rock Creek

Spring Creek

151

Southern Ute

Indian Reservation

N

W   E

S

172

151

LaBoca

0 1 2 3 4 5 MILES

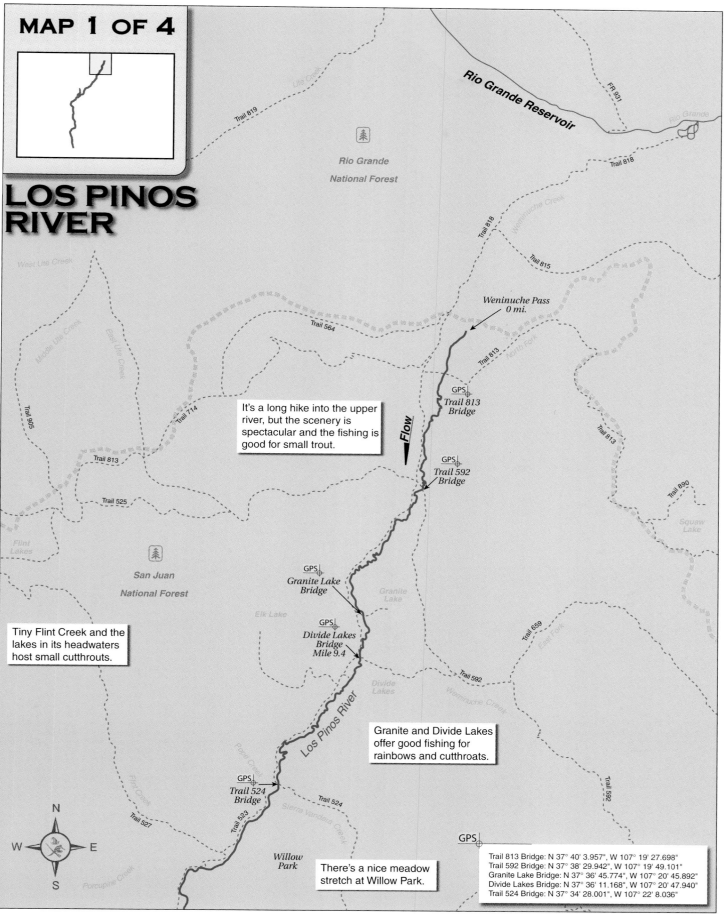

MAP 1 OF 4

LOS PINOS RIVER

Rio Grande National Forest

San Juan National Forest

Rio Grande Reservoir

FR 931

Rio Grande

Trail 819

Trail 818

Trail 815

Ute Creek

Weninuche Creek

West Ute Creek

Middle Ute Creek

East Ute Creek

Trail 564

Weninuche Pass 0 mi.

Trail 813

North Fork

GPS Trail 813 Bridge

Trail 813

Trail 890

Squaw Lake

Trail 714

Flow

GPS Trail 592 Bridge

It's a long hike into the upper river, but the scenery is spectacular and the fishing is good for small trout.

Trail 905

Trail 813

Trail 525

Flint Lakes

Elk Lake

GPS Granite Lake Bridge

Granite Lake

Trail 659

East Fork

GPS Divide Lakes Bridge Mile 9.4

Divide Lakes

Tiny Flint Creek and the lakes in its headwaters host small cutthrouts.

Trail 592

Weninuche Creek

Granite and Divide Lakes offer good fishing for rainbows and cutthroats.

Los Pinos River

Pope Creek

GPS Trail 524 Bridge

Trail 524

Flint Creek

Trail 523

Trail 527

Sierra Vandera Creek

Trail 592

N W E S

Willow Park

Porcupine Creek

There's a nice meadow stretch at Willow Park.

GPS

Trail 813 Bridge: N 37° 40' 3.957", W 107° 19' 27.698"
Trail 592 Bridge: N 37° 38' 29.942", W 107° 19' 49.101"
Granite Lake Bridge: N 37° 36' 45.774", W 107° 20' 45.892"
Divide Lakes Bridge: N 37° 36' 11.168", W 107° 20' 47.940"
Trail 524 Bridge: N 37° 34' 28.001", W 107° 22' 8.036"

© 2008 Wilderness Adventures Press, Inc.

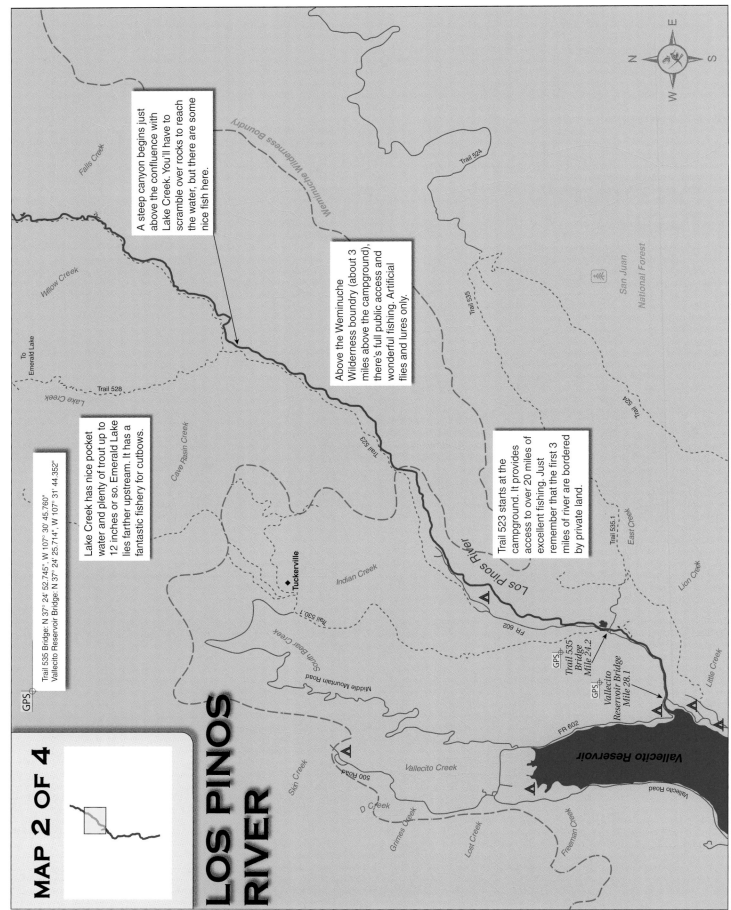

A steep canyon begins just above the confluence with Lake Creek. You'll have to scramble over rocks to reach the water, but there are some nice fish here.

Above the Weminuche Wilderness boundry (about 3 miles above the campground), there's full public access and wonderful fishing. Artificial flies and lures only.

Lake Creek has nice pocket water and plenty of trout up to 12 inches or so. Emerald Lake lies farther upstream. It has a fantastic fishery for cutbows.

Trail 523 starts at the campground. It provides access to over 20 miles of excellent fishing. Just remember that the first 3 miles of river are bordered by private land.

Trail 535 Bridge: N 37° 24' 52.745", W 107° 30' 45.760"
Vallecito Reservoir Bridge: N 37° 24' 25.714", W 107° 31' 44.352"

GPS

Weminuche Wilderness Boundry

Trail 524

San Juan
National Forest

Falls Creek

Willow Creek

To Emerald Lake

Trail 528

Lake Creek

Trail 535

Trail 524

Cave Rasin Creek

Trail 523

East Creek

Trail 535.1

Lion Creek

Tuckerville

Indian Creek

Los Pinos River

FR 602

GPS
Trail 535 Bridge Mile 24.2

GPS
Vallecito Reservoir Bridge Mile 28.1

Little Creek

Trail 530.1

South Bear Creek

Middle Mountain Road

500 Road

Skin Creek

FR 602

Vallecito Creek

Vallecito Reservoir

D Creek

Grimes Creek

Lost Creek

Freeman Creek

Vallecito Road

MAP 2 OF 4

LOS PINOS RIVER

© 2008 Wilderness Adventures Press, Inc.

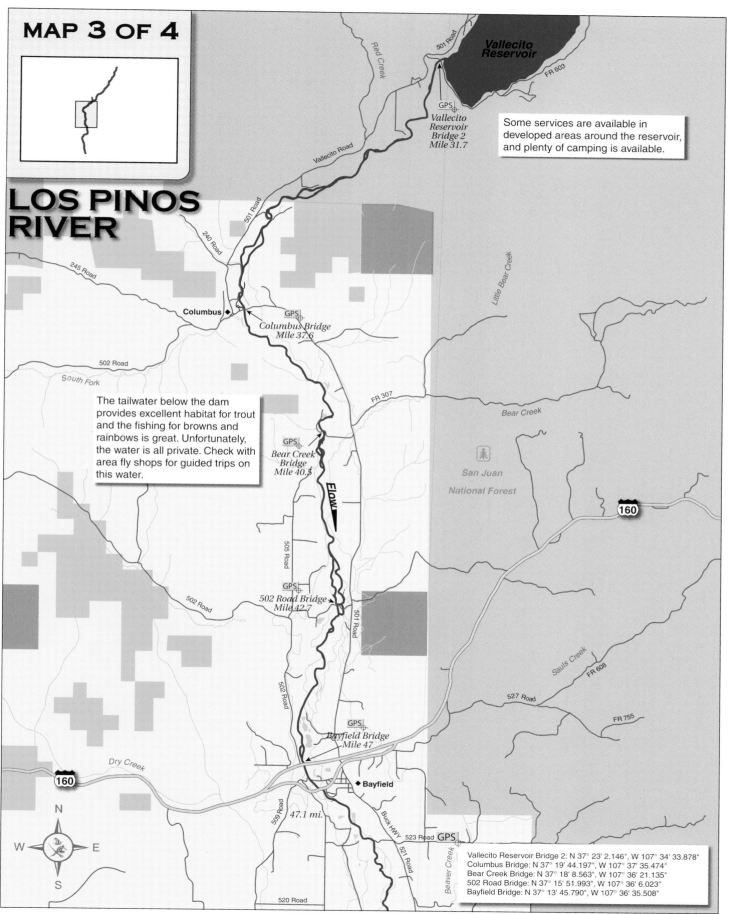

MAP 3 OF 4

LOS PINOS RIVER

Vallecito Reservoir

Red Creek

501 Road

FR 603

Vallecito Road

GPS ⊕
*Vallecito
Reservoir
Bridge 2
Mile 31.7*

Some services are available in
developed areas around the reservoir,
and plenty of camping is available.

240 Road

501 Road

245 Road

Little Bear Creek

Columbus ◆

GPS ⊕
*Columbus Bridge
Mile 37.6*

502 Road

South Fork

FR 307

Bear Creek

The tailwater below the dam
provides excellent habitat for trout
and the fishing for browns and
rainbows is great. Unfortunately,
the water is all private. Check with
area fly shops for guided trips on
this water.

GPS ⊕
*Bear Creek
Bridge
Mile 40.5*

🌲
*San Juan
National Forest*

160

Flow ▼

505 Road

502 Road

GPS ⊕
*502 Road Bridge
Mile 42.7*

501 Road

Sauls Creek

FR 608

527 Road

FR 755

502 Road

GPS ⊕
*Bayfield Bridge
Mile 47*

Dry Creek

160

◆ *Bayfield*

509 Road

47.1 mi.

Buck HWY

523 Road GPS ⊕

N
W ✦ E
S

521 Road

Beaver Creek

520 Road

Vallecito Reservoir Bridge 2: N 37° 23' 2.146", W 107° 34' 33.878"
Columbus Bridge: N 37° 19' 44.197", W 107° 37' 35.474"
Bear Creek Bridge: N 37° 18' 8.563", W 107° 36' 21.135"
502 Road Bridge: N 37° 15' 51.993", W 107° 36' 6.023"
Bayfield Bridge: N 37° 13' 45.790", W 107° 36' 35.508"

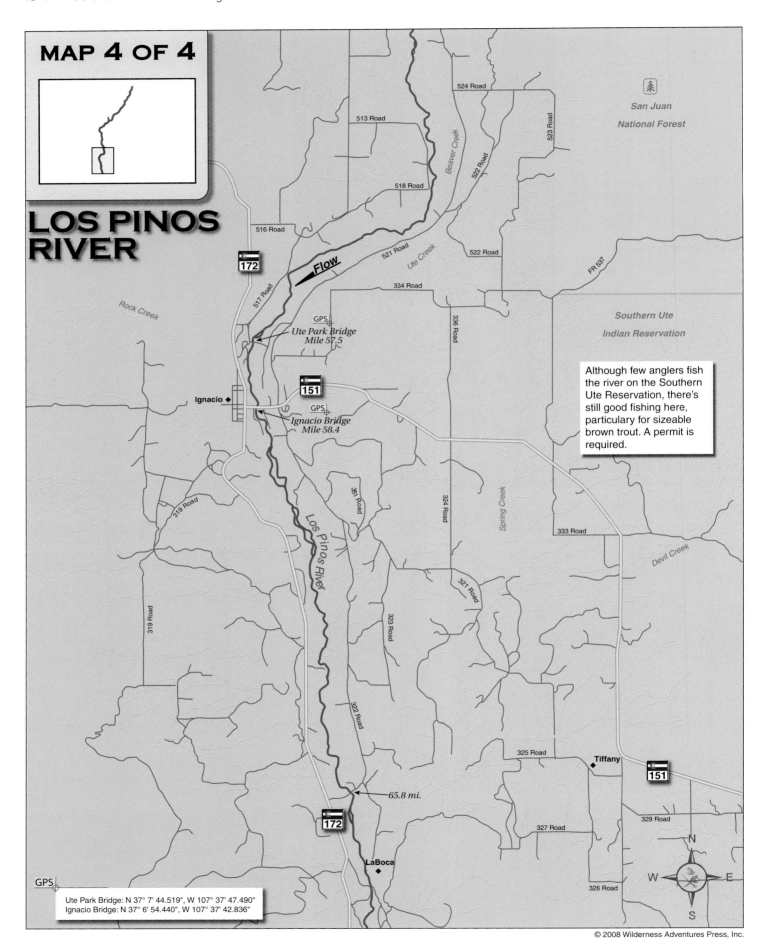

MAP 4 OF 4

LOS PINOS RIVER

Flow

524 Road

513 Road

518 Road

516 Road

San Juan
National Forest

523 Road

522 Road

Beaver Creek

521 Road

Ute Creek

522 Road

FR 537

334 Road

172

517 Road

Rock Creek

GPS
Ute Park Bridge
Mile 57.5

Southern Ute

Indian Reservation

336 Road

151

Ignacio ♦

GPS
Ignacio Bridge
Mile 58.4

Although few anglers fish
the river on the Southern
Ute Reservation, there's
still good fishing here,
particulary for sizeable
brown trout. A permit is
required.

319 Road

351 Road

324 Road

Spring Creek

333 Road

Devil Creek

Los Pinos River

321 Road

319 Road

323 Road

322 Road

325 Road

Tiffany ♦

151

65.8 mi.

172

327 Road

329 Road

N

LaBoca ♦

W   E

S

GPS

326 Road

Ute Park Bridge: N 37° 7' 44.519", W 107° 37' 47.490"
Ignacio Bridge: N 37° 6' 54.440", W 107° 37' 42.836"

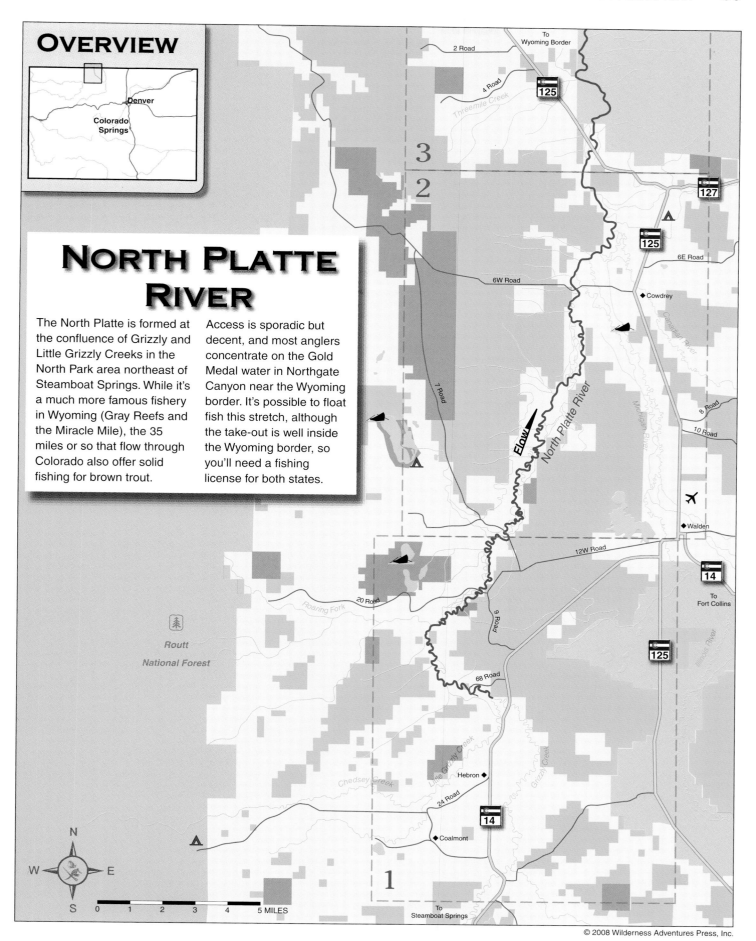

OVERVIEW

NORTH PLATTE RIVER

The North Platte is formed at the confluence of Grizzly and Little Grizzly Creeks in the North Park area northeast of Steamboat Springs. While it's a much more famous fishery in Wyoming (Gray Reefs and the Miracle Mile), the 35 miles or so that flow through Colorado also offer solid fishing for brown trout.

Access is sporadic but decent, and most anglers concentrate on the Gold Medal water in Northgate Canyon near the Wyoming border. It's possible to float fish this stretch, although the take-out is well inside the Wyoming border, so you'll need a fishing license for both states.

Denver
Colorado Springs

To Wyoming Border
2 Road
4 Road
125
Threemile Creek
3
2
127
6E Road
125
6W Road
Cowdrey
7 Road
Canadian River
Flow
North Platte River
Michigan River
8 Road
10 Road
Walden
12W Road
14
To Fort Collins
20 Road
Roaring Fork
9 Road
Illinois River
Routt National Forest
68 Road
125
Little Grizzly Creek
Grizzly Creek
Chedsey Creek
Hebron
24 Road
14
Coalmont
N
W   E
S
0 1 2 3 4 5 MILES
To Steamboat Springs

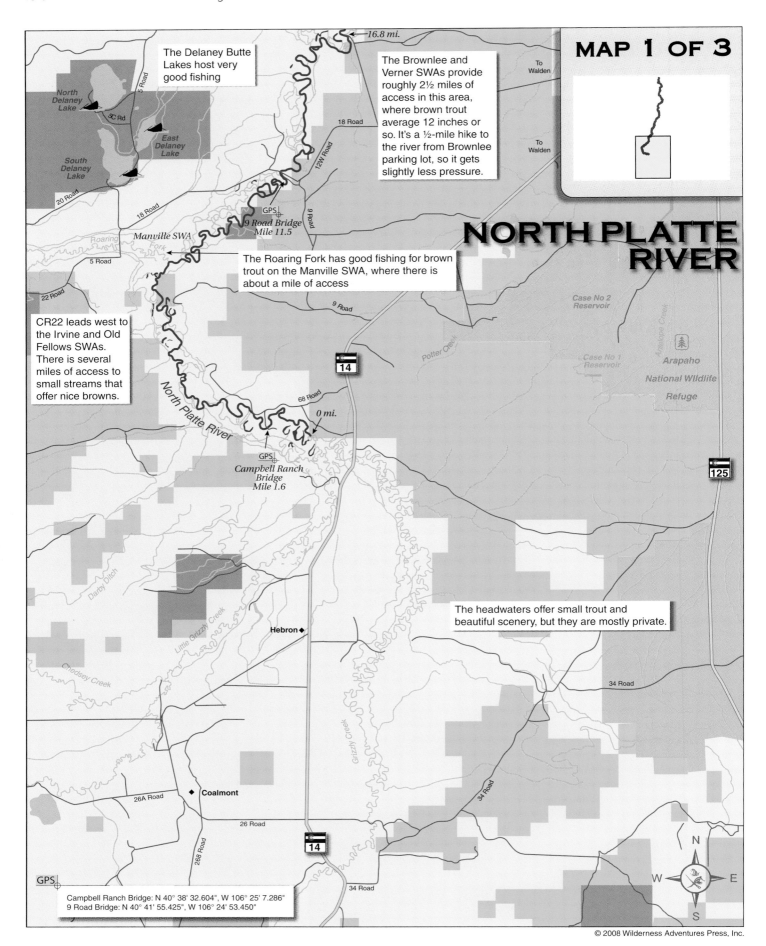

The Delaney Butte Lakes host very good fishing

The Brownlee and Verner SWAs provide roughly 2½ miles of access in this area, where brown trout average 12 inches or so. It's a ½-mile hike to the river from Brownlee parking lot, so it gets slightly less pressure.

MAP 1 OF 3

North Delaney Lake

5C Rd

East Delaney Lake

South Delaney Lake

20 Road

5 Road

18 Road

18 Road

12W Road

9 Road

To Walden

To Walden

GPS
9 Road Bridge
Mile 11.5

Manville SWA

Roaring Fork

5 Road

22 Road

The Roaring Fork has good fishing for brown trout on the Manville SWA, where there is about a mile of access

NORTH PLATTE RIVER

9 Road

Case No 2 Reservoir

Potter Creek

Case No 1 Reservoir

Antelope Creek

Arapaho National Wildlife Refuge

CR22 leads west to the Irvine and Old Fellows SWAs. There is several miles of access to small streams that offer nice browns.

14

68 Road

0 mi.

North Platte River

GPS
Campbell Ranch Bridge
Mile 1.6

125

Darby Ditch

Little Grizzly Creek

Chedsey Creek

Hebron

The headwaters offer small trout and beautiful scenery, but they are mostly private.

34 Road

Grizzly Creek

26A Road

Coalmont

26 Road

268 Road

34 Road

14

34 Road

N
W   E
S

GPS

Campbell Ranch Bridge: N 40° 38' 32.604", W 106° 25' 7.286"
9 Road Bridge: N 40° 41' 55.425", W 106° 24' 53.450"

16.8 mi.

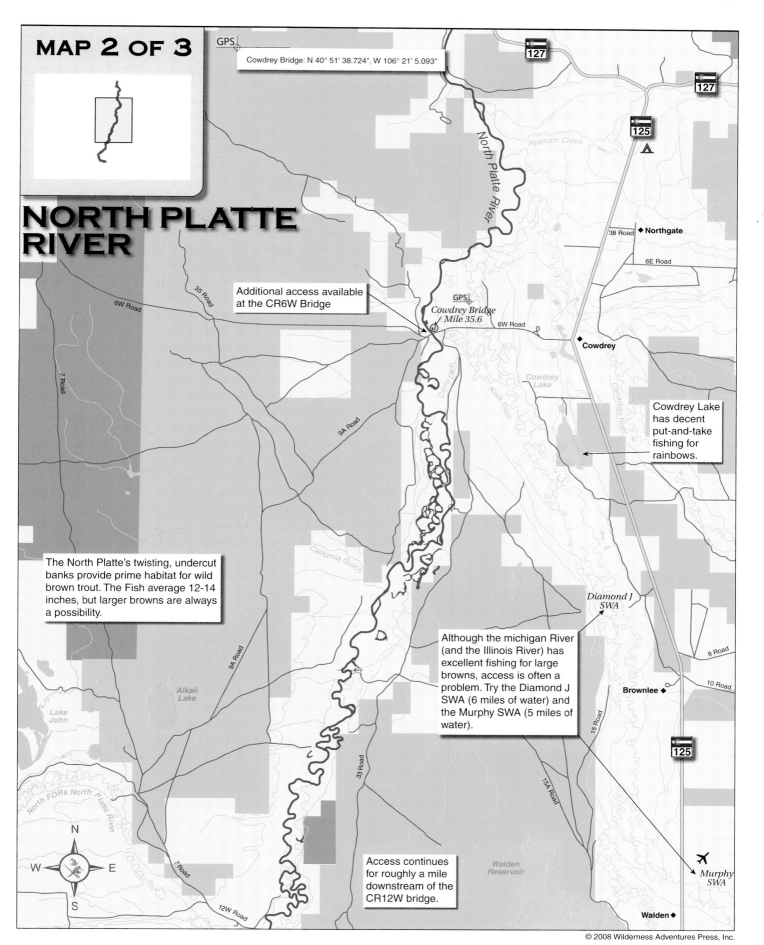

MAP 2 OF 3

NORTH PLATTE RIVER

Cowdrey Bridge: N 40° 51' 38.724", W 106° 21' 5.093"

Additional access available at the CR6W Bridge

Cowdrey Bridge / Mile 35.6

Cowdrey Lake has decent put-and-take fishing for rainbows.

The North Platte's twisting, undercut banks provide prime habitat for wild brown trout. The Fish average 12-14 inches, but larger browns are always a possibility.

Although the michigan River (and the Illinois River) has excellent fishing for large browns, access is often a problem. Try the Diamond J SWA (6 miles of water) and the Murphy SWA (5 miles of water).

Access continues for roughly a mile downstream of the CR12W bridge.

Diamond J SWA

Murphy SWA

North Platte River

Pinkham Creek

Northgate

Cowdrey

Cowdrey Lake

Davis Ditch

Kiwa Ditch

Canadian River

Brownlee

California Gulch

Alkali Lake

Lake John

North FORk North Platte River

Walden Reservoir

Walden

38 Road
6E Road
6W Road
6W Road
35 Road
7 Road
9A Road
9A Road
8 Road
10 Road
15 Road
15A Road
.33 Road
7 Road
12W Road

127
127
125
125

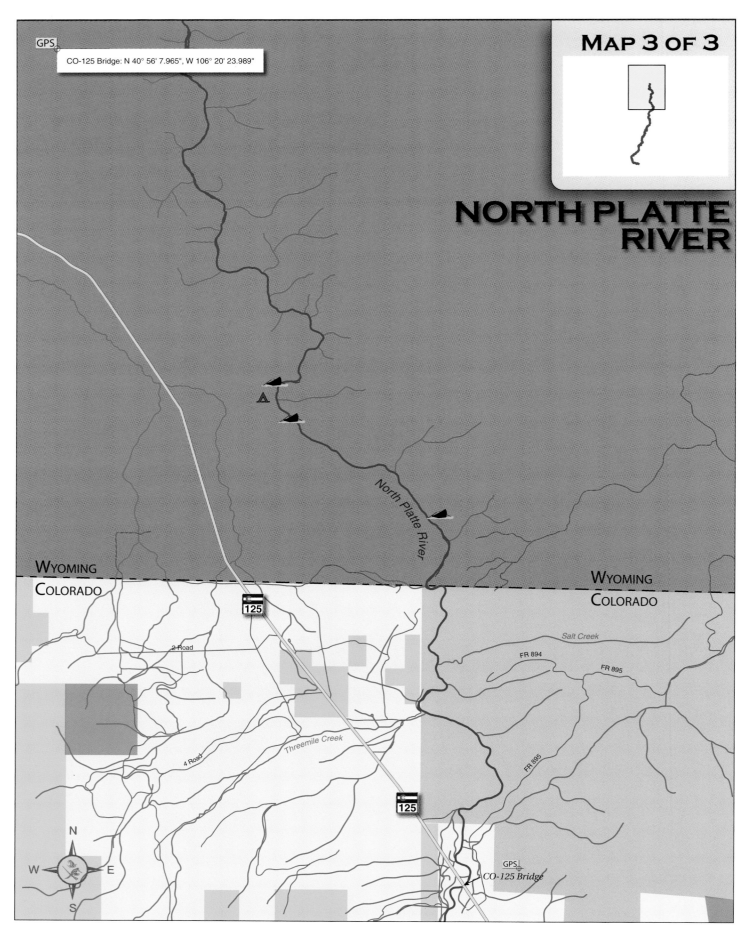

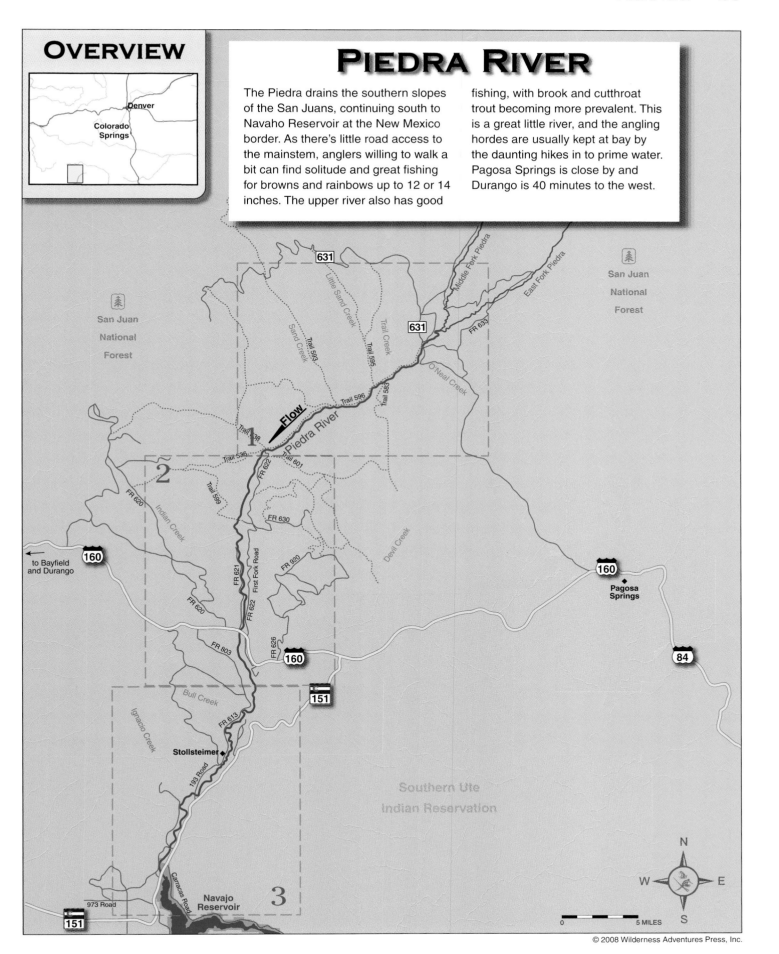

OVERVIEW

Denver

Colorado
Springs

PIEDRA RIVER

The Piedra drains the southern slopes of the San Juans, continuing south to Navaho Reservoir at the New Mexico border. As there's little road access to the mainstem, anglers willing to walk a bit can find solitude and great fishing for browns and rainbows up to 12 or 14 inches. The upper river also has good fishing, with brook and cutthroat trout becoming more prevalent. This is a great little river, and the angling hordes are usually kept at bay by the daunting hikes in to prime water. Pagosa Springs is close by and Durango is 40 minutes to the west.

631

631

Middle Fork Piedra

East Fork Piedra

San Juan

National

Forest

FR 633

O'Neal Creek

San Juan

National

Forest

Little Sand Creek

Trail Creek

Sand Creek

Trail 593

Trail 595

Trail 583

Trail 596

Flow

Trail 138

Trail 536

Piedra River

Trail 622

Trail 601

FR 622

Trail 599

FR 620

Indian Creek

FR 630

Devil Creek

160

to Bayfield
and Durango

FR 620

FR 621

First Fork Road

FR 622

FR 920

160

Pagosa
Springs

84

FR 803

FR 626

160

151

Bull Creek

Ignacio Creek

FR 613

Stollsteimer

193 Road

Southern Ute

Indian Reservation

Caracas Road

Navajo
Reservoir

973 Road

151

N

W   E

S

0   5 MILES

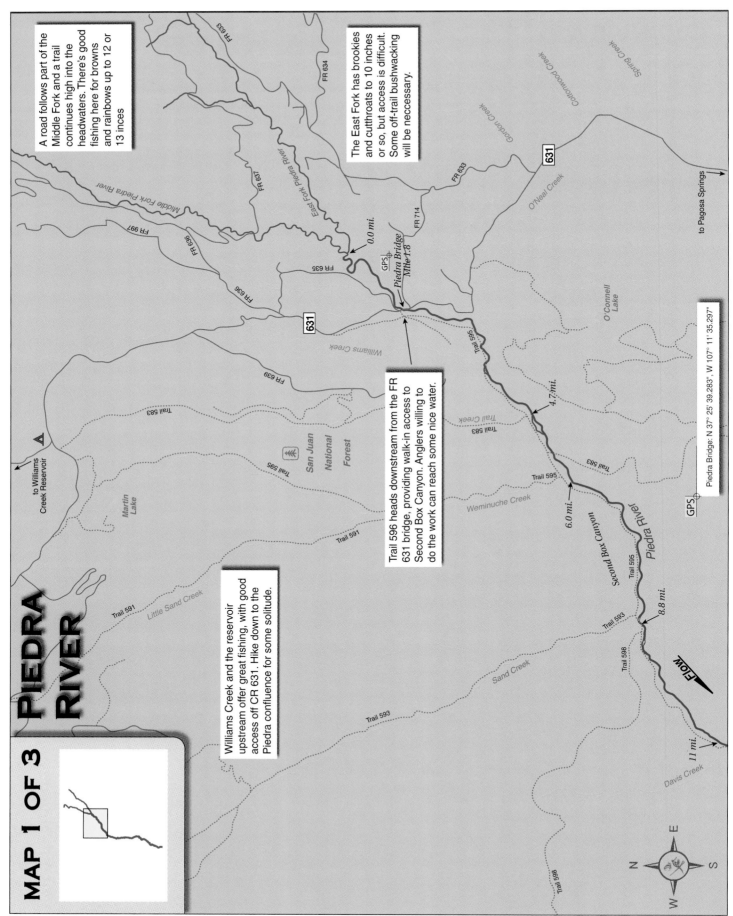

MAP 1 OF 3

PIEDRA RIVER

A road follows part of the Middle Fork and a trail continues high into the headwaters. There's good fishing here for browns and rainbows up to 12 or 13 inces

The East Fork has brookies and cutthroats to 10 inches or so, but access is difficult. Some off-trail bushwacking will be neccessary.

Trail 596 heads downstream from the FR 631 bridge, providing walk-in access to Second Box Canyon. Anglers willing to do the work can reach some nice water.

Williams Creek and the reservoir upstream offer great fishing, with good access off CR 631. Hike down to the Piedra confluence for some solitude.

Piedra Bridge: N 37° 25' 39.283", W 107° 11' 35.297"

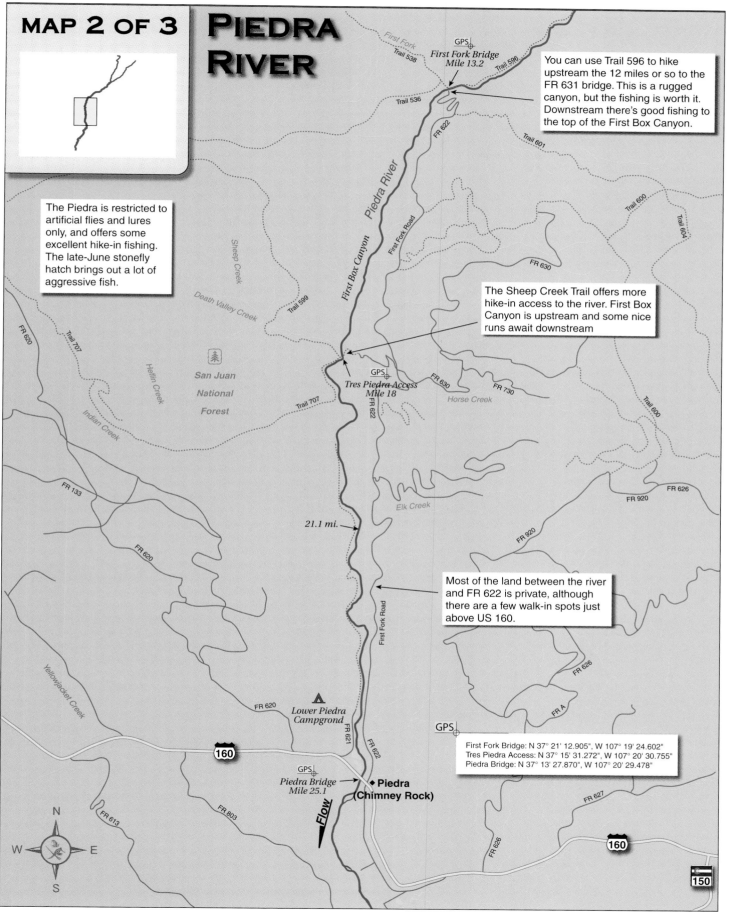

MAP 2 OF 3 PIEDRA RIVER

You can use Trail 596 to hike upstream the 12 miles or so to the FR 631 bridge. This is a rugged canyon, but the fishing is worth it. Downstream there's good fishing to the top of the First Box Canyon.

The Piedra is restricted to artificial flies and lures only, and offers some excellent hike-in fishing. The late-June stonefly hatch brings out a lot of aggressive fish.

The Sheep Creek Trail offers more hike-in access to the river. First Box Canyon is upstream and some nice runs await downstream

Most of the land between the river and FR 622 is private, although there are a few walk-in spots just above US 160.

First Fork Bridge
Mile 13.2

GPS

Tres Piedra Access
Mile 18

21.1 mi.

Lower Piedra
Campgrond

Piedra Bridge
Mile 25.1

♦ Piedra
(Chimney Rock)

Flow

First Fork Bridge: N 37° 21' 12.905", W 107° 19' 24.602"
Tres Piedra Access: N 37° 15' 31.272", W 107° 20' 30.755"
Piedra Bridge: N 37° 13' 27.870", W 107° 20' 29.478"

Piedra River

First Fork

Trail 538

Trail 536

Trail 596

FR 622

Trail 601

Trail 600

Trail 604

FR 630

First Fork Road

First Box Canyon

Sheep Creek

Death Valley Creek

Trail 599

FR 620

Trail 707

Heflin Creek

San Juan National Forest

Trail 707

FR 622

FR 630

FR 730

Horse Creek

Trail 600

Indian Creek

FR 133

FR 620

Elk Creek

FR 920

FR 920

FR 626

FR 626

FR 626

FR A

GPS

First Fork Road

Yellowjacket Creek

FR 620

FR 621

FR 622

160

GPS

FR 613

FR 803

FR 626

FR 627

160

150

N
W   E
S

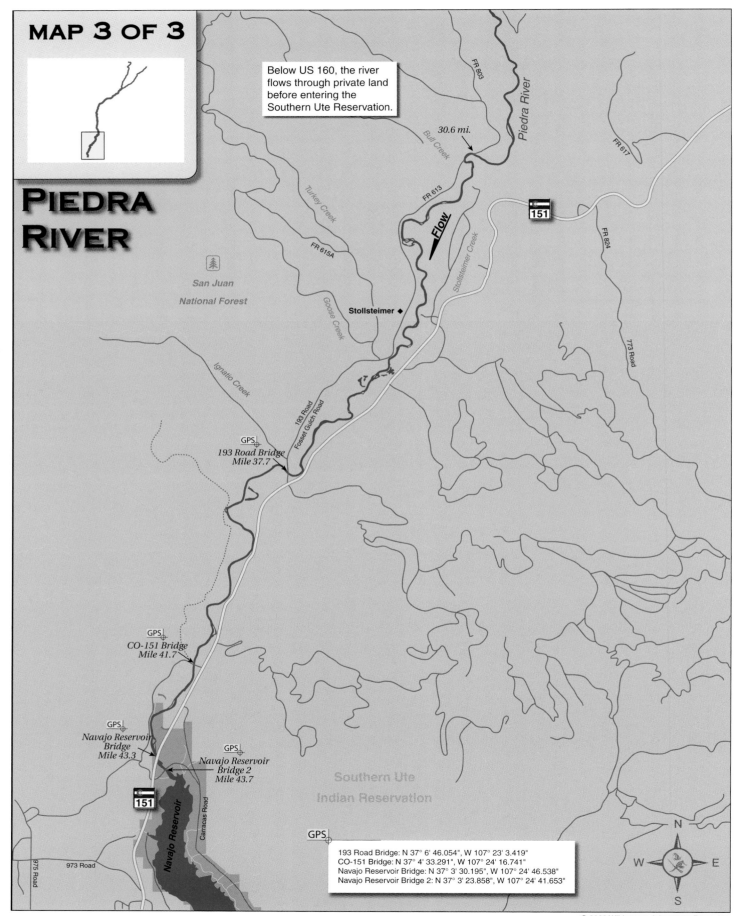

MAP 3 OF 3

PIEDRA RIVER

Below US 160, the river flows through private land before entering the Southern Ute Reservation.

30.6 mi.

Flow

Piedra River

FR 803

FR 617

FR 824

773 Road

151

FR 613

Bull Creek

Stollsteimer Creek

Turkey Creek

FR 615A

San Juan
National Forest

Goose Creek

Stollsteimer ◆

Ignatio Creek

193 Road

Fosset Gulch Road

GPS
193 Road Bridge
Mile 37.7

GPS
CO-151 Bridge
Mile 41.7

GPS
Navajo Reservoir
Bridge
Mile 43.3

GPS
Navajo Reservoir
Bridge 2
Mile 43.7

Southern Ute
Indian Reservation

GPS

151

Carracas Road

975 Road

973 Road

Navajo Reservoir

N

W   E

S

193 Road Bridge: N 37° 6' 46.054", W 107° 23' 3.419"
CO-151 Bridge: N 37° 4' 33.291", W 107° 24' 16.741"
Navajo Reservoir Bridge: N 37° 3' 30.195", W 107° 24' 46.538"
Navajo Reservoir Bridge 2: N 37° 3' 23.858", W 107° 24' 41.653"

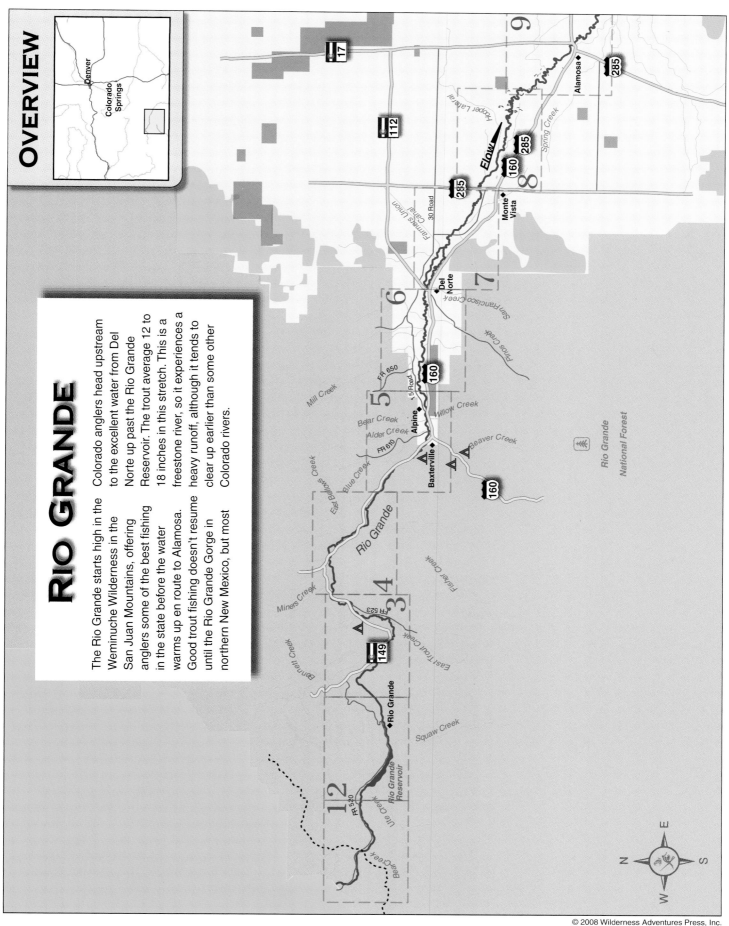

OVERVIEW

RIO GRANDE

The Rio Grande starts high in the Weminuche Wilderness in the San Juan Mountains, offering anglers some of the best fishing in the state before the water warms up en route to Alamosa. Good trout fishing doesn't resume until the Rio Grande Gorge in northern New Mexico, but most

Colorado anglers head upstream to the excellent water from Del Norte up past the Rio Grande Reservoir. The trout average 12 to 18 inches in this stretch. This is a freestone river, so it experiences a heavy runoff, although it tends to clear up earlier than some other Colorado rivers.

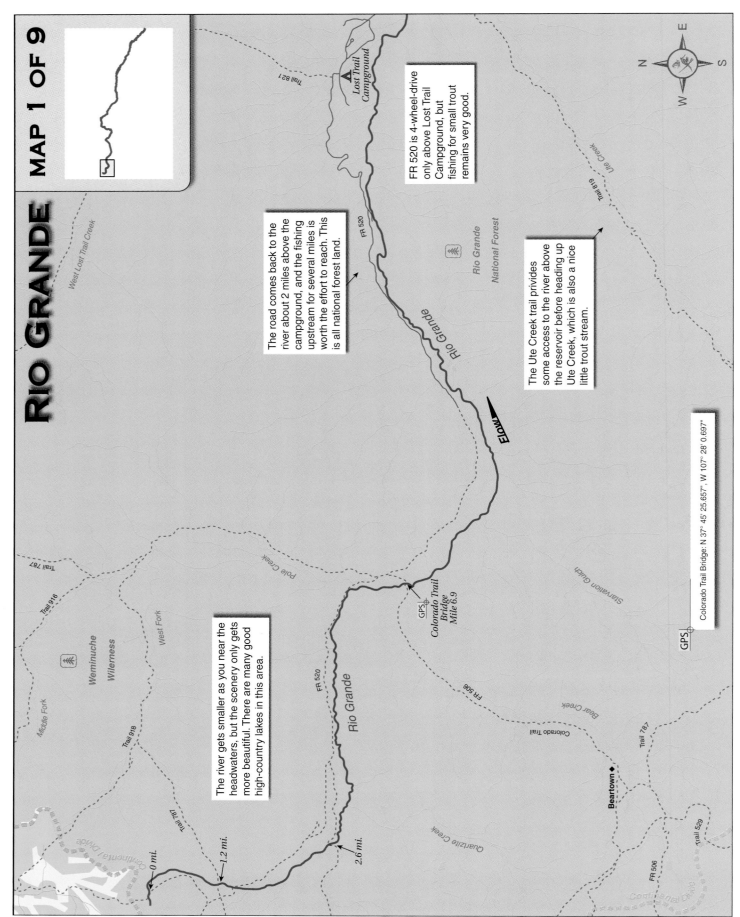

MAP 1 OF 9

RIO GRANDE

Lost Trail Campground

Trail 821

FR 520 is 4-wheel-drive only above Lost Trail Campground, but fishing for small trout remains very good.

Ute Creek

Trail 819

Rio Grande National Forest

The road comes back to the river about 2 miles above the campground, and the fishing upstream for several miles is worth the effort to reach. This is all national forest land.

Rio Grande

FR 520

West Lost Trail Creek

FLOW

The Ute Creek trail privides some access to the river above the reservoir before heading up Ute Creek, which is also a nice little trout stream.

Pole Creek

Trail 787

Trail 916

Weminuche Wilerness

West Fork

Trail 918

The river gets smaller as you near the headwaters, but the scenery only gets more beautiful. There are many good high-country lakes in this area.

Middle Fork

Starvation Gulch

Colorado Trail Bridge: N 37° 45' 25.657", W 107° 28' 0.697"

GPS

Colorado Trail Bridge Mile 6.9

GPS

FR 506

Bear Creek

Colorado Trail

Trail 787

Trail 787

Beartown

Quartzite Creek

FR 506

Trail 529

Rio Grande

FR 520

0 mi.

1.2 mi.

2.6 mi.

Continental Divide

Continental Divide

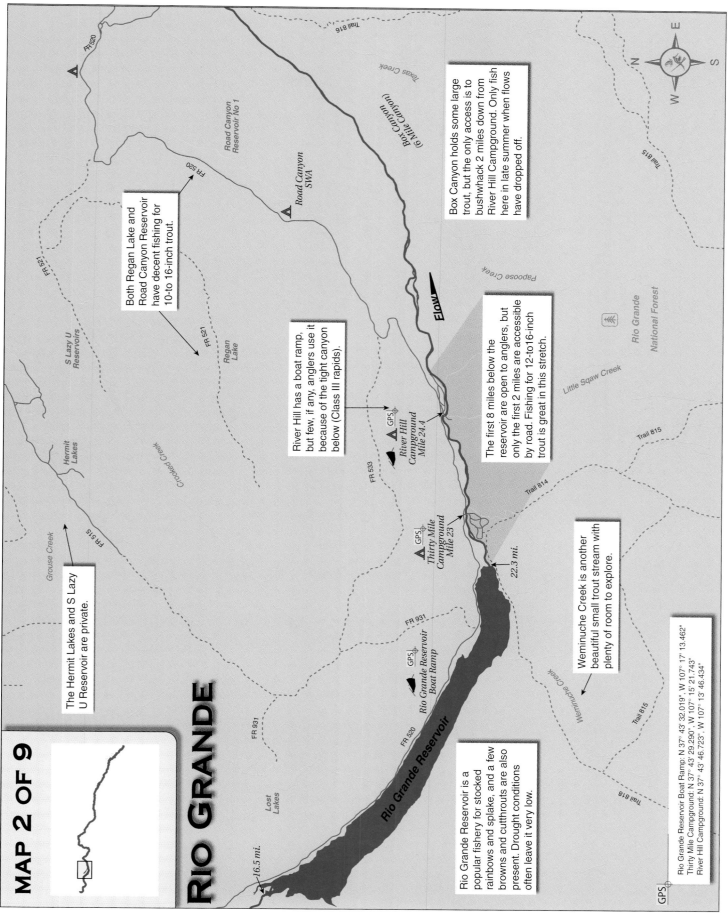

MAP 2 OF 9

RIO GRANDE

Both Regan Lake and Road Canyon Reservoir have decent fishing for 10-to 16-inch trout.

Box Canyon holds some large trout, but the only access is to bushwhack 2 miles down from River Hill Campground. Only fish here in late summer when flows have dropped off.

River Hill has a boat ramp, but few, if any, anglers use it because of the tight canyon below (Class III rapids).

The first 8 miles below the reservoir are open to anglers, but only the first 2 miles are accessible by road. Fishing for 12-to16-inch trout is great in this stretch.

The Hermit Lakes and S Lazy U Reservoir are private.

Weminuche Creek is another beautiful small trout stream with plenty of room to explore.

Rio Grande Reservoir is a popular fishery for stocked rainbows and splake, and a few browns and cutthroats are also present. Drought conditions often leave it very low.

Rio Grande Reservoir Boat Ramp: N 37° 43' 32.019", W 107° 17' 13.462"
Thirty Mile Campground: N 37° 43' 29.290", W 107° 15' 21.743"
River Hill Campground: N 37° 43' 46.723", W 107° 13' 46.434"

River Hill Campground Mile 24.4

Thirty Mile Campground Mile 23

22.3 mi.

16.5 mi.

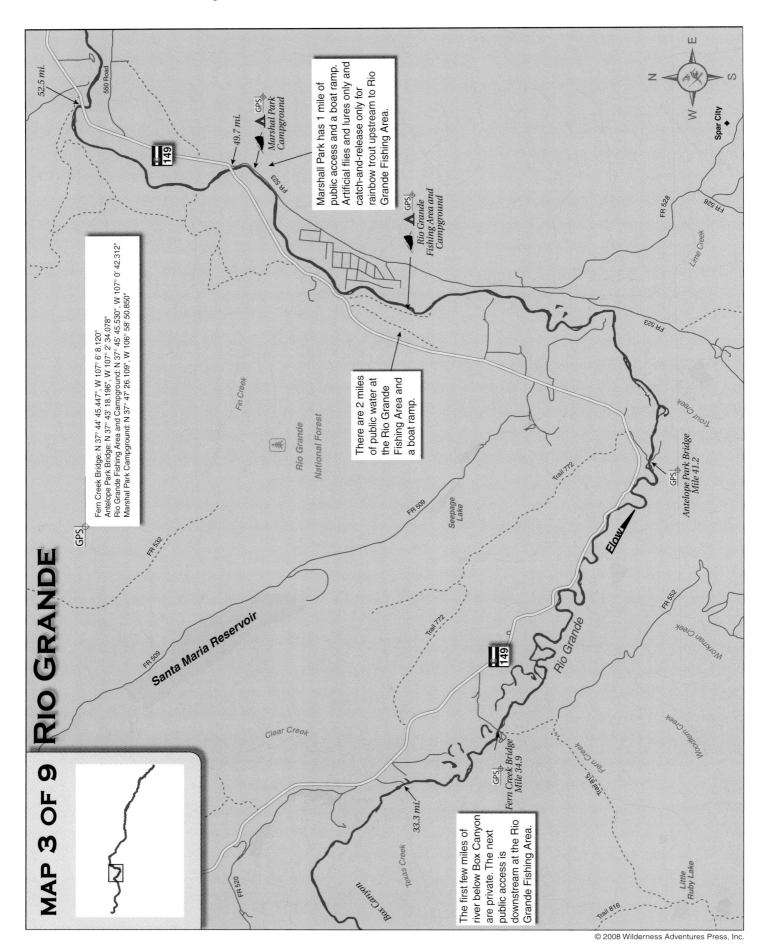

MAP 3 OF 9

RIO GRANDE

52.5 mi.

550 Road

49.7 mi.

149

GPS
Marshal Park
Campground

FR 523

Marshall Park has 1 mile of public access and a boat ramp. Artificial flies and lures only and catch-and-release only for rainbow trout upstream to Rio Grande Fishing Area.

GPS
Rio Grande
Fishing Area and
Campground

FR 528

FR 526

Lime Creek

GPS

Fern Creek Bridge: N 37° 44' 45.447", W 107° 6' 8.120"
Antelope Park Bridge: N 37° 43' 18.196", W 107° 2' 34.078"
Rio Grande Fishing Area and Campground: N 37° 45' 45.530", W 107° 0' 42.312"
Marshal Park Campground: N 37° 47' 26.109", W 106° 58' 50.850"

There are 2 miles of public water at the Rio Grande Fishing Area and a boat ramp.

FR 523

Fin Creek

Rio Grande
National Forest

FR 532

FR 509

Seepage
Lake

Trail 772

Trout Creek

GPS

Antelope Park Bridge
Mile 41.2

Flow

FR 552

Workman Creek

Santa Maria Reservoir

FR 509

Trail 772

149

Rio Grande

Clear Creek

GPS
Fern Creek Bridge
Mile 34.9

Fern Creek

Woodlem Creek

33.3 mi.

The first few miles of river below Box Canyon are private. The next public access is downstream at the Rio Grande Fishing Area.

Box Canyon

Texas Creek

FR 520

Trail 815

Little
Ruby Lake

Trail 816

N E S W

Spar City

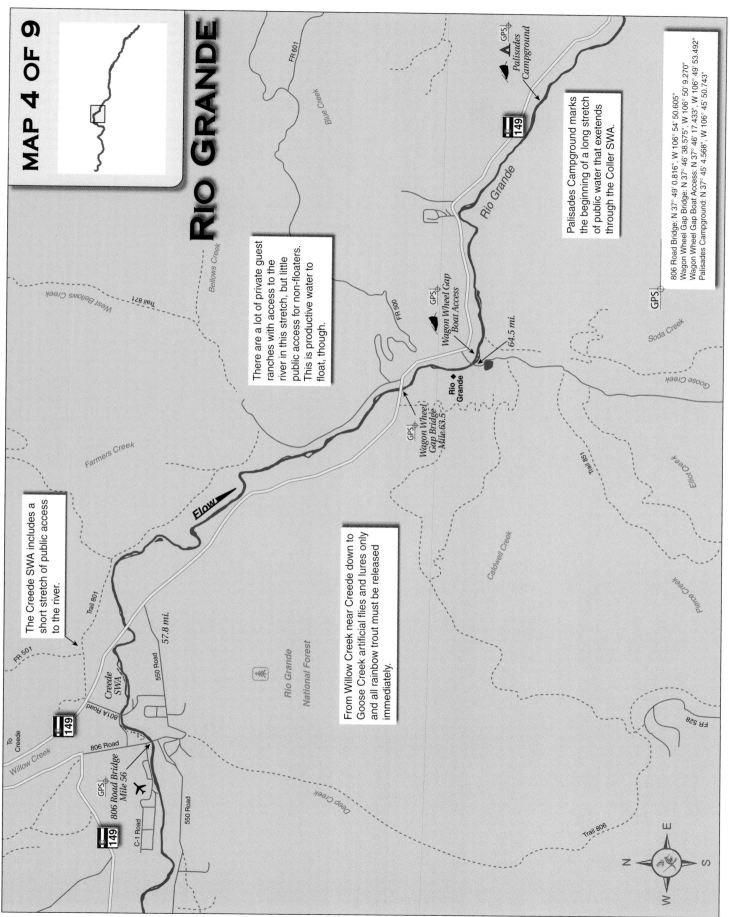

MAP 4 OF 9

RIO GRANDE

There are a lot of private guest ranches with access to the river in this stretch, but little public access for non-floaters. This is productive water to float, though.

Palisades Campground marks the beginning of a long stretch of public water that exetends through the Coller SWA.

The Creede SWA includes a short stretch of public access to the river.

From Willow Creek near Creede down to Goose Creek artificial flies and lures only and all rainbow trout must be released immediately.

806 Road Bridge: N 37° 49' 0.816", W 106° 54' 50.605"
Wagon Wheel Gap Bridge: N 37° 46' 38.575", W 106° 50' 9.270"
Wagon Wheel Gap Boat Access: N 37° 46' 17.433", W 106° 49' 53.492"
Palisades Campground: N 37° 45' 4.568", W 106° 45' 50.743"

Palisades Campground

Wagon Wheel Gap Boat Access

Wagon Wheel Gap Bridge Mile 63.5

Rio Grande

64.5 mi.

Rio Grande

Blue Creek

Bellows Creek

West Bellows Creek

Trail 871

Farmers Creek

FR 601

FR 500

Soda Creek

Goose Creek

Elliott Creek

Trail 851

Pierce Creek

Caldwell Creek

Rio Grande National Forest

Flow

57.8 mi.

Trail 801

Creede SWA

550 Road

801A Road

806 Road

806 Road Bridge Mile 56

C-1 Road

550 Road

FR 501

To Creede

Willow Creek

Deep Creek

FR 528

Trail 806

GPS

N E S W

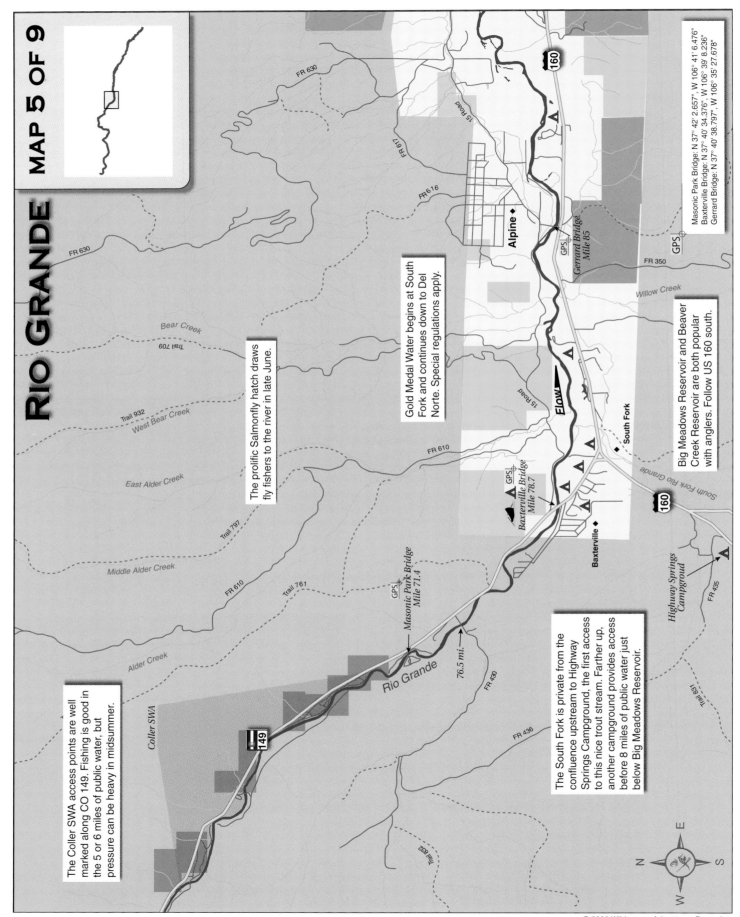

MAP 5 OF 9

RIO GRANDE

Masonic Park Bridge: N 37° 42' 2.657", W 106° 41' 6.476"
Baxterville Bridge: N 37° 40' 34.376", W 106° 39' 8.236"
Gerrard Bridge: N 37° 40' 38.797", W 106° 35' 27.678"

Gold Medal Water begins at South Fork and continues down to Del Norte. Special regulations apply.

The prolific Salmonfly hatch draws fly fishers to the river in late June.

Big Meadows Reservoir and Beaver Creek Reservoir are both popular with anglers. Follow US 160 south.

The Coller SWA access points are well marked along CO 149. Fishing is good in the 5 or 6 miles of public water, but pressure can be heavy in midsummer.

The South Fork is private from the confluence upstream to Highway Springs Campground, the first access to this nice trout stream. Farther up, another campground provides access before 8 miles of public water just below Big Meadows Reservoir.

Bear Creek

Trail 709

Trail 932

West Bear Creek

East Alder Creek

Middle Alder Creek

Trail 797

Trail 761

FR 610

Alder Creek

FR 630

FR 630

FR 616

FR 617

15 Road

15 Road

FR 630

Alpine

Gerrard Bridge
Mile 85

GPS

Willow Creek

FR 350

GPS

Flow

South Fork

FR 610

Baxterville Bridge
Mile 78.7

GPS

Baxterville

South Fork Rio Grande

160

160

Highway Springs Campground

FR 435

Trail 831

Masonic Park Bridge
Mile 71.4

GPS

Rio Grande

76.5 mi.

FR 430

FR 436

Coller SWA

149

Trail 838

Coller SWA

N
W   E
S

© 2008 Wilderness Adventures Press, Inc.

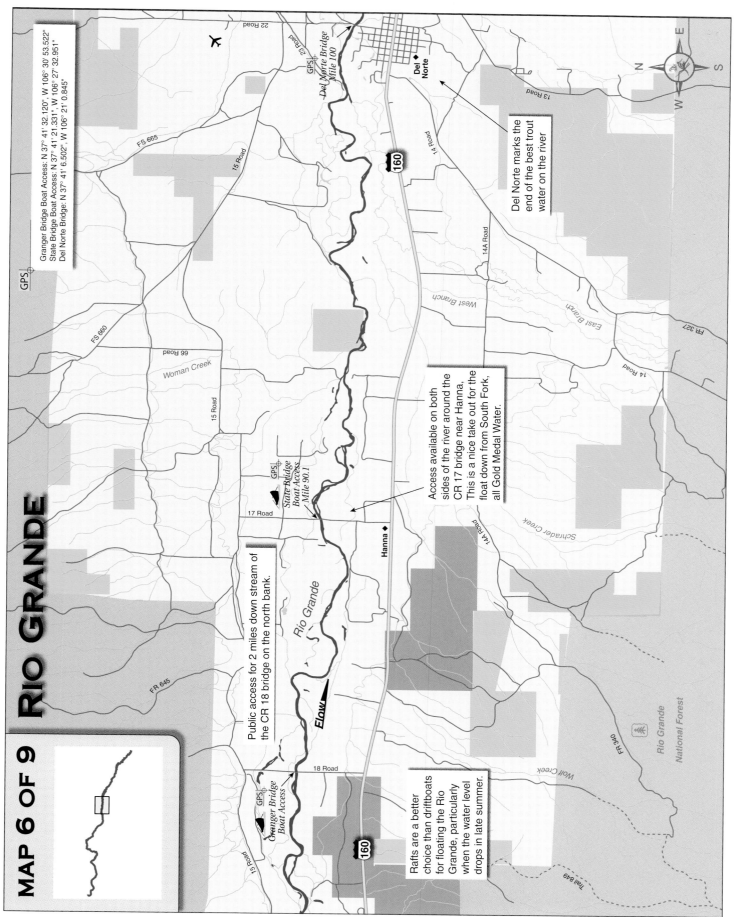

RIO GRANDE

MAP 6 OF 9

Granger Bridge Boat Access: N 37° 41' 32.120", W 106° 30' 53.522"
State Bridge Boat Access: N 37° 41' 21.331", W 106° 27' 32.951"
Del Norte Bridge: N 37° 41' 6.502", W 106° 21' 0.845"

GPS

FS 665

15 Road

FS 660

66 Road

Woman Creek

15 Road

17 Road

State Bridge Boat Access Mile 90.1

GPS

Rio Grande

Flow

FR 645

Public access for 2 miles down stream of the CR 18 bridge on the north bank.

18 Road

Granger Bridge Boat Access

GPS

15 Road

160

Rafts are a better choice than driftboats for floating the Rio Grande, particularly when the water level drops in late summer.

22 Road

23 Road

GPS

Del Norte Bridge Mile 100

Del Norte

160

14 Road

14A Road

West Branch

East Branch

14 Road

13 Road

FR 327

Del Norte marks the end of the best trout water on the river

Hanna

14A Road

Access available on both sides of the river around the CR 17 bridge near Hanna. This is a nice take out for the float down from South Fork, all Gold Medal Water.

Schrader Creek

Wolf Creek

FR 340

Rio Grande National Forest

Trail 849

N E S W

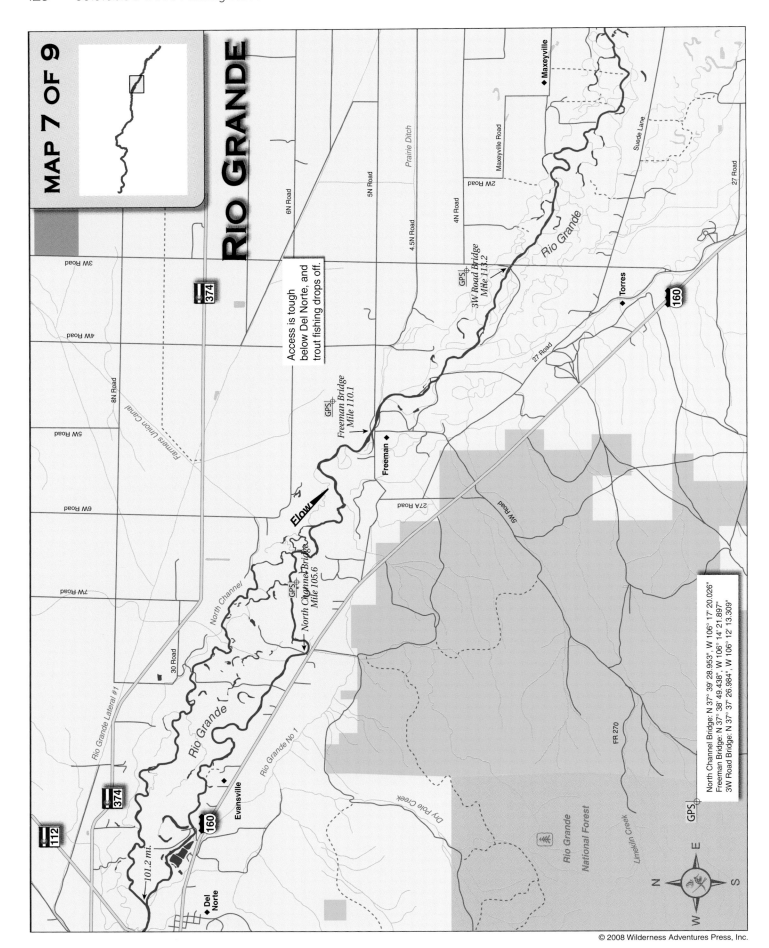

MAP 7 OF 9

RIO GRANDE

Access is tough below Del Norte, and trout fishing drops off.

3W Road Bridge
Mile 113.2

Freeman Bridge
Mile 110.1

Flow

North Channel Bridge
Mile 105.6

101.2 mi.

North Channel Bridge: N 37° 39' 28.953", W 106° 17' 20.026"
Freeman Bridge: N 37° 38' 49.438", W 106° 14' 21.897"
3W Road Bridge: N 37° 37' 26.984", W 106° 12' 13.309"

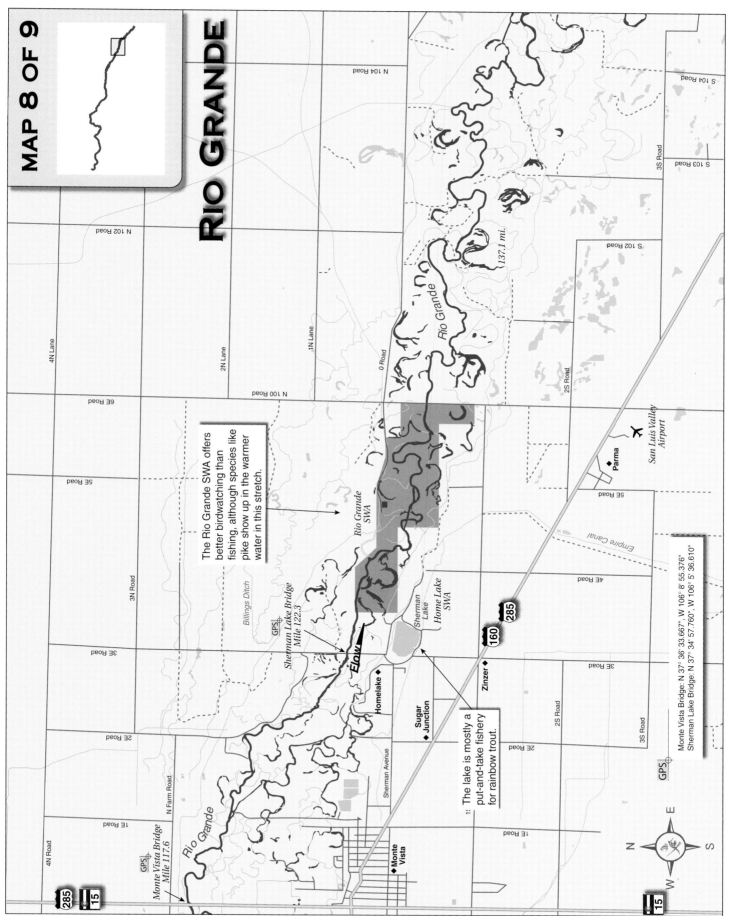

MAP 8 OF 9

RIO GRANDE

137.1 mi.

Rio Grande

N 104 Road
N 102 Road
4N Lane
2N Lane
1N Lane
0 Road
N 100 Road
6E Road
5E Road
3N Road
3E Road
2E Road
1E Road
N Farm Road
4N Road

S 104 Road
S 103 Road
S 102 Road
2S Road
5E Road
4E Road
3E Road
2S Road
2E Road
3S Road
1E Road

The Rio Grande SWA offers better birdwatching than fishing, although species like pike show up in the warmer water in this stretch.

Rio Grande SWA

Billings Ditch

GPS

Sherman Lake Bridge Mile 122.3

Flow

Homelake ◆

Sherman Lake

Home Lake SWA

Sugar Junction ◆

Zinzer ◆

160
285

Sherman Avenue

The lake is mostly a put-and-take fishery for rainbow trout.

San Luis Valley Airport

Parma ◆

Empire Canal

GPS

Monte Vista Bridge: N 37° 36' 33.667", W 106° 8' 55.376"
Sherman Lake Bridge: N 37° 34' 57.760", W 106° 5' 36.610"

N
E
W
S

Rio Grande

GPS

Monte Vista Bridge Mile 117.6

285
15

◆ Monte Vista

15

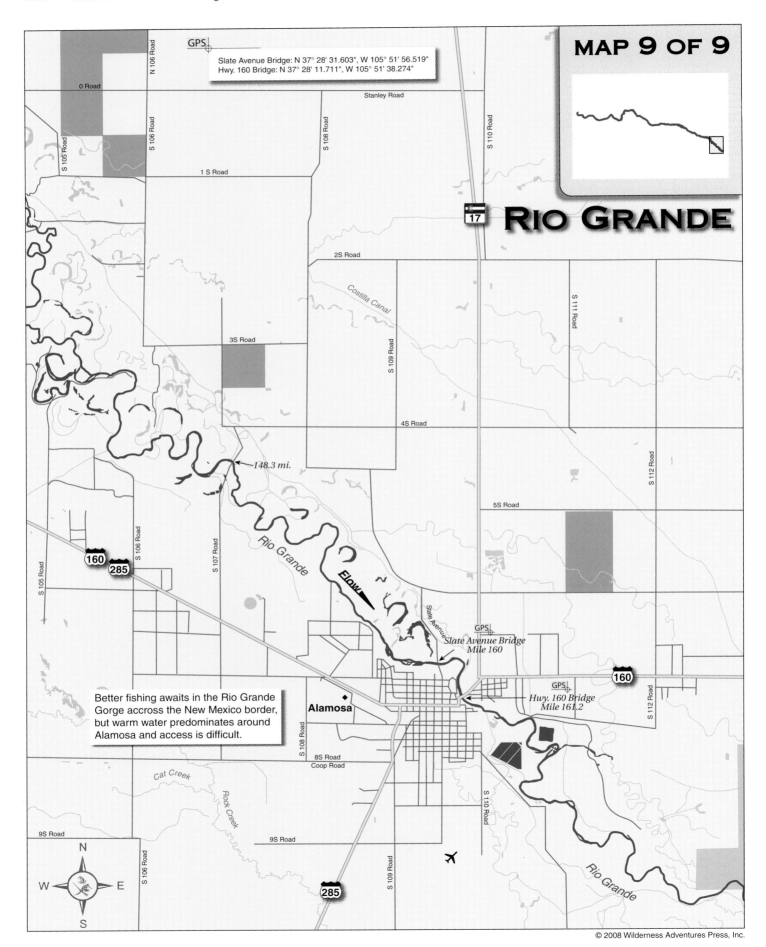

MAP 9 OF 9

RIO GRANDE

Slate Avenue Bridge: N 37° 28' 31.603", W 105° 51' 56.519"
Hwy. 160 Bridge: N 37° 28' 11.711", W 105° 51' 38.274"

0 Road
N 106 Road
S 105 Road
S 106 Road
1 S Road
S 108 Road
Stanley Road
S 110 Road
GPS
17
2S Road
Costilla Canal
S 111 Road
3S Road
S 109 Road
4S Road
148.3 mi.
5S Road
S 112 Road
Rio Grande
S 106 Road
S 107 Road
Flow
~
Slate Avenue
GPS
Slate Avenue Bridge
Mile 160
160
285
S 105 Road
GPS
Hwy. 160 Bridge
Mile 161.2
160
S 112 Road

Better fishing awaits in the Rio Grande
Gorge accross the New Mexico border,
but warm water predominates around
Alamosa and access is difficult.

Alamosa
S 108 Road
8S Road
Coop Road
Cat Creek
Rock Creek
S 110 Road
9S Road
9S Road
S 106 Road
S 109 Road
285
Rio Grande

N
W E
S

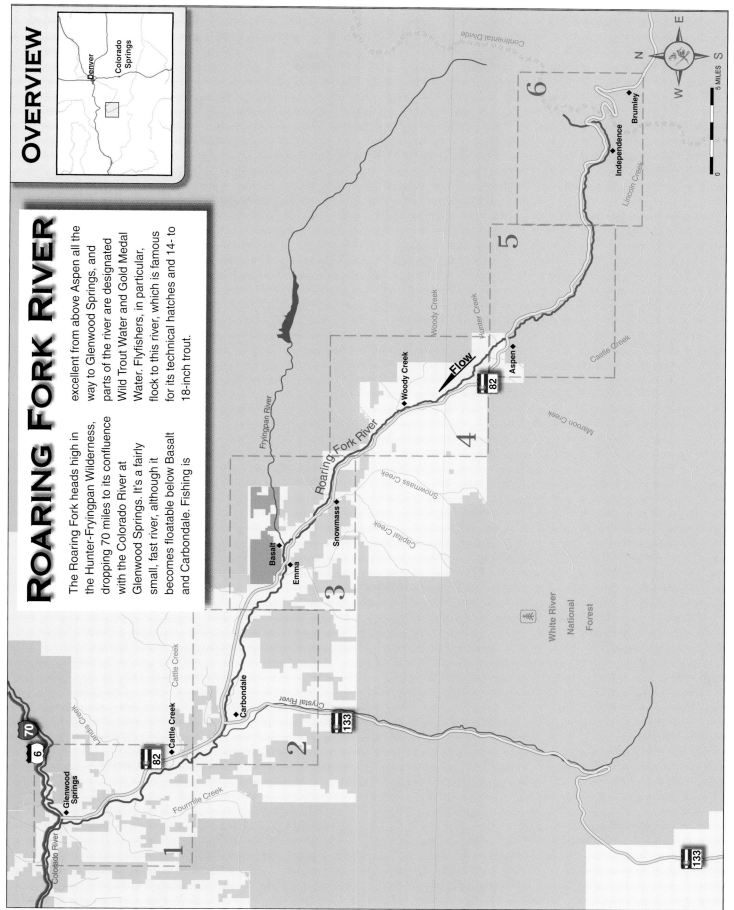

OVERVIEW

ROARING FORK RIVER

The Roaring Fork heads high in the Hunter-Fryingpan Wilderness, dropping 70 miles to its confluence with the Colorado River at Glenwood Springs. It's a fairly small, fast river, although it becomes floatable below Basalt and Carbondale. Fishing is excellent from above Aspen all the way to Glenwood Springs, and parts of the river are designated Wild Trout Water and Gold Medal Water. Flyfishers, in particular, flock to this river, which is famous for its technical hatches and 14- to 18-inch trout.

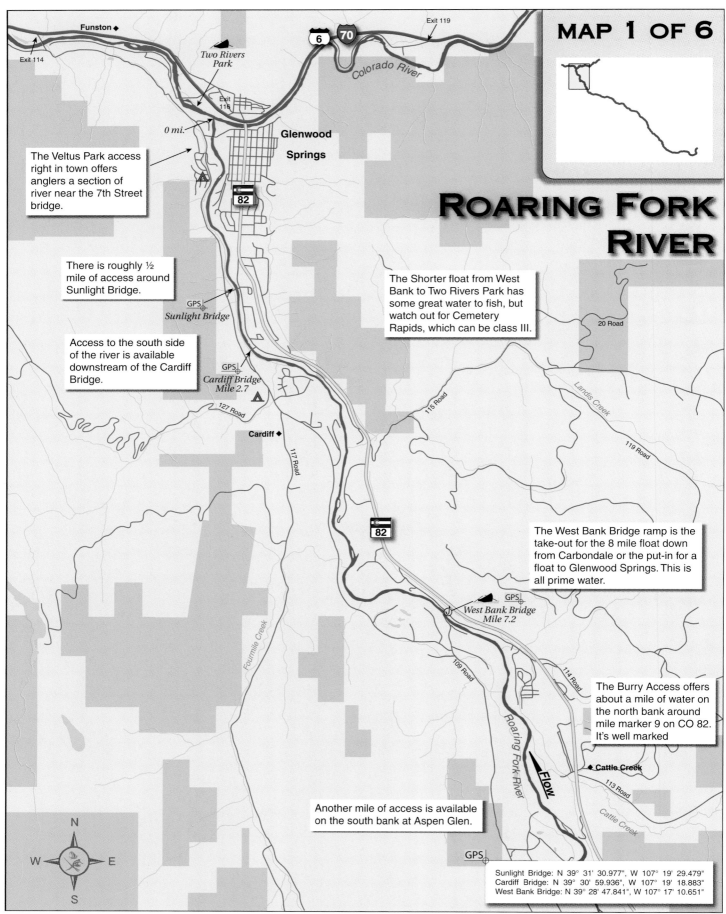

MAP 1 OF 6

ROARING FORK RIVER

Funston ◆

Exit 114

Two Rivers Park

Exit 119

Colorado River

6 70

Exit 116

0 mi.

Glenwood Springs

82

The Veltus Park access right in town offers anglers a section of river near the 7th Street bridge.

There is roughly ½ mile of access around Sunlight Bridge.

GPS
Sunlight Bridge

The Shorter float from West Bank to Two Rivers Park has some great water to fish, but watch out for Cemetery Rapids, which can be class III.

20 Road

Access to the south side of the river is available downstream of the Cardiff Bridge.

GPS
Cardiff Bridge
Mile 2.7

127 Road

Cardiff ◆

117 Road

115 Road

Landis Creek

119 Road

82

The West Bank Bridge ramp is the take-out for the 8 mile float down from Carbondale or the put-in for a float to Glenwood Springs. This is all prime water.

GPS
West Bank Bridge
Mile 7.2

109 Road

114 Road

The Burry Access offers about a mile of water on the north bank around mile marker 9 on CO 82. It's well marked

Fourmile Creek

Roaring Fork River

Flow

◆ Cattle Creek

113 Road

Cattle Creek

Another mile of access is available on the south bank at Aspen Glen.

N
W E
S

GPS

Sunlight Bridge: N 39° 31' 30.977", W 107° 19' 29.479"
Cardiff Bridge: N 39° 30' 59.936", W 107° 19' 18.883"
West Bank Bridge: N 39° 28' 47.841", W 107° 17' 10.651"

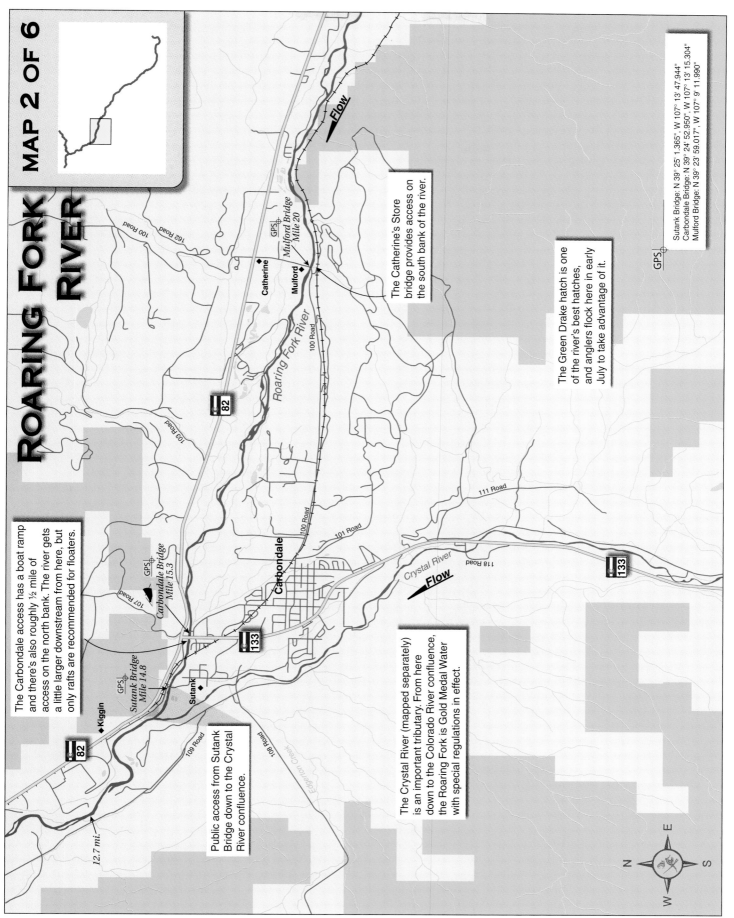

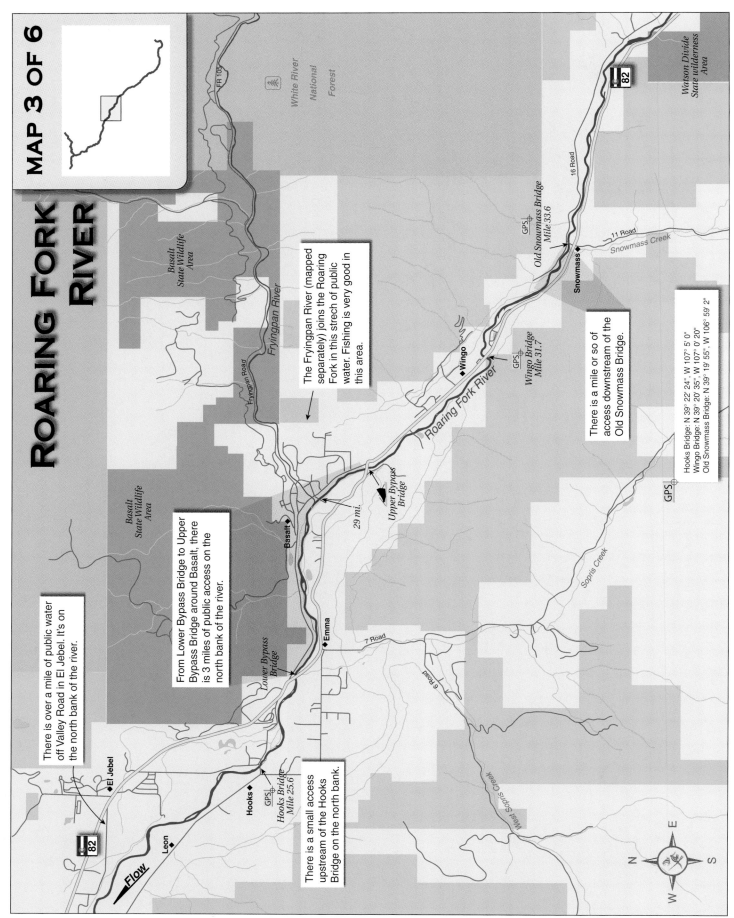

MAP 3 OF 6

ROARING FORK RIVER

White River National Forest

Basalt State Wildlife Area

Basalt State Wildlife Area

There is over a mile of public water off Valley Road in El Jebel. It's on the north bank of the river.

From Lower Bypass Bridge to Upper Bypass Bridge around Basalt, there is 3 miles of public access on the north bank of the river.

The Fryingpan River (mapped separately) joins the Roaring Fork in this strech of public water. Fishing is very good in this area.

There is a mile or so of access downstream of the Old Snowmass Bridge.

Fryingpan River

Fryingpan Road

FR 105

Wingo

Roaring Fork River

Wingo Bridge Mile 31.7
GPS

GPS
Old Snowmass Bridge Mile 33.6

11 Road

Snowmass Creek

Snowmass

16 Road

82

Watson Divide State wilderness Area

Upper Bypass Bridge

29 mi.

Basalt

Lower Bypass Bridge

Emma

7 Road

6 Road

Sopris Creek

West Sopris Creek

El Jebel

Leon

Hooks
GPS
Hooks Bridge Mile 25.6

There is a small access upstream of the Hooks Bridge on the north bank.

82

Flow

GPS

Hooks Bridge: N 39° 22' 24", W 107° 5' 0"
Wingo Bridge: N 39° 20' 35", W 107° 0' 20"
Old Snowmass Bridge: N 39° 19' 55", W 106° 59' 2"

N E S W

ROARING FORK RIVER

MAP 4 OF 6

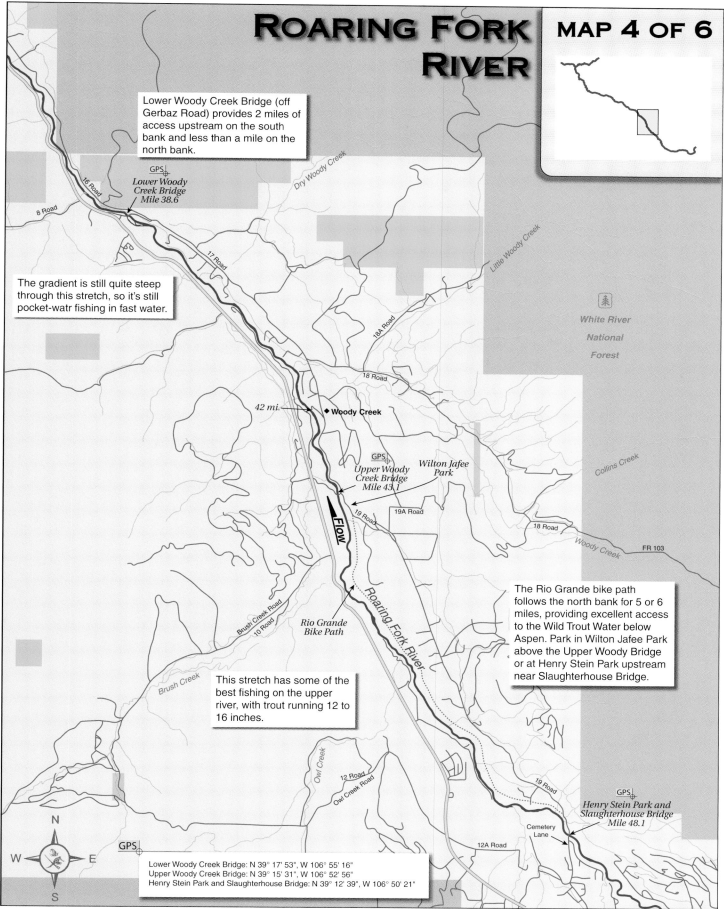

Lower Woody Creek Bridge (off Gerbaz Road) provides 2 miles of access upstream on the south bank and less than a mile on the north bank.

GPS
Lower Woody Creek Bridge Mile 38.6

16 Road

8 Road

Dry Woody Creek

17 Road

The gradient is still quite steep through this stretch, so it's still pocket-watr fishing in fast water.

Little Woody Creek

18A Road

White River

National

Forest

18 Road

42 mi. ◆ **Woody Creek**

GPS
Upper Woody Creek Bridge Mile 43.1

Wilton Jafee Park

Collins Creek

19A Road

19 Road

18 Road

Woody Creek   FR 103

Flow

Brush Creek Road
10 Road

Rio Grande Bike Path

Roaring Fork River

The Rio Grande bike path follows the north bank for 5 or 6 miles, providing excellent access to the Wild Trout Water below Aspen. Park in Wilton Jafee Park above the Upper Woody Bridge or at Henry Stein Park upstream near Slaughterhouse Bridge.

Brush Creek

This stretch has some of the best fishing on the upper river, with trout running 12 to 16 inches.

Owl Creek

12 Road

Owl Creek Road

19 Road

GPS
Henry Stein Park and Slaughterhouse Bridge Mile 48.1

Cemetery Lane

12A Road

N
W   E
S

GPS

Lower Woody Creek Bridge: N 39° 17' 53", W 106° 55' 16"
Upper Woody Creek Bridge: N 39° 15' 31", W 106° 52' 56"
Henry Stein Park and Slaughterhouse Bridge: N 39° 12' 39", W 106° 50' 21"

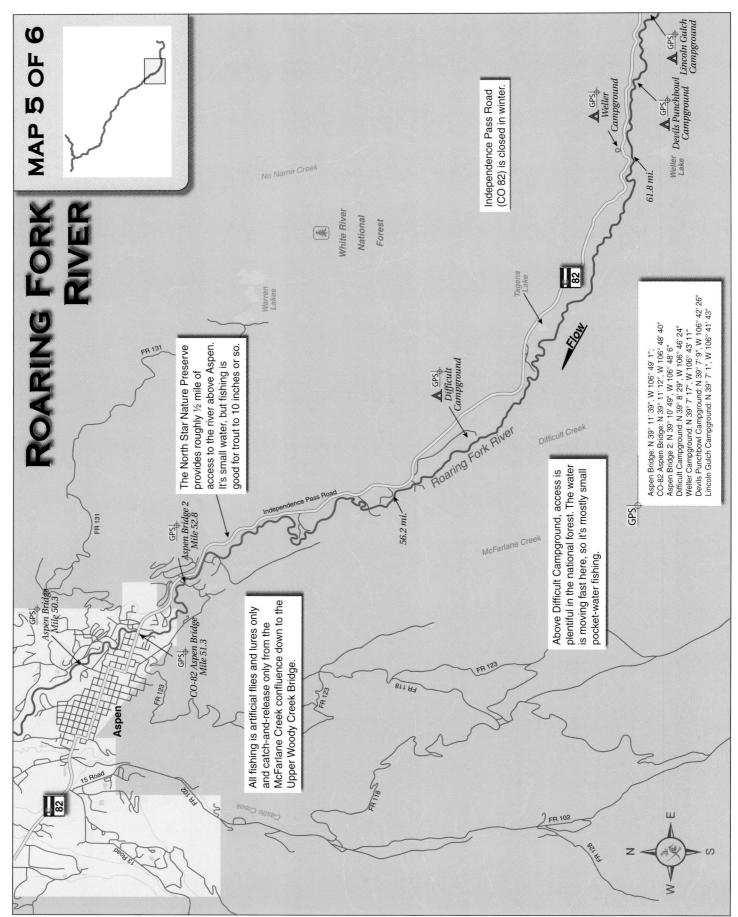

MAP 5 OF 6

ROARING FORK RIVER

No Name Creek

White River National Forest

Warren Lakes

FR 131

Independence Pass Road (CO 82) is closed in winter.

The North Star Nature Preserve provides roughly ½ mile of access to the river above Aspen. It's small water, but fishing is good for trout to 10 inches or so.

GPS Aspen Bridge 2 Mile 52.8

Aspen Bridge Mile 50.3

GPS

CO-82 Aspen Bridge Mile 51.3

GPS

Aspen

All fishing is artificial flies and lures only and catch-and-release only from the McFarlane Creek confluence down to the Upper Woody Creek Bridge.

15 Road

FR 102

Castle Creek

13 Road

Independence Pass Road

Roaring Fork River

56.2 mi.

Difficult Creek

GPS Difficult Campground

McFarlane Creek

Above Difficult Campground, access is plentiful in the national forest. The water is moving fast here, so it's mostly small pocket-water fishing.

GPS

FR 123

FR 118

FR 123

FR 118

FR 102

FR 128

82

Tagens Lake

Flow

82

GPS Weller Campground

Weller Lake

61.8 mi.

GPS Devils Punchbowl Campground

GPS Lincoln Gulch Campground

Aspen Bridge: N 39° 11' 39", W 106° 49' 1";
CO-82 Aspen Bridge: N 39° 11' 12", W 106° 48' 40"
Aspen Bridge 2: N 39° 10' 49", W 106° 48' 6"
Difficult Campground: N 39° 8' 29", W 106° 46' 24"
Weller Campground: N 39° 7' 17", W 106° 43' 11"
Devils Punchbowl Campground: N 39° 7' 9", W 106° 42' 26"
Lincoln Gulch Campground: N 39° 7' 1", W 106° 41' 43"

N E S W

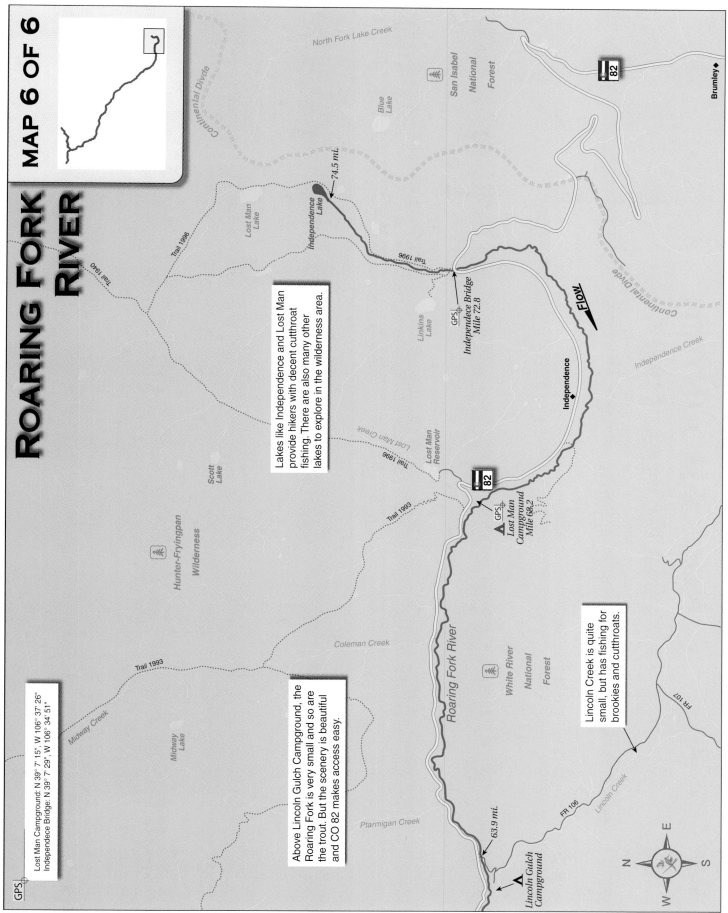

MAP 6 OF 6

ROARING FORK RIVER

North Fork Lake Creek

San Isabel National Forest

82

Brumley ◆

Continental Divide

Blue Lake

74.5 mi.

Lost Man Lake

Independence Lake

Trail 1996

Trail 1940

Independence Creek

Continental Divide

FLOW

GPS ⊕

Independece Bridge Mile 72.8

Linkins Lake

Lakes like Independence and Lost Man provide hikers with decent cutthroat fishing. There are also many other lakes to explore in the wilderness area.

Lost Man Creek

Trail 1996

Lost Man Reservoir

Scott Lake

Independence ◆

Hunter-Fryingpan Wilderness

82

GPS ⊕

Lost Man Campground Mile 68.2

Trail 1993

Coleman Creek

White River National Forest

Lincoln Creek is quite small, but has fishing for brookies and cutthroats.

Roaring Fork River

Trail 1993

Midway Creek

Midway Lake

Above Lincoln Gulch Campground, the Roaring Fork is very small and so are the trout. But the scenery is beautiful and CO 82 makes access easy.

FR 107

FR 106

Lincoln Creek

63.9 mi.

Ptarmigan Creek

Lincoln Gulch Campground

N E W S

GPS ⊕

Lost Man Campground: N 39° 7′ 15″, W 106° 37′ 26″
Independece Bridge: N 39° 7′ 29″, W 106° 34′ 51″

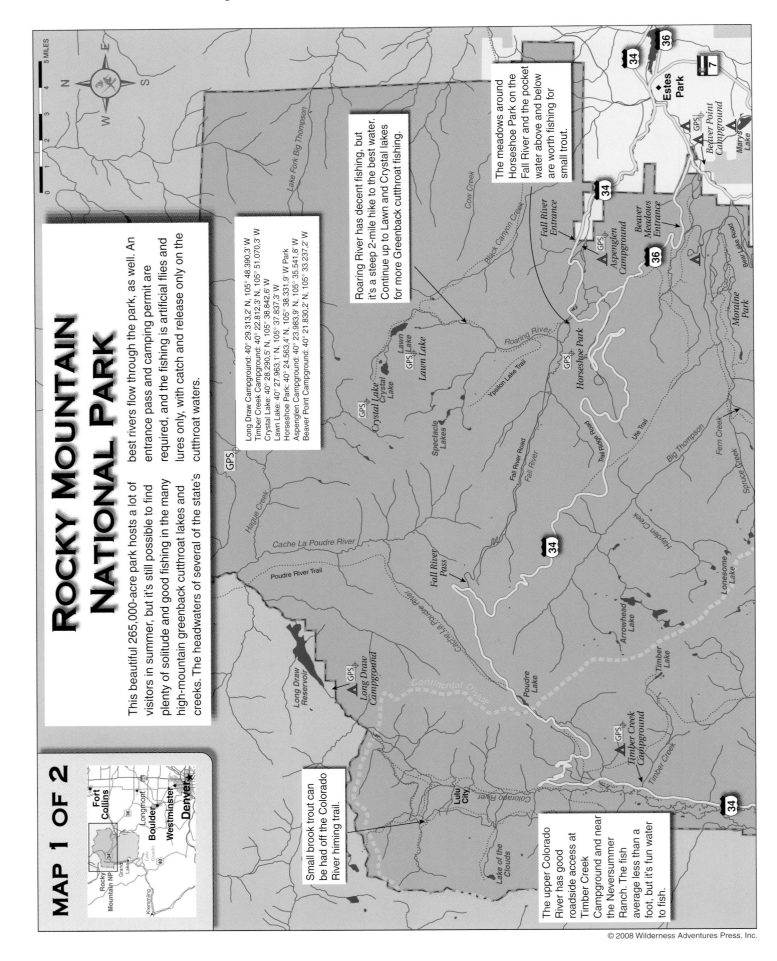

ROCKY MOUNTAIN NATIONAL PARK

This beautiful 265,000-acre park hosts a lot of visitors in summer, but it's still possible to find plenty of solitude and good fishing in the many high-mountain greenback cutthroat lakes and creeks. The headwaters of several of the state's best rivers flow through the park, as well. An entrance pass and camping permit are required, and the fishing is artificial flies and lures only, with catch and release only on the cutthroat waters.

Long Draw Campground: 40° 29.313,2' N, 105° 48.390,3' W
Timber Creek Campground: 40° 22.812,3' N, 105° 51.070,3' W
Crystal Lake: 40° 28.290,5' N, 105° 38.842,6' W
Lawn Lake: 40° 27.963,1' N, 105° 37.837,3' W
Horseshoe Park: 40° 24.563,4' N, 105° 38.331,9' W Park
Aspenglen Campground: 40° 23.983,9' N, 105° 35.541,8' W
Beaver Point Campground: 40° 21.830,2 N, 105° 33.237,2' W

The meadows around Horseshoe Park on the Fall River and the pocket water above and below are worth fishing for small trout.

Roaring River has decent fishing, but it's a steep 2-mile hike to the best water. Continue up to Lawn and Crystal lakes for more Greenback cutthroat fishing.

Small brook trout can be had off the Colorado River himing trail.

The upper Colorado River has good roadside access at Timber Creek Campground and near the Neversummer Ranch. The fish average less than a foot, but it's fun water to fish.

MAP 1 OF 2

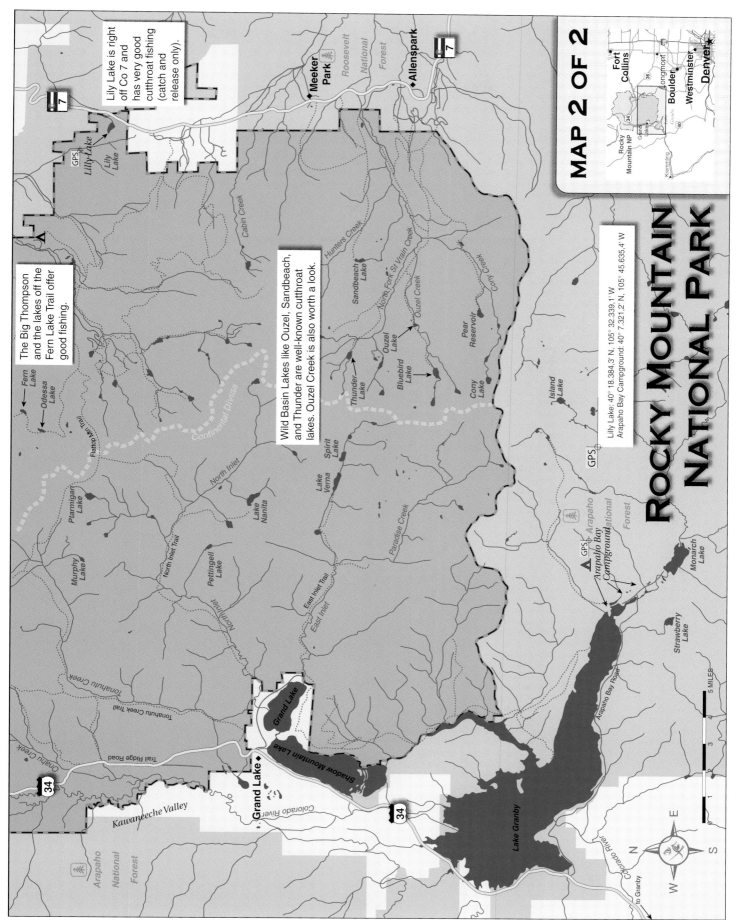

Lily Lake is right off Co 7 and has very good cutthroat fishing (catch and release only).

The Big Thompson and the lakes off the Fern Lake Trail offer good fishing.

Wild Basin Lakes like Ouzel, Sandbeach, and Thunder are well-known cutthroat lakes. Ouzel Creek is also worth a look.

Lily Lake: 40° 18.384.3' N, 105° 32.339.1' W
Arapaho Bay Campground: 40° 7.321,2' N, 105° 45.635,4' W

ROCKY MOUNTAIN NATIONAL PARK

MAP 2 OF 2

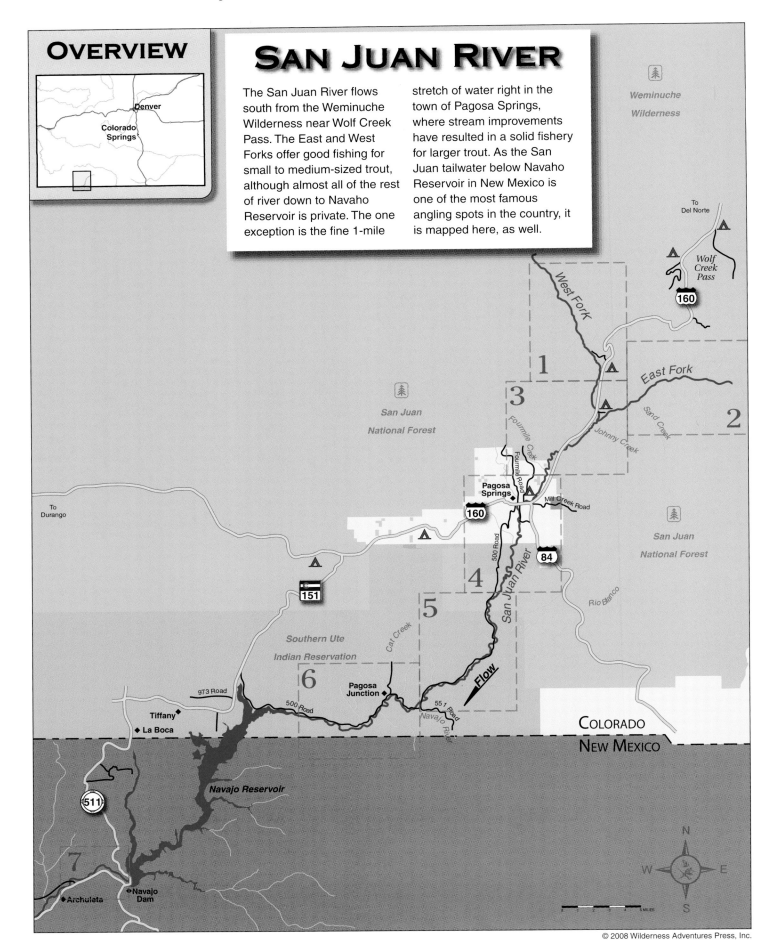

OVERVIEW

Denver

Colorado
Springs

SAN JUAN RIVER

The San Juan River flows south from the Weminuche Wilderness near Wolf Creek Pass. The East and West Forks offer good fishing for small to medium-sized trout, although almost all of the rest of river down to Navaho Reservoir is private. The one exception is the fine 1-mile stretch of water right in the town of Pagosa Springs, where stream improvements have resulted in a solid fishery for larger trout. As the San Juan tailwater below Navaho Reservoir in New Mexico is one of the most famous angling spots in the country, it is mapped here, as well.

Weminuche
Wilderness

To
Del Norte

Wolf
Creek
Pass

160

West Fork

East Fork

Sand Creek

1

3

2

San Juan

National Forest

Fourmile Creek

Johnny Creek

Fourmile Road

Pagosa
Springs

160

Mill Creek Road

84

San Juan
National Forest

To
Durango

500 Road

San Juan River

Rio Blanco

151

4

5

Cat Creek

Southern Ute

Indian Reservation

6

Pagosa
Junction

Flow

973 Road

500 Road

551 Road

Navajo River

COLORADO

NEW MEXICO

Tiffany

La Boca

Navajo Reservoir

511

7

Archuleta

Navajo
Dam

N

W   E

S

0   1   2   3   4   5 MILES

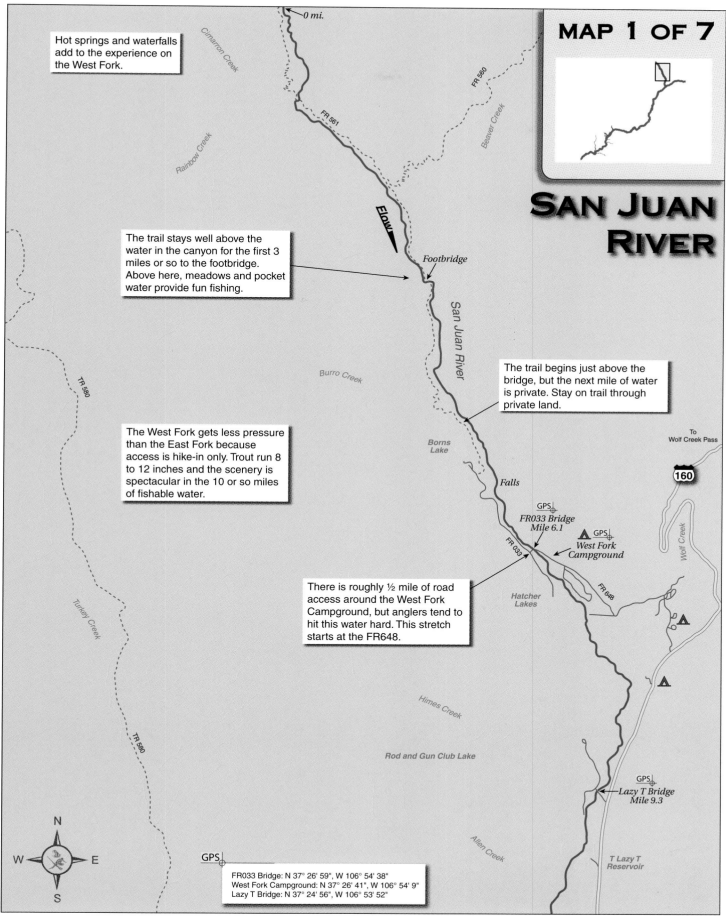

MAP 1 OF 7

SAN JUAN RIVER

Hot springs and waterfalls add to the experience on the West Fork.

The trail stays well above the water in the canyon for the first 3 miles or so to the footbridge. Above here, meadows and pocket water provide fun fishing.

The trail begins just above the bridge, but the next mile of water is private. Stay on trail through private land.

The West Fork gets less pressure than the East Fork because access is hike-in only. Trout run 8 to 12 inches and the scenery is spectacular in the 10 or so miles of fishable water.

There is roughly ½ mile of road access around the West Fork Campground, but anglers tend to hit this water hard. This stretch starts at the FR648.

Flow

Footbridge

San Juan River

Cimarron Creek

Rainbow Creek

Burro Creek

FR 561

FR 560

Beaver Creek

TR 580

Borns Lake

Falls

GPS
FR033 Bridge Mile 6.1

GPS
West Fork Campground

FR 033

Hatcher Lakes

FR 648

Wolf Creek

To Wolf Creek Pass

160

Turkey Creek

TR 580

Himes Creek

Rod and Gun Club Lake

Allen Creek

GPS
Lazy T Bridge Mile 9.3

T Lazy T Reservoir

N
W E
S

GPS

FR033 Bridge: N 37° 26' 59", W 106° 54' 38"
West Fork Campground: N 37° 26' 41", W 106° 54' 9"
Lazy T Bridge: N 37° 24' 56", W 106° 53' 52"

0 mi.

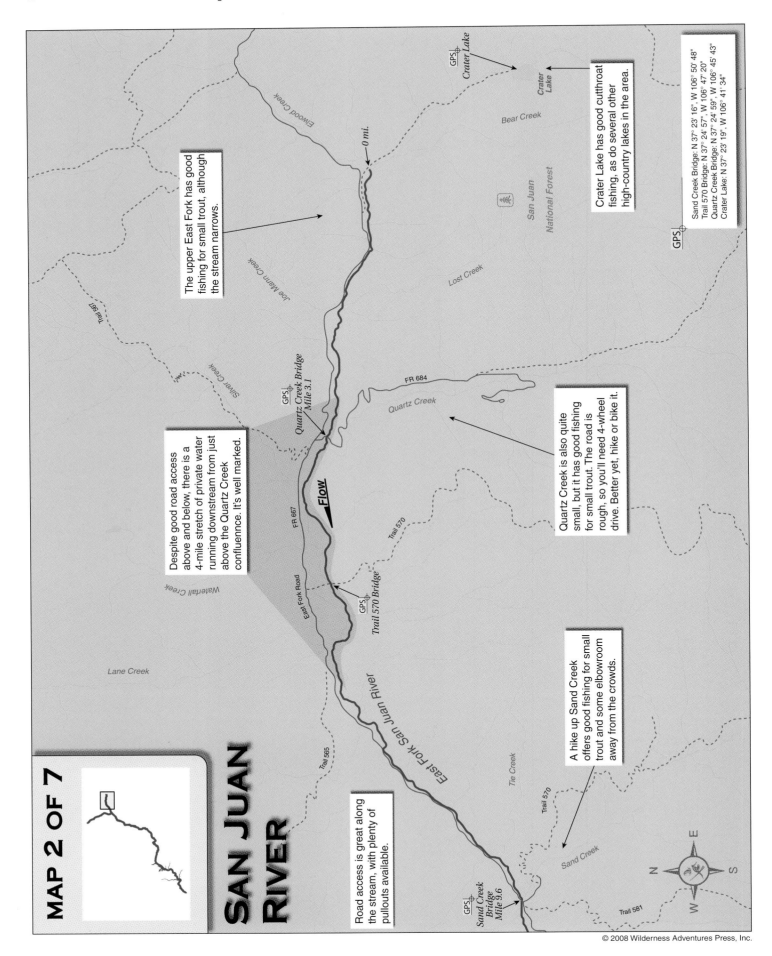

The upper East Fork has good fishing for small trout, although the stream narrows.

Crater Lake has good cutthroat fishing, as do several other high-country lakes in the area.

Sand Creek Bridge: N 37° 23' 16", W 106° 50' 48"
Trail 570 Bridge: N 37° 24' 57", W 106° 47' 20"
Quartz Creek Bridge: N 37° 24' 59", W 106° 45' 43"
Crater Lake: N 37° 23' 19", W 106° 41' 34"

Despite good road access above and below, there is a 4-mile stretch of private water running downstream from just above the Quartz Creek confluence. It's well marked.

Quartz Creek is also quite small, but it has good fishing for small trout. The road is rough, so you'll need 4-wheel drive. Better yet, hike or bike it.

A hike up Sand Creek offers good fishing for small trout and some elbowroom away from the crowds.

Road access is great along the stream, with plenty of pullouts available.

MAP 2 OF 7

SAN JUAN RIVER

© 2008 Wilderness Adventures Press, Inc.

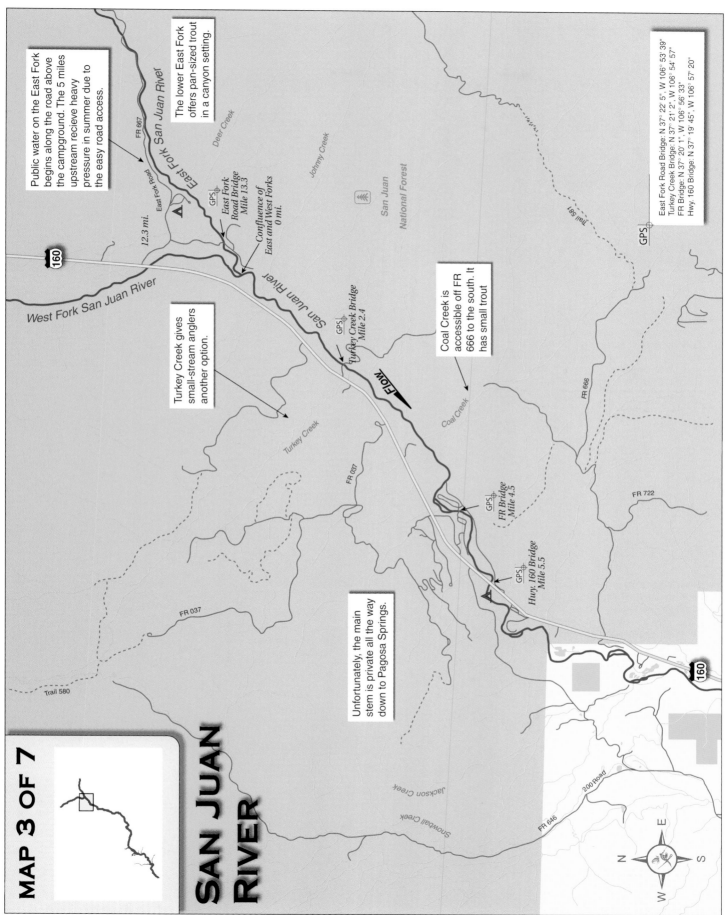

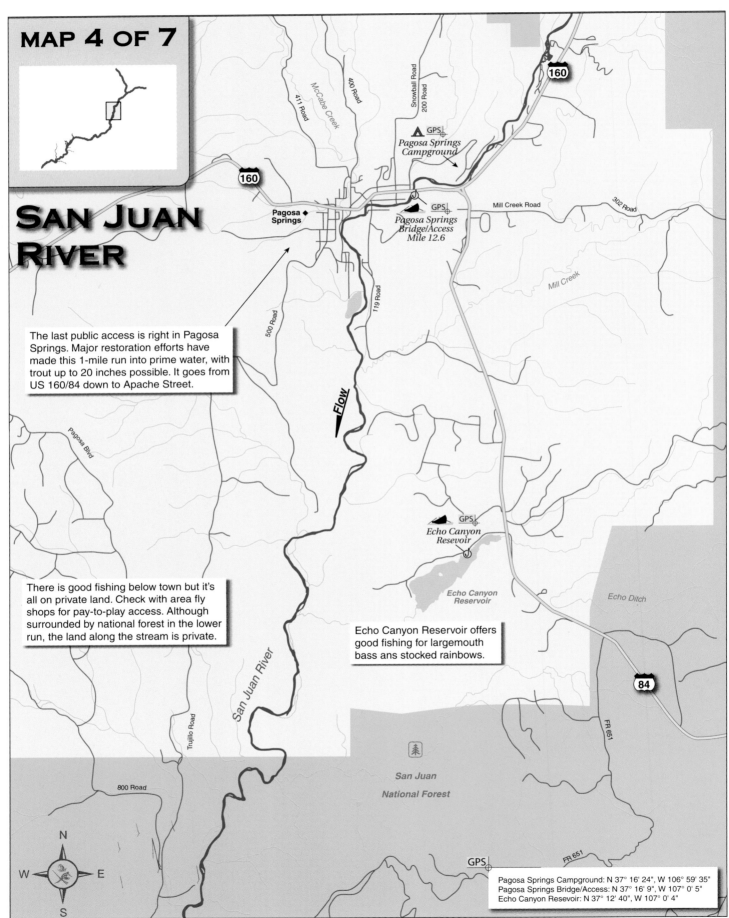

MAP 4 OF 7

SAN JUAN RIVER

The last public access is right in Pagosa Springs. Major restoration efforts have made this 1-mile run into prime water, with trout up to 20 inches possible. It goes from US 160/84 down to Apache Street.

There is good fishing below town but it's all on private land. Check with area fly shops for pay-to-play access. Although surrounded by national forest in the lower run, the land along the stream is private.

Echo Canyon Reservoir offers good fishing for largemouth bass ans stocked rainbows.

Pagosa Springs Campground: N 37° 16' 24", W 106° 59' 35"
Pagosa Springs Bridge/Access: N 37° 16' 9", W 107° 0' 5"
Echo Canyon Resevoir: N 37° 12' 40", W 107° 0' 4"

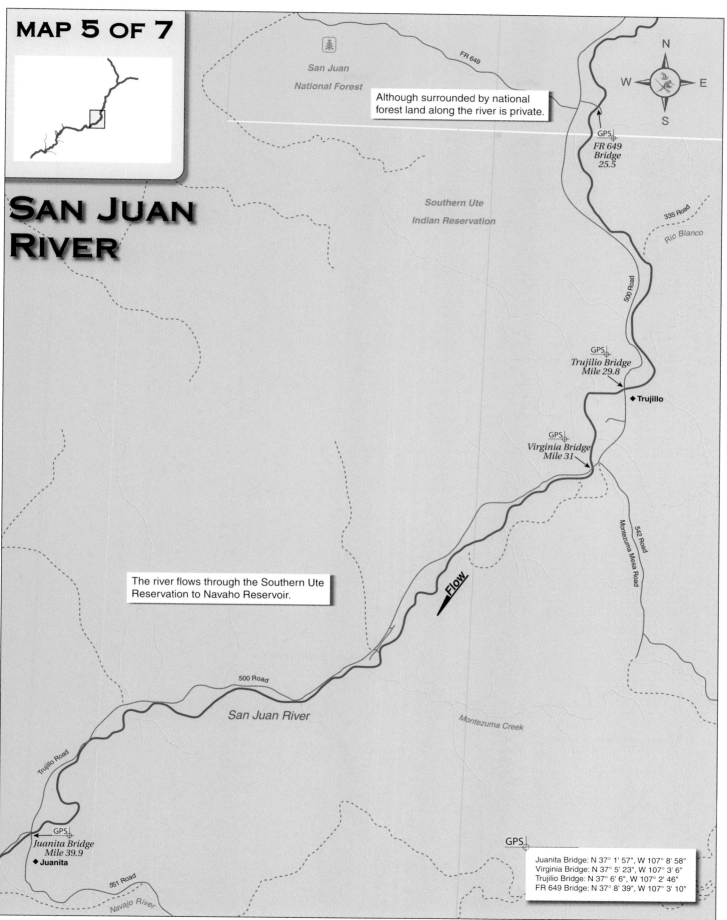

MAP 5 OF 7

SAN JUAN RIVER

FR 649

San Juan
National Forest

Although surrounded by national
forest land along the river is private.

N
W   E
S

GPS
FR 649
Bridge
25.5

335 Road

Southern Ute
Indian Reservation

Rio Blanco

500 Road

GPS
Trujilio Bridge
Mile 29.8

◆ Trujillo

GPS
Virginia Bridge
Mile 31

542 Road

Montezuma Mesa Road

Flow

The river flows through the Southern Ute
Reservation to Navaho Reservoir.

500 Road

San Juan River

Montezuma Creek

Trujillo Road

GPS
Juanita Bridge
Mile 39.9
◆ Juanita

551 Road

Navajo River

GPS

Juanita Bridge: N 37° 1' 57", W 107° 8' 58"
Virginia Bridge: N 37° 5' 23", W 107° 3' 6"
Trujilio Bridge: N 37° 6' 6", W 107° 2' 46"
FR 649 Bridge: N 37° 8' 39", W 107° 3' 10"

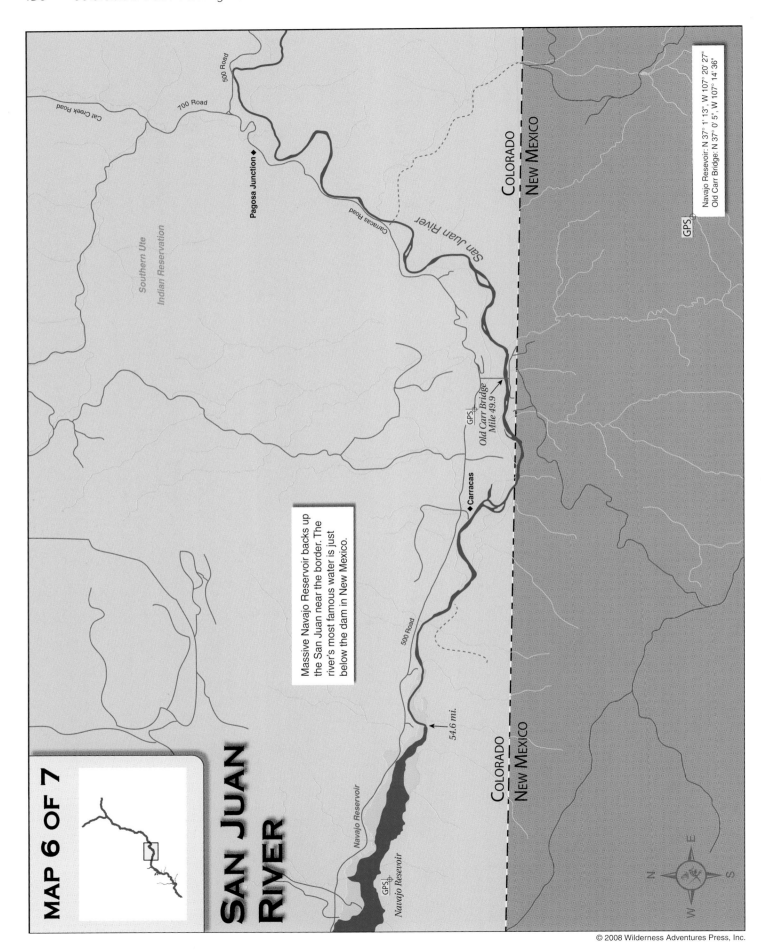

Massive Navajo Reservoir backs up the San Juan near the border. The river's most famous water is just below the dam in New Mexico.

Navajo Resevoir: N 37° 1' 13", W 107° 20' 27"
Old Carr Bridge: N 37° 0' 5', W 107° 14' 36"

MAP 6 OF 7

SAN JUAN RIVER

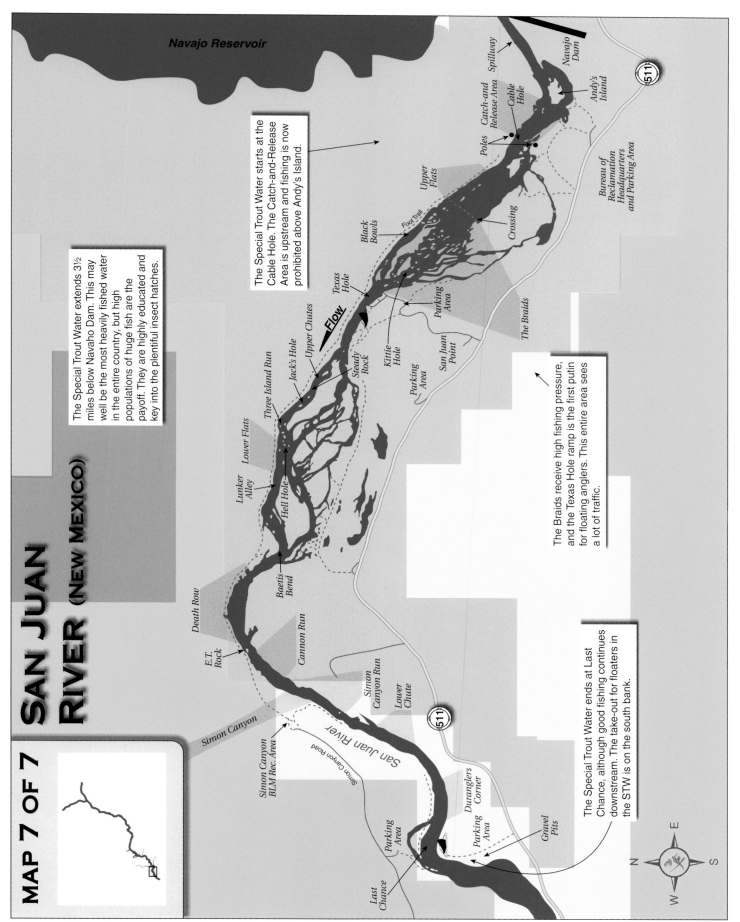

MAP 7 OF 7

SAN JUAN RIVER (NEW MEXICO)

The Special Trout Water extends 3½ miles below Navaho Dam. This may well be the most heavily fished water in the entire country, but high populations of huge fish are the payoff. They are highly educated and key into the plentiful insect hatches.

The Special Trout Water starts at the Cable Hole. The Catch-and-Release Area is upstream and fishing is now prohibited above Andy's Island.

The Braids receive high fishing pressure, and the Texas Hole ramp is the first putin for floating anglers. This entire area sees a lot of traffic.

The Special Trout Water ends at Last Chance, although good fishing continues downstream. The take-out for floaters in the STW is on the south bank.

Navajo Reservoir

Navajo Dam

Spillway

Andy's Island

Catch-and-Release Area

Cable Hole

Poles

Bureau of Reclamation Headquarters and Parking Area

Upper Flats

Crossing

Black Bowls

Foot Trail

The Braids

Texas Hole

Flow

Parking Area

Kittie Hole

San Juan Point

Parking Area

Upper Chutes

Jack's Hole

Three Island Run

Steady Rock

Lower Flats

Lunker Alley

Hell Hole

Baetis Bend

Death Row

E.T. Rock

Cannon Run

Simon Canyon Run

Lower Chute

Simon Canyon

Simon Canyon BLM Rec. Area

Simon Canyon Road

San Juan River

Duranglers Corner

Parking Area

Gravel Pits

Parking Area

Last Chance

N E S W

OVERVIEW

SAN MIGUEL RIVER

The San Miguel begins where Bridal Veil and Ingram Creeks join just outside Telluride and flows over 70 miles northwest to meet the Dolores River. It's a fast little stream, with good fishing for medium-sized rainbow, brown, and cutthroat trout in the plentiful pocket water. The river is still rebounding from mining pollution, but it's a fun river to fish and it continues to improve. There is also a wealth of good fishing in the high-country lakes and tiny feeder streams in the surrounding national forest.

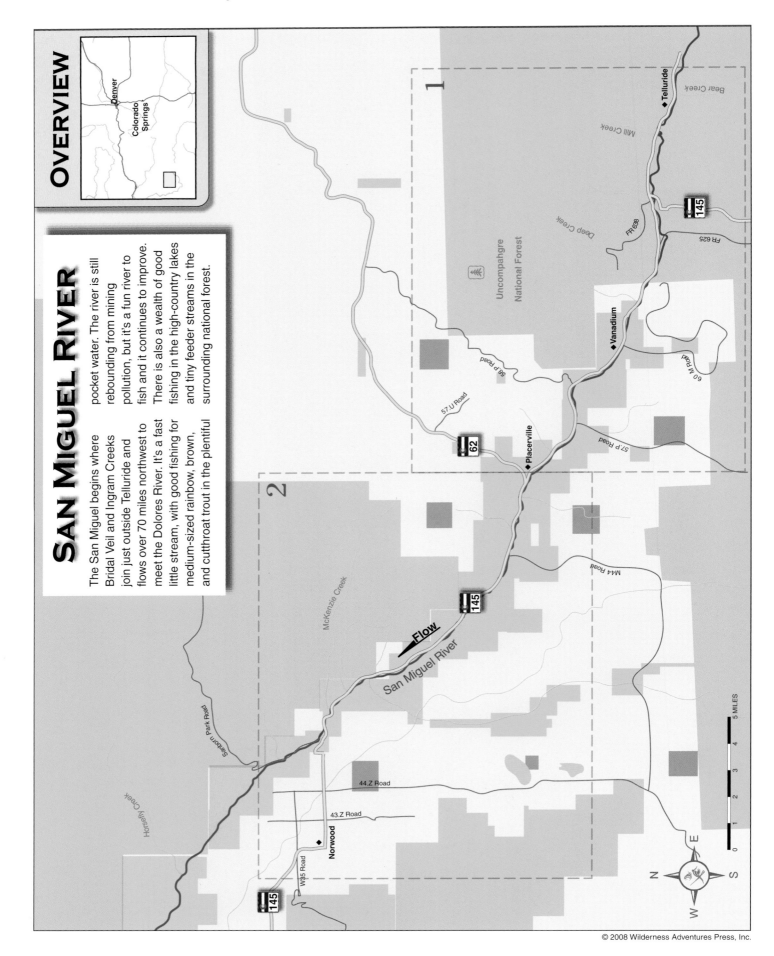

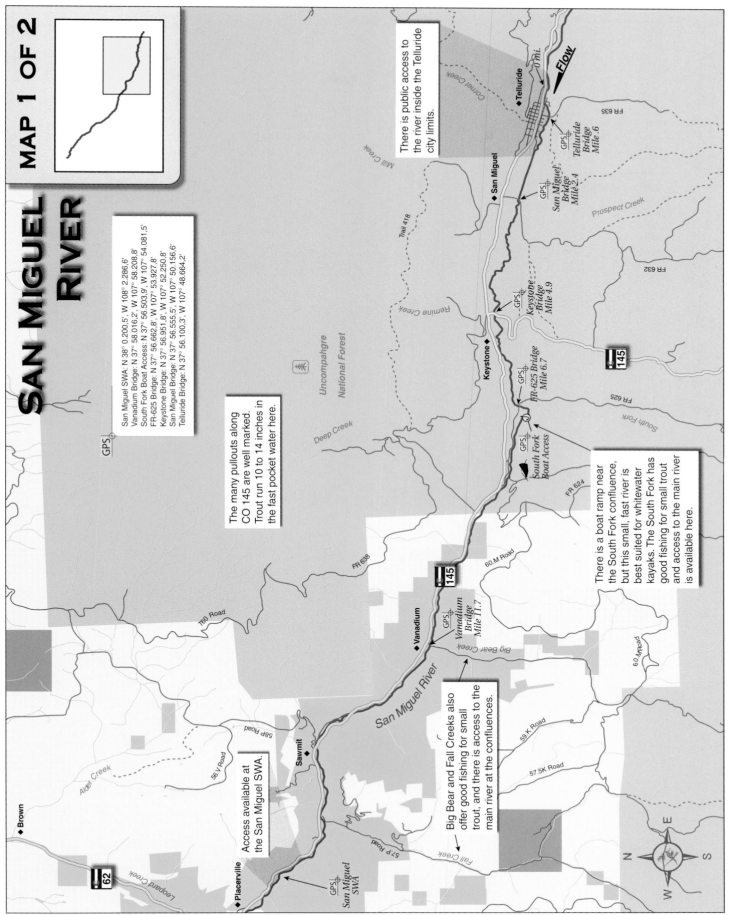

MAP 1 OF 2

SAN MIGUEL RIVER

San Miguel SWA: N 38° 0.200,5', W 108° 2.286,6'
Vanadium Bridge: N 37° 58.016,2', W 107° 58.208,8'
South Fork Boat Access: N 37° 56.503,9', W 107° 54.081,5'
FR-625 Bridge: N 37° 56.662,8', W 107° 53.927,8'
Keystone Bridge: N 37° 56.951,8', W 107° 52.250,8'
San Miguel Bridge: N 37° 56.555,5', W 107° 50.156,6'
Telluride Bridge: N 37° 56.100,3', W 107° 48.664,2'

There is public access to the river inside the Telluride city limits.

The many pullouts along CO 145 are well marked. Trout run 10 to 14 inches in the fast pocket water here.

There is a boat ramp near the South Fork confluence, but this small, fast river is best suited for whitewater kayaks. The South Fork has good fishing for small trout and access to the main river is available here.

Big Bear and Fall Creeks also offer good fishing for small trout, and there is access to the main river at the confluences.

Access available at the San Miguel SWA.

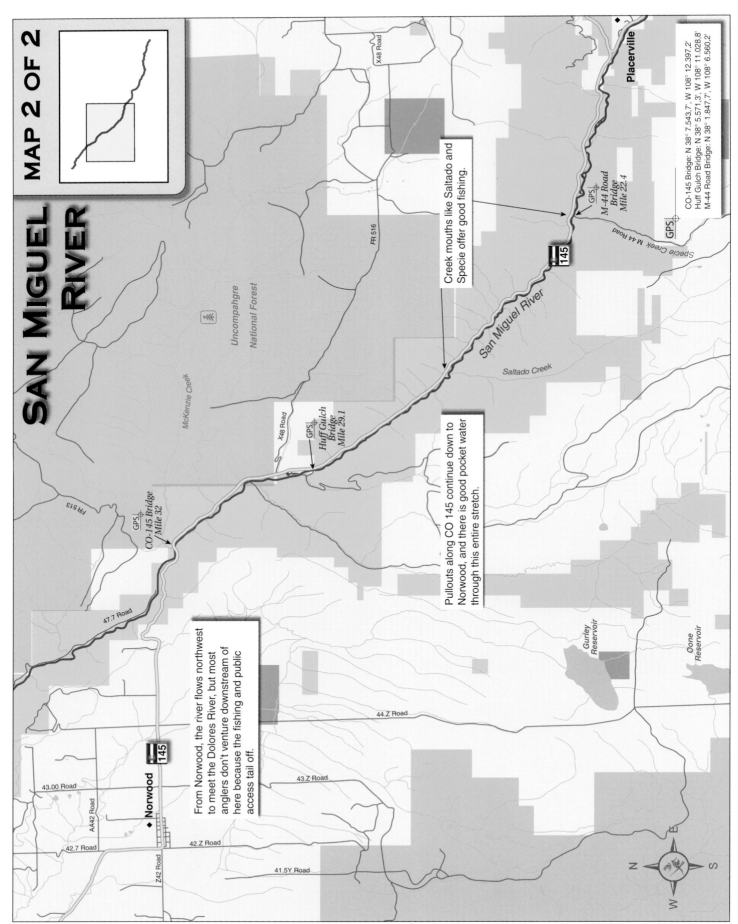

SAN MIGUEL RIVER

MAP 2 OF 2

CO-145 Bridge: N 38° 7.543.7', W 108° 12.397.2'
Huff Gulch Bridge: N 38° 5.571.3', W 108° 11.028.8'
M-44 Road Bridge: N 38° 1.847.7', W 108° 6.560.2'

Placerville

GPS
M-44 Road Bridge
Mile 22.4

Specie Creek M 44 Road

GPS

San Miguel River

Saltado Creek

Creek mouths like Saltado and Specie offer good fishing.

X48 Road

FR 516

Uncompahgre National Forest

McKenzie Creek

X48 Road

GPS
Huff Gulch Bridge
Mile 29.1

GPS
CO-145 Bridge
Mile 32

FR 513

Pullouts along CO 145 continue down to Norwood, and there is good pocket water through this entire stretch.

47.7 Road

Gurley Reservoir

Oone Reservoir

From Norwood, the river flows northwest to meet the Dolores River, but most anglers don't venture downstream of here because the fishing and public access tail off.

Norwood

145

43.00 Road

AA42 Road

42.7 Road

Z42 Road

42.Z Road

43.Z Road

44.Z Road

41.5Y Road

N
E
W
S

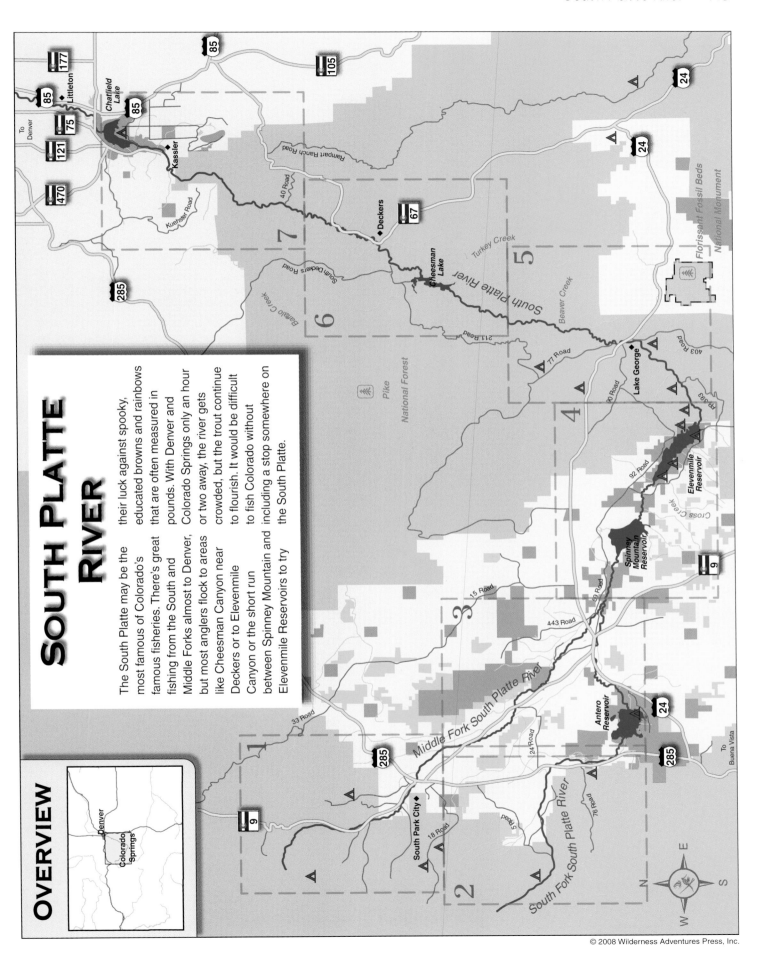

SOUTH PLATTE RIVER

The South Platte may be the most famous of Colorado's famous fisheries. There's great fishing from the South and Middle Forks almost to Denver, but most anglers flock to areas like Cheesman Canyon near Deckers or to Elevenmile Canyon or the short run between Spinney Mountain and Elevenmile Reservoirs to try their luck against spooky, educated browns and rainbows that are often measured in pounds. With Denver and Colorado Springs only an hour or two away, the river gets crowded, but the trout continue to flourish. It would be difficult to fish Colorado without including a stop somewhere on the South Platte.

OVERVIEW

MAP 1 OF 7

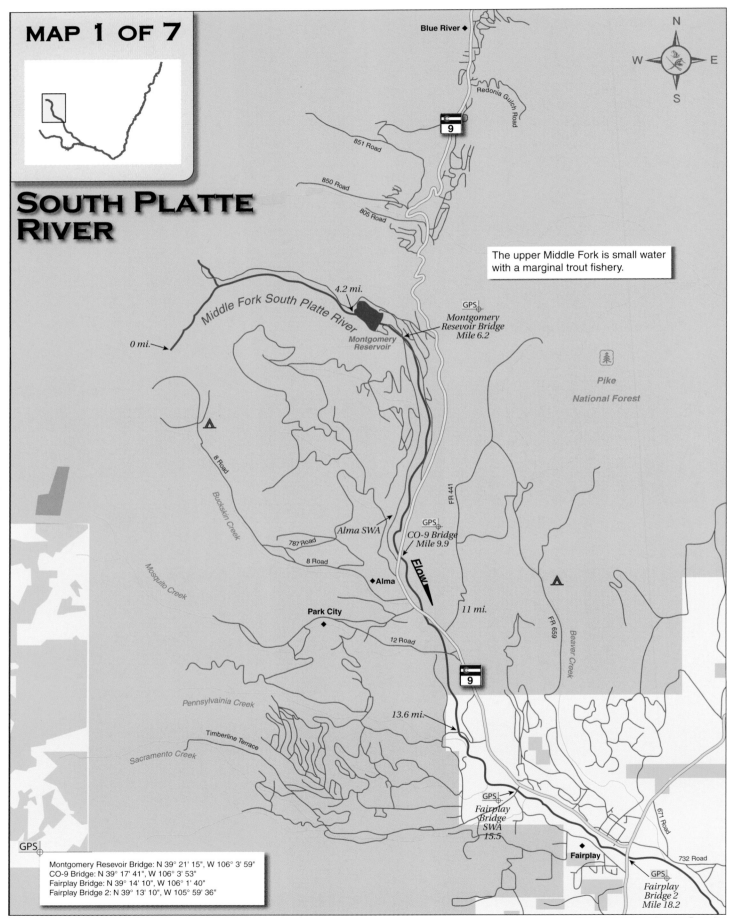

SOUTH PLATTE RIVER

Blue River ◆

9

851 Road

850 Road

805 Road

Redonia Gulch Road

N
W E
S

The upper Middle Fork is small water with a marginal trout fishery.

Middle Fork South Platte River

4.2 mi.

0 mi.

GPS
Montgomery Resevoir Bridge Mile 6.2

Montgomery Reservoir

Pike
National Forest

8 Road

Buckskin Creek

787 Road

8 Road

Alma SWA

GPS
CO-9 Bridge Mile 9.9

FR 441

Flow

◆ Alma

11 mi.

FR 659

Beaver Creek

Mosquito Creek

Park City

12 Road

Pennsylvainia Creek

Timberline Terrace

Sacramento Creek

9

13.6 mi.

GPS
Fairplay Bridge SWA 15.5

671 Road

◆ Fairplay

732 Road

GPS
Fairplay Bridge 2 Mile 18.2

Montgomery Resevoir Bridge: N 39° 21' 15", W 106° 3' 59"
CO-9 Bridge: N 39° 17' 41", W 106° 3' 53"
Fairplay Bridge: N 39° 14' 10", W 106° 1' 40"
Fairplay Bridge 2: N 39° 13' 10", W 105° 59' 36"

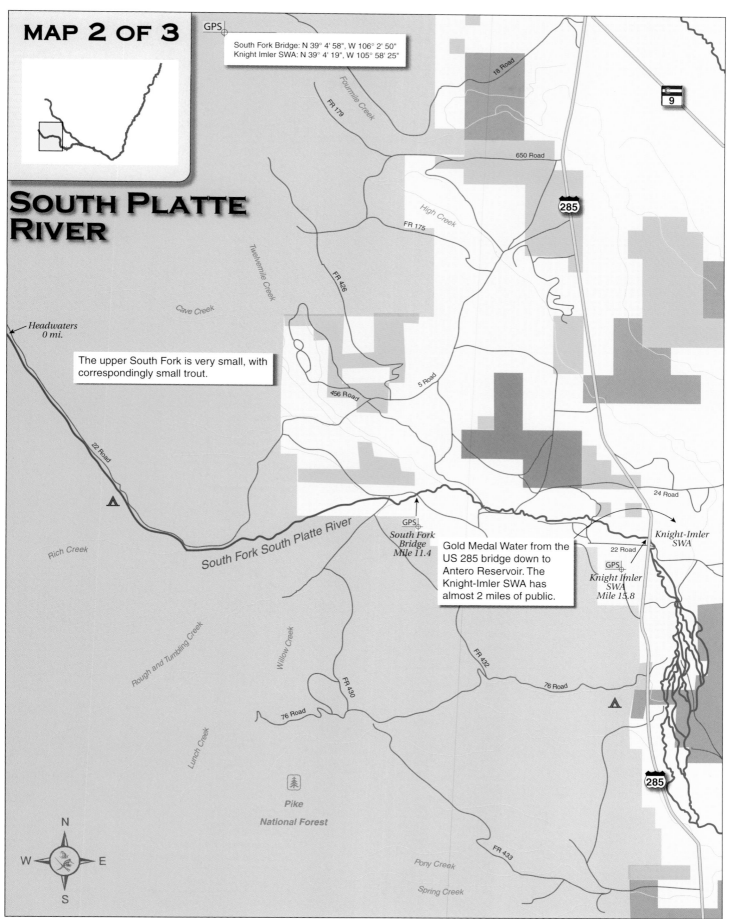

MAP 2 OF 3

SOUTH PLATTE RIVER

South Fork Bridge: N 39° 4' 58", W 106° 2' 50"
Knight Imler SWA: N 39° 4' 19", W 105° 58' 25"

The upper South Fork is very small, with correspondingly small trout.

Headwaters 0 mi.

Gold Medal Water from the US 285 bridge down to Antero Reservoir. The Knight-Imler SWA has almost 2 miles of public.

GPS
South Fork Bridge
Mile 11.4

Knight-Imler SWA

GPS
Knight Imler SWA
Mile 15.8

South Fork South Platte River

Pike National Forest

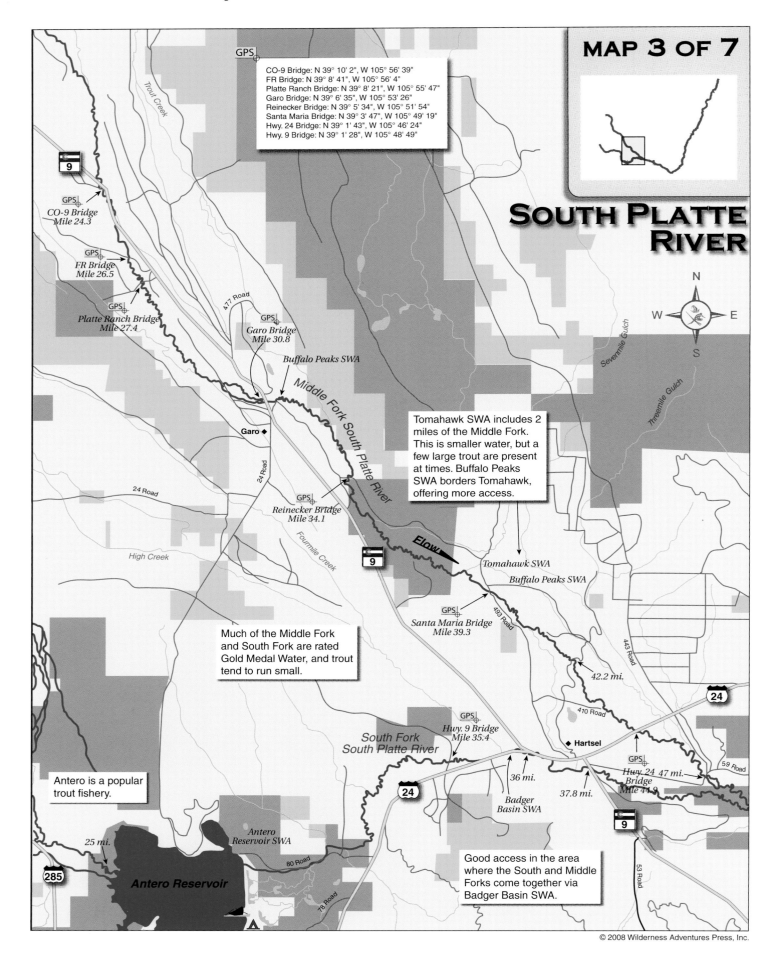

MAP 3 OF 7

SOUTH PLATTE RIVER

CO-9 Bridge: N 39° 10' 2", W 105° 56' 39"
FR Bridge: N 39° 8' 41", W 105° 56' 4"
Platte Ranch Bridge: N 39° 8' 21", W 105° 55' 47"
Garo Bridge: N 39° 6' 35", W 105° 53' 26"
Reinecker Bridge: N 39° 5' 34", W 105° 51' 54"
Santa Maria Bridge: N 39° 3' 47", W 105° 49' 19"
Hwy. 24 Bridge: N 39° 1' 43", W 105° 46' 24"
Hwy. 9 Bridge: N 39° 1' 28", W 105° 48' 49"

CO-9 Bridge
Mile 24.3

FR Bridge
Mile 26.5

Platte Ranch Bridge
Mile 27.4

Garo Bridge
Mile 30.8

Buffalo Peaks SWA

Middle Fork South Platte River

Garo ◆

Tomahawk SWA includes 2 miles of the Middle Fork. This is smaller water, but a few large trout are present at times. Buffalo Peaks SWA borders Tomahawk, offering more access.

Reinecker Bridge
Mile 34.1

Flow

Tomahawk SWA
Buffalo Peaks SWA

High Creek

Fourmile Creek

Santa Maria Bridge
Mile 39.3

Much of the Middle Fork and South Fork are rated Gold Medal Water, and trout tend to run small.

42.2 mi.

24 Road

Hwy. 9 Bridge
Mile 35.4

South Fork
South Platte River

◆ Hartsel

Hwy. 24 47 mi.
Bridge
Mile 44.9

Antero is a popular trout fishery.

36 mi.

37.8 mi.

Badger
Basin SWA

Good access in the area where the South and Middle Forks come together via Badger Basin SWA.

25 mi.

Antero
Reservoir SWA

Antero Reservoir

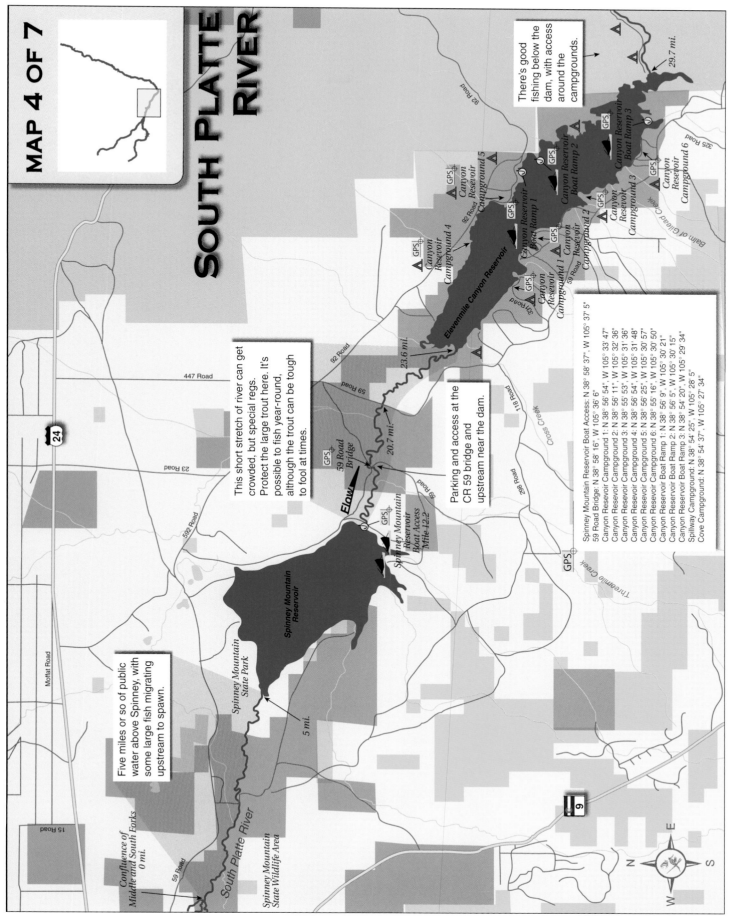

MAP 4 OF 7

SOUTH PLATTE RIVER

There's good fishing below the dam, with access around the campgrounds.

29.7 mi.

92 Road

325 Road

Balm of Gilead Creek

Canyon Reservoir Campground 5

Canyon Reservoir Campground 4

Canyon Reservoir Boat Ramp 2

Canyon Reservoir Boat Ramp 3

Canyon Reservoir Campground 6

Canyon Reservoir Boat Ramp 1

Canyon Reservoir Campground 3

Canyon Reservoir Campground 2

Canyon Reservoir Campground 1

Elevenmile Canyon Reservoir

59 Road

92 Road

23.6 mi.

This short stretch of river can get crowded, but special regs. Protect the large trout here. It's possible to fish year-round, although the trout can be tough to fool at times.

447 Road

92 Road

59 Road

20.7 mi.

59 Road Bridge

118 Road

Cross Creek

298 Road

69 Road

Parking and access at the CR 59 bridge and upstream near the dam.

23 Road

Flow

Spinney Mountain Reservoir Boat Access Mile 12.2

Threemile Creek

Spinney Mountain Reservoir Boat Access: N 38° 58' 37", W 105° 37' 5"
59 Road Bridge: N 38° 58' 16", W 105° 36' 6"
Canyon Reservoir Campground 1: N 38° 56' 54", W 105° 33' 47"
Canyon Reservoir Campground 2: N 38° 56' 11", W 105° 32' 36"
Canyon Reservoir Campground 3: N 38° 55' 53", W 105° 31' 36"
Canyon Reservoir Campground 4: N 38° 56' 54", W 105° 31' 48"
Canyon Reservoir Campground 5: N 38° 56' 25", W 105° 30' 57"
Canyon Reservoir Campground 6: N 38° 55' 16", W 105° 30' 50"
Canyon Reservoir Boat Ramp 1: N 38° 56' 9", W 105° 30' 21"
Canyon Reservoir Boat Ramp 2: N 38° 56' 5", W 105° 30' 15"
Canyon Reservoir Boat Ramp 3: N 38° 54' 20", W 105° 29' 34"
Spillway Campground: N 38° 54' 25", W 105° 28' 5"
Cove Campground: N 38° 54' 37", W 105° 27' 34"

592 Road

Moffat Road

24

Five miles or so of public water above Spinney, with some large fish migrating upstream to spawn.

Spinney Mountain Reservoir

Spinney Mountain State Park

5 mi.

Spinney Mountain State Wildlife Area

15 Road

59 Road

Confluence of Middle and South Forks 0 mi.

South Platte River

9

N
E
W
S

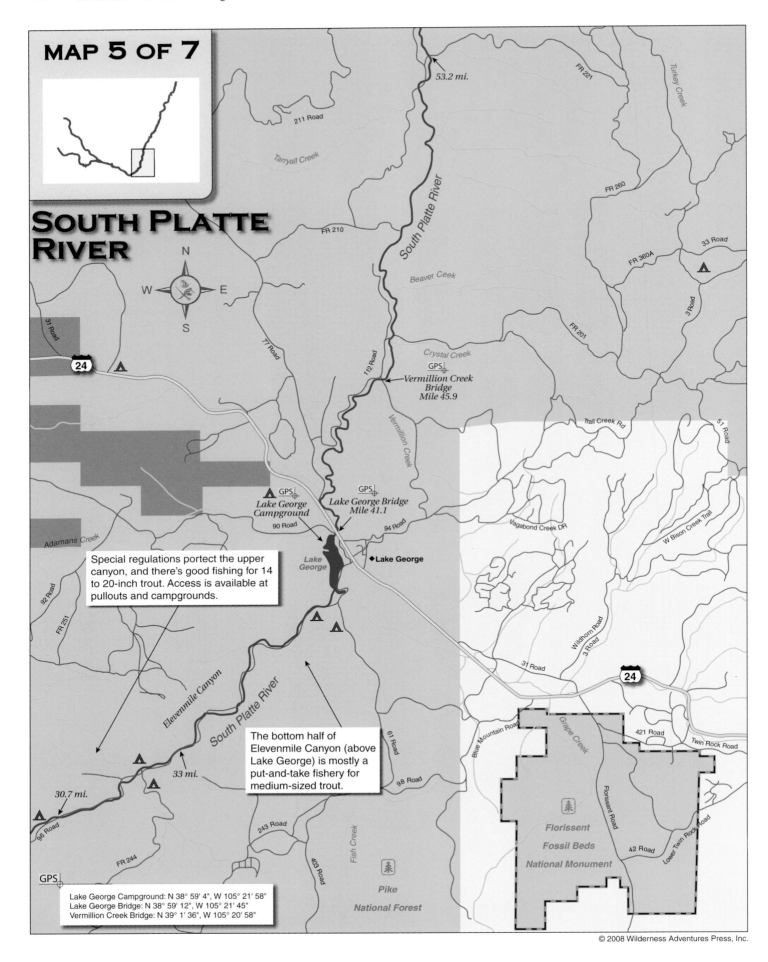

MAP 5 OF 7

SOUTH PLATTE RIVER

53.2 mi.

Turkey Creek

FR 221

211 Road

FR 260

Tarryall Creek

33 Road

FR 210

FR 360A

South Platte River

Beaver Ceek

31 Road

FR 201

3 Road

77 Road

Crystal Creek

1 1/2 Road

GPS
Vermillion Creek Bridge
Mile 45.9

Trail Creek Rd

51 Road

Vermillion Creek

GPS
Lake George Campground

GPS
Lake George Bridge Mile 41.1

90 Road

94 Road

Vagabond Creek DR

W Bison Creek Trail

Adamans Creek

Special regulations portect the upper canyon, and there's good fishing for 14 to 20-inch trout. Access is available at pullouts and campgrounds.

Lake George

◆ **Lake George**

92 Road

FR 251

Wildhorn Road

3 Road

31 Road

Elevenmile Canyon

South Platte River

The bottom half of Elevenmile Canyon (above Lake George) is mostly a put-and-take fishery for medium-sized trout.

61 Road

Blue Mountain Road

Grape Creek

421 Road

Twin Rock Road

33 mi.

9.8 Road

Florissant Road

30.7 mi.

243 Road

403 Road

42 Road

Lower Twin Rock Road

96 Road

FR 244

Fish Creek

Florissant

Fossil Beds

National Monument

GPS

Lake George Campground: N 38° 59' 4", W 105° 21' 58"
Lake George Bridge: N 38° 59' 12", W 105° 21' 45"
Vermillion Creek Bridge: N 39° 1' 36", W 105° 20' 58"

Pike

National Forest

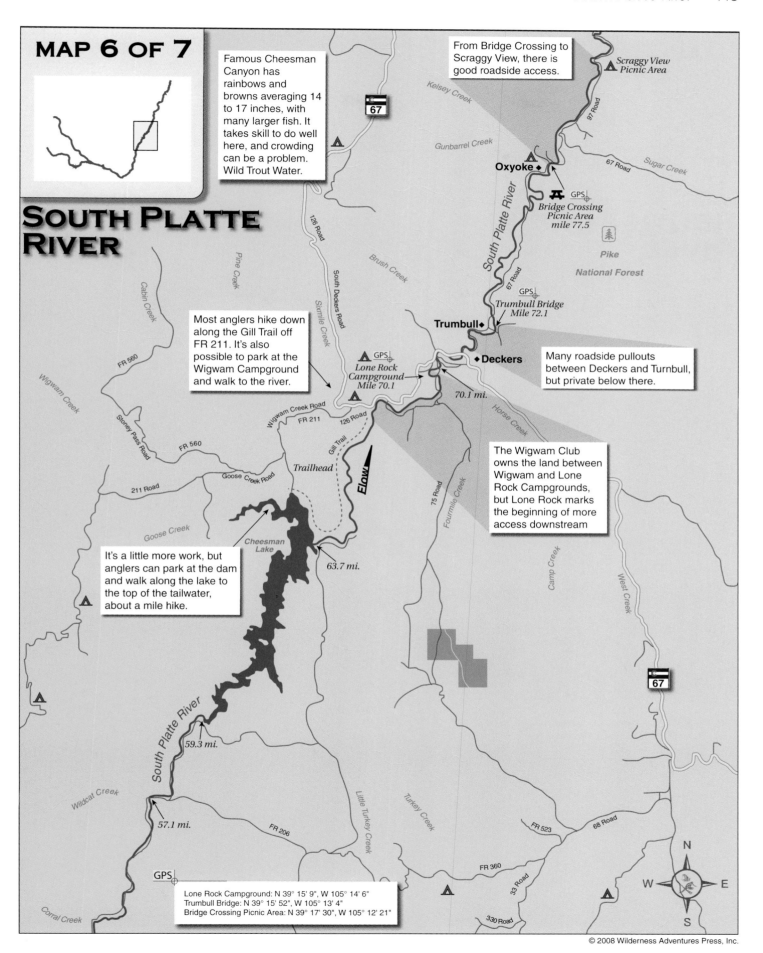

MAP 6 OF 7

SOUTH PLATTE RIVER

Famous Cheesman Canyon has rainbows and browns averaging 14 to 17 inches, with many larger fish. It takes skill to do well here, and crowding can be a problem. Wild Trout Water.

From Bridge Crossing to Scraggy View, there is good roadside access.

Most anglers hike down along the Gill Trail off FR 211. It's also possible to park at the Wigwam Campground and walk to the river.

Many roadside pullouts between Deckers and Turnbull, but private below there.

The Wigwam Club owns the land between Wigwam and Lone Rock Campgrounds, but Lone Rock marks the beginning of more access downstream

It's a little more work, but anglers can park at the dam and walk along the lake to the top of the tailwater, about a mile hike.

Scraggy View Picnic Area

Oxyoke

Bridge Crossing Picnic Area mile 77.5

Pike National Forest

Trumbull Bridge Mile 72.1

Trumbull

Deckers

Lone Rock Campground Mile 70.1

70.1 mi.

Cheesman Lake

63.7 mi.

South Platte River

59.3 mi.

57.1 mi.

GPS

Lone Rock Campground: N 39° 15' 9", W 105° 14' 6"
Trumbull Bridge: N 39° 15' 52", W 105° 13' 4"
Bridge Crossing Picnic Area: N 39° 17' 30", W 105° 12' 21"

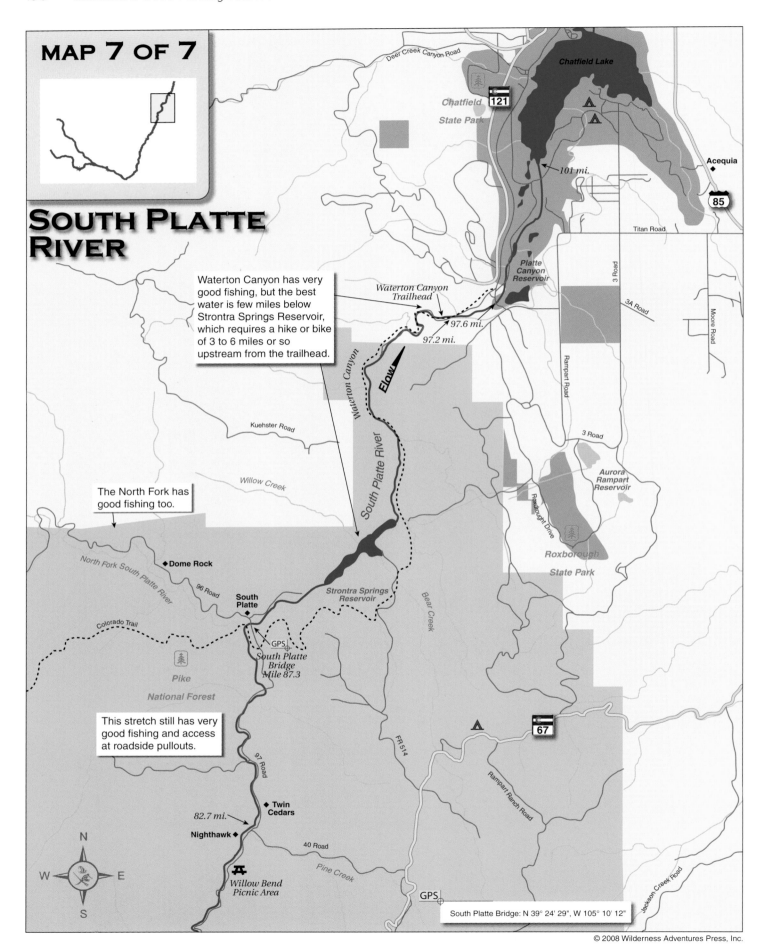

MAP 7 OF 7

SOUTH PLATTE RIVER

Deer Creek Canyon Road

Chatfield Lake

Chatfield State Park

121

Acequia

101 mi.

85

Titan Road

Platte Canyon Reservoir

3 Road

3A Road

Moore Road

Waterton Canyon has very good fishing, but the best water is few miles below Strontra Springs Reservoir, which requires a hike or bike of 3 to 6 miles or so upstream from the trailhead.

Waterton Canyon Trailhead

97.6 mi.

97.2 mi.

Flow

Rampart Road

Kuehster Road

Waterton Canyon

South Platte River

Willow Creek

3 Road

Aurora Rampart Reservoir

Roxborough Drive

The North Fork has good fishing too.

North Fork South Platte River

Dome Rock

96 Road

Roxborough State Park

Strontra Springs Reservoir

Bear Creek

South Platte

Colorado Trail

GPS

South Platte Bridge Mile 87.3

Pike National Forest

67

This stretch still has very good fishing and access at roadside pullouts.

97 Road

FR 514

Rampart Ranch Road

82.7 mi.

Twin Cedars

Nighthawk

40 Road

Pine Creek

Jackson Creek Road

N W E S

Willow Bend Picnic Area

GPS

South Platte Bridge: N 39° 24' 29", W 105° 10' 12"

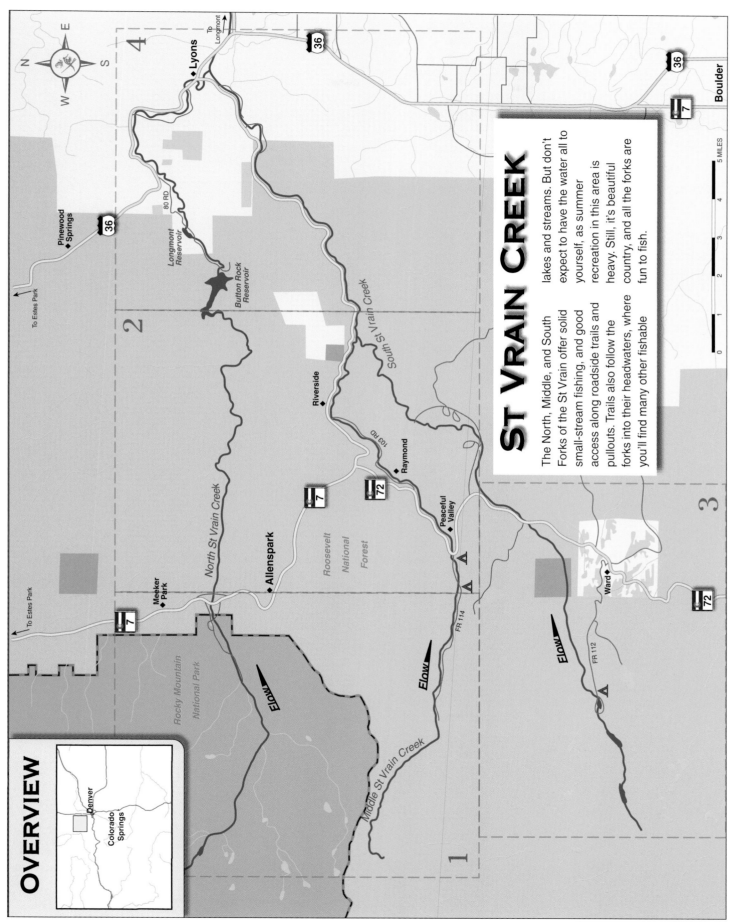

OVERVIEW

ST VRAIN CREEK

The North, Middle, and South Forks of the St Vrain offer solid small-stream fishing, and good access along roadside trails and pullouts. Trails also follow the forks into their headwaters, where you'll find many other fishable lakes and streams. But don't expect to have the water all to yourself, as summer recreation in this area is heavy. Still, it's beautiful country, and all the forks are fun to fish.

MAP 1 OF 4

ST VRAIN CREEK

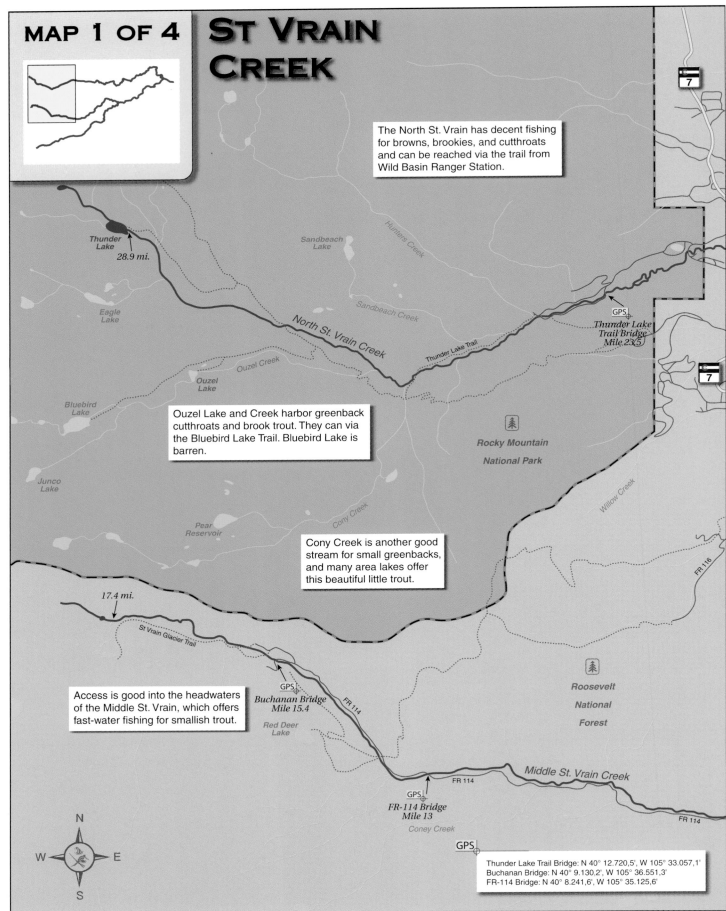

The North St. Vrain has decent fishing for browns, brookies, and cutthroats and can be reached via the trail from Wild Basin Ranger Station.

Ouzel Lake and Creek harbor greenback cutthroats and brook trout. They can via the Bluebird Lake Trail. Bluebird Lake is barren.

Cony Creek is another good stream for small greenbacks, and many area lakes offer this beautiful little trout.

Access is good into the headwaters of the Middle St. Vrain, which offers fast-water fishing for smallish trout.

Thunder Lake
28.9 mi.

Sandbeach Lake

Hunters Creek

Sandbeach Creek

North St. Vrain Creek

Eagle Lake

Ouzel Creek

Ouzel Lake

Thunder Lake Trail

GPS
Thunder Lake Trail Bridge
Mile 23.5

Bluebird Lake

Rocky Mountain National Park

Junco Lake

Willow Creek

Cony Creek

Pear Reservoir

FR 116

17.4 mi.

St Vrain Glacier Trail

GPS
Buchanan Bridge
Mile 15.4

FR 114

Red Deer Lake

Roosevelt National Forest

Middle St. Vrain Creek

GPS
FR-114 Bridge
Mile 13

FR 114

FR 114

Coney Creek

GPS

Thunder Lake Trail Bridge: N 40° 12.720,5', W 105° 33.057,1'
Buchanan Bridge: N 40° 9.130,2', W 105° 36.551,3'
FR-114 Bridge: N 40° 8.241,6', W 105° 35.125,6'

N W E S

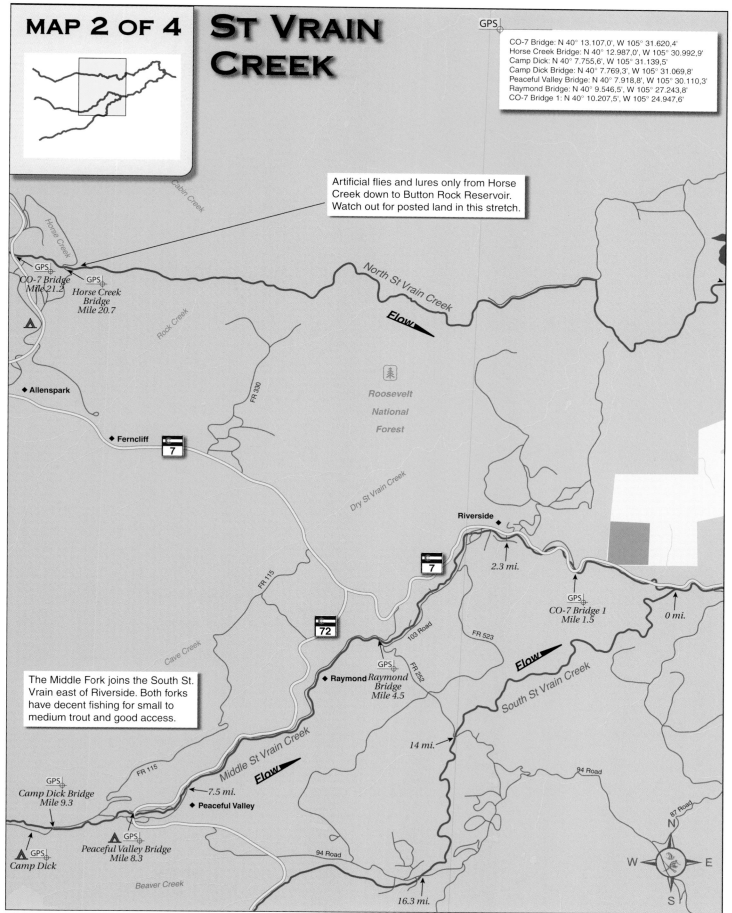

MAP 2 OF 4

ST VRAIN CREEK

CO-7 Bridge: N 40° 13.107.0', W 105° 31.620,4'
Horse Creek Bridge: N 40° 12.987,0', W 105° 30.992,9'
Camp Dick: N 40° 7.755,6', W 105° 31.139,5'
Camp Dick Bridge: N 40° 7.769,3', W 105° 31.069,8'
Peaceful Valley Bridge: N 40° 7.918,8', W 105° 30.110,3'
Raymond Bridge: N 40° 9.546,5', W 105° 27.243,8'
CO-7 Bridge 1: N 40° 10.207,5', W 105° 24.947,6'

Artificial flies and lures only from Horse Creek down to Button Rock Reservoir. Watch out for posted land in this stretch.

North St Vrain Creek

Flow

Cabin Creek

Horse Creek

CO-7 Bridge Mile 21.2

GPS

Horse Creek Bridge Mile 20.7

Rock Creek

Roosevelt National Forest

◆ Allenspark

FR 330

◆ Ferncliff

7

Dry St Vrain Creek

Riverside

2.3 mi.

GPS
CO-7 Bridge 1 Mile 1.5

0 mi.

FR 115

72

103 Road

FR 523

Flow

Cave Creek

GPS

◆ Raymond Raymond Bridge Mile 4.5

FR 252

South St Vrain Creek

The Middle Fork joins the South St. Vrain east of Riverside. Both forks have decent fishing for small to medium trout and good access.

14 mi.

94 Road

Middle St Vrain Creek

Flow

FR 115

87 Road

GPS
Camp Dick Bridge Mile 9.3

7.5 mi.

◆ Peaceful Valley

N

GPS

94 Road

GPS
Peaceful Valley Bridge Mile 8.3

W   E

GPS
Camp Dick

Beaver Creek

16.3 mi.

S

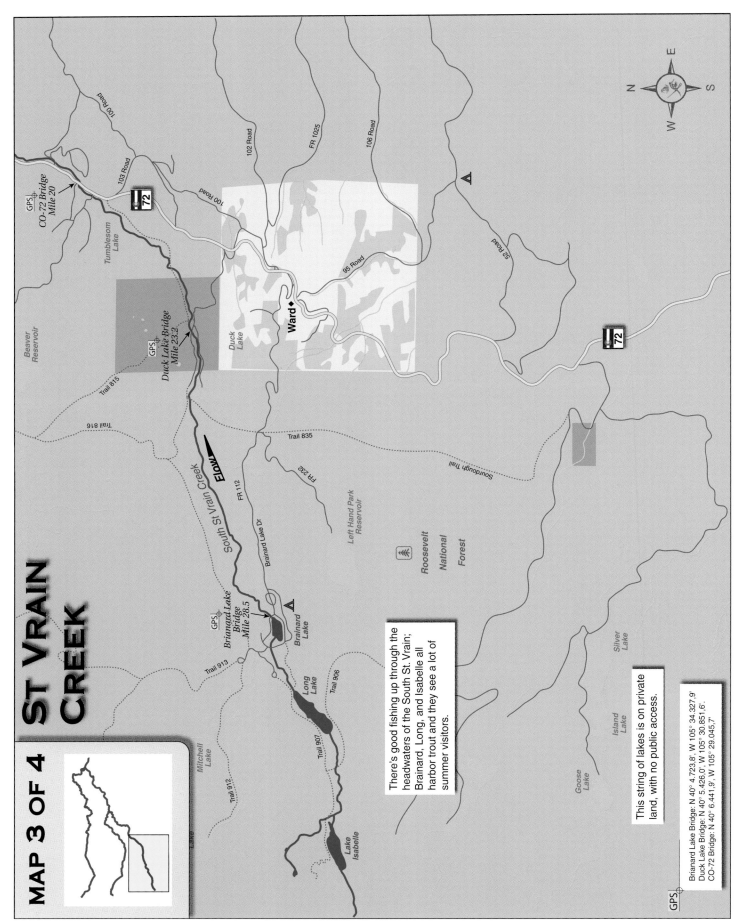

MAP 3 OF 4

St Vrain Creek

There's good fishing up through the headwaters of the South St. Vrain; Brainard, Long, and Isabelle all harbor trout and they see a lot of summer visitors.

This string of lakes is on private land, with no public access.

GPS
Brianard Lake Bridge: N 40° 4.723,8', W 105° 34.327,9'
Duck Lake Bridge: N 40° 5.426,0', W 105° 30.851,6'.
CO-72 Bridge: N 40° 6.441,9', W 105° 29.045,7'

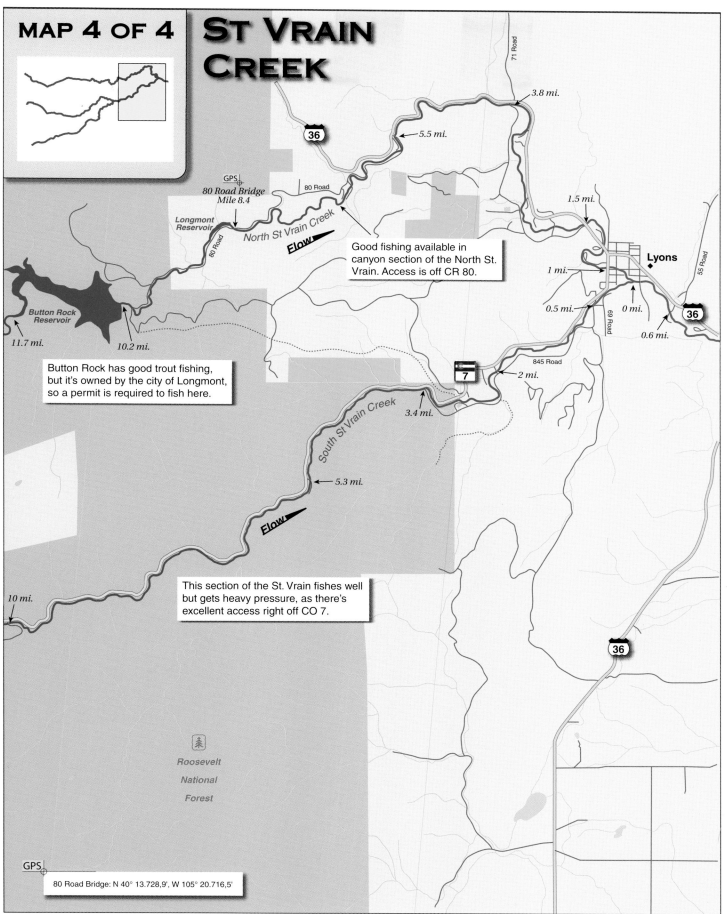

MAP 4 OF 4 ST VRAIN CREEK

3.8 mi.

5.5 mi.

71 Road

36

GPS

80 Road Bridge Mile 8.4

80 Road

1.5 mi.

Longmont Reservoir

80 Road

North St Vrain Creek

Flow

Good fishing available in canyon section of the North St. Vrain. Access is off CR 80.

Lyons

1 mi.

55 Road

Button Rock Reservoir

0.5 mi.

69 Road

0 mi.

36

11.7 mi.

10.2 mi.

0.6 mi.

Button Rock has good trout fishing, but it's owned by the city of Longmont, so a permit is required to fish here.

845 Road

7

2 mi.

3.4 mi.

South St Vrain Creek

5.3 mi.

Flow

10 mi.

This section of the St. Vrain fishes well but gets heavy pressure, as there's excellent access right off CO 7.

36

Roosevelt

National

Forest

GPS

80 Road Bridge: N 40° 13.728,9', W 105° 20.716,5'

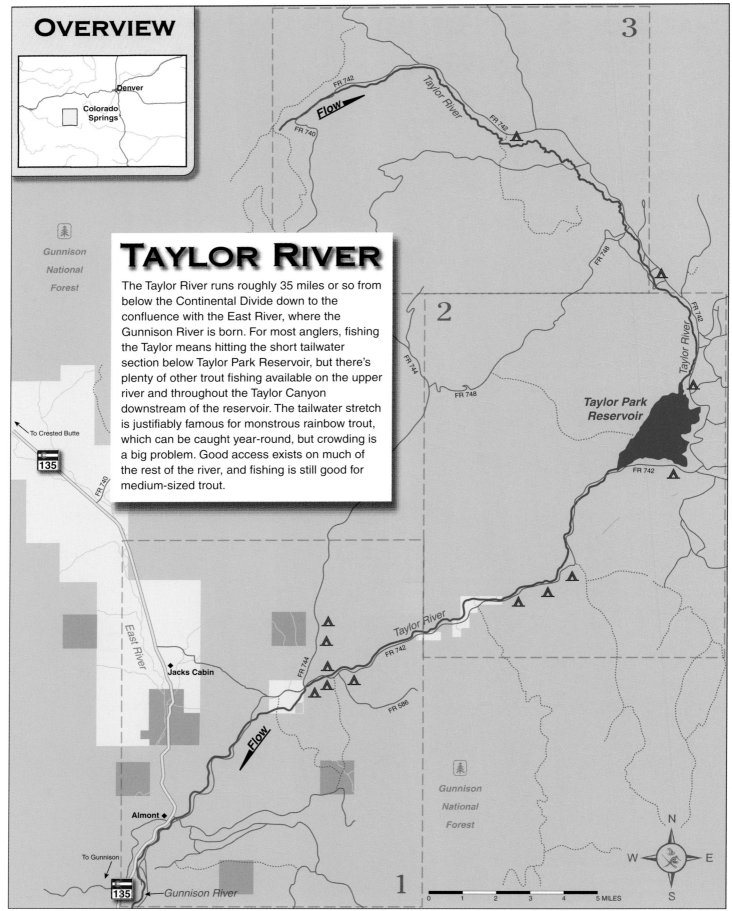

OVERVIEW

Denver

Colorado Springs

Gunnison National Forest

To Crested Butte

135

FR 740

TAYLOR RIVER

The Taylor River runs roughly 35 miles or so from below the Continental Divide down to the confluence with the East River, where the Gunnison River is born. For most anglers, fishing the Taylor means hitting the short tailwater section below Taylor Park Reservoir, but there's plenty of other trout fishing available on the upper river and throughout the Taylor Canyon downstream of the reservoir. The tailwater stretch is justifiably famous for monstrous rainbow trout, which can be caught year-round, but crowding is a big problem. Good access exists on much of the rest of the river, and fishing is still good for medium-sized trout.

3

Flow

FR 742

FR 740

Taylor River

FR 742

2

FR 748

FR 744

FR 748

Taylor River

FR 742

Taylor Park Reservoir

FR 742

East River

Jacks Cabin

Taylor River

FR 744

FR 742

FR 586

Flow

Almont

Gunnison National Forest

To Gunnison

135

Gunnison River

1

0 1 2 3 4 5 MILES

N W E S

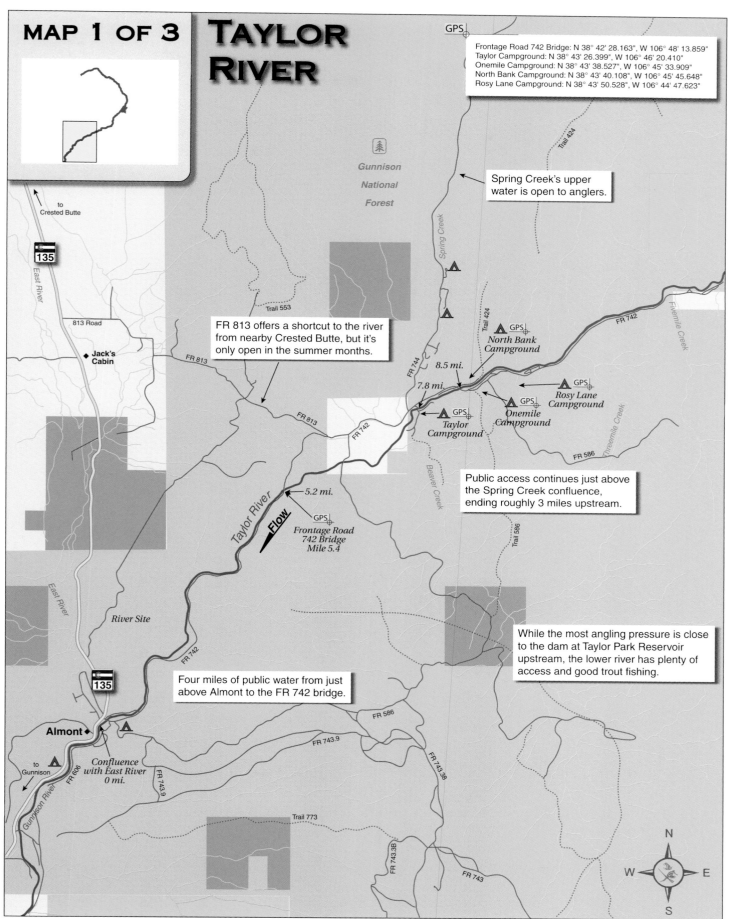

MAP 1 OF 3 TAYLOR RIVER

Frontage Road 742 Bridge: N 38° 42' 28.163", W 106° 48' 13.859"
Taylor Campground: N 38° 43' 26.399", W 106° 46' 20.410"
Onemile Campground: N 38° 43' 38.527", W 106° 45' 33.909"
North Bank Campground: N 38° 43' 40.108", W 106° 45' 45.648"
Rosy Lane Campground: N 38° 43' 50.528", W 106° 44' 47.623"

to Crested Butte

135

East River

813 Road

Jack's Cabin

Gunnison National Forest

Trail 553

Spring Creek

Trail 424

FR 742

Fivemile Creek

Spring Creek's upper water is open to anglers.

FR 813 offers a shortcut to the river from nearby Crested Butte, but it's only open in the summer months.

FR 744

8.5 mi.

7.8 mi.

GPS North Bank Campground

GPS Rosy Lane Campground

GPS Onemile Campground

GPS Taylor Campground

FR 813

FR 742

Threemile Creek

FR 586

Beaver Creek

Taylor River

5.2 mi.

Flow

GPS Frontage Road 742 Bridge Mile 5.4

Trail 424

Public access continues just above the Spring Creek confluence, ending roughly 3 miles upstream.

Trail 586

East River

River Site

FR 742

While the most angling pressure is close to the dam at Taylor Park Reservoir upstream, the lower river has plenty of access and good trout fishing.

135

FR 586

Four miles of public water from just above Almont to the FR 742 bridge.

Almont

to Gunnison

Gunnison River

FR 606

Confluence with East River 0 mi.

FR 743.9

FR 743.9

FR 743.38

FR 743.38B

Trail 773

FR 743.38B

FR 743

N
W   E
S

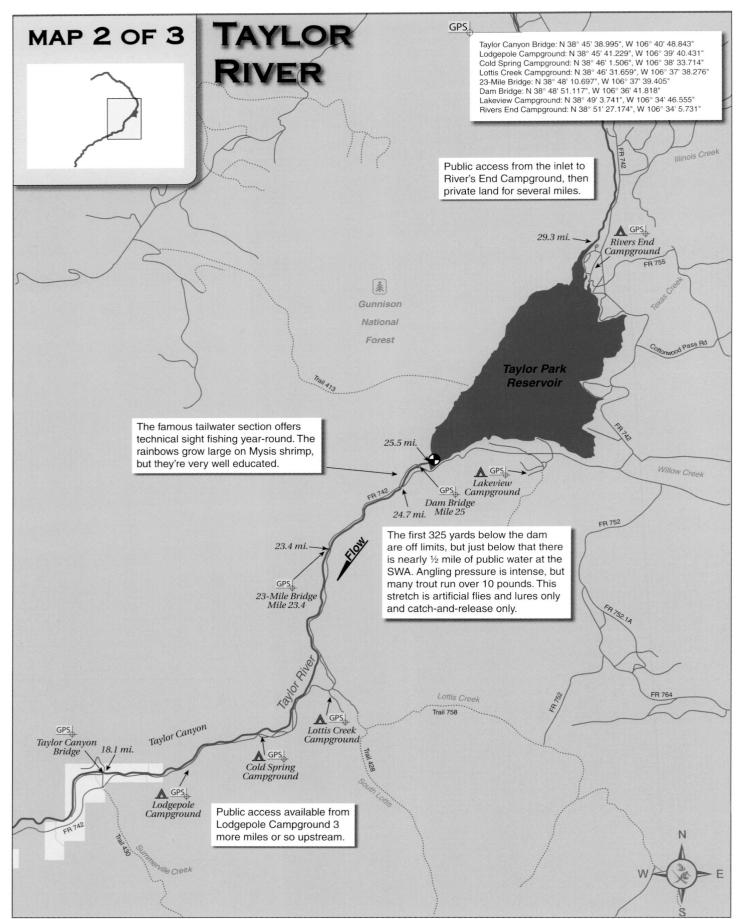

MAP 2 OF 3 TAYLOR RIVER

Taylor Canyon Bridge: N 38° 45' 38.995", W 106° 40' 48.843"
Lodgepole Campground: N 38° 45' 41.229", W 106° 39' 40.431"
Cold Spring Campground: N 38° 46' 1.506", W 106° 38' 33.714"
Lottis Creek Campground: N 38° 46' 31.659", W 106° 37' 38.276"
23-Mile Bridge: N 38° 48' 10.697", W 106° 37' 39.405"
Dam Bridge: N 38° 48' 51.117", W 106° 36' 41.818"
Lakeview Campground: N 38° 49' 3.741", W 106° 34' 46.555"
Rivers End Campground: N 38° 51' 27.174", W 106° 34' 5.731"

Illinois Creek

Public access from the inlet to River's End Campground, then private land for several miles.

29.3 mi. — Rivers End Campground

FR 755

Texas Creek

Gunnison National Forest

Cottonwood Pass Rd

Trail 413

Taylor Park Reservoir

FR 742

The famous tailwater section offers technical sight fishing year-round. The rainbows grow large on Mysis shrimp, but they're very well educated.

25.5 mi.

Willow Creek

FR 742

Lakeview Campground

FR 742

GPS

Dam Bridge Mile 25

24.7 mi.

FR 752

The first 325 yards below the dam are off limits, but just below that there is nearly ½ mile of public water at the SWA. Angling pressure is intense, but many trout run over 10 pounds. This stretch is artificial flies and lures only and catch-and-release only.

23.4 mi.

Flow

GPS

23-Mile Bridge Mile 23.4

FR 752.1A

Taylor River

Lottis Creek

FR 764

Trail 758

GPS

Lottis Creek Campground

Trail 428

FR 752

Taylor Canyon

South Lottis

GPS

Taylor Canyon Bridge

18.1 mi.

GPS

Cold Spring Campground

GPS

Lodgepole Campground

Public access available from Lodgepole Campground 3 more miles or so upstream.

FR 742

Trail 430

Summerville Creek

N

W E

S

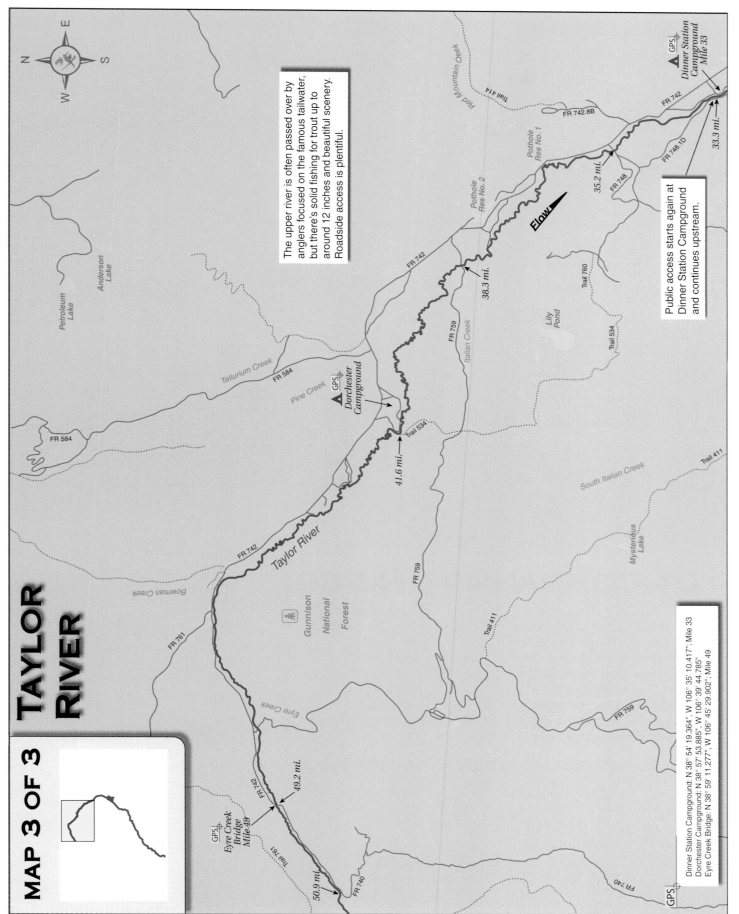

The upper river is often passed over by anglers focused on the famous tailwater, but there's solid fishing for trout up to around 12 inches and beautiful scenery. Roadside access is plentiful.

Public access starts again at Dinner Station Campground and continues upstream.

Dinner Station Campground: N 38° 54' 19.364", W 106° 35' 10.417"; Mile 33
Dorchester Campground: N 38° 57' 53.885", W 106° 39' 44.785"
Eyre Creek Bridge: N 38° 59' 11.277", W 106° 45' 29.902"; Mile 49

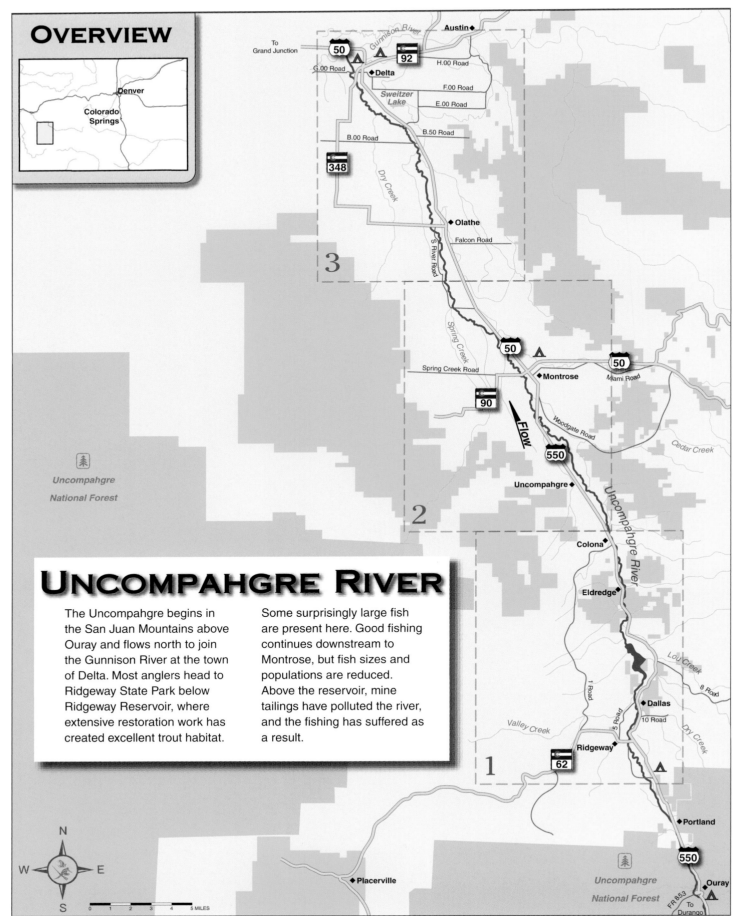

OVERVIEW

Denver

Colorado
Springs

To
Grand Junction

50

G.00 Road

Gunnison River

Austin

92

H.00 Road

◆ Delta

Sweitzer
Lake

F.00 Road

E.00 Road

B.00 Road

B.50 Road

348

Dry Creek

◆ Olathe

Falcon Road

3

S. River Road

Spring Creek

50

Spring Creek Road

◆ Montrose

50

Miami Road

Flow

90

Woodgate Road

Cedar Creek

550

Uncompahgre
National Forest

Uncompahgre ◆

2

Colona ●

1 Road

Eldredge ◆

UNCOMPAHGRE RIVER

The Uncompahgre begins in
the San Juan Mountains above
Ouray and flows north to join
the Gunnison River at the town
of Delta. Most anglers head to
Ridgeway State Park below
Ridgeway Reservoir, where
extensive restoration work has
created excellent trout habitat.

Some surprisingly large fish
are present here. Good fishing
continues downstream to
Montrose, but fish sizes and
populations are reduced.
Above the reservoir, mine
tailings have polluted the river,
and the fishing has suffered as
a result.

Lou Creek

8 Road

◆ Dallas

10 Road

Valley Creek

5 Road

Dry Creek

Uncompahgre River

62

Ridgeway ●

1

◆ Portland

N
W   E
S

0   1   2   3   4   5 MILES

Uncompahgre

National Forest

550

FR 853

Ouray ◆

To
Durango

◆ Placerville

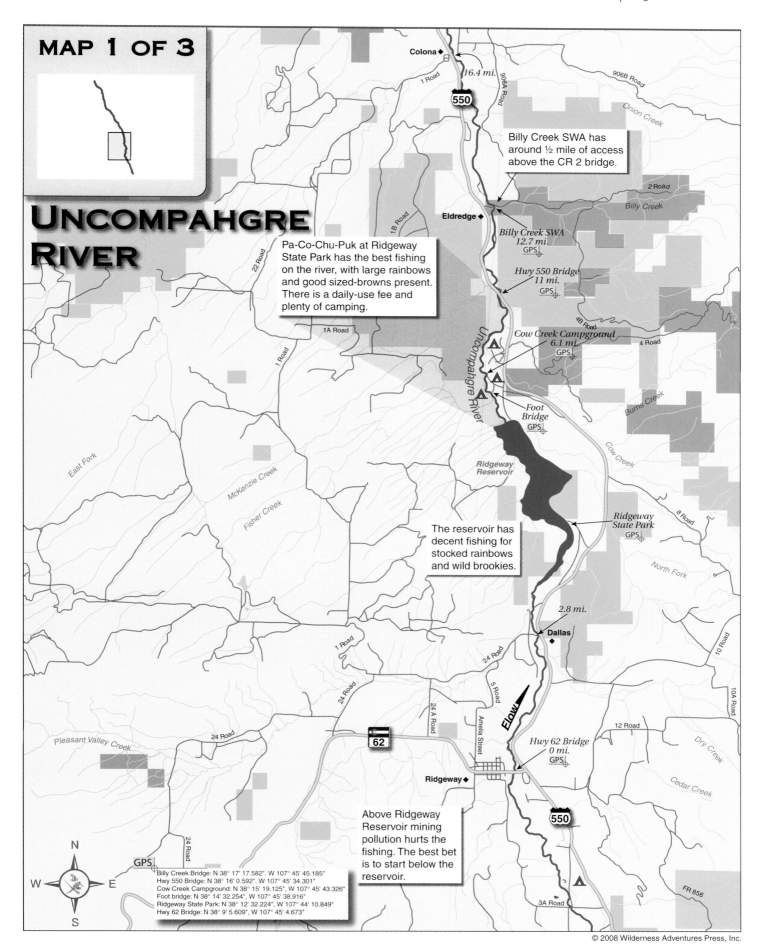

MAP 1 OF 3

UNCOMPAHGRE RIVER

Colona ◆

16.4 mi.

1 Road

550

906A Road

906B Road

Onion Creek

2 Road

Billy Creek

Billy Creek SWA has around ½ mile of access above the CR 2 bridge.

Eldredge ◆

Billy Creek SWA
12.7 mi.
GPS

1B Road

Pa-Co-Chu-Puk at Ridgeway State Park has the best fishing on the river, with large rainbows and good sized-browns present. There is a daily-use fee and plenty of camping.

Hwy 550 Bridge
11 mi.
GPS

4B Road

4 Road

22 Road

Cow Creek Campground
6.1 mi.
GPS

Uncompahgre River

Burns Creek

1A Road

Foot Bridge
GPS

1 Road

Ridgeway Reservoir

Cow Creek

East Fork

McKenzie Creek

Fisher Creek

8 Road

Ridgeway State Park
GPS

The reservoir has decent fishing for stocked rainbows and wild brookies.

North Fork

2.8 mi.

10 Road

1 Road

Dallas ◆

24 Road

10A Road

24 Road

24 A Road

5 Road

Flow

Dry Creek

12 Road

Pleasant Valley Creek

24 Road

62

Amelia Street

Hwy 62 Bridge
0 mi.
GPS

24 Road

Ridgeway ◆

Cedar Creek

550

Above Ridgeway Reservoir mining pollution hurts the fishing. The best bet is to start below the reservoir.

N
W E
S

GPS

Billy Creek Bridge: N 38° 17' 17.582", W 107° 45' 45.185"
Hwy 550 Bridge: N 38° 16' 0.592", W 107° 45' 34.301"
Cow Creek Campground: N 38° 15' 19.125", W 107° 45' 43.326"
Foot bridge: N 38° 14' 32.254", W 107° 45' 38.916"
Ridgeway State Park: N 38° 12' 32.224", W 107° 44' 10.849"
Hwy 62 Bridge: N 38° 9' 5.609", W 107° 45' 4.673"

24 Road

3A Road

FR 856

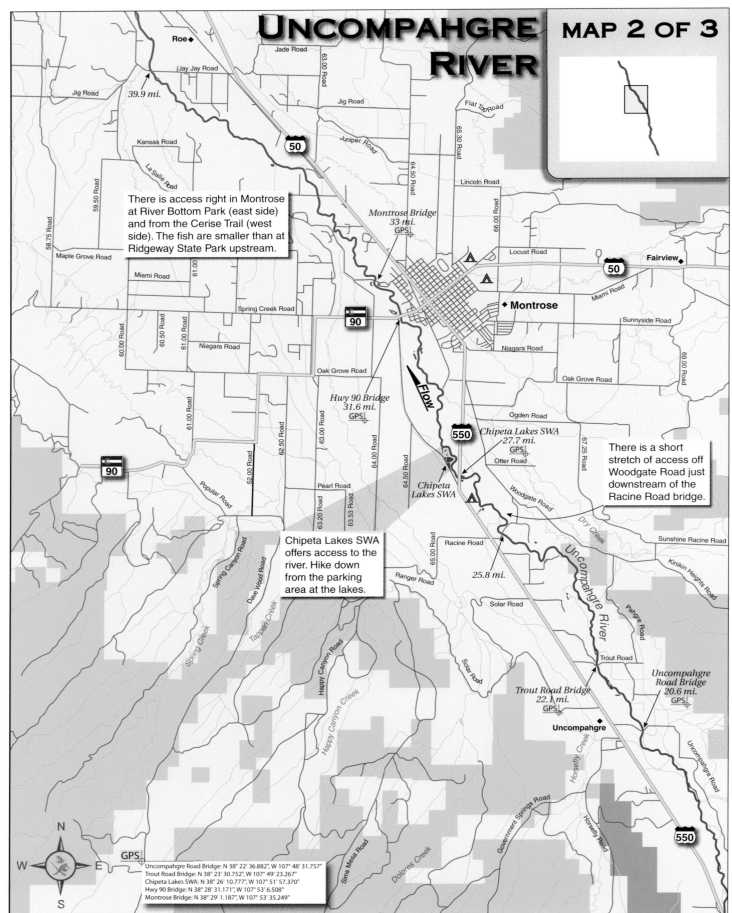

UNCOMPAHGRE RIVER
MAP 2 OF 3

Roe

Jade Road

Jay Jay Road

Jig Road

39.9 mi.

Jig Road

Juniper Road

63.00 Road

Flat Top Road

Kansas Road

La Salle Road

50

Lincoln Road

65.30 Road

58.75 Road

59.50 Road

Maple Grove Road

Miami Road

61.00 Road

64.50 Road

66.00 Road

There is access right in Montrose at River Bottom Park (east side) and from the Cerise Trail (west side). The fish are smaller than at Ridgeway State Park upstream.

Montrose Bridge 33 mi. GPS

Locust Road

50 Fairview

Miami Road

Montrose

60.50 Road

61.00 Road

Niagara Road

Spring Creek Road

90

Sunnyside Road

Niagara Road

60.00 Road

Oak Grove Road

Flow

Oak Grove Road

69.00 Road

61.00 Road

Hwy 90 Bridge 31.6 mi. GPS

63.00 Road

64.00 Road

Ogden Road

550

Chipeta Lakes SWA 27.7 mi. GPS

Otter Road

67.25 Road

There is a short stretch of access off Woodgate Road just downstream of the Racine Road bridge.

90

52.00 Road

Pearl Road

63.20 Road

63.53 Road

64.50 Road

Chipeta Lakes SWA

Woodgate Road

Dry Creek

Sunshine Racine Road

Popular Road

Spring Canyon Road

Dave Wood Road

Chipeta Lakes SWA offers access to the river. Hike down from the parking area at the lakes.

Ranger Road

Racine Road

65.00 Road

25.8 mi.

Solar Road

Uncompahgre River

Pahgre Road

Kinikin Heights Road

Tappan Creek

Spring Creek

Happy Canyon Road

Happy Canyon Creek

Solar Road

Trout Road

Trout Road Bridge 22.1 mi. GPS

Uncompahgre Road Bridge 20.6 mi. GPS

Horsefly Creek

Uncompahgre

Government Springs Road

Sims Mesa Road

Dolores Creek

Horsefly Road

Uncompahgre Road

550

N
W E
S

GPS

Uncompahgre Road Bridge: N 38° 22' 36.882", W 107° 48' 31.757"
Trout Road Bridge: N 38° 23' 30.752", W 107° 49' 23.267"
Chipeta Lakes SWA: N 38° 26' 10.777", W 107° 51' 57.370"
Hwy 90 Bridge: N 38° 28' 31.171", W 107° 53' 6.508"
Montrose Bridge: N 38° 29' 1.187", W 107° 53' 35.249"

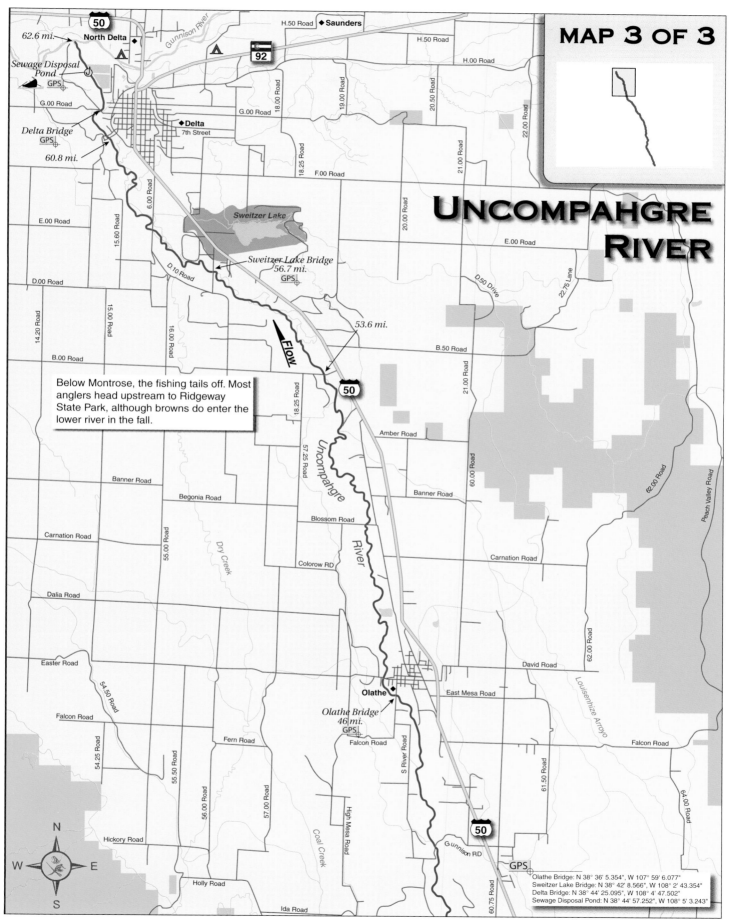

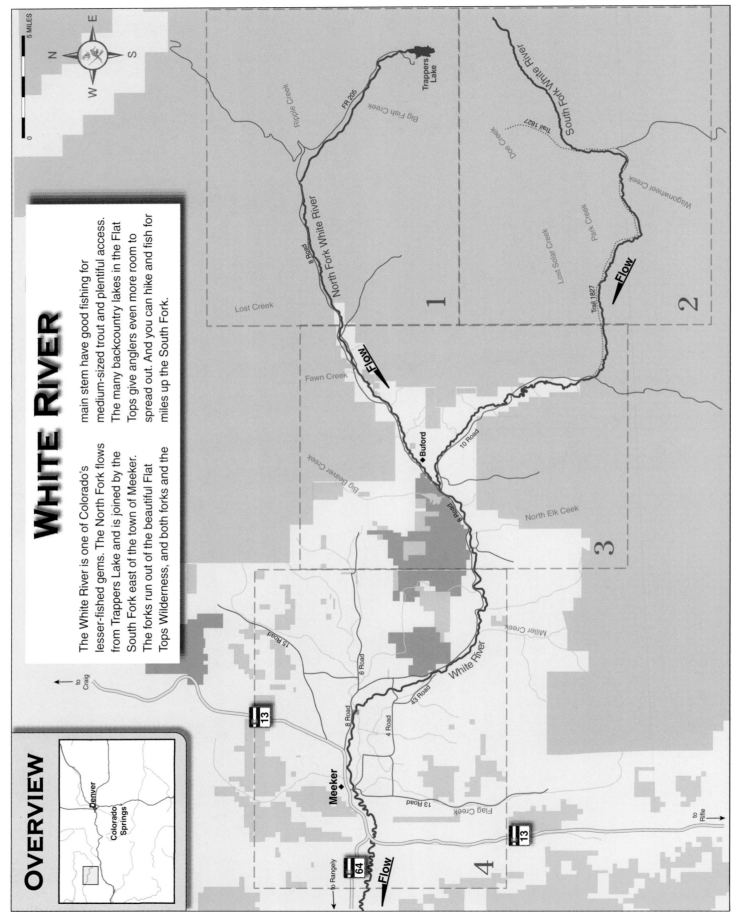

WHITE RIVER

The White River is one of Colorado's lesser-fished gems. The North Fork flows from Trappers Lake and is joined by the South Fork east of the town of Meeker. The forks run out of the beautiful Flat Tops Wilderness, and both forks and the main stem have good fishing for medium-sized trout and plentiful access. The many backcountry lakes in the Flat Tops give anglers even more room to spread out. And you can hike and fish for miles up the South Fork.

OVERVIEW

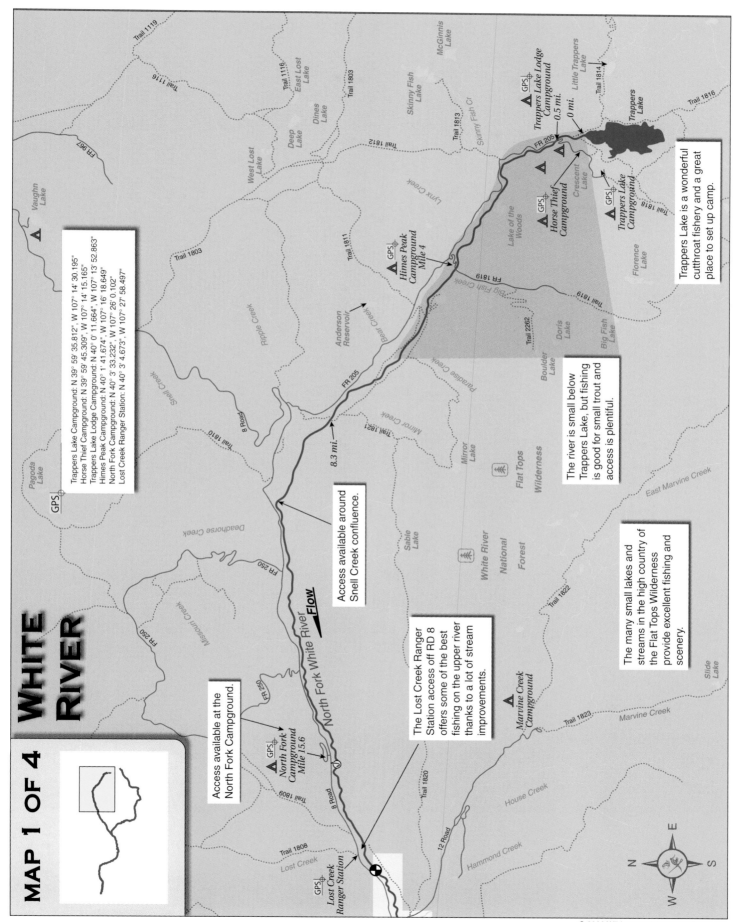

MAP 1 OF 4

WHITE RIVER

Trappers Lake Campground: N 39° 59' 35.812", W 107° 14' 30.195"
Horse Thief Campground: N 39° 59' 45.309", W 107° 14' 15.165"
Trappers Lake Lodge Campground: N 40° 0' 11.664", W 107° 13' 52.863"
Himes Peak Campground: N 40° 1' 41.674", W 107° 16' 18.649"
North Fork Campground: N 40° 3' 33.232", W 107° 26' 0.102"
Lost Creek Ranger Station: N 40° 3' 4.673", W 107° 27' 58.497"

Trappers Lake is a wonderful cutthroat fishery and a great place to set up camp.

The river is small below Trappers Lake, but fishing is good for small trout and access is plentiful.

The many small lakes and streams in the high country of the Flat Tops Wilderness provide excellent fishing and scenery.

Access available around Snell Creek confluence.

The Lost Creek Ranger Station access off RD 8 offers some of the best fishing on the upper river thanks to a lot of stream improvements.

Access available at the North Fork Campground.

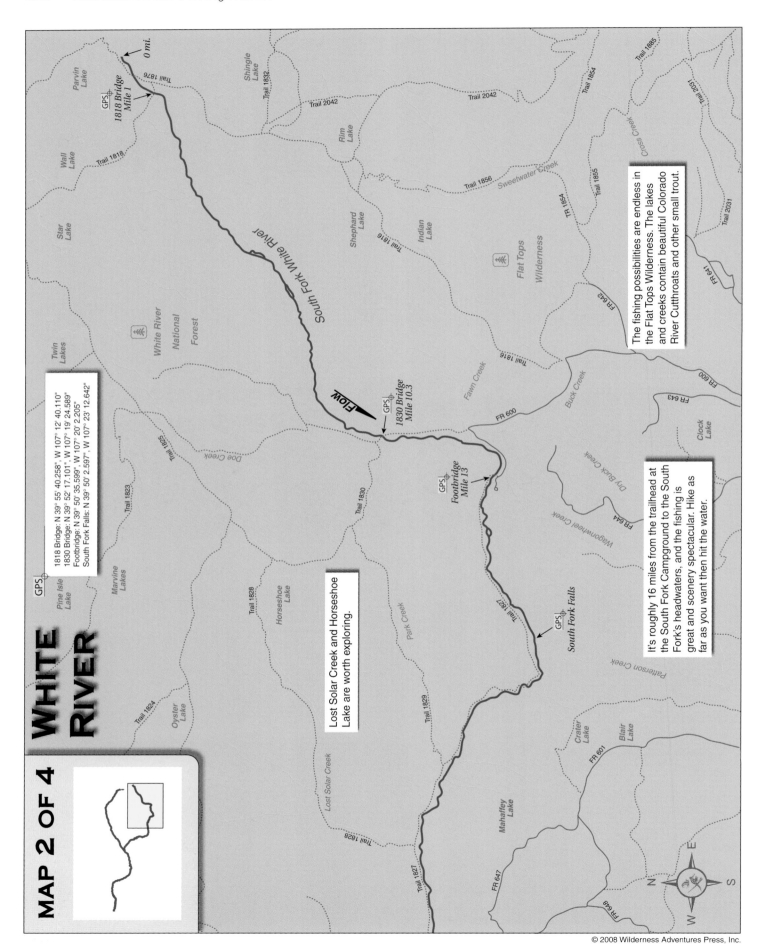

WHITE RIVER

MAP 2 OF 4

The fishing possibilities are endless in the Flat Tops Wilderness. The lakes and creeks contain beautiful Colorado River Cutthroats and other small trout.

It's roughly 16 miles from the trailhead at the South Fork Campground to the South Fork's headwaters, and the fishing is great and scenery spectacular. Hike as far as you want then hit the water.

Lost Solar Creek and Horseshoe Lake are worth exploring.

1818 Bridge: N 39° 55' 40.258", W 107° 12' 40.110"
1830 Bridge: N 39° 52' 17.101", W 107° 19' 24.589"
Footbridge: N 39° 50' 35.599", W 107° 20' 2.205"
South Fork Falls: N 39° 50' 2.597", W 107° 23' 12.642"

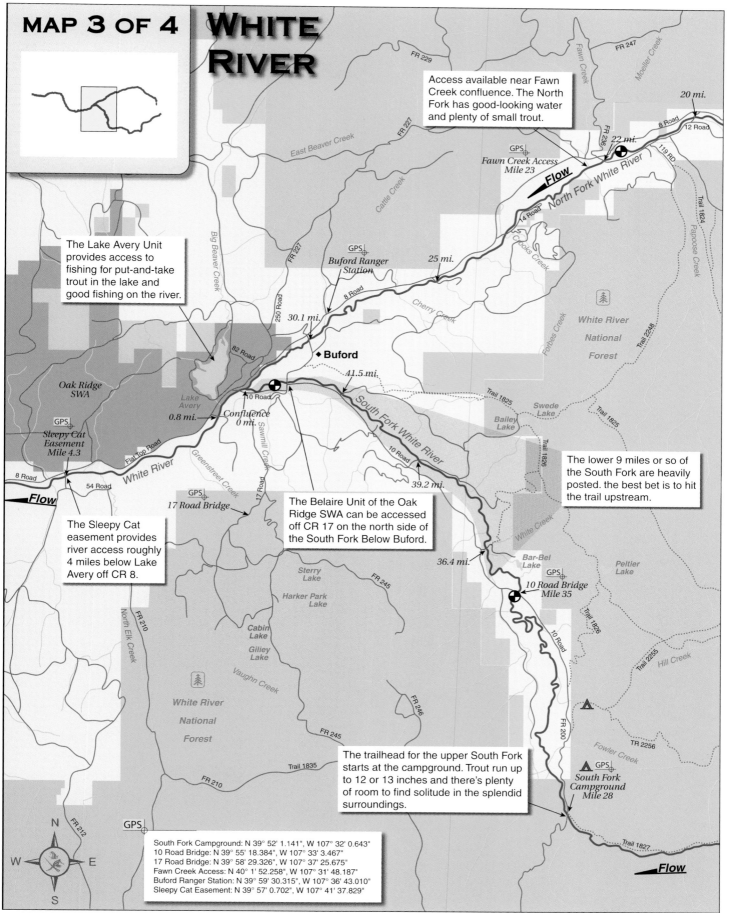

MAP 3 OF 4 WHITE RIVER

Access available near Fawn Creek confluence. The North Fork has good-looking water and plenty of small trout.

20 mi.

22 mi.

GPS
Fawn Creek Access Mile 23

Flow

North Fork White River

The Lake Avery Unit provides access to fishing for put-and-take trout in the lake and good fishing on the river.

GPS
Buford Ranger Station

25 mi.

30.1 mi.

White River National Forest

◆ **Buford**

41.5 mi.

Oak Ridge SWA

Lake Avery

0.8 mi.

Confluence 0 mi.

GPS
Sleepy Cat Easement Mile 4.3

Swede Lake

Bailey Lake

The lower 9 miles or so of the South Fork are heavily posted. the best bet is to hit the trail upstream.

White River

Flow

8 Road

54 Road

White River

GPS
17 Road Bridge

The Belaire Unit of the Oak Ridge SWA can be accessed off CR 17 on the north side of the South Fork Below Buford.

39.2 mi.

36.4 mi.

Bar-Bel Lake

Peltier Lake

GPS
10 Road Bridge Mile 35

The Sleepy Cat easement provides river access roughly 4 miles below Lake Avery off CR 8.

Sterry Lake

Harker Park Lake

Cabin Lake

Gilley Lake

White River National Forest

The trailhead for the upper South Fork starts at the campground. Trout run up to 12 or 13 inches and there's plenty of room to find solitude in the splendid surroundings.

Fowler Creek

GPS
South Fork Campground Mile 28

GPS

N
W E
S

South Fork Campground: N 39° 52' 1.141", W 107° 32' 0.643"
10 Road Bridge: N 39° 55' 18.384", W 107° 33' 3.467"
17 Road Bridge: N 39° 58' 29.326", W 107° 37' 25.675"
Fawn Creek Access: N 40° 1' 52.258", W 107° 31' 48.187"
Buford Ranger Station: N 39° 59' 30.315", W 107° 36' 43.010"
Sleepy Cat Easement: N 39° 57' 0.702", W 107° 41' 37.829"

Flow

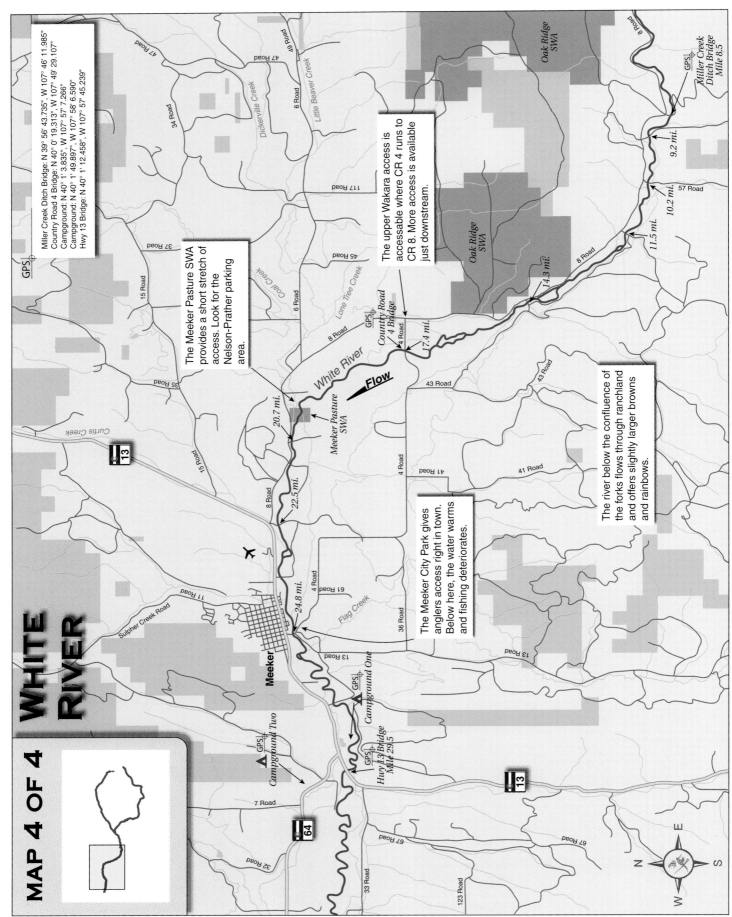

MAP 4 OF 4

WHITE RIVER

Miller Creek Ditch Bridge: N 39° 56' 43.735", W 107° 46' 11.985"
Country Road 4 Bridge: N 40° 0' 19.313", W 107° 49' 29.107"
Campground: N 40° 1' 3.835", W 107° 57' 7.266"
Campground: N 40° 1' 49.897", W 107° 58' 6.590"
Hwy 13 Bridge: N 40° 1' 12.458", W 107° 57' 45.239"

The Meeker Pasture SWA provides a short stretch of access. Look for the Nelson-Prather parking area.

The upper Wakara access is accessible where CR 4 runs to CR 8. More access is available just downstream.

The river below the confluence of the forks flows through ranchland and offers slightly larger browns and rainbows.

The Meeker City Park gives anglers access right in town. Below here, the water warms and fishing deteriorates.

Flow

© 2008 Wilderness Adventures Press, Inc.

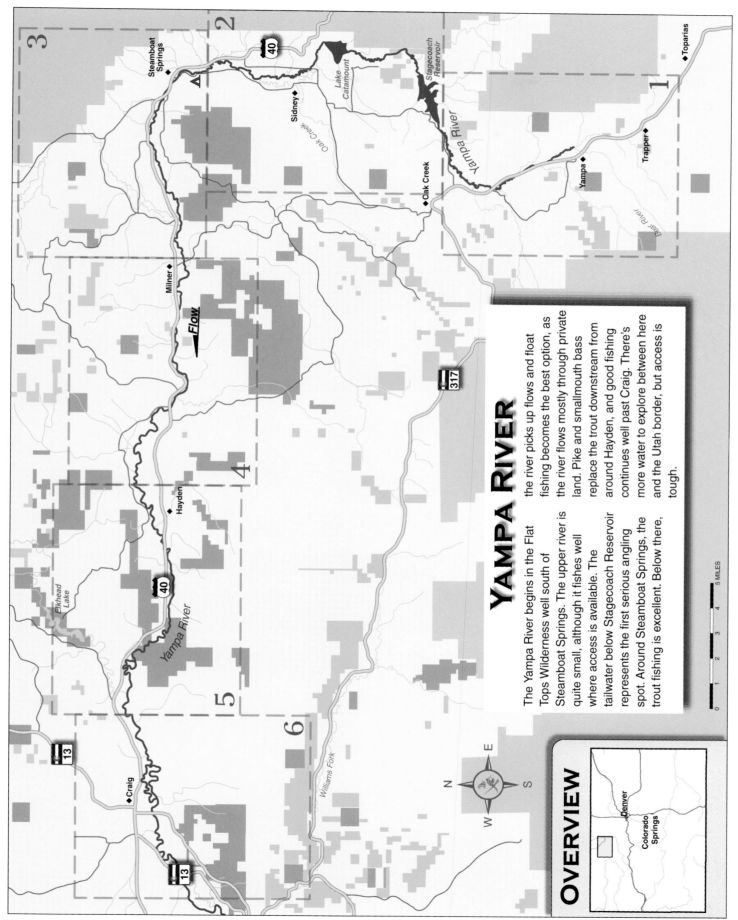

YAMPA RIVER

The Yampa River begins in the Flat Tops Wilderness well south of Steamboat Springs. The upper river is quite small, although it fishes well where access is available. The tailwater below Stagecoach Reservoir represents the first serious angling spot. Around Steamboat Springs, the trout fishing is excellent. Below there, the river picks up flows and float fishing becomes the best option, as the river flows mostly through private land. Pike and smallmouth bass replace the trout downstream from around Hayden, and good fishing continues well past Craig. There's more water to explore between here and the Utah border, but access is tough.

OVERVIEW

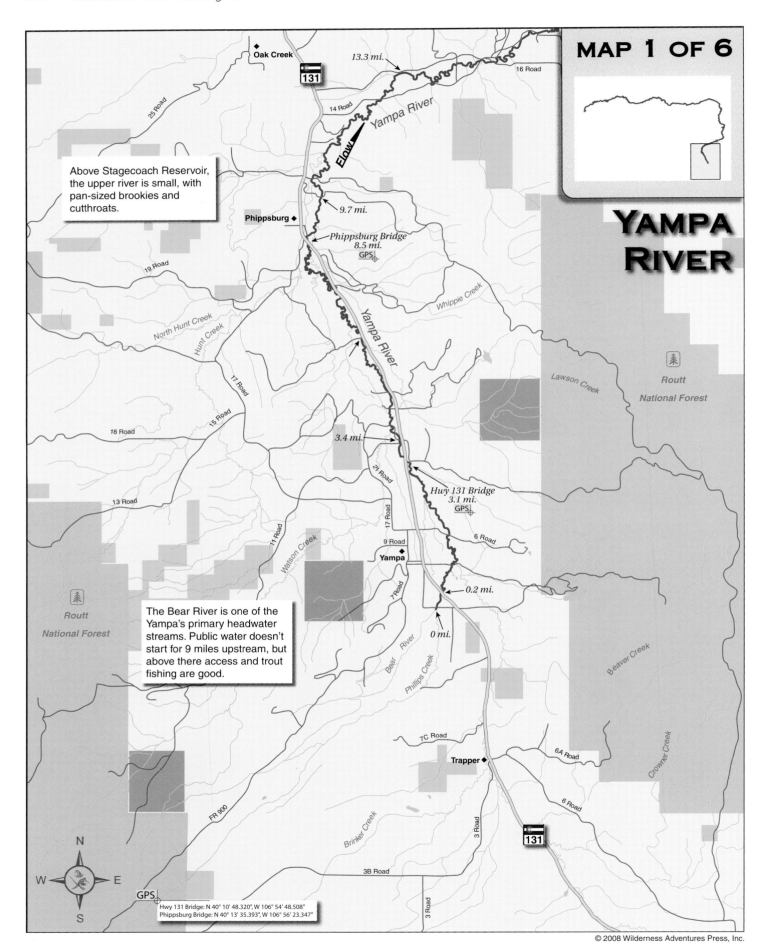

MAP 1 OF 6

YAMPA RIVER

Above Stagecoach Reservoir, the upper river is small, with pan-sized brookies and cutthroats.

The Bear River is one of the Yampa's primary headwater streams. Public water doesn't start for 9 miles upstream, but above there access and trout fishing are good.

Oak Creek

131

13.3 mi.

16 Road

25 Road

14 Road

Yampa River

Flow

9.7 mi.

Phippsburg ♦

Phippsburg Bridge 8.5 mi.
GPS

19 Road

Whippie Creek

North Hunt Creek

Hunt Creek

Yampa River

17 Road

Lawson Creek

Routt National Forest

15 Road

18 Road

3.4 mi.

21 Road

13 Road

17 Road

Hwy 131 Bridge 3.1 mi.
GPS

6 Road

11 Road

9 Road

Yampa ♦

7 Road

0.2 mi.

Routt National Forest

Watson Creek

Bear River

Phillips Creek

0 mi.

Beaver Creek

7C Road

6A Road

Trapper ♦

Crowner Creek

FR 900

3 Road

6 Road

Brinker Creek

131

N
W · E
S

GPS

3B Road

3 Road

Hwy 131 Bridge: N 40° 10' 48.320", W 106° 54' 48.508"
Phippsburg Bridge: N 40° 13' 35.393", W 106° 56' 23.347"

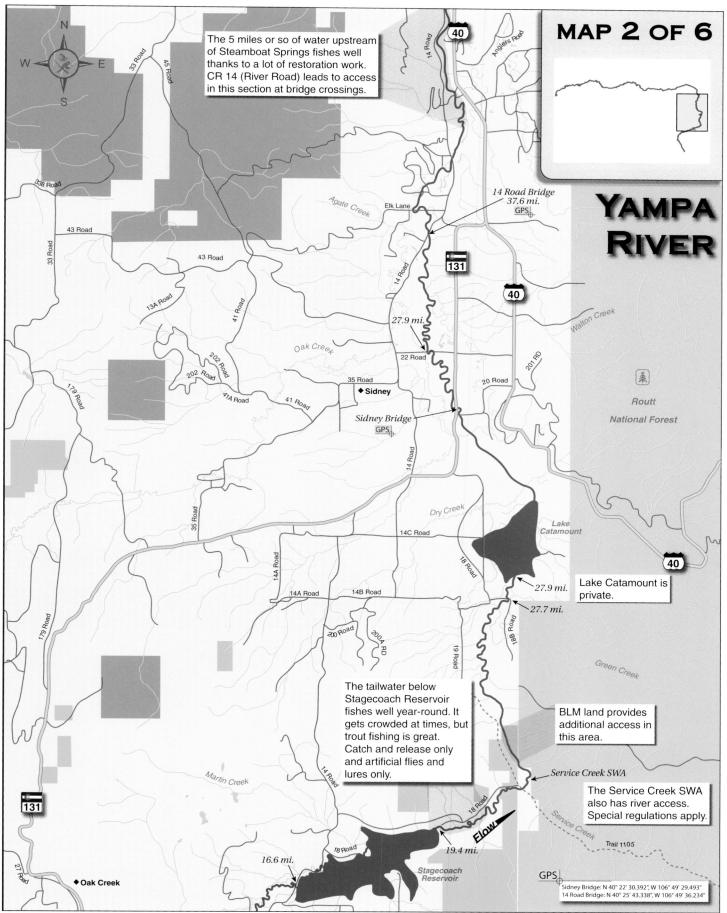

MAP 2 OF 6

YAMPA RIVER

The 5 miles or so of water upstream of Steamboat Springs fishes well thanks to a lot of restoration work. CR 14 (River Road) leads to access in this section at bridge crossings.

14 Road Bridge
37.6 mi.
GPS

27.9 mi.

Sidney Bridge
GPS

Routt National Forest

27.9 mi. Lake Catamount is private.

27.7 mi.

The tailwater below Stagecoach Reservoir fishes well year-round. It gets crowded at times, but trout fishing is great. Catch and release only and artificial flies and lures only.

BLM land provides additional access in this area.

Service Creek SWA

The Service Creek SWA also has river access. Special regulations apply.

Trail 1105

Flow

19.4 mi.

16.6 mi.

Stagecoach Reservoir

◆ Oak Creek

GPS

Sidney Bridge: N 40° 22' 30.392", W 106° 49' 29.493"
14 Road Bridge: N 40° 25' 43.338", W 106° 49' 36.234"

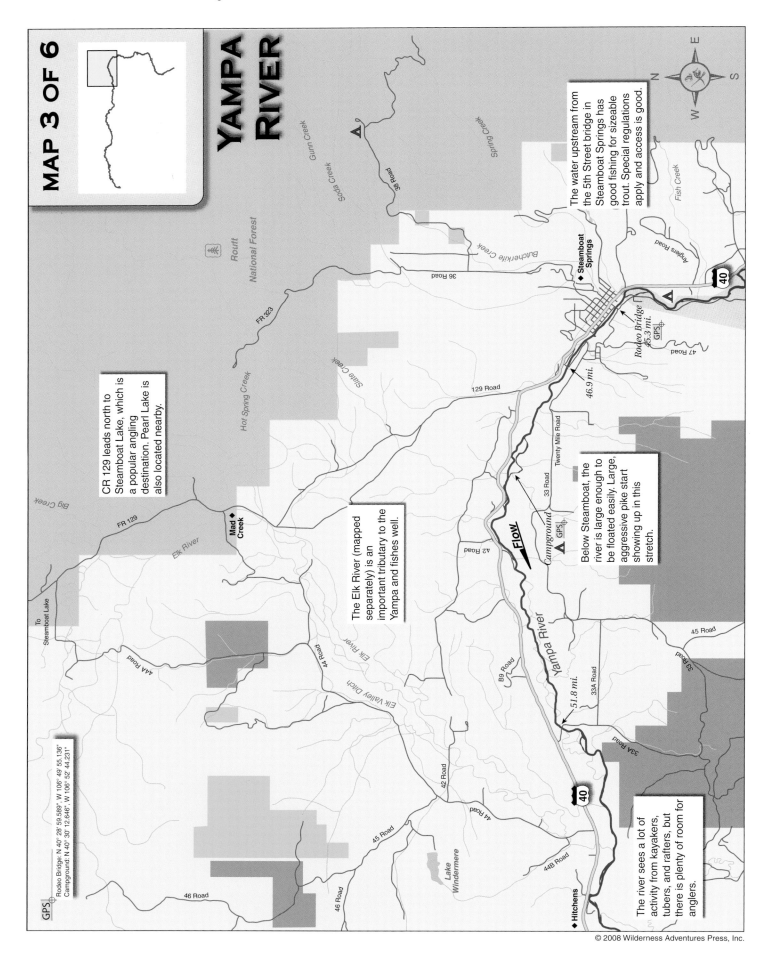

MAP 3 OF 6

YAMPA RIVER

The water upstream from the 5th Street bridge in Steamboat Springs has good fishing for sizeable trout. Special regulations apply and access is good.

CR 129 leads north to Steamboat Lake, which is a popular angling destination. Pearl Lake is also located nearby.

The Elk River (mapped separately) is an important tributary to the Yampa and fishes well.

Below Steamboat, the river is large enough to be floated easily. Large, aggressive pike start showing up in this stretch.

The river sees a lot of activity from kayakers, tubers, and rafters, but there is plenty of room for anglers.

Rodeo Bridge: N 40° 28' 59.589'; W 106° 49' 55.136"
Campground: N 40° 30' 12.646'; W 106° 52' 44.231"

Routt National Forest

Steamboat Springs

Rodeo Bridge
45.3 mi. GPS

46.9 mi.

51.8 mi.

Campground GPS

Flow

Yampa River

Hitchens

To Steamboat Lake

Mad Creek

Lake Windermere

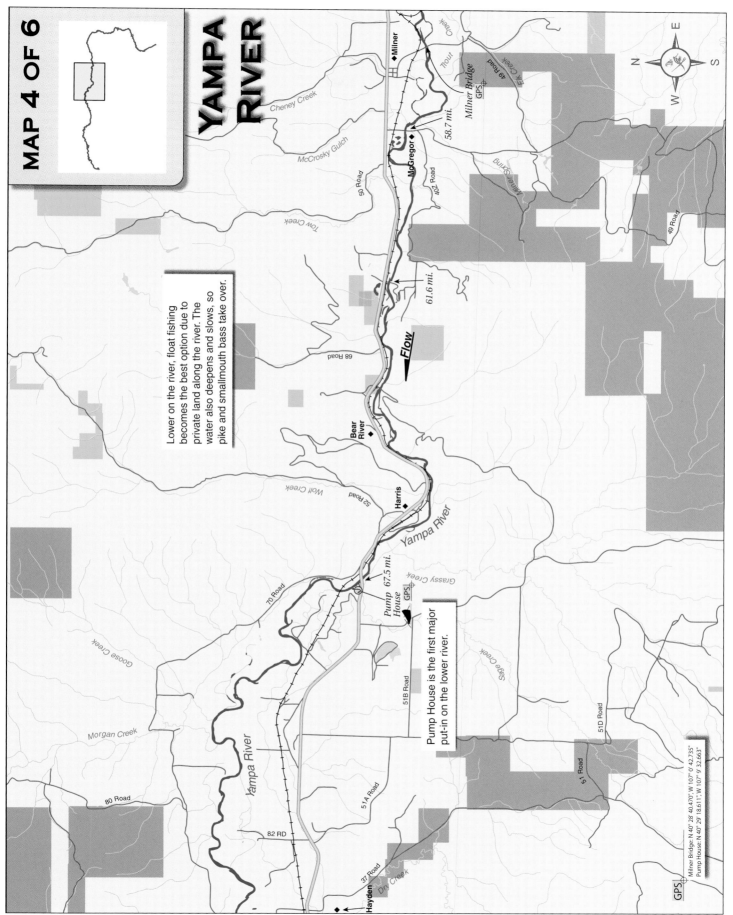

MAP 4 OF 6

YAMPA RIVER

Lower on the river, float fishing becomes the best option due to private land along the river. The water also deepens and slows, so pike and smallmouth bass take over.

Flow

Milner

Milner Bridge
GPS

McGregor

58.7 mi.

61.6 mi.

Bear River

Harris

Yampa River

Pump House
GPS

67.5 mi.

Pump House is the first major put-in on the lower river.

Cheney Creek

McCrosky Gulch

Tow Creek

Wolf Creek

Grassy Creek

Goose Creek

Morgan Creek

Yampa River

Dry Creek

Sage Creek

Trout Creek

Elk Creek

Miner Spring

50 Road

68 Road

52 Road

70 Road

80 Road

82 RD

37 Road

51A Road

51B Road

51 Road

51D Road

49 Road

40Z Road

Hayden

GPS
Milner Bridge: N 40° 28' 40.470'; W 107° 0' 42.735"
Pump House: N 40° 29' 18.611'; W 107° 9' 32.663"

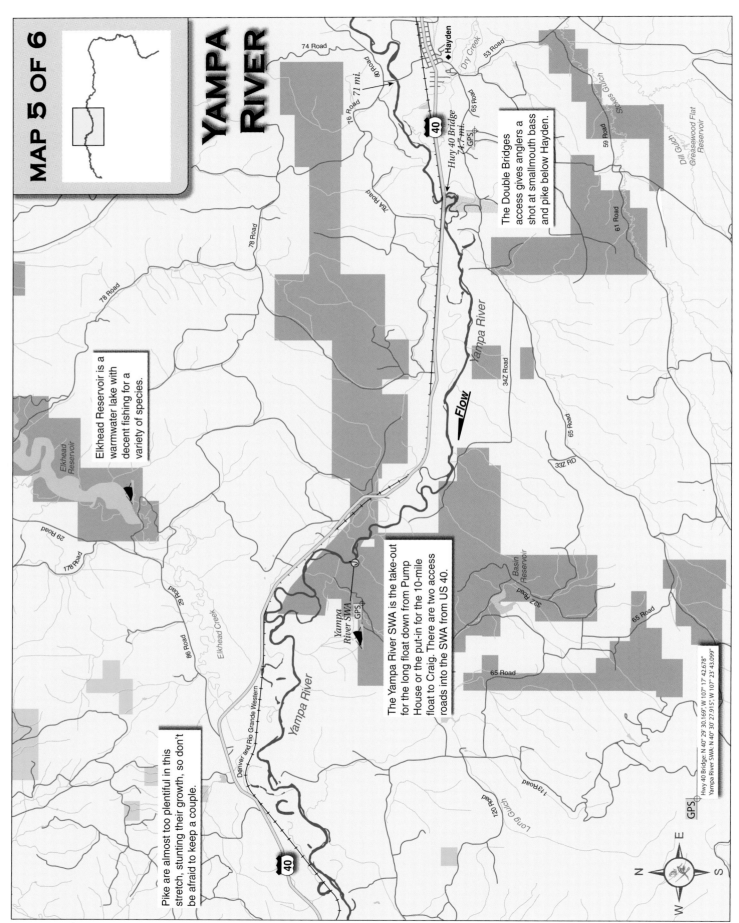

MAP 5 OF 6

YAMPA RIVER

Elkhead Reservoir is a warmwater lake with decent fishing for a variety of species.

The Double Bridges access gives anglers a shot at smallmouth bass and pike below Hayden.

The Yampa River SWA is the take-out for the long float down from Pump House or the put-in for the 10-mile float to Craig. There are two access roads into the SWA from US 40.

Pike are almost too plentiful in this stretch, stunting their growth, so don't be afraid to keep a couple.

GPS | Hwy 40 Bridge: N 40° 29' 30.169'; W 107° 17' 42.678"
Yampa River SWA: N 40° 30' 27.915'; W 107° 23' 43.099"

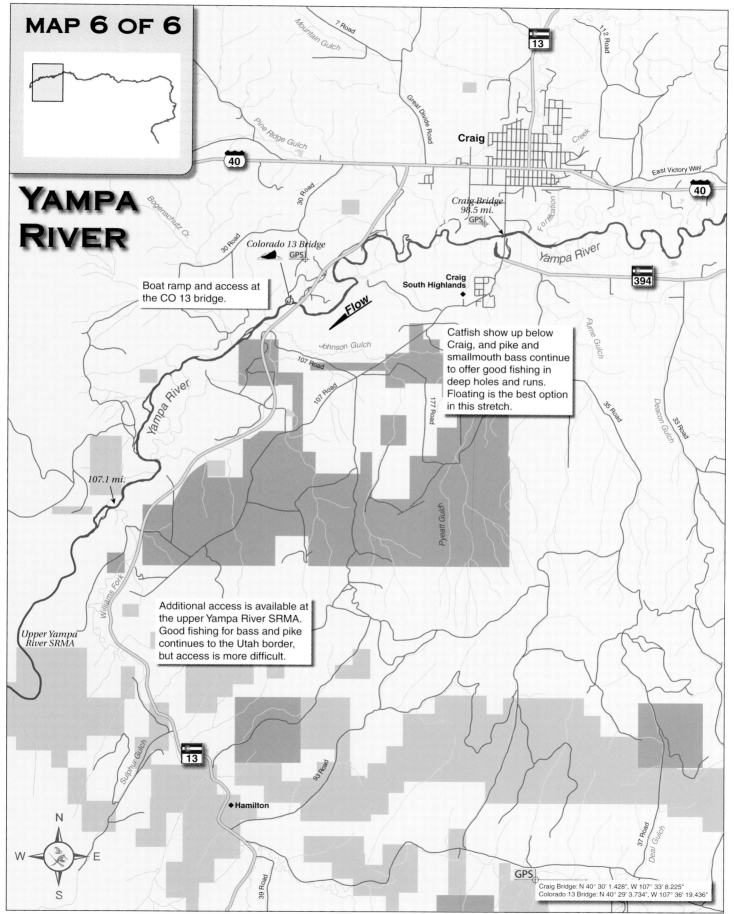

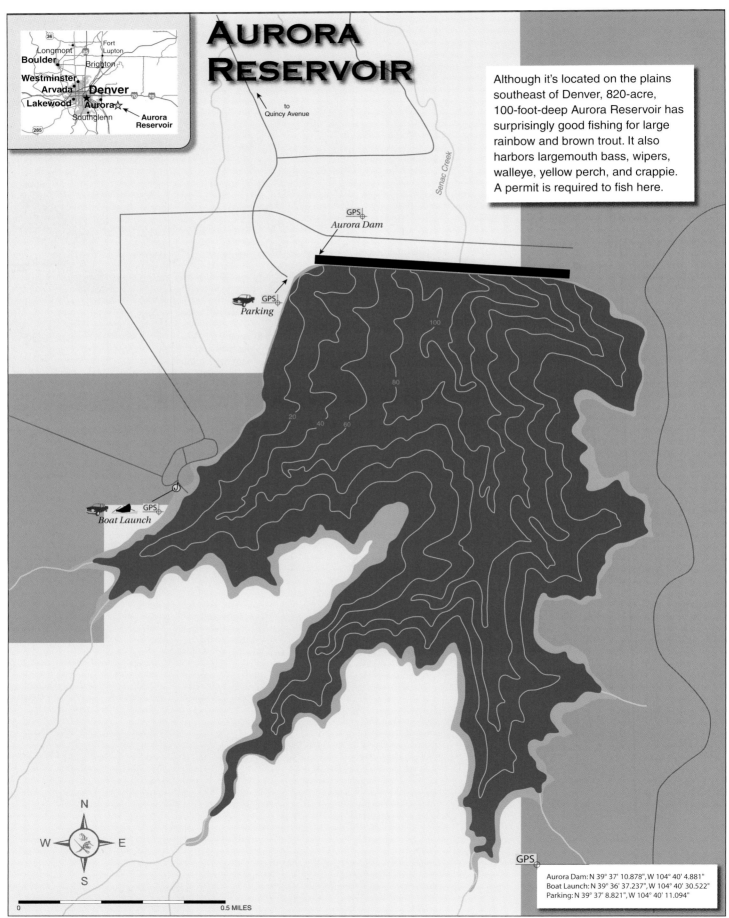

AURORA RESERVOIR

Although it's located on the plains southeast of Denver, 820-acre, 100-foot-deep Aurora Reservoir has surprisingly good fishing for large rainbow and brown trout. It also harbors largemouth bass, wipers, walleye, yellow perch, and crappie. A permit is required to fish here.

to Quincy Avenue

Senac Creek

GPS
Aurora Dam

GPS
Parking

GPS
Boat Launch

100

80

20 40 60

GPS

Aurora Dam: N 39° 37' 10.878", W 104° 40' 4.881"
Boat Launch: N 39° 36' 37.237", W 104° 40' 30.522"
Parking: N 39° 37' 8.821", W 104° 40' 11.094"

N
W   E
S

0   0.5 MILES

© 2008 Wilderness Adventures Press, Inc.

BLUE MESA RESERVOIR

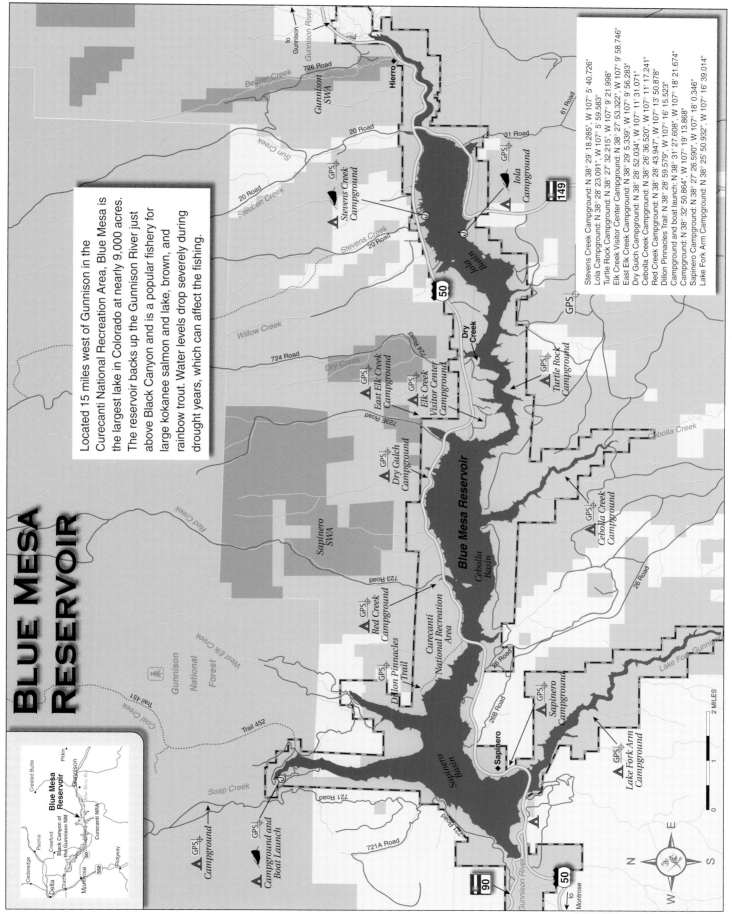

Located 15 miles west of Gunnison in the Curecanti National Recreation Area, Blue Mesa is the largest lake in Colorado at nearly 9,000 acres. The reservoir backs up the Gunnison River just above Black Canyon and is a popular fishery for large kokanee salmon and lake, brown, and rainbow trout. Water levels drop severely during drought years, which can affect the fishing.

Stevens Creek Campground: N 38° 29' 18.285", W 107° 5' 40.726"
Lola Campground: N 38° 28' 23.091", W 107° 5' 59.583"
Turtle Rock Campground: N 38° 27' 32.215", W 107° 9' 21.998"
Elk Creek Visitor Center Campground: N 38° 27' 53.322", W 107° 9' 58.746"
East Elk Creek Campground: N 38° 29' 5.339", W 107° 9' 56.283"
Dry Gulch Campground: N 38° 28' 52.034", W 107° 11' 31.071"
Cebolla Creek Campground: N 38° 26' 36.520", W 107° 11' 17.241"
Red Creek Campground: N 38° 28' 43.947", W 107° 13' 50.878"
Dillon Pinnacles Trail: N 38° 28' 59.579", W 107° 16' 15.523"
Campground and boat launch: N 38° 31' 27.608", W 107° 17' 21.674"
Campground: N 38° 32' 50.864", W 107° 19' 13.868"
Sapinero Campground: N 38° 27' 26.590", W 107° 18' 0.346"
Lake Fork Arm Campground: N 38° 25' 50.932", W 107° 16' 39.014"

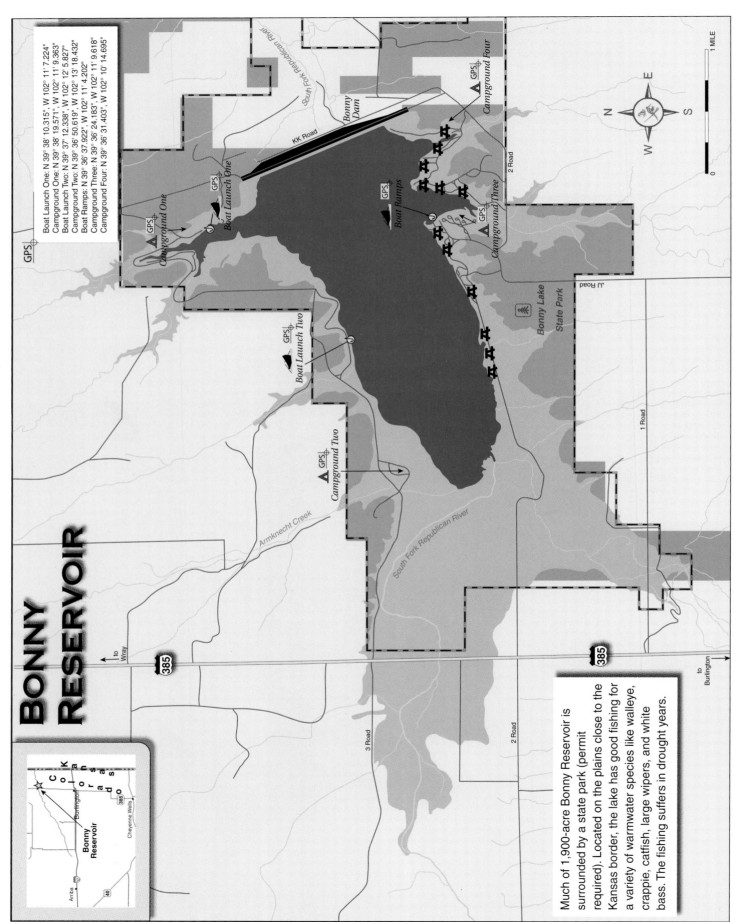

BONNY RESERVOIR

Boat Launch One: N 39° 38' 10.315", W 102° 11' 7.224"
Campground One: N 39° 38' 19.571", W 102° 11' 9.363"
Boat Launch Two: N 39° 37' 12.338", W 102° 12' 5.827"
Campground Two: N 39° 36' 50.619", W 102° 13' 18.432"
Boat Ramps: N 39° 36' 37.922", W 102° 11' 4.202"
Campground Three: N 39° 36' 24.183", W 102° 11' 9.618"
Campground Four: N 39° 36' 31.403", W 102° 10' 14.695"

Much of 1,900-acre Bonny Reservoir is surrounded by a state park (permit required). Located on the plains close to the Kansas border, the lake has good fishing for a variety of warmwater species like walleye, crappie, catfish, large wipers, and white bass. The fishing suffers in drought years.

© 2008 Wilderness Adventures Press, Inc.

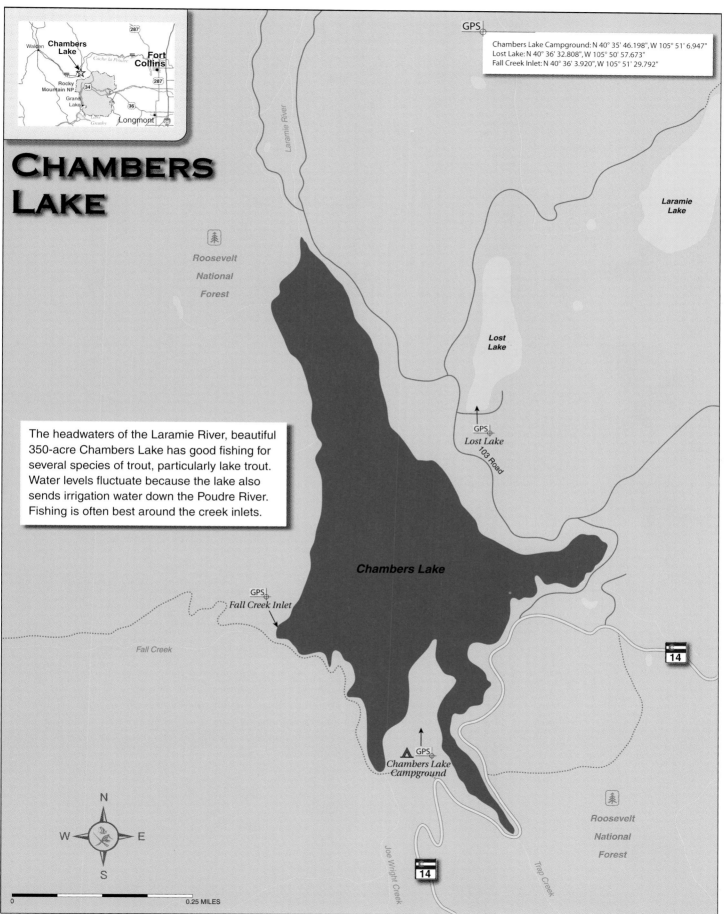

CHAMBERS LAKE

Chambers Lake Campground: N 40° 35' 46.198", W 105° 51' 6.947"
Lost Lake: N 40° 36' 32.808", W 105° 50' 57.673"
Fall Creek Inlet: N 40° 36' 3.920", W 105° 51' 29.792"

Laramie Lake

Roosevelt National Forest

Lost Lake

GPS
Lost Lake
103 Road

The headwaters of the Laramie River, beautiful 350-acre Chambers Lake has good fishing for several species of trout, particularly lake trout. Water levels fluctuate because the lake also sends irrigation water down the Poudre River. Fishing is often best around the creek inlets.

Chambers Lake

GPS
Fall Creek Inlet

Fall Creek

14

GPS
Chambers Lake Campground

Roosevelt National Forest

N
W   E
S

Joe Wright Creek

14

Trap Creek

0   0.25 MILES

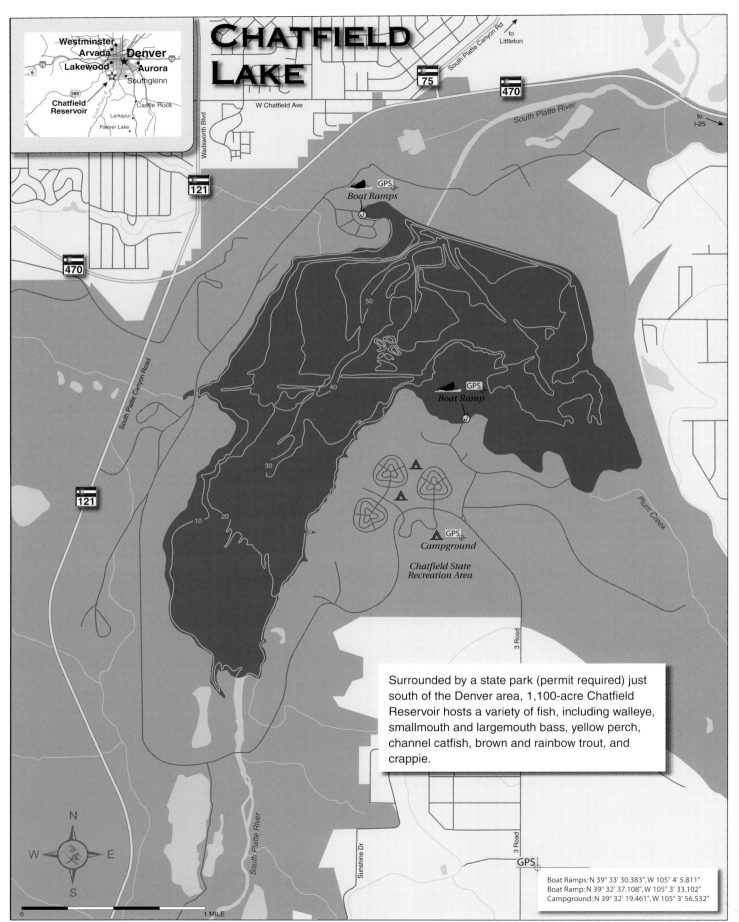

CHATFIELD LAKE

Westminster
Arvada
Lakewood
Denver
Aurora
Southglenn

Chatfield
Reservoir

Larkspur
Castle Rock

Palmer Lake

to
Littleton

South Platte Canyon Rd

75

470

South Platte River

to
I-25

W Chatfield Ave

Wadsworth Blvd

121

470

GPS
Boat Ramps

50

40

30

GPS
Boat Ramp

Plum Creek

121

10   20

Campground
GPS

Chatfield State
Recreation Area

3 Road

South Platte Canyon Road

South Platte River

Sunshine Dr

3 Road

GPS

Surrounded by a state park (permit required) just
south of the Denver area, 1,100-acre Chatfield
Reservoir hosts a variety of fish, including walleye,
smallmouth and largemouth bass, yellow perch,
channel catfish, brown and rainbow trout, and
crappie.

N
W   E
S

0   1 MILE

Boat Ramps: N 39° 33' 30.383", W 105° 4' 5.811"
Boat Ramp: N 39° 32' 37.108", W 105° 3' 33.102"
Campground: N 39° 32' 19.461", W 105° 3' 56.532"

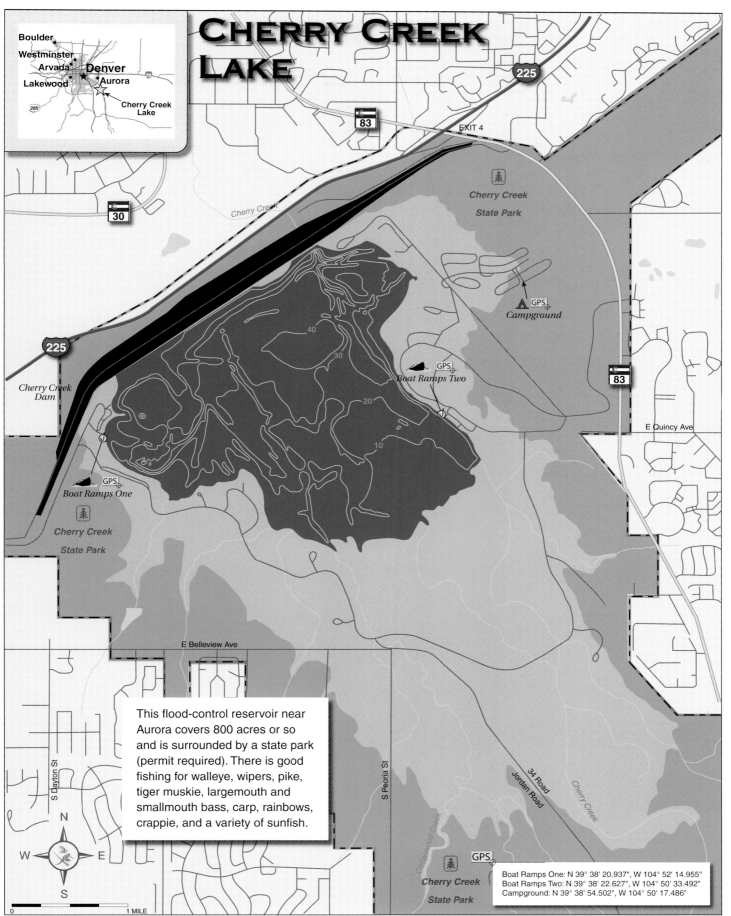

CHERRY CREEK LAKE

Boulder
Westminster
Arvada
Denver
Lakewood
Aurora
Cherry Creek
Lake

225

83

EXIT 4

30

Cherry Creek
State Park

Campground
GPS

Cherry Creek

40

30

GPS
Boat Ramps Two

20

225

10

Cherry Creek
Dam

83

E Quincy Ave

GPS
Boat Ramps One

Cherry Creek
State Park

E Belleview Ave

This flood-control reservoir near Aurora covers 800 acres or so and is surrounded by a state park (permit required). There is good fishing for walleye, wipers, pike, tiger muskie, largemouth and smallmouth bass, carp, rainbows, crappie, and a variety of sunfish.

S Dayton St

S Peoria St

34 Road

Jordan Road

Cherry Creek

Cottonwood Creek

N
W E
S

0   1 MILE

GPS
Cherry Creek
State Park

Boat Ramps One: N 39° 38' 20.937", W 104° 52' 14.955"
Boat Ramps Two: N 39° 38' 22.627", W 104° 50' 33.492"
Campground: N 39° 38' 54.502", W 104° 50' 17.486"

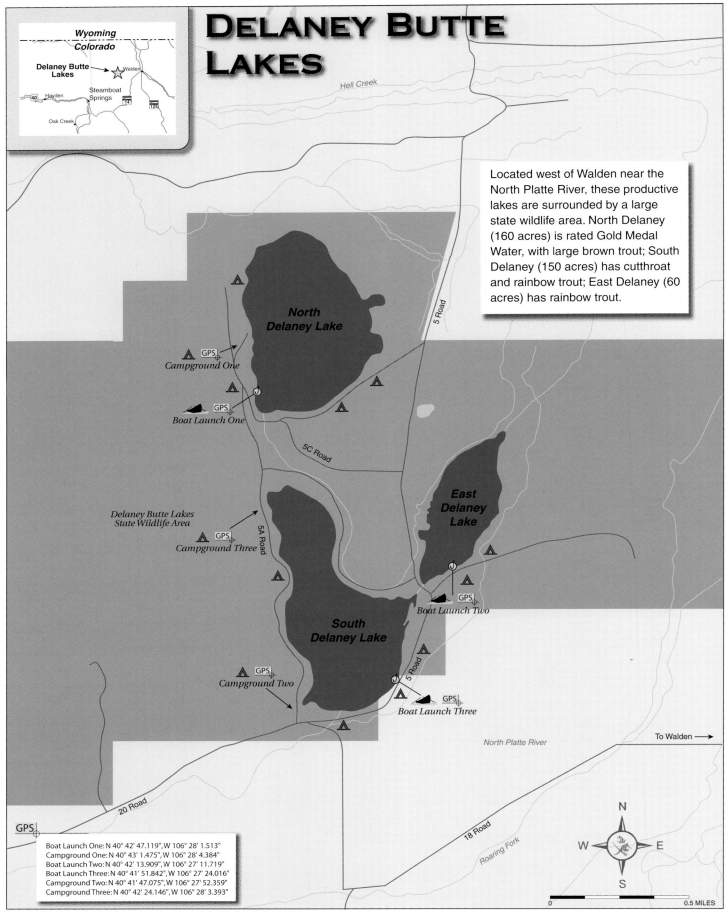

DELANEY BUTTE LAKES

Wyoming
Colorado

Delaney Butte Lakes → Walden

Steamboat Springs

40 Hayden   14   125

Oak Creek

Hell Creek

Located west of Walden near the North Platte River, these productive lakes are surrounded by a large state wildlife area. North Delaney (160 acres) is rated Gold Medal Water, with large brown trout; South Delaney (150 acres) has cutthroat and rainbow trout; East Delaney (60 acres) has rainbow trout.

North Delaney Lake

5 Road

GPS
Campground One

GPS
Boat Launch One

5C Road

East Delaney Lake

Delaney Butte Lakes State Wildlife Area

5A Road

GPS
Campground Three

GPS
Boat Launch Two

South Delaney Lake

GPS
Campground Two

5 Road

GPS
Boat Launch Three

North Platte River

To Walden →

20 Road

GPS

18 Road

Roaring Fork

N
W   E
S

0   0.5 MILES

Boat Launch One: N 40° 42' 47.119", W 106° 28' 1.513"
Campground One: N 40° 43' 1.475", W 106° 28' 4.384"
Boat Launch Two: N 40° 42' 13.909", W 106° 27' 11.719"
Boat Launch Three: N 40° 41' 51.842", W 106° 27' 24.016"
Campground Two: N 40° 41' 47.075", W 106° 27' 52.359"
Campground Three: N 40° 42' 24.146", W 106° 28' 3.393"

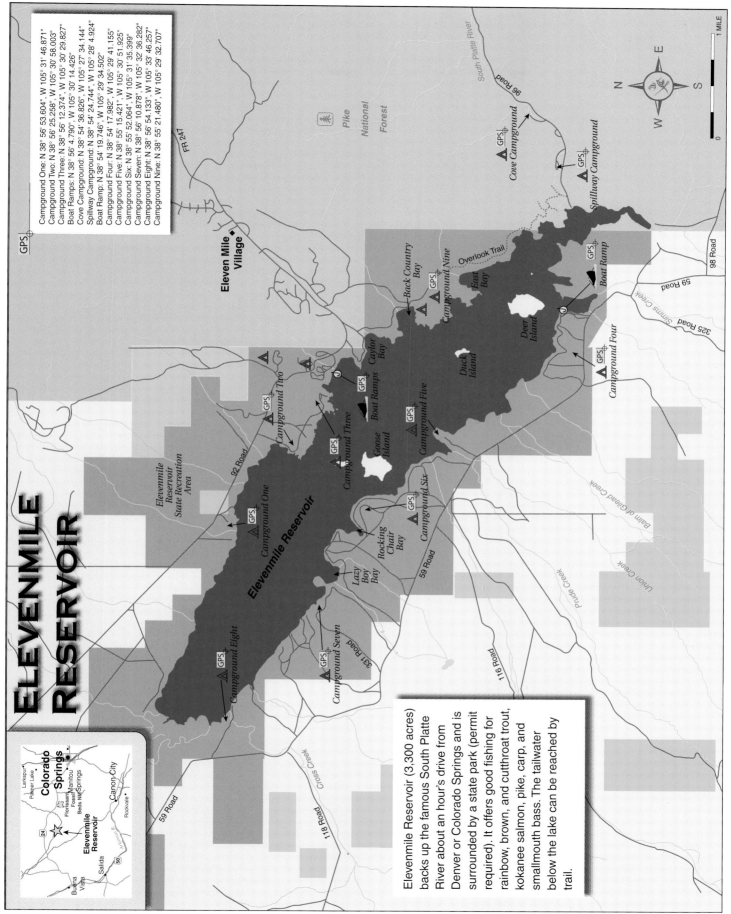

ELEVENMILE RESERVOIR

Campground One: N 38° 56' 53.604", W 105° 31' 46.871"
Campground Two: N 38° 56' 25.258", W 105° 30' 58.003"
Campground Three: N 38° 56' 12.374", W 105° 30' 29.827"
Boat Ramps: N 38° 56' 4.790", W 105° 30' 14.426"
Cove Campground: N 38° 54' 36.826", W 105° 27' 34.144"
Spillway Campground: N 38° 54' 24.744", W 105° 28' 4.924"
Boat Ramp: N 38° 54' 19.746", W 105° 29' 34.502"
Campground Four: N 38° 54' 17.982", W 105° 29' 41.155"
Campground Five: N 38° 55' 15.421", W 105° 30' 51.925"
Campground Six: N 38° 55' 52.064", W 105° 31' 35.399"
Campground Seven: N 38° 56' 52.064", W 105° 32' 36.282"
Campground Eight: N 38° 56' 54.133", W 105° 33' 46.257"
Campground Nine: N 38° 55' 21.480", W 105° 29' 32.707"

Elevenmile Reservoir (3,300 acres) backs up the famous South Platte River about an hour's drive from Denver or Colorado Springs and is surrounded by a state park (permit required). It offers good fishing for rainbow, brown, and cutthroat trout, kokanee salmon, pike, carp, and smallmouth bass. The tailwater below the lake can be reached by trail.

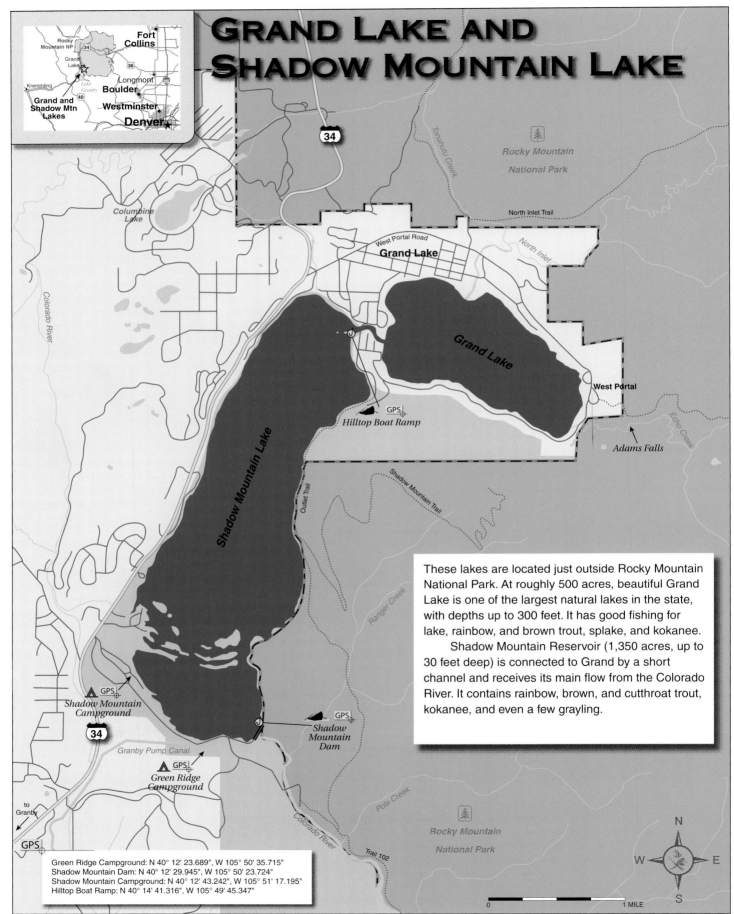

GRAND LAKE AND SHADOW MOUNTAIN LAKE

Rocky Mountain NP

Fort Collins

Grand Lakes

Kremmling

Lake Granby

Boulder

Longmont

Westminster

Denver

Grand and Shadow Mtn Lakes

Columbine Lake

Tonahutu Creek

Rocky Mountain National Park

North Inlet Trail

West Portal Road

Grand Lake

North Inlet

Colorado River

Grand Lake

West Portal

GPS

Hilltop Boat Ramp

Adams Falls

Echo Creek

Shadow Mountain Lake

Outlet Trail

Shadow Mountain Trail

Ranger Creek

These lakes are located just outside Rocky Mountain National Park. At roughly 500 acres, beautiful Grand Lake is one of the largest natural lakes in the state, with depths up to 300 feet. It has good fishing for lake, rainbow, and brown trout, splake, and kokanee.

Shadow Mountain Reservoir (1,350 acres, up to 30 feet deep) is connected to Grand by a short channel and receives its main flow from the Colorado River. It contains rainbow, brown, and cutthroat trout, kokanee, and even a few grayling.

GPS
Shadow Mountain Campground

GPS

Shadow Mountain Dam

Granby Pump Canal

GPS
Green Ridge Campground

Pole Creek

to Granby

GPS

Colorado River

Trail 102

Rocky Mountain National Park

N
W E
S

Green Ridge Campground: N 40° 12' 23.689", W 105° 50' 35.715"
Shadow Mountain Dam: N 40° 12' 29.945", W 105° 50' 23.724"
Shadow Mountain Campground: N 40° 12' 43.242", W 105° 51' 17.195"
Hilltop Boat Ramp: N 40° 14' 41.316", W 105° 49' 45.347"

0   1 MILE

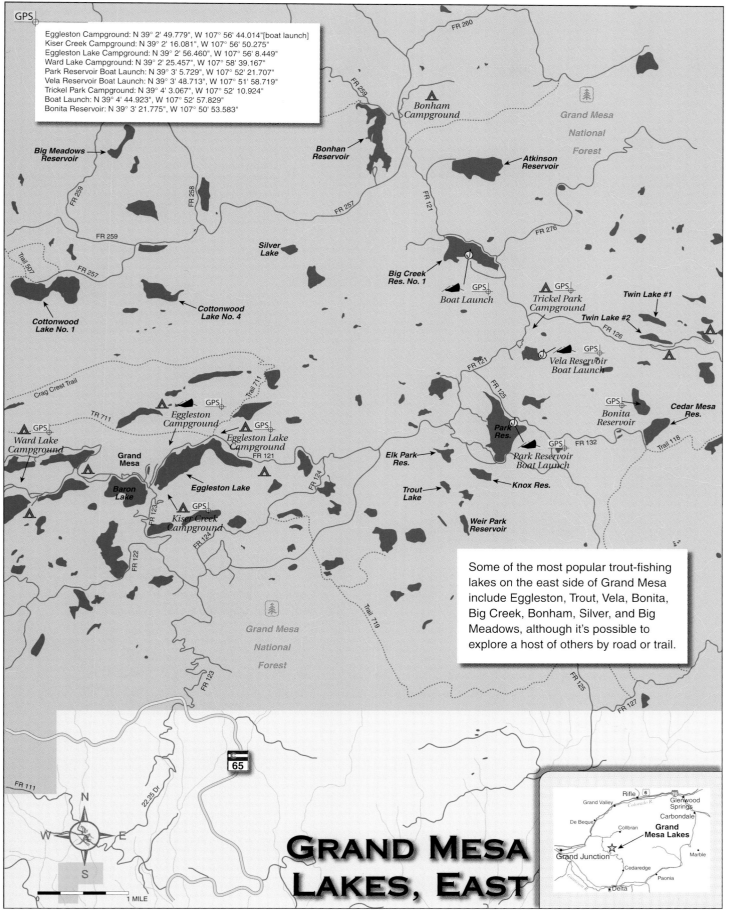

GPS

Eggleston Campground: N 39° 2' 49.779", W 107° 56' 44.014"[boat launch]
Kiser Creek Campground: N 39° 2' 16.081", W 107° 56' 50.275"
Eggleston Lake Campground: N 39° 2' 56.460", W 107° 56' 8.449"
Ward Lake Campground: N 39° 2' 25.457", W 107° 58' 39.167"
Park Reservoir Boat Launch: N 39° 3' 5.729", W 107° 52' 21.707"
Vela Reservoir Boat Launch: N 39° 3' 48.713", W 107° 51' 58.719"
Trickel Park Campground: N 39° 4' 3.067", W 107° 52' 10.924"
Boat Launch: N 39° 4' 44.923", W 107° 52' 57.829"
Bonita Reservoir: N 39° 3' 21.775", W 107° 50' 53.583"

FR 260

Bonham
Campground

Grand Mesa

National

Forest

FR 259

Big Meadows
Reservoir

Bonhan
Reservoir

Atkinson
Reservoir

FR 259

FR 258

FR 121

FR 257

FR 276

FR 259

FR 257

Silver
Lake

Big Creek
Res. No. 1

GPS

GPS

Trail 507

Boat Launch

Trickel Park
Campground

Twin Lake #1

Cottonwood
Lake No. 4

Twin Lake #2

FR 126

Cottonwood
Lake No. 1

Crag Crest Trail

FR 121

Vela Reservoir
Boat Launch

GPS

TR 711

Trail 711

FR 125

GPS

Bonita
Reservoir

Cedar Mesa
Res.

GPS

Eggleston
Campground

GPS

GPS

Trail 118

Eggleston Lake
Campground

Park
Res.

Ward Lake
Campground

FR 121

Elk Park
Res.

GPS

FR 132

Park Reservoir
Boat Launch

Grand
Mesa

Knox Res.

Baron
Lake

Eggleston Lake

Trout
Lake

FR 123

GPS

Kiser Creek
Campground

FR 124

Weir Park
Reservoir

Some of the most popular trout-fishing
lakes on the east side of Grand Mesa
include Eggleston, Trout, Vela, Bonita,
Big Creek, Bonham, Silver, and Big
Meadows, although it's possible to
explore a host of others by road or trail.

FR 122

FR 124

Grand Mesa

National

Forest

Trail 719

FR 123

FR 125

FR 127

65

FR 111

22.25 Dr.

N

W   E

S

0   1 MILE

GRAND MESA
LAKES, EAST

Rifle 6

Grand Valley   Colorado R.   Glenwood
                                        Springs

De Beque   Carbondale

        Collbran   **Grand**
                        Mesa Lakes

Grand Junction   Marble

                Cedaredge

                        Paonia

        Gunnison R.   Delta

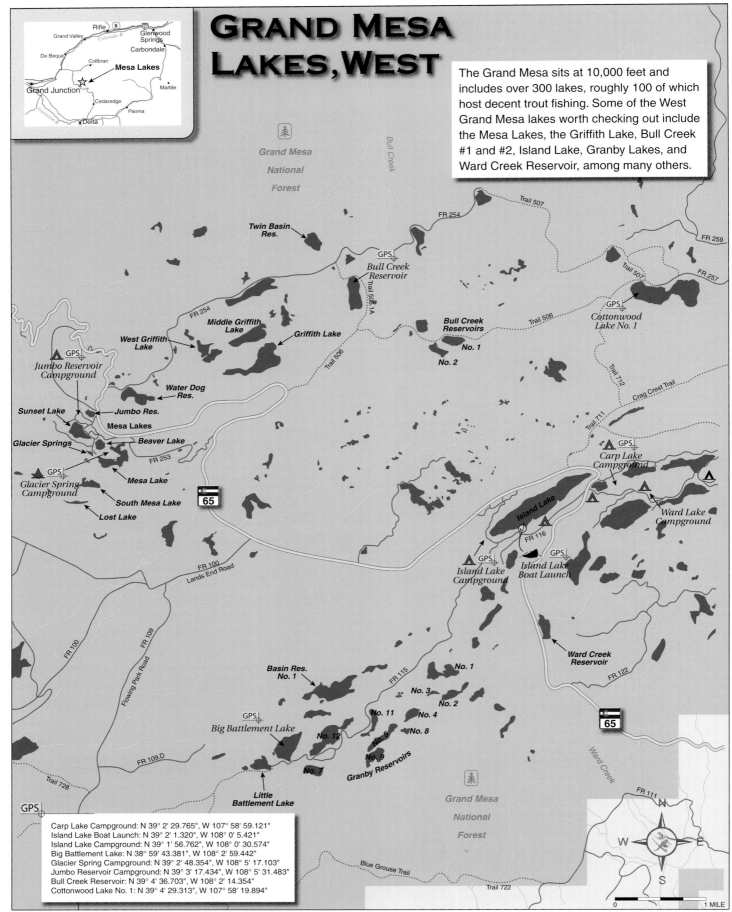

GRAND MESA LAKES, WEST

The Grand Mesa sits at 10,000 feet and includes over 300 lakes, roughly 100 of which host decent trout fishing. Some of the West Grand Mesa lakes worth checking out include the Mesa Lakes, the Griffith Lake, Bull Creek #1 and #2, Island Lake, Granby Lakes, and Ward Creek Reservoir, among many others.

Carp Lake Campground: N 39° 2' 29.765", W 107° 58' 59.121"
Island Lake Boat Launch: N 39° 2' 1.320", W 108° 0' 5.421"
Island Lake Campground: N 39° 1' 56.762", W 108° 0' 30.574"
Big Battlement Lake: N 38° 59' 43.381", W 108° 2' 59.442"
Glacier Spring Campground: N 39° 2' 48.354", W 108° 5' 17.103"
Jumbo Reservoir Campground: N 39° 3' 17.434", W 108° 5' 31.483"
Bull Creek Reservoir: N 39° 4' 36.703", W 108° 2' 14.354"
Cottonwood Lake No. 1: N 39° 4' 29.313", W 107° 58' 19.894"

© 2008 Wilderness Adventures Press, Inc.

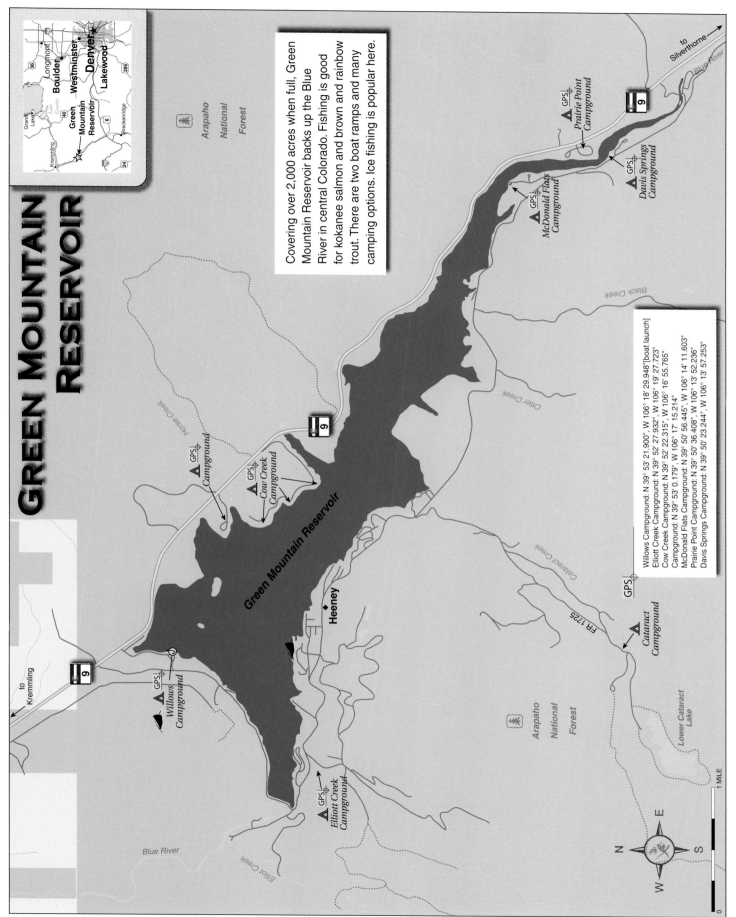

GREEN MOUNTAIN RESERVOIR

Covering over 2,000 acres when full, Green Mountain Reservoir backs up the Blue River in central Colorado. Fishing is good for kokanee salmon and brown and rainbow trout. There are two boat ramps and many camping options. Ice fishing is popular here.

Arapaho National Forest

to Silverthorne

Blue River

GPS
Prairie Point Campground

GPS
Davis Springs Campground

9

GPS
McDonald Flats Campground

Black Creek

Otter Creek

Horse Creek

GPS
Campground

GPS
Cow Creek Campground

9

Green Mountain Reservoir

Cataract Creek

Willows Campground: N 39° 53' 21.900", W 106° 18' 29.948"[boat launch]
Elliott Creek Campground: N 39° 52' 27.932", W 106° 19' 27.723"
Cow Creek Campground: N 39° 52' 22.315", W 106° 16' 55.765"
Campground: N 39° 53' 0.179", W 106° 17' 15.214"
McDonald Flats Campground: N 39° 50' 56.445", W 106° 14' 11.603"
Prairie Point Campground: N 39° 50' 36.408", W 106° 13' 52.236"
Davis Springs Campground: N 39° 50' 23.244", W 106° 13' 57.253"

GPS

FR 1725

Cataract Campground

Heeney

to Kremmling

9

GPS
Willows Campground

Elliott Creek

GPS
Elliott Creek Campground

Blue River

Arapaho National Forest

Lower Cataract Lake

N E S W

1 MILE

0

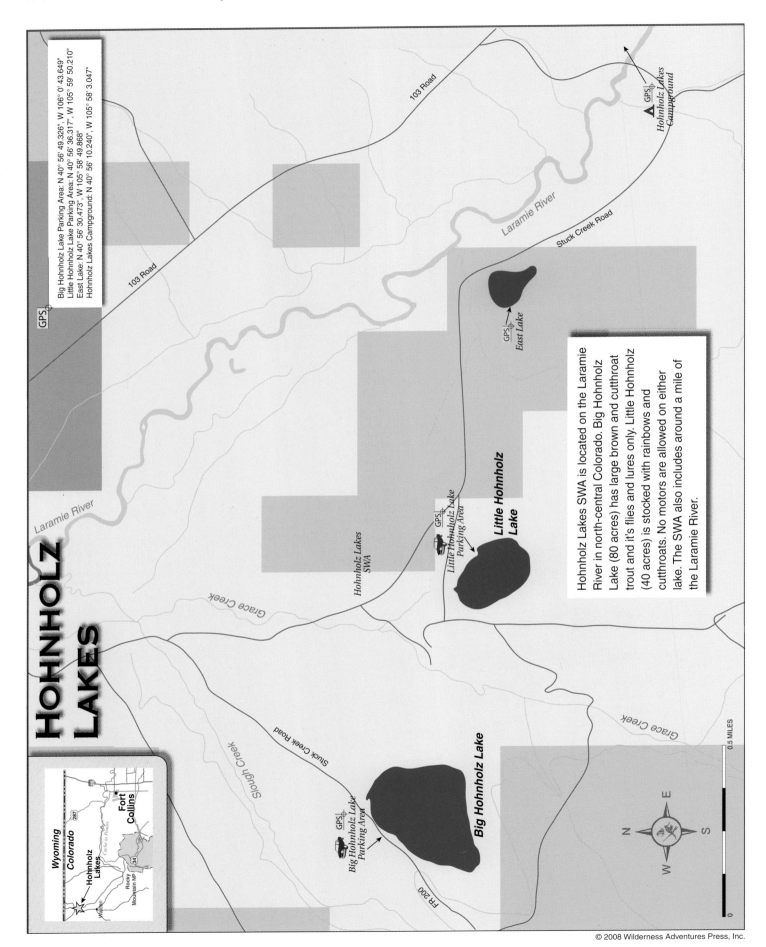

HOHNHOLZ LAKES

Big Hohnholz Lake Parking Area: N 40° 56' 49.326", W 106° 0' 43.649"
Little Hohnholz Lake Parking Area: N 40° 56' 36.317", W 105° 59' 50.210"
East Lake: N 40° 56' 30.473", W 105° 58' 49.868"
Hohnholz Lakes Campground: N 40° 56' 10.240", W 105° 58' 3.047"

GPS

103 Road

103 Road

Laramie River

Stuck Creek Road

GPS
Hohnholz Lakes Campground

Laramie River

GPS
East Lake

Hohnholz Lakes SWA

GPS
Little Hohnholz Lake Parking Area

Little Hohnholz Lake

Grace Creek

Hohnholz Lakes SWA is located on the Laramie River in north-central Colorado. Big Hohnholz Lake (80 acres) has large brown and cutthroat trout and it's flies and lures only. Little Hohnholz (40 acres) is stocked with rainbows and cutthroats. No motors are allowed on either lake. The SWA also includes around a mile of the Laramie River.

Slough Creek

Stuck Creek Road

GPS
Big Hohnholz Lake Parking Area

Big Hohnholz Lake

Grace Creek

FR 200

Wyoming
Colorado

287

Fort Collins

Cache la Poudre

Hohnholz Lakes

34

Rocky Mountain NP

Walden

N E S W

0   0.5 MILES

© 2008 Wilderness Adventures Press, Inc.

HORSESHOE AND MARTIN LAKES

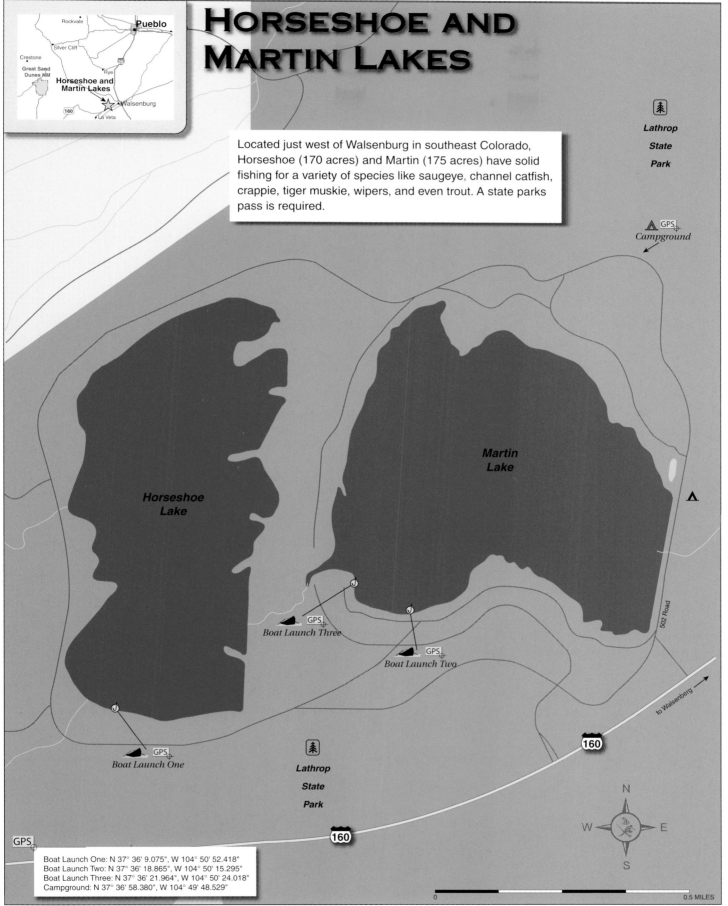

Located just west of Walsenburg in southeast Colorado, Horseshoe (170 acres) and Martin (175 acres) have solid fishing for a variety of species like saugeye, channel catfish, crappie, tiger muskie, wipers, and even trout. A state parks pass is required.

Lathrop State Park

Campground

Martin Lake

Horseshoe Lake

Boat Launch Three
GPS

Boat Launch Two
GPS

502 Road

Boat Launch One
GPS

to Walsenberg

160

Lathrop State Park

160

N
W E
S

GPS

Boat Launch One: N 37° 36' 9.075", W 104° 50' 52.418"
Boat Launch Two: N 37° 36' 18.865", W 104° 50' 15.295"
Boat Launch Three: N 37° 36' 21.964", W 104° 50' 24.018"
Campground: N 37° 36' 58.380", W 104° 49' 48.529"

0   0.5 MILES

© 2008 Wilderness Adventures Press, Inc.

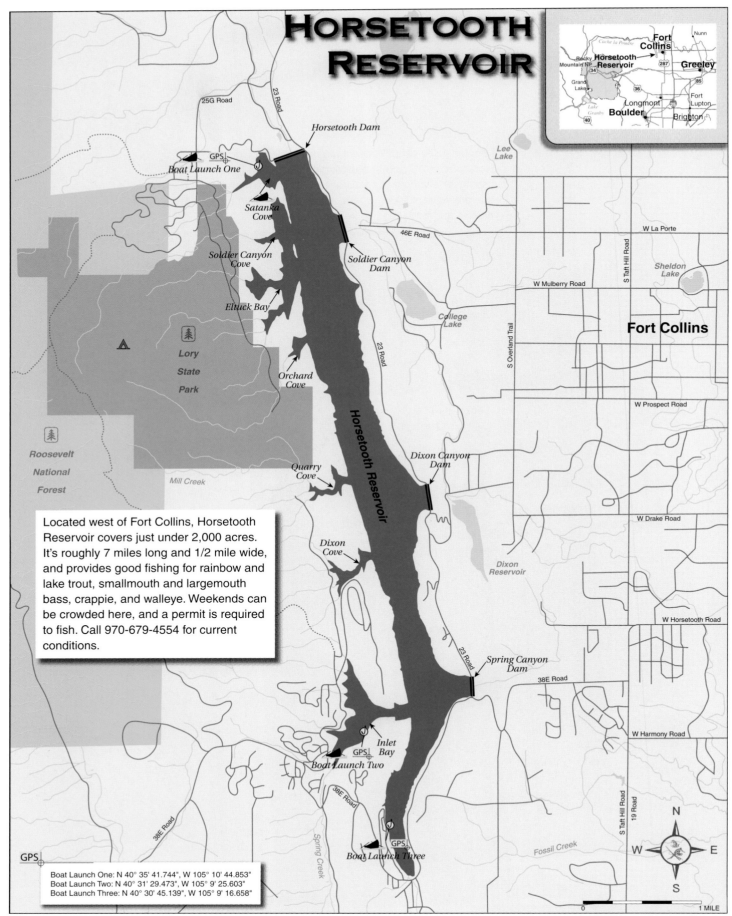

HORSETOOTH RESERVOIR

Horsetooth Dam

GPS

Boat Launch One

Satanka Cove

Soldier Canyon Cove

Soldier Canyon Dam

Eltuck Bay

Lory State Park

Orchard Cove

Roosevelt National Forest

Mill Creek

Quarry Cove

Dixon Canyon Dam

Horsetooth Reservoir

Dixon Cove

Located west of Fort Collins, Horsetooth Reservoir covers just under 2,000 acres. It's roughly 7 miles long and 1/2 mile wide, and provides good fishing for rainbow and lake trout, smallmouth and largemouth bass, crappie, and walleye. Weekends can be crowded here, and a permit is required to fish. Call 970-679-4554 for current conditions.

Dixon Reservoir

Spring Canyon Dam

Inlet Bay

GPS

Boat Launch Two

Spring Creek

GPS

Boat Launch Three

Fossil Creek

GPS

Boat Launch One: N 40° 35' 41.744", W 105° 10' 44.853"
Boat Launch Two: N 40° 31' 29.473", W 105° 9' 25.603"
Boat Launch Three: N 40° 30' 45.139", W 105° 9' 16.658"

Lee Lake

W La Porte

46E Road

S Taft Hill Road

Sheldon Lake

W Mulberry Road

College Lake

S Overland Trail

Fort Collins

23 Road

W Prospect Road

W Drake Road

W Horsetooth Road

38E Road

W Harmony Road

19 Road

N / E / S / W

0 — 1 MILE

25G Road

23 Road

Fort Collins

Nunn

287

Greeley

Rocky Mountain NP — Horsetooth Reservoir

34

Grand Lake

Lake Granby

40

Longmont

36

85

Fort Lupton

Boulder

Brighton

© 2008 Wilderness Adventures Press, Inc.

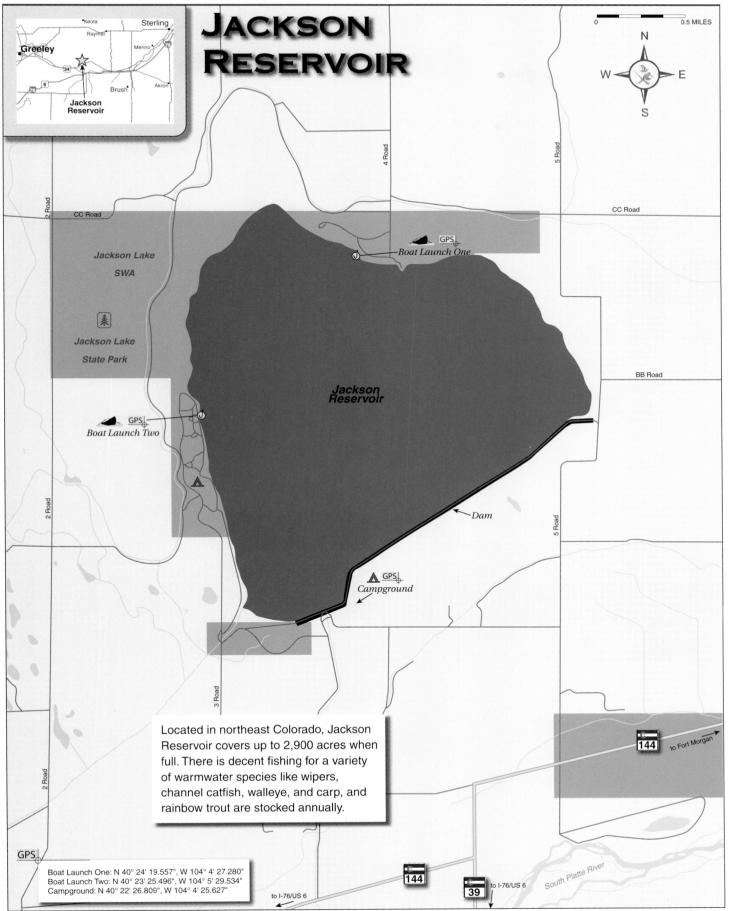

JACKSON RESERVOIR

Keota

Sterling

Raymer

Merino

Greeley

Brush

Akron

Jackson Reservoir

0   0.5 MILES

N
W — E
S

4 Road

5 Road

2 Road

CC Road

CC Road

Jackson Lake
SWA

Boat Launch One
GPS

Jackson Lake
State Park

BB Road

Boat Launch Two
GPS

Jackson
Reservoir

2 Road

Dam

5 Road

Campground
GPS

3 Road

Located in northeast Colorado, Jackson
Reservoir covers up to 2,900 acres when
full. There is decent fishing for a variety
of warmwater species like wipers,
channel catfish, walleye, and carp, and
rainbow trout are stocked annually.

144
to Fort Morgan

2 Road

GPS

Boat Launch One: N 40° 24' 19.557", W 104° 4' 27.280"
Boat Launch Two: N 40° 23' 25.496", W 104° 5' 29.534"
Campground: N 40° 22' 26.809", W 104° 4' 25.627"

144

39   to I-76/US 6

to I-76/US 6

South Platte River

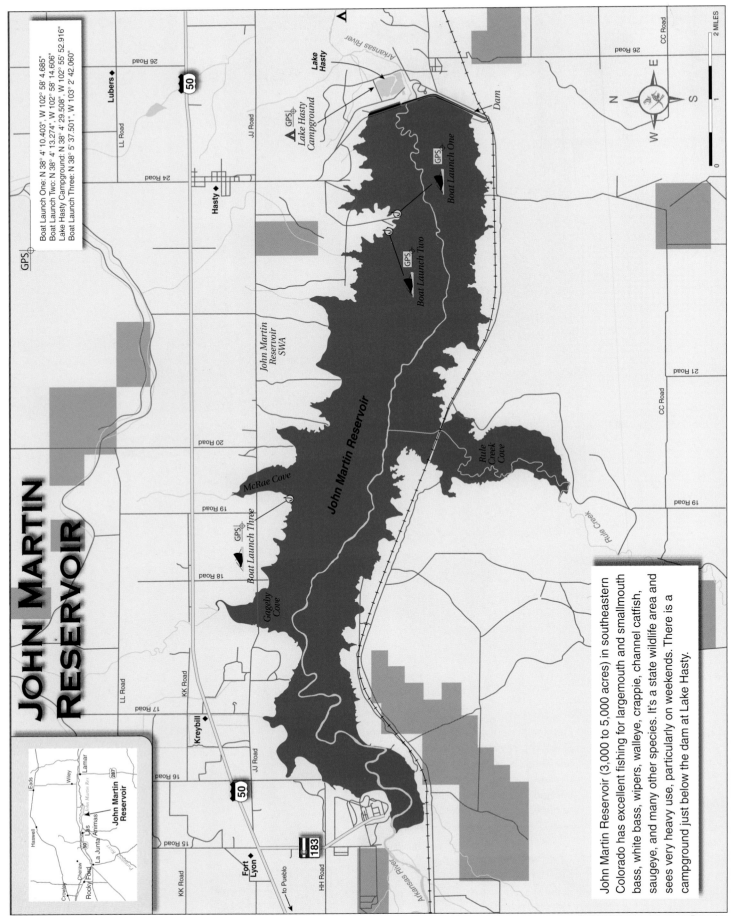

JOHN MARTIN RESERVOIR

Boat Launch One: N 38° 4' 10.403', W 102° 58' 4.685"
Boat Launch Two: N 38° 4' 13.274', W 102° 58' 14.606"
Lake Hasty Campground: N 38° 4' 29.508", W 102° 55' 52.916"
Boat Launch Three: N 38° 5' 37.501", W 103° 2' 42.060"

John Martin Reservoir (3,000 to 5,000 acres) in southeastern Colorado has excellent fishing for largemouth and smallmouth bass, white bass, wipers, walleye, crappie, channel catfish, saugeye, and many other species. It's a state wildlife area and sees very heavy use, particularly on weekends. There is a campground just below the dam at Lake Hasty.

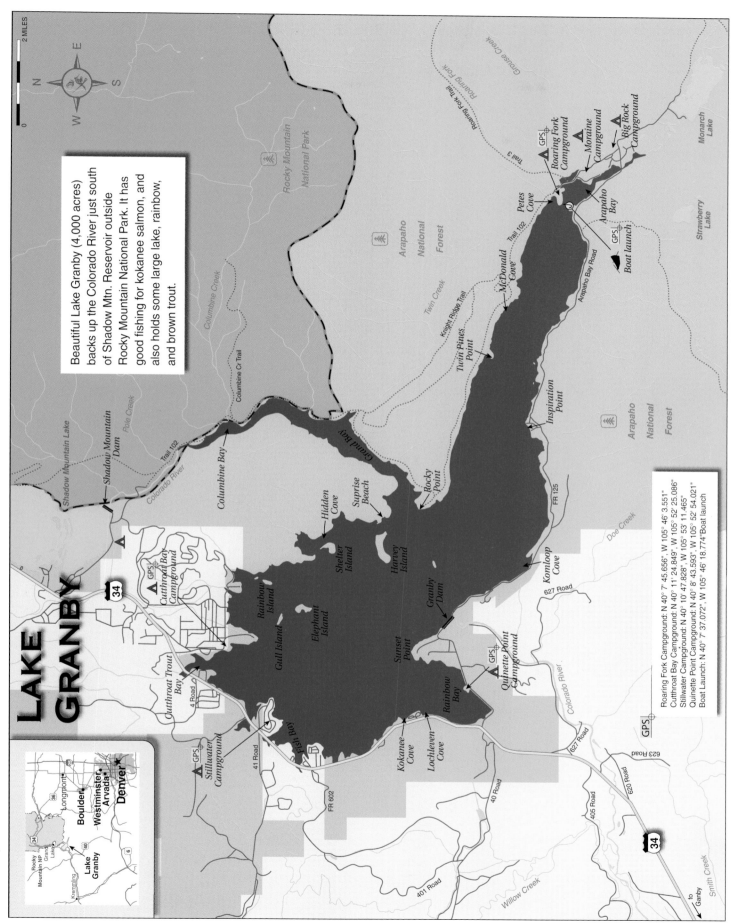

LAKE GRANBY

Beautiful Lake Granby (4,000 acres) backs up the Colorado River just south of Shadow Mtn. Reservoir outside Rocky Mountain National Park. It has good fishing for kokanee salmon, and also holds some large lake, rainbow, and brown trout.

Roaring Fork Campground: N 40° 7' 45.656", W 105° 46' 3.551"
Cutthroat Bay Campground: N 40° 11' 24.849", W 105° 52' 25.086"
Stillwater Campground: N 40° 10' 47.828", W 105° 53' 11.465"
Quinette Point Campground: N 40° 8' 43.593", W 105° 52' 54.021"
Boat Launch: N 40° 7' 37.072", W 105° 46' 18.774"Boat launch

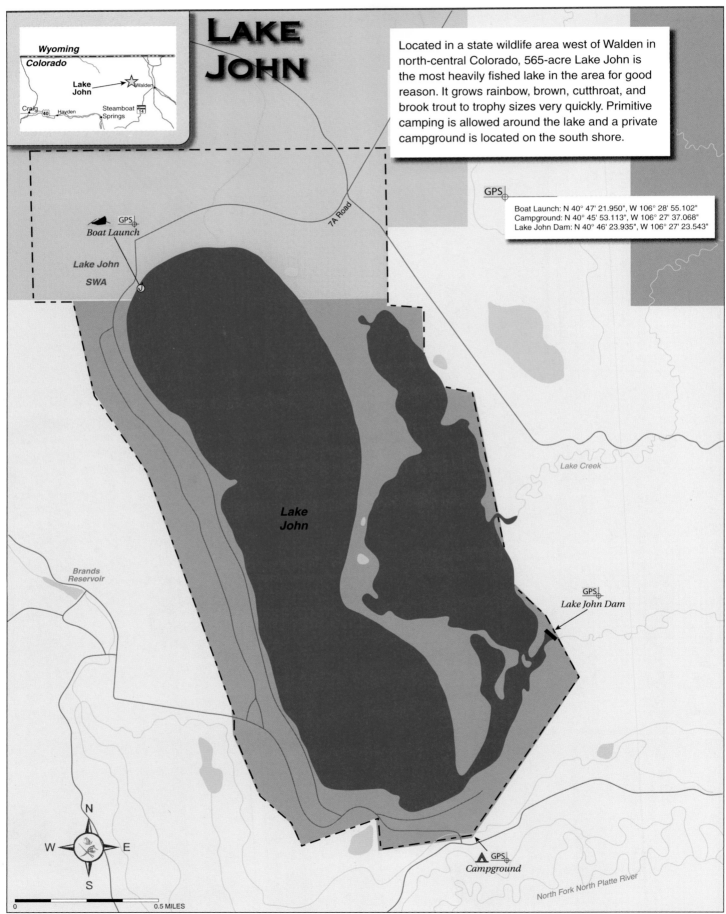

LAKE JOHN

Located in a state wildlife area west of Walden in north-central Colorado, 565-acre Lake John is the most heavily fished lake in the area for good reason. It grows rainbow, brown, cutthroat, and brook trout to trophy sizes very quickly. Primitive camping is allowed around the lake and a private campground is located on the south shore.

Wyoming
Colorado
Lake John
Walden
Craig
40
Hayden
Steamboat Springs
14

GPS
Boat Launch: N 40° 47' 21.950", W 106° 28' 55.102"
Campground: N 40° 45' 53.113", W 106° 27' 37.068"
Lake John Dam: N 40° 46' 23.935", W 106° 27' 23.543"

GPS
Boat Launch

7A Road

Lake John SWA

Lake Creek

Lake John

Brands Reservoir

GPS
Lake John Dam

N
W E
S

GPS
Campground

North Fork North Platte River

0   0.5 MILES

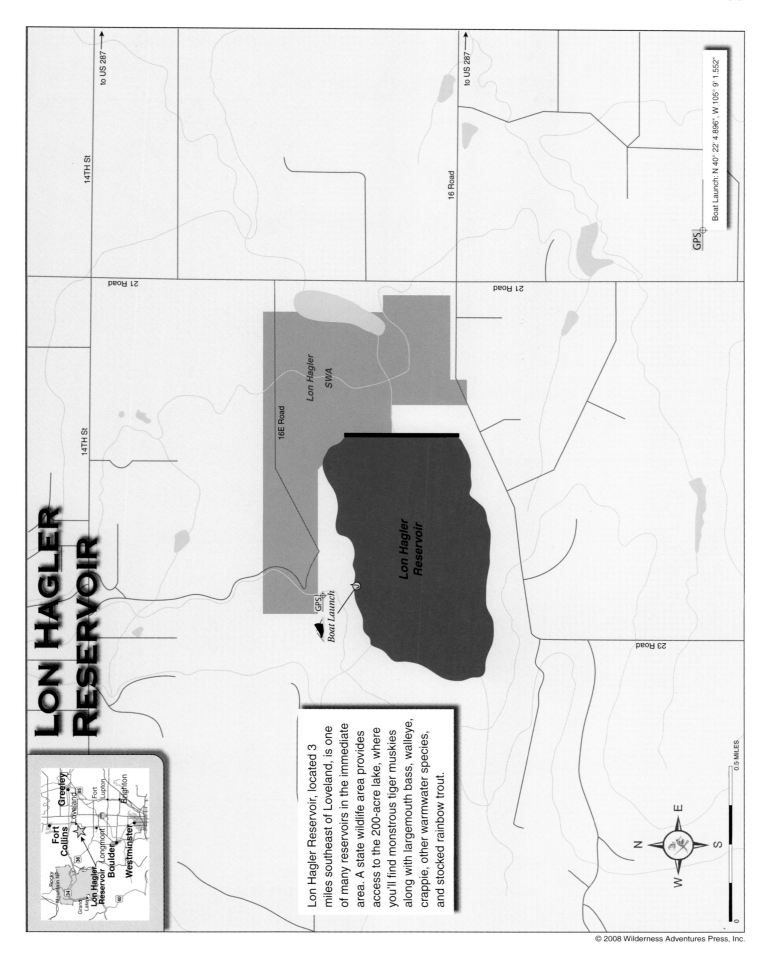

LON HAGLER RESERVOIR

Lon Hagler Reservoir, located 3 miles southeast of Loveland, is one of many reservoirs in the immediate area. A state wildlife area provides access to the 200-acre lake, where you'll find monstrous tiger muskies along with largemouth bass, walleye, crappie, other warmwater species, and stocked rainbow trout.

Lon Hagler SWA

Lon Hagler Reservoir

Boat Launch

GPS

14TH St

14TH St

16E Road

21 Road

21 Road

16 Road

23 Road

to US 287

to US 287

Boat Launch: N 40° 22' 4.896", W 105° 9' 1.552"

GPS

N
W   E
S

0   0.5 MILES

Fort Collins
Greeley
Loveland
Fort Lupton
Brighton
Lon Hagler Reservoir
Longmont
Boulder
Westminster
Rocky Mountain NP
Grand Lake

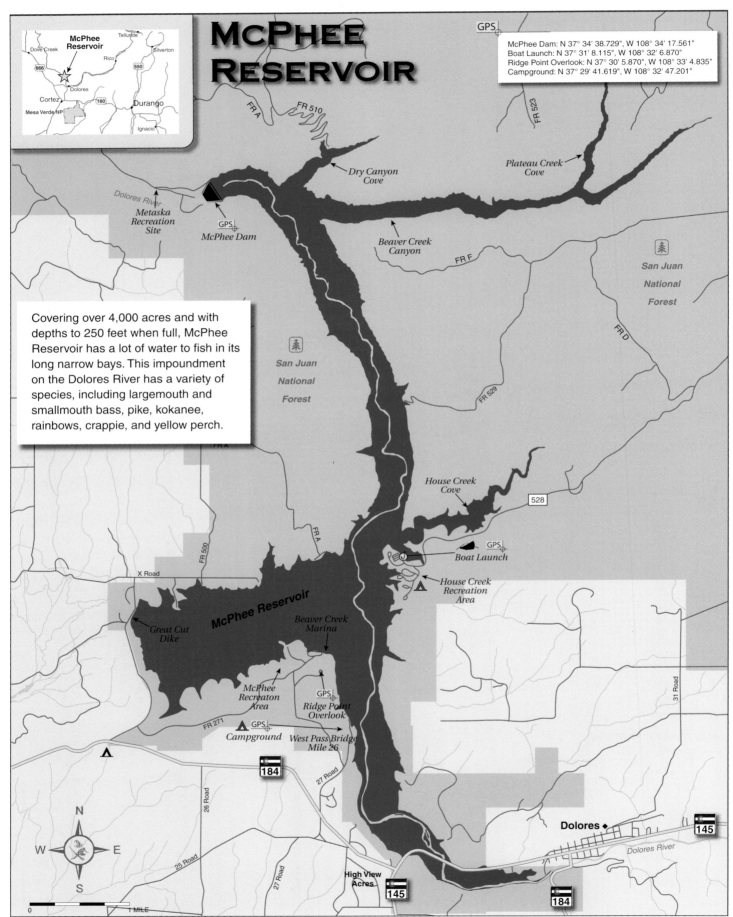

McPhee Reservoir

McPhee Dam: N 37° 34' 38.729", W 108° 34' 17.561"
Boat Launch: N 37° 31' 8.115", W 108° 32' 6.870"
Ridge Point Overlook: N 37° 30' 5.870", W 108° 33' 4.835"
Campground: N 37° 29' 41.619", W 108° 32' 47.201"

Covering over 4,000 acres and with depths to 250 feet when full, McPhee Reservoir has a lot of water to fish in its long narrow bays. This impoundment on the Dolores River has a variety of species, including largemouth and smallmouth bass, pike, kokanee, rainbows, crappie, and yellow perch.

© 2008 Wilderness Adventures Press, Inc.

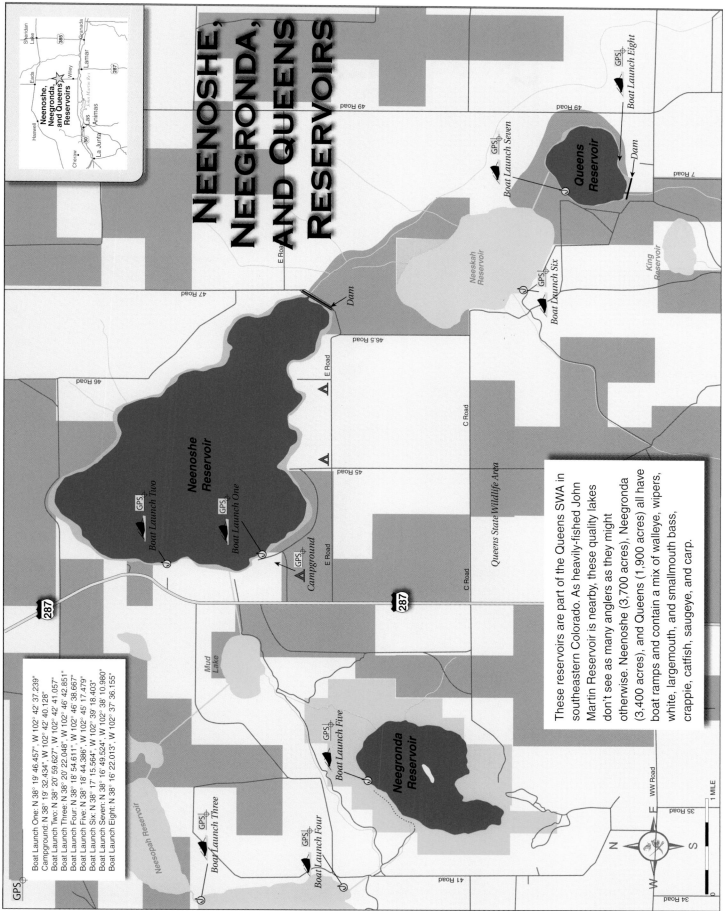

NEENOSHE, NEEGRONDA, AND QUEENS RESERVOIRS

Boat Launch One: N 38° 19' 46.457", W 102° 42' 37.239"
Campground: N 38° 19' 32.434", W 102° 42' 40.128"
Boat Launch Two: N 38° 20' 59.627", W 102° 42' 41.057"
Boat Launch Three: N 38° 20' 22.048", W 102° 46' 42.851"
Boat Launch Four: N 38° 18' 54.611", W 102° 46' 38.667"
Boat Launch Five: N 38° 18' 44.386", W 102° 45' 17.479"
Boat Launch Six: N 38° 17' 15.564", W 102° 39' 18.403"
Boat Launch Seven: N 38° 16' 49.524", W 102° 38' 10.980"
Boat Launch Eight: N 38° 16' 22.013", W 102° 37' 36.155"

These reservoirs are part of the Queens SWA in southeastern Colorado. As heavily-fished John Martin Reservoir is nearby, these quality lakes don't see as many anglers as they might otherwise. Neenoshe (3,700 acres), Neegronda (3,400 acres), and Queens (1,900 acres) all have boat ramps and contain a mix of walleye, wipers, white, largemouth, and smallmouth bass, crappie, catfish, saugeye, and carp.

Queens Reservoir

Neeskah Reservoir

King Reservoir

Neenoshe Reservoir

Neegronda Reservoir

Neesopah Reservoir

Mud Lake

Queens State Wildlife Area

Boat Launch Eight

Boat Launch Seven

Boat Launch Six

Boat Launch One

Boat Launch Two

Boat Launch Three

Boat Launch Four

Boat Launch Five

Campground

Dam

Dam

287

287

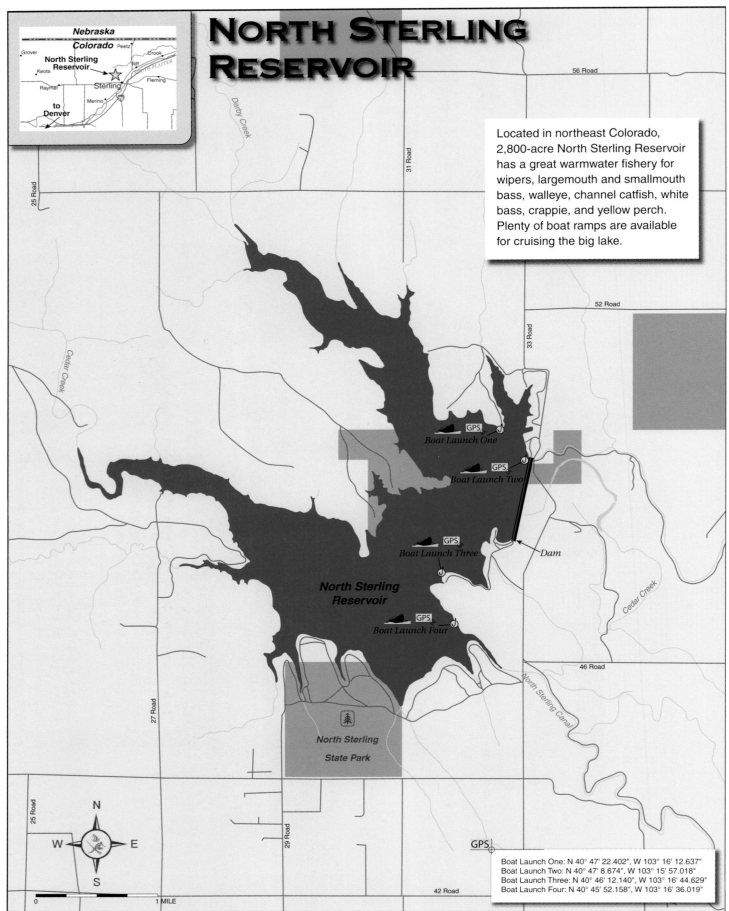

NORTH STERLING RESERVOIR

Nebraska
Colorado

Grover • Peetz
North Sterling
Reservoir
Keota •
Crook
Iliff
Fleming
NORTH PLATTER
Raymer •
Sterling
Merino
to
Denver

Located in northeast Colorado, 2,800-acre North Sterling Reservoir has a great warmwater fishery for wipers, largemouth and smallmouth bass, walleye, channel catfish, white bass, crappie, and yellow perch. Plenty of boat ramps are available for cruising the big lake.

56 Road

Darby Creek

31 Road

52 Road

25 Road

33 Road

Cedar Creek

GPS
Boat Launch One

GPS
Boat Launch Two

GPS
Boat Launch Three

Dam

North Sterling Reservoir

Cedar Creek

GPS
Boat Launch Four

46 Road

27 Road

North Sterling Canal

🌲

North Sterling
State Park

N
W + E
S

25 Road

29 Road

GPS

42 Road

0   1 MILE

Boat Launch One: N 40° 47' 22.402", W 103° 16' 12.637"
Boat Launch Two: N 40° 47' 8.674", W 103° 15' 57.018"
Boat Launch Three: N 40° 46' 12.140", W 103° 16' 44.629"
Boat Launch Four: N 40° 45' 52.158", W 103° 16' 36.019"

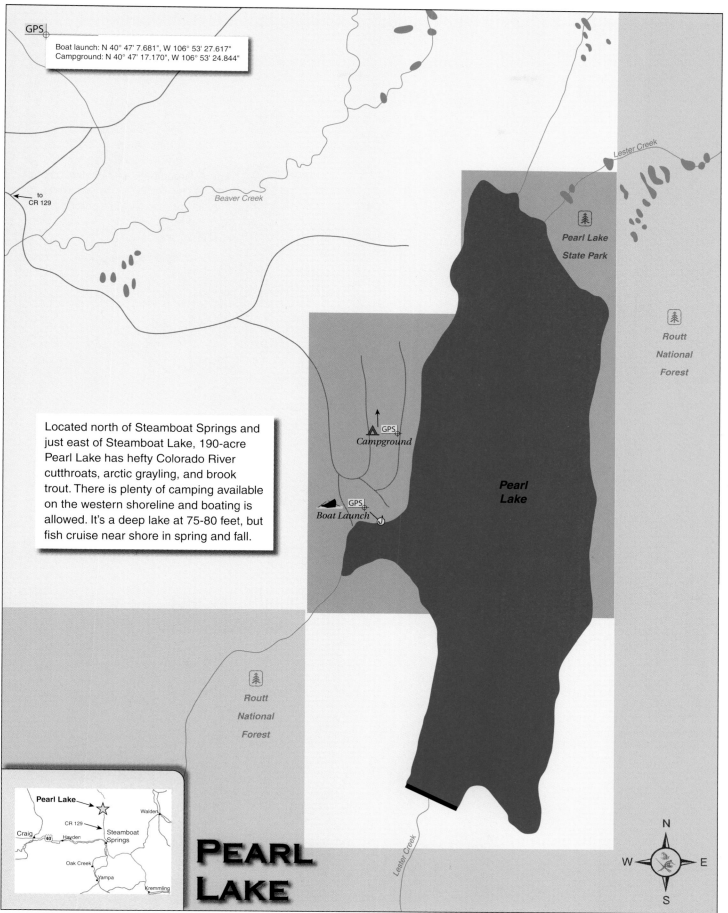

GPS

Boat launch: N 40° 47' 7.681", W 106° 53' 27.617"
Campground: N 40° 47' 17.170", W 106° 53' 24.844"

to
CR 129

Beaver Creek

Lester Creek

Pearl Lake
State Park

Routt
National
Forest

GPS
Campground

Located north of Steamboat Springs and just east of Steamboat Lake, 190-acre Pearl Lake has hefty Colorado River cutthroats, arctic grayling, and brook trout. There is plenty of camping available on the western shoreline and boating is allowed. It's a deep lake at 75-80 feet, but fish cruise near shore in spring and fall.

Pearl
Lake

GPS
Boat Launch

Routt
National
Forest

Pearl Lake

Walden

CR 129

Craig
40
Hayden
Steamboat
Springs

Oak Creek

Yampa

Kremmling

Lester Creek

PEARL
LAKE

N
W   E
S

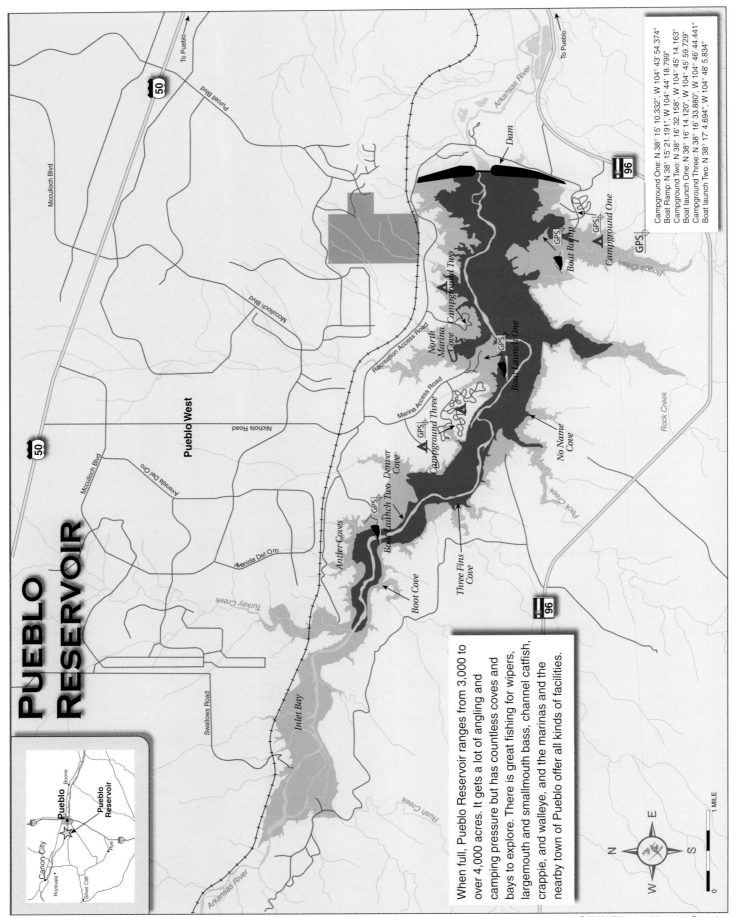

PUEBLO RESERVOIR

Campground One: N 38° 15' 10.332", W 104° 43' 54.374"
Boat Ramp: N 38° 15' 21.191", W 104° 44' 18.799"
Campground Two: N 38° 16' 32.158", W 104° 45' 14.163"
Boat launch One: N 38° 16' 14.120", W 104° 45' 59.729"
Campground Three: N 38° 16' 33.880", W 104° 46' 44.441"
Boat launch Two: N 38° 17' 4.694", W 104° 48' 5.834"

When full, Pueblo Reservoir ranges from 3,000 to over 4,000 acres. It gets a lot of angling and camping pressure but has countless coves and bays to explore. There is great fishing for wipers, largemouth and smallmouth bass, channel catfish, crappie, and walleye, and the marinas and the nearby town of Pueblo offer all kinds of facilities.

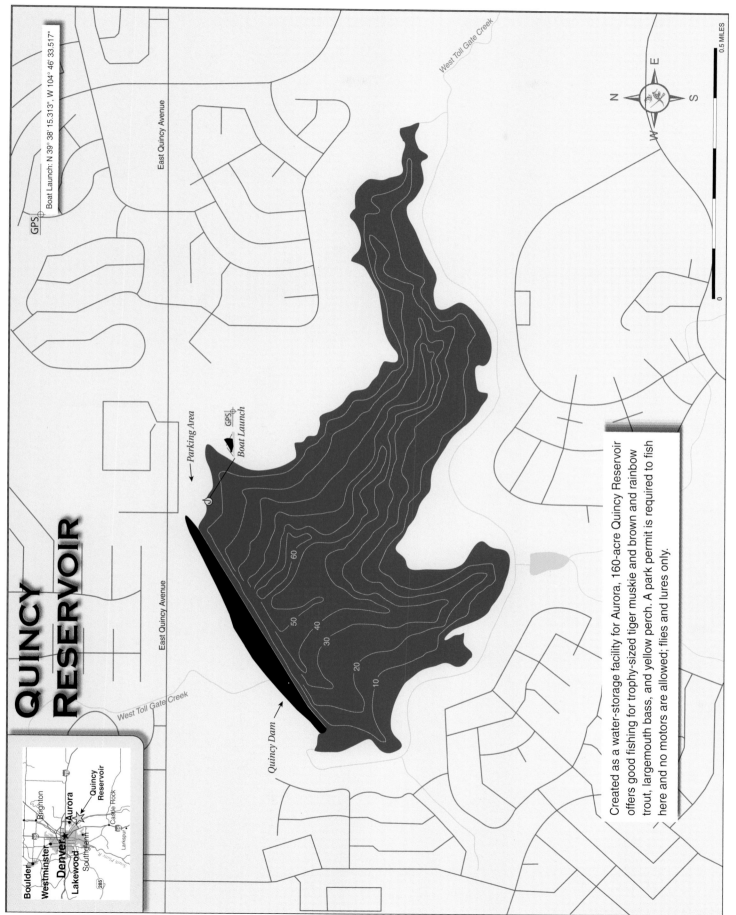

QUINCY RESERVOIR

GPS
Boat Launch: N 39° 38' 15.313"; W 104° 46' 33.517"

East Quincy Avenue

West Toll Gate Creek

Parking Area

GPS
Boat Launch

East Quincy Avenue

60

50

40

30

20

10

Quincy Dam

West Toll Gate Creek

N
W — E
S

0.5 MILES
0

Boulder
Westminster
Denver
Lakewood
Brighton
Aurora
Southglenn
Quincy Reservoir
Castle Rock
Larkspur
South Platte R.
285

Created as a water-storage facility for Aurora, 160-acre Quincy Reservoir offers good fishing for trophy-sized tiger muskie and brown and rainbow trout, largemouth bass, and yellow perch. A park permit is required to fish here and no motors are allowed; flies and lures only.

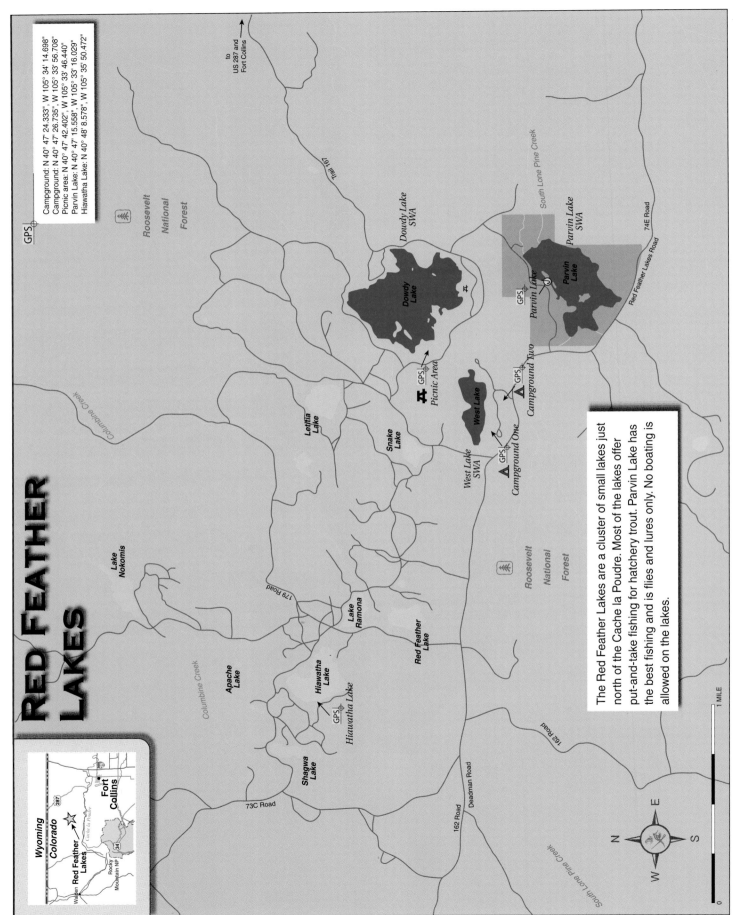

RED FEATHER LAKES

Campground: N 40° 47' 24.333", W 105° 34' 14.698"
Campground: N 40° 47' 26.735", W 105° 33' 56.708"
Picnic area: N 40° 47' 42.402", W 105° 33' 46.440"
Parvin Lake: N 40° 47' 15.558", W 105° 33' 16.029"
Hiawatha Lake: N 40° 48' 8.578", W 105° 35' 50.472"

The Red Feather Lakes are a cluster of small lakes just north of the Cache la Poudre. Most of the lakes offer put-and-take fishing for hatchery trout. Parvin Lake has the best fishing and is flies and lures only. No boating is allowed on the lakes.

SANCHEZ RESERVOIR

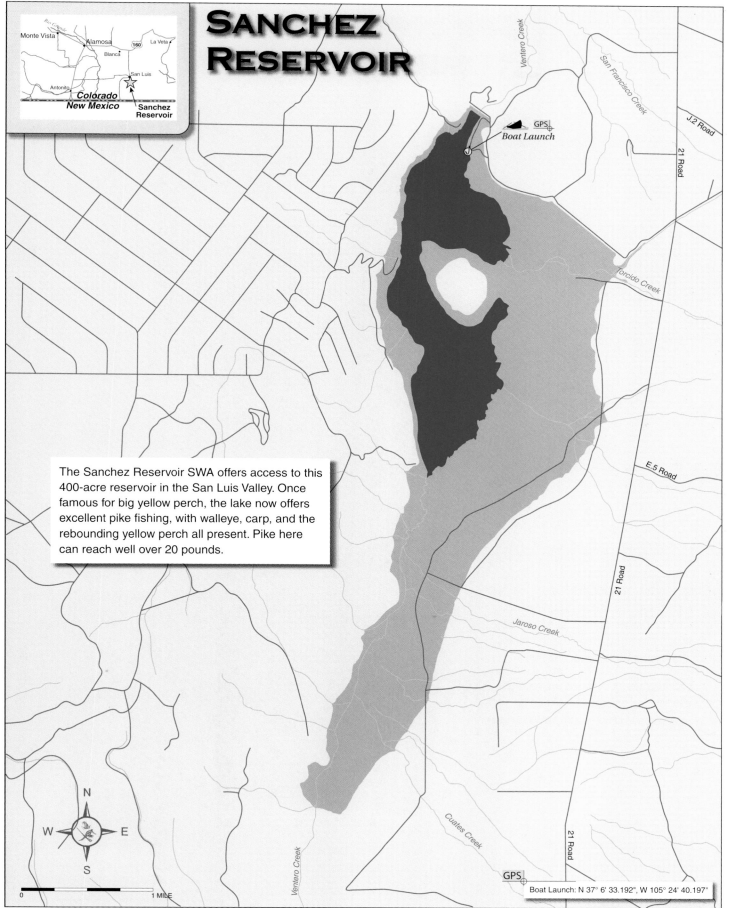

The Sanchez Reservoir SWA offers access to this 400-acre reservoir in the San Luis Valley. Once famous for big yellow perch, the lake now offers excellent pike fishing, with walleye, carp, and the rebounding yellow perch all present. Pike here can reach well over 20 pounds.

Boat Launch: N 37° 6' 33.192", W 105° 24' 40.197"

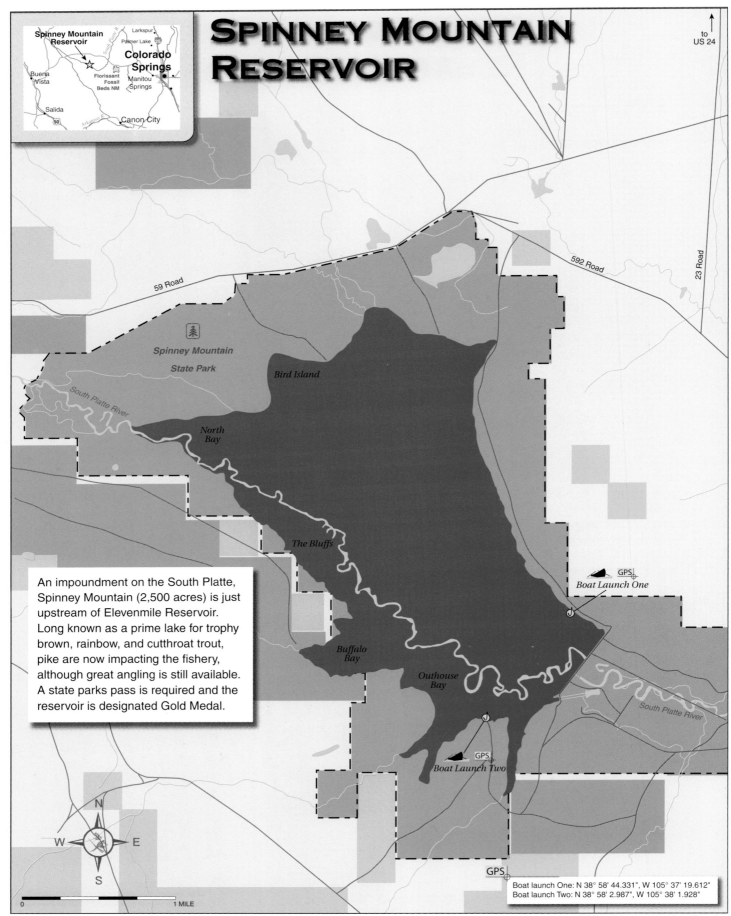

SPINNEY MOUNTAIN RESERVOIR

Spinney Mountain Reservoir

Larkspur
Palmer Lake
Colorado Springs
Buena Vista
Florissant Fossil Beds NM
Manitou Springs
Salida
Canon City

to US 24

592 Road

23 Road

59 Road

Spinney Mountain State Park

South Platte River

Bird Island

North Bay

The Bluffs

Buffalo Bay

Outhouse Bay

Boat Launch One
GPS

Boat Launch Two
GPS

South Platte River

An impoundment on the South Platte, Spinney Mountain (2,500 acres) is just upstream of Elevenmile Reservoir. Long known as a prime lake for trophy brown, rainbow, and cutthroat trout, pike are now impacting the fishery, although great angling is still available. A state parks pass is required and the reservoir is designated Gold Medal.

N
W   E
S

0   1 MILE

GPS

Boat launch One: N 38° 58' 44.331", W 105° 37' 19.612"
Boat launch Two: N 38° 58' 2.987", W 105° 38' 1.928"

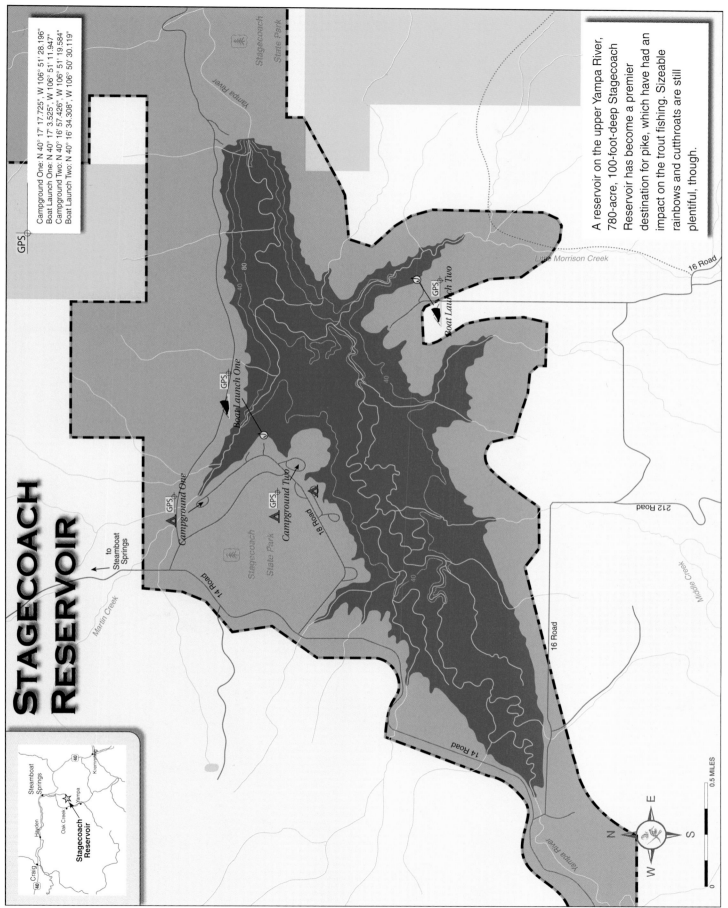

STAGECOACH RESERVOIR

Campground One: N 40° 17' 17.725", W 106° 51' 28.196"
Boat Launch One: N 40° 17' 3.525", W 106° 51' 11.947"
Campground Two: N 40° 16' 57.426", W 106° 51' 19.584"
Boat Launch Two: N 40° 16' 34.308", W 106° 50' 30.119"

A reservoir on the upper Yampa River, 780-acre, 100-foot-deep Stagecoach Reservoir has become a premier destination for pike, which have had an impact on the trout fishing. Sizeable rainbows and cutthroats are still plentiful, though.

to Steamboat Springs

Stagecoach State Park

Campground One
Boat Launch One
Campground Two
Boat Launch Two

Martin Creek

Yampa River

Little Morrison Creek

16 Road

212 Road

14 Road

18 Road

Middle Creek

Steamboat Springs
Hayden
Craig
Oak Creek
Yampa
Kremmling
Stagecoach Reservoir

0.5 MILES

© 2008 Wilderness Adventures Press, Inc.

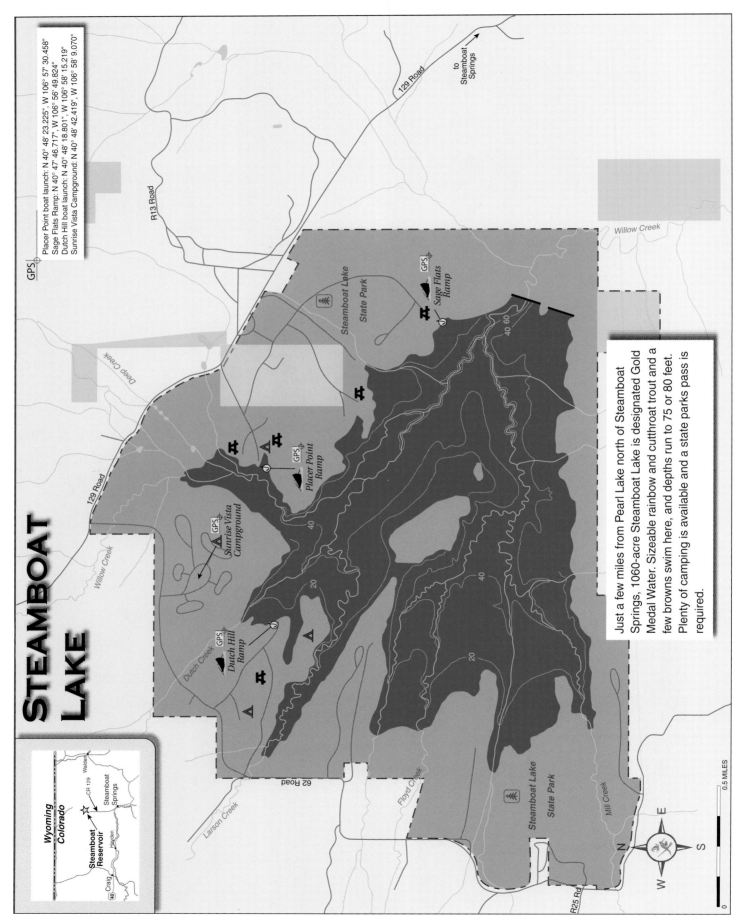

STEAMBOAT LAKE

Just a few miles from Pearl Lake north of Steamboat Springs, 1060-acre Steamboat Lake is designated Gold Medal Water. Sizeable rainbow and cutthroat trout and a few browns swim here, and depths run to 75 or 80 feet. Plenty of camping is available and a state parks pass is required.

Placer Point boat launch: N 40° 48' 23.225", W 106° 57' 30.458"
Sage Flats Ramp: N 40° 47' 46.717", W 106° 56' 49.824"
Dutch Hill boat launch: N 40° 48' 18.801", W 106° 58' 15.219"
Sunrise Vista Campground: N 40° 48' 42.419", W 106° 58' 9.070"

Sage Flats Ramp
Placer Point Ramp
Sunrise Vista Campground
Dutch Hill Ramp
Steamboat Lake State Park

Willow Creek
Deep Creek
Larson Creek
Dutch Creek
Floyd Creek
Mill Creek

129 Road
R13 Road
62 Road
R25 Rd
to Steamboat Springs

Wyoming
Colorado
Walden
CR 129
Steamboat Springs
Steamboat Reservoir
Hayden
Craig

0.5 MILES

TAYLOR PARK RESERVOIR

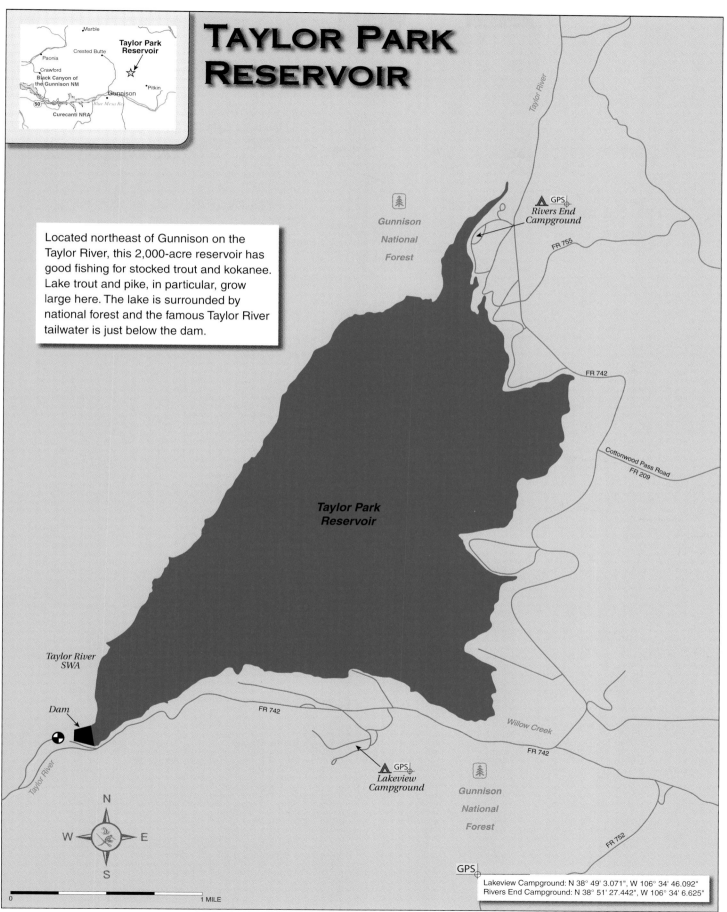

Located northeast of Gunnison on the Taylor River, this 2,000-acre reservoir has good fishing for stocked trout and kokanee. Lake trout and pike, in particular, grow large here. The lake is surrounded by national forest and the famous Taylor River tailwater is just below the dam.

Marble
Crested Butte
Paonia
Crawford
Black Canyon of the Gunnison NM
Curecanti NRA
50
Gunnison
Pitkin
Blue Mesa Res.
Taylor Park Reservoir

Taylor River

Gunnison National Forest

Rivers End Campground
GPS
FR 755

FR 742

Cottonwood Pass Road
FR 209

Taylor Park Reservoir

Taylor River SWA

Dam

FR 742

Willow Creek

FR 742

Lakeview Campground
GPS

Gunnison National Forest

FR 752

Taylor River

N
W   E
S

GPS

0   1 MILE

Lakeview Campground: N 38° 49' 3.071", W 106° 34' 46.092"
Rivers End Campground: N 38° 51' 27.442", W 106° 34' 6.625"

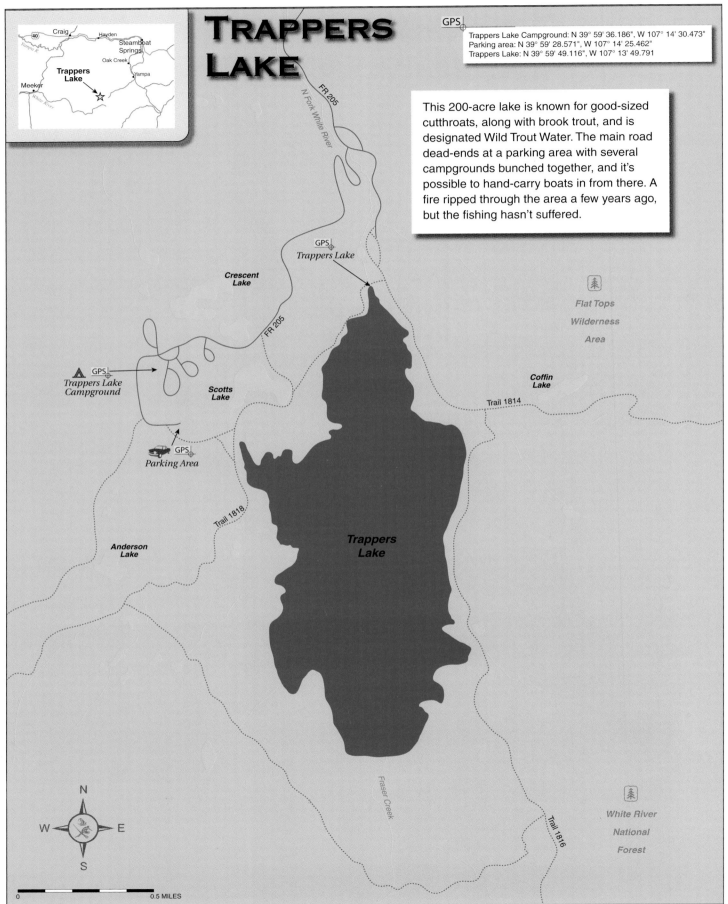

TRAPPERS LAKE

GPS

Trappers Lake Campground: N 39° 59' 36.186", W 107° 14' 30.473"
Parking area: N 39° 59' 28.571", W 107° 14' 25.462"
Trappers Lake: N 39° 59' 49.116", W 107° 13' 49.791

This 200-acre lake is known for good-sized cutthroats, along with brook trout, and is designated Wild Trout Water. The main road dead-ends at a parking area with several campgrounds bunched together, and it's possible to hand-carry boats in from there. A fire ripped through the area a few years ago, but the fishing hasn't suffered.

Craig
Hayden
Steamboat Springs
40
Yampa R.
Oak Creek
Trappers Lake
Yampa
Meeker
White River

N Fork White River

FR 205

GPS
Trappers Lake

Crescent Lake

FR 205

Flat Tops

Wilderness

Area

Coffin Lake

Trail 1814

GPS
Trappers Lake Campground

Scotts Lake

GPS
Parking Area

Trail 1818

Trappers Lake

Anderson Lake

Fraser Creek

White River

National

Forest

Trail 1816

N
W E
S

0   0.5 MILES

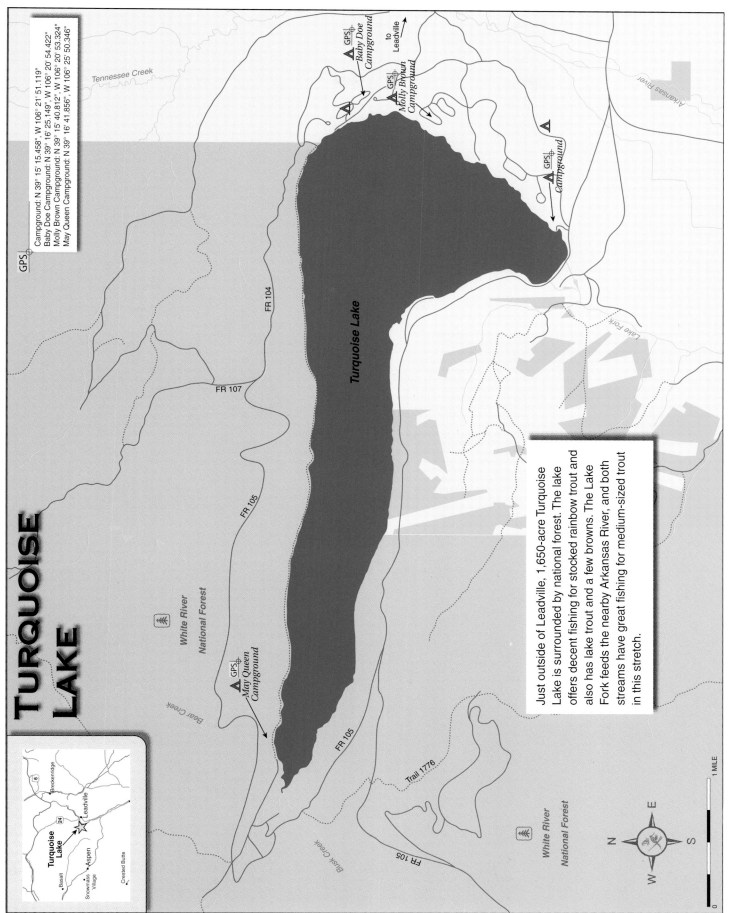

TURQUOISE LAKE

Campground: N 39° 15' 15.458", W 106° 21' 51.119"
Baby Doe Campground: N 39° 16' 25.149", W 106° 20' 54.422"
Molly Brown Campground: N 39° 15' 40.812", W 106° 20' 53.324"
May Queen Campground: N 39° 16' 41.856", W 106° 25' 50.346"

GPS

Baby Doe Campground
Molly Brown Campground
GPS Campground
to Leadville

Turquoise Lake

FR 104
FR 107
FR 105
White River National Forest
May Queen Campground
Bear Creek
FR 105
Trail 1776
Busk Creek
FR 105
White River National Forest
Lake Fork
Arkansas River
Tennessee Creek

Just outside of Leadville, 1,650-acre Turquoise Lake is surrounded by national forest. The lake offers decent fishing for stocked rainbow trout and also has lake trout and a few browns. The Lake Fork feeds the nearby Arkansas River, and both streams have great fishing for medium-sized trout in this stretch.

Breckenridge
Leadville
Turquoise Lake
Basalt
Aspen
Snowmass Village
Crested Butte

1 MILE

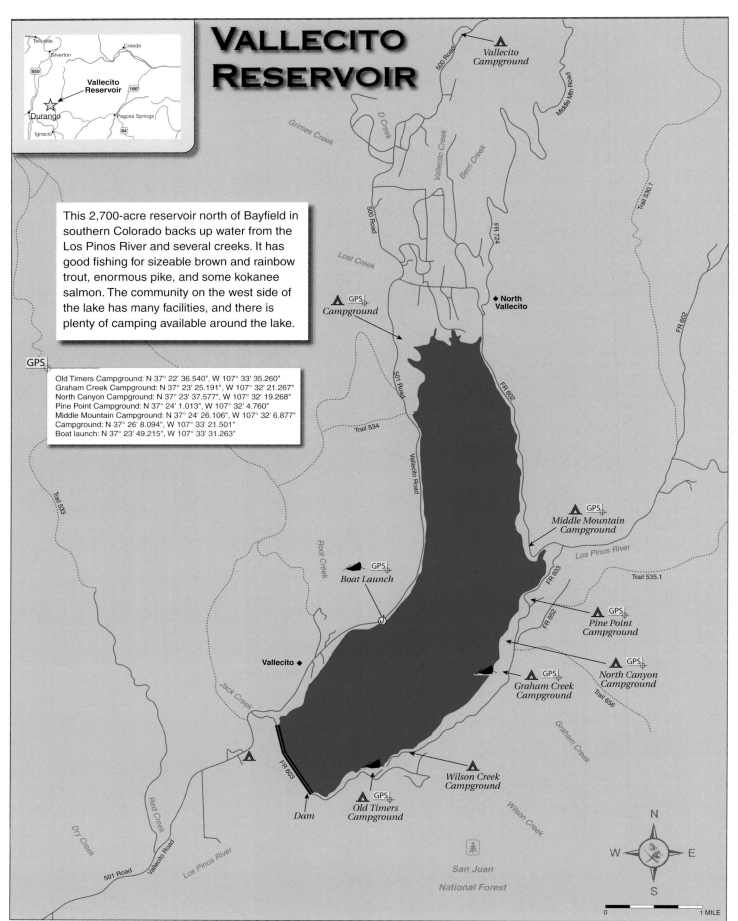

VALLECITO RESERVOIR

This 2,700-acre reservoir north of Bayfield in southern Colorado backs up water from the Los Pinos River and several creeks. It has good fishing for sizeable brown and rainbow trout, enormous pike, and some kokanee salmon. The community on the west side of the lake has many facilities, and there is plenty of camping available around the lake.

GPS

Old Timers Campground: N 37° 22' 36.540", W 107° 33' 35.260"
Graham Creek Campground: N 37° 23' 25.191", W 107° 32' 21.267"
North Canyon Campground: N 37° 23' 37.577", W 107° 32' 19.268"
Pine Point Campground: N 37° 24' 1.013", W 107° 32' 4.760"
Middle Mountain Campground: N 37° 24' 26.106", W 107° 32' 6.877"
Campground: N 37° 26' 8.094", W 107° 33' 21.501"
Boat launch: N 37° 23' 49.215", W 107° 33' 31.263"

Telluride
Silverton
Creede
550
Vallecito Reservoir
160
Durango
Ignacio
Pagosa Springs
84

Vallecito Campground

Grimes Creek
D Creek
Vallecito Creek
Bern Creek
Middle Mtn Road
Trail 530.1
500 Road
FR 724
FR 602
500 Road
Last Creek
501 Road
North Vallecito
GPS
Campground
Trail 534
Vallecito Road
Middle Mountain Campground
GPS
Los Pinos River
Root Creek
Trail 535.1
Boat Launch
GPS
FR 603
Pine Point Campground
GPS
FR 852
Vallecito
North Canyon Campground
GPS
Graham Creek Campground
GPS
Trail 656
Jack Creek
Trail 553
Graham Creek
Wilson Creek Campground
Dam
FR 603
Old Timers Campground
GPS
Wilson Creek
Red Creek
Dry Creek
501 Road
Vallecito Road
Los Pinos River
San Juan National Forest

N
W   E
S

0   1 MILE

© 2008 Wilderness Adventures Press, Inc.

VEGA RESERVOIR

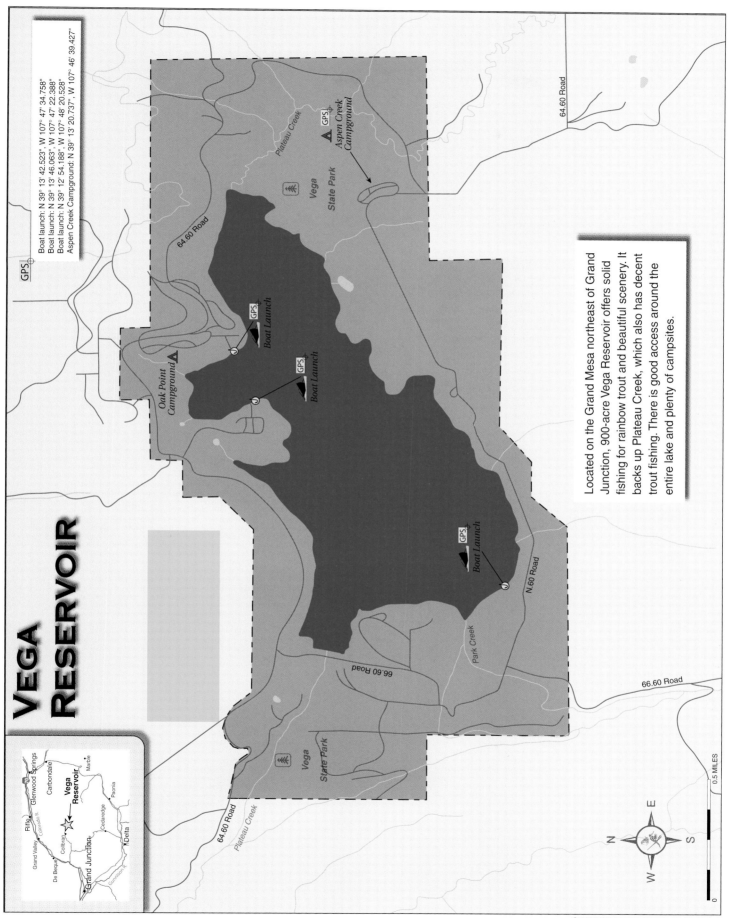

Boat launch: N 39° 13' 42.523", W 107° 47' 34.758"
Boat launch: N 39° 13' 46.063", W 107° 47' 22.388"
Boat launch: N 39° 12' 54.188" W 107° 48' 20.528"
Aspen Creek Campground: N 39° 13' 20.737", W 107° 46' 39.427"

GPS

Oak Point Campground

Boat Launch
GPS

Boat Launch
GPS

Boat Launch
GPS

Aspen Creek Campground
GPS

Vega State Park

Plateau Creek

64.60 Road

64.60 Road

66.60 Road

N.60 Road

Park Creek

Vega State Park

Plateau Creek

66.60 Road

64.60 Road

Located on the Grand Mesa northeast of Grand Junction, 900-acre Vega Reservoir offers solid fishing for rainbow trout and beautiful scenery. It backs up Plateau Creek, which also has decent trout fishing. There is good access around the entire lake and plenty of campsites.

Glenwood Springs
Rifle
Grand Valley
Colorado R.
Carbondale
Marble
Vega Reservoir
De Beque
Collbran
Paonia
Cedaredge
Grand Junction
Delta
Gunnison R.

N
W   E
S

0   0.5 MILES

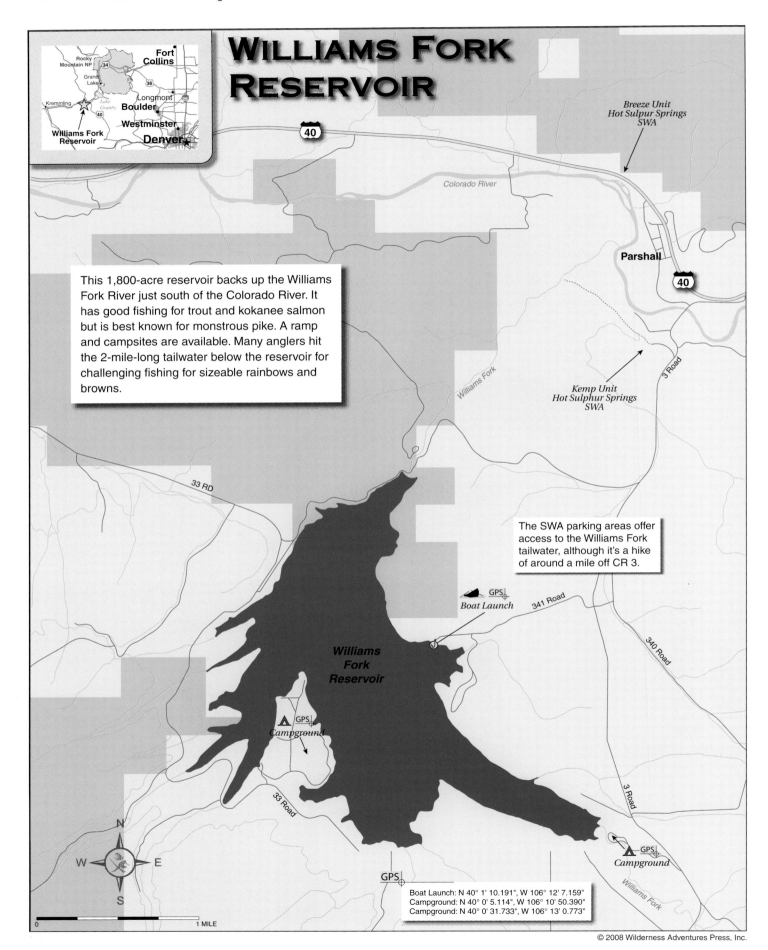

WILLIAMS FORK RESERVOIR

This 1,800-acre reservoir backs up the Williams Fork River just south of the Colorado River. It has good fishing for trout and kokanee salmon but is best known for monstrous pike. A ramp and campsites are available. Many anglers hit the 2-mile-long tailwater below the reservoir for challenging fishing for sizeable rainbows and browns.

The SWA parking areas offer access to the Williams Fork tailwater, although it's a hike of around a mile off CR 3.

*Breeze Unit
Hot Sulpur Springs
SWA*

*Kemp Unit
Hot Sulphur Springs
SWA*

Parshall

Colorado River

Williams Fork

Boat Launch

Williams Fork Reservoir

Campground

Campground

Williams Fork

33 RD

33 Road

341 Road

340 Road

3 Road

3 Road

Boat Launch: N 40° 1' 10.191", W 106° 12' 7.159"
Campground: N 40° 0' 5.114", W 106° 10' 50.390"
Campground: N 40° 0' 31.733", W 106° 13' 0.773"

0   1 MILE

© 2008 WILDERNESS ADVENTURES PRESS, Inc.

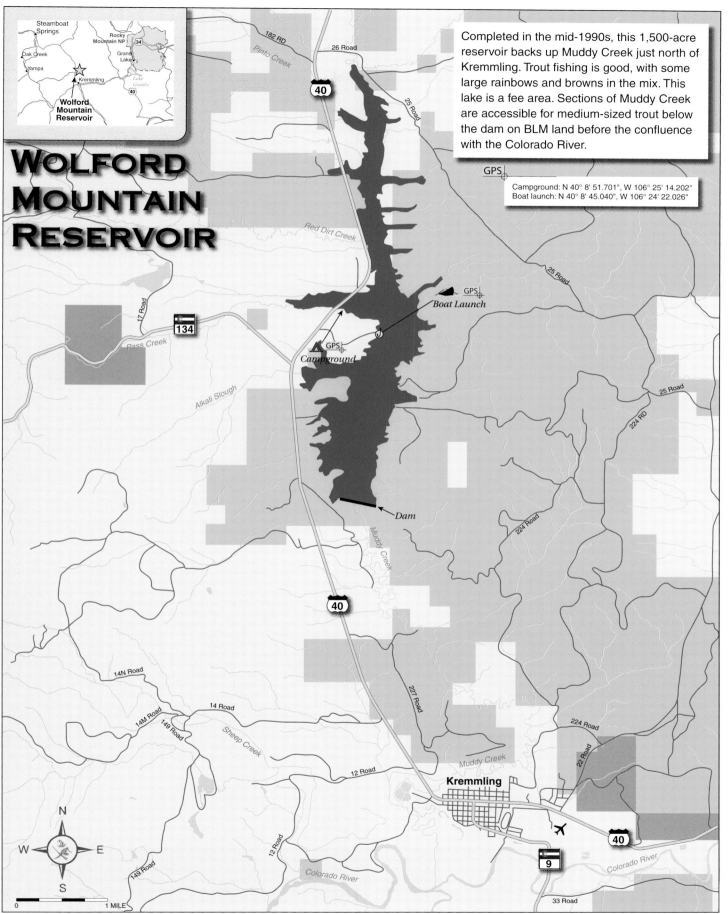

WOLFORD MOUNTAIN RESERVOIR

Completed in the mid-1990s, this 1,500-acre reservoir backs up Muddy Creek just north of Kremmling. Trout fishing is good, with some large rainbows and browns in the mix. This lake is a fee area. Sections of Muddy Creek are accessible for medium-sized trout below the dam on BLM land before the confluence with the Colorado River.

Campground: N 40° 8' 51.701", W 106° 25' 14.202"
Boat launch: N 40° 8' 45.040", W 106° 24' 22.026"

Boat Launch

Campground

Dam

Kremmling

0   1 MILE

N
W   E
S

Notes

NOTES

NOTES

NOTES

Fishing Titles Available from Wilderness Adventures Press, Inc.™

Flyfishers Guide to™

Flyfisher's Guide to Alaska

Flyfisher's Guide to Arizona

Flyfisher's Guide to Chesapeake Bay

Flyfisher's Guide to Colorado

Flyfisher's Guide to the Florida Keys

Flyfisher's Guide to Freshwater Florida

Flyfisher's Guide to Idaho

Flyfisher's Guide to Montana

Flyfisher's Guide to Michigan

Flyfisher's Guide to Minnesota

Flyfisher's Guide to Missouri & Arkansas

Flyfisher's Guide to New York

Flyfisher's Guide to New Mexico

Flyfisher's Guide to Northern California

Flyfisher's Guide to Northern New England

Flyfisher's Guide to Oregon

Flyfisher's Guide to Pennsylvania

Flyfisher's Guide to Saltwater Florida

Flyfisher's Guide to Texas

Flyfisher's Guide to Utah

Flyfisher's Guide to Virginia

Flyfisher's Guide to Washington

Flyfisher's Guide to Wisconsin & Iowa

Flyfisher's Guide to Wyoming

Flyfisher's Guide to Yellowstone National Park

Best Fishing Waters™

California's Best Fishing Waters

Colorado's Best Fishing Waters

Idaho's Best Fishing Waters

Montana's Best Fishing Waters

Oregon's Best Fishing Waters

Washington's Best Fishing Waters

Anglers Guide to™

Complete Anglers Guide to Oregon

Saltwater Angler's Guide to the Southeast

Saltwater Angler's Guide to Southern California

On the Fly Guide to™

On the Fly Guide to the Northwest

On the Fly Guide to the Northern Rockies

Field Guide to™

Field Guide to Fishing Knots

Fly Tying

Go-To Flies™